CHANGING FAMILIES

A Family Therapy Reader

CHANGING FAMILIES

A Family Therapy Reader

Edited by

JAY HALEY

Director of Family Research
Philadelphia Child Guidance Clinic
Philadelphia, Pennsylvania

GRUNE & STRATTON *New York and London*

Library of Congress Catalog Card Number 72-118654
International Standard Book Number 0-8089-0681-x
Printed in the United States of America (PC-B)

Contents

Contributors

Ian Alger, M.D.
Training Psychoanalyst, New York Medical College, New York, New York

Carolyn L. Attneave, Ph.D.
Director, New Personnel Training Program, Department of Education,
Boston State Hospital, Boston, Massachusetts

Sidney W. Bijou, Ph.D.
Director, Child Behavior Laboratory, Professor of Psychology, and member of the
Institute for Research in Exceptional Children, University of Illinois,
Champaign-Urbana, Illinois

Murray Bowen, M.D.
Clinical Professor of Psychiatry, Georgetown University Medical Center,
Washington, D. C., and Clinical Professor and Chairman, Division of Family
and Social Psychiatry, Medical College of Virginia, Virginia Commonwealth
University, Richmond, Virginia

Juliana Day, M.D.
Formerly Chief, Family Study Section, Adult Psychiatry Branch,
National Institute of Mental Health, Bethesda, Maryland

Carol D. DeYoung, R.N., M.S.
Associate Director of Nursing, Tri-County District Health Department,
Aurora, Colorado

Milton H. Erickson, M.D.
Private practice, Phoenix, Arizona

Kalman Flomenhaft, D.S.W.
Assistant Professor, School of Social Work, University of Maryland, Baltimore, Maryland

Alexander Gralnick, M.D.
Medical Director, High Point Hospital, Port Chester, New York

George H. Grosser, Ph.D.
Assistant Commissioner, Department of Mental Health, Commonwealth of Massachusetts, Boston, Massachusetts

Jay Haley
Director of Family Research, Philadelphia Child Guidance Clinic, Philadelphia, Pennsylvania

Alexander Halperin, M.D.
Training and Supervising Analyst, Washington Psychoanalytic Institute, and Consultant, National Institute of Mental Health, Bethesda, Maryland

Robert P. Hawkins, Ph.D.
Director, School Adjustment Research Project, Kalamazoo Valley Intermediate School District, and Adjunct Assistant Professor, Western Michigan University, Kalamazoo, Michigan

Lynn Hoffman
Brooklyn, New York

Peter Hogan, M.D.
Assistant Clinical Professor of Psychiatry, New York University-Bellevue Medical Center, New York, New York

Don D. Jackson, M.D.
Former Director of the Mental Research Institute, Palo Alto, California

David M. Kaplan, Ph.D.
Director, Division of Clinical Social Work, Stanford University School of Medicine, Palo Alto, California

Walter Kempler, M.D.
Director, Kempler Institute, Los Angeles, California

Harry A. LaBurt, M.D.
Former Director, Creedmoor State Hospital, Queens Village, New York

Donald G. Langsley, M.D.
Chairman, Department of Psychiatry, University of California School of Medicine, Davis, California

H. Peter Laqueur, M.D.
Director, Family Study and Treatment Unit, Vermont State Hospital, Waterbury, Vermont, and Associate Clinical Professor of Psychiatry, University of Vermont Medical College, Burlington, Vermont

Pavel Machotka, Ph.D.
University of California, Santa Cruz, California

Milton H. Miller, M.D.
Professor of Psychiatry, Department of Psychiatry, University of Wisconsin, Madison, Wisconsin

Salvador Minuchin, M.D.
Director, Philadelphia Child Guidance Clinic, Philadelphia, Pennsylvania

Hans Molinski, M.D.
Staff Psychiatrist, High Point Hospital, Port Chester, New York

Braulio Montalvo, M.A.
Co-ordinator of School Consultations, Philadelphia Child Guidance Clinic, Philadelphia, Pennsylvania

Eugene Morong, M.D.
Assistant Physician, Department of Community Medicine, and Medical Director, Methadone Maintenance Unit, The Bronx-Lebanon Hospital Center, Bronx, New York

Norman Paul, M.D.
Assistant Clinical Professor, Department of Psychiatry, Harvard Medical School, and Research Assistant Professor of Neurology, Boston University School of Medicine, Boston, Massachusetts

Robert F. Peterson, Ph.D.
Associate Professor of Psychology, University of Illinois, Champaign-Urbana, Illinois

Frank S. Pittman, III, M.D.
Director of Psychiatric Services, Grady Memorial Hospital, Atlanta, Georgia

Edwin L. Rabiner, M.D.
Research Consultant, High Point Hospital, Port Chester, New York, and Assistant Clinical Professor of Psychiatry, Albert Einstein College of Medicine of Yeshiva University, Bronx, New York

Agnes Ritchie, A.C.S.W.
Chief Psychiatric Social Worker, Division of Child and Adolescent Psychiatry, University of Texas Medical Branch, Galveston, Texas

Irving M. Ryckoff, M.D.
Consultant, National Institute of Mental Health, Bethesda, Maryland, and Director of Training and Research, Washington School of Psychiatry, Washington, D.C.

Virginia Satir, A.C.S.W.
San Francisco, California

Edda Schweid, Ph.D.
Psychologist, Children's Orthopedic Hospital and Medical Center, Seattle, Washington

Leslie Schaffer, M.D.
Consultant, National Institute of Mental Health, Bethesda, Maryland, and Washington School of Psychiatry, Washington, D.C., and Editor, *Review of Existential Psychology and Psychiatry*

Ross V. Speck, M.D.
Fellow of the Center for the Study of Social Change, New York, New York

John H. Weakland
Research Associate, Mental Research Institute, Palo Alto, California

Carl A. Whitaker, M.D.
Professor of Psychiatry, Department of Psychiatry, University of Wisconsin, Madison, Wisconsin

Lyman C. Wynne, M.D.
Chief, Adult Psychiatry Branch, National Institute of Mental Health, Bethesda, Maryland

Gerald H. Zuk, Ph.D.
Research Scientist, Department of Clinical Research, and Member, Division of Family Psychiatry, Eastern Pennsylvania Psychiatric Institute, Philadelphia, Pennsylvania

Preface

This collection brings together the better papers on family therapy which have been published in various journals over the years along with several new articles not previously published. The arrangement of the articles is roughly chronological according to the year published so the reader can see how ideas evolved in this field over the last decade. Although the focus of the collection is upon therapy technique more than upon family diagnosis or dynamics, many authors emphasize the problems to be changed as well as the experience of being a family therapist. The articles were selected for their quality but also to present the wide range of approaches which are called family therapy today.

Jay Haley

I

A Review of the
Family Therapy Field

JAY HALEY

The idea of trying to change a family appeared in the 1950's at the same time as other happenings in the social sciences in America. At midcentury the social sciences became more social: the study of small groups flourished, animals were observed in their natural environments instead of in the zoo or laboratory, psychological experiments were seen as social situations in experimenter-bias studies, businesses began to be thought of as complex systems, mental hospitals were studied as total institutions, and ecology developed as a special field, with man and other creatures looked upon as inseparable from their environments. As part of this shift to a social view, research investigators and people-changers took the unprecedented step of bringing whole families under direct observation. Instead of depending upon what a person said about his family life, the investigator actually observed him interacting with his family. This kind of observation let to a breakthrough in thinking about human problems which has had many consequences. One consequence was the idea of a therapist's intervening to change the ways in which family members deal with one another.

Before observational family research and therapy, no one had tried to describe and measure the habitual behavior of a group of intimates who had a history together and would have a future association. Small group research had been carried out with artificial collections of strangers, and family research had depended upon opinion surveys of family members about their lives. Therapeutic intervention was focused upon changing individuals.

Then for unexplained reasons a number of therapists began to deal with whole families in the 1950's, often without knowing that anyone else was doing so. Many of these people did not write for professional journals or attend meetings, so their work was known only locally, if at all. Curiously, a decade later many experienced family therapists still had not met each other. If they had been introduced, they still had not sat down together to discuss their work and seek a common view on what changing a family is all about.

This movement toward therapy with whole families occurred just when the dynamic concept of the individual, and psychoanalytic treatment, had won power and prestige in the psychiatric establishment after a long struggle. Everyone who was respectable wished to practice psychoanalysis or at least to give psychoanalytically oriented treatment. Consequently, therapy was defined as a form of medical treatment and psychiatrists held the highest status. Social workers and psychologists tended to be thought of as auxiliary personnel (and lay therapists were outside the pale, despite Freud's efforts).

An essential part of the medical model was the idea that a person could be changed if he were plucked out of his social situation and treated individually in a private office or inside a hospital. Once changed, he would return to his social milieu transformed because he had been "cleared" of the intrapsychic problems causing his difficulties. In this model, primary change was effected by providing the "patient" with insight into his unconscious conflicts, thus eliminating the repressive forces which were incapacitating him. The real world of the patient was considered secondary since what was important was his perception of it, his affect, his attitudes, the objects he had introjected, and the conflicts within him programmed by his past. While a science of human behavior was being conceptualized in social terms under the influence of systems theory, the people who were trying to change people were determinedly disregarding the social environment.

Just why a few people-changers broke away from the established ideas about psychopathology and change in the 1950's is unclear. Often treating whole families caused them to be penalized by professional isolation. It would be comfortable to assume that such therapists turned to family treatment because they were not getting results with psychoanalytically oriented therapy, yet that fact has not persuaded other therapists to change their ways. Sometimes family treatment seems to have come about because a therapist brought family members together when he was puzzled by something said by his patient. Though the family was interviewed only to gain information to help one individual belonging to it, what the therapist saw happening among the family members caused him to arrive at a new concept of the cause of human problems. Or sometimes a therapist noticed that, when his patient did change in individual therapy, there were consequences within the family—someone else developed symptoms, or the family began to come apart. Concern over this kind of change forced the therapist to think of the social function of psychopathology.

Often the shift to a family orientation was caused by a combination of factors. In my own case, two sets of circumstances occurred at the same time. I was a member of Gregory Bateson's project on communication, and we were doing research on schizophrenia. We had brought a schizophrenic patient together with his parents to try to find out why the patient could not be with them on visiting day for more than a few minutes without collapsing in an anxiety state. It was an information-gathering session, not a family treatment interview. Yet what we observed so changed our views about treating schizophrenics that by the beginning of the next year we had started a systematic program of treating families of schizophrenics. Simultaneously, I was doing brief therapy in private practice, and it became impossible for me not to notice that rapid change of a severe symptom in a patient produced instability in a marriage and family. Looking back on that period now, everyone was groping not only toward the idea that the family had something to do with pathology in a patient but also toward the idea that one could attempt to change the family. We began to learn that a number of therapists in different parts of the country, quite independent of one another, were also treating families. They were gaining considerable experience in this new endeavor, were collecting disciples, and were becoming more confident about their results.

As family therapists began to see a psychiatric problem as an expression of a family, they found that they had to reconceptualize therapy. To change an individual required one way of thinking, and to change the interaction among family members required quite another. While groping toward a new notion of what therapy was about, some family therapists thought at first that individual therapy might be appropriate for some cases and family therapy for others. Family therapy was beginning to be defined as interviewing a whole family together, and individual therapy as the treatment of one person. However, as family therapists began to be more flexible in their practices and clearer in their ideas, they realized that traditional individual therapy was actually *one* way to intervene in a family, whether the therapist thought of it that way or not. It was the intrusion of an outsider into a family even if the therapist considered himself to be dealing only with one person's fantasies. Some family therapists developed this view when they had to deal with families after one member had been in long-term individual therapy with consequences to the whole family.

By the end of the 1950's it was becoming clearer that family therapy was a different concept of change, rather than merely an additional method of treatment to be added to individual and group therapy. The focus of family treatment was no longer on changing an individual's perception, his affect, or his behavior, but on changing the structure of a family and the sequences of behavior among a group of intimates. With this shift, it became clearer that neither traditional individual therapy nor group therapy with artificial groups was relevant to the goals and techniques of family therapists. The problem was to change the living situation of a person, not to pluck him out of that situation and try to change *him*.

In the process of thinking in new ways about a human problem, family therapists had to revise their views on the importance of the real world. Often this meant unlearning what they had been taught in training. Thinking that a person's problem was with his maternal introject was different from thinking his problem was with his wife. Although it seems strange now, a child with a school phobia might be diagnosed and treated with no concern for the real situation in his home or, for that matter, in his school. An adolescent acting out in a hospital was examined with no consideration of his situation in the hospital. It was necessary to discard many of the notions about the causes and cures of phobias when it was discovered that a wife who feared to leave her home alone had a problem with a marital relationship which was confining her. Previously it had been assumed that everyone faces much the same situation and that people could be classified as normal, neurotic, or psychotic on the basis of how they handled that situation. Now it was discovered that everyone does not face the same situation but is adapting to a unique one.

A theoretical framework for these new ways of thinking was difficult to conceptualize. Actually observing families and trying to change them produced information which had never been gathered before. Rather than family therapy's developing because of a theory, it appeared that people were struggling to find a theory to fit their practices. There was no theoretical model which could be used to describe behavior in natural, ongoing groups, and there was no language for describing their relationships.

Moreover, investigators in the 1950's faced a continually changing unit of observation. They first shifted from the individual to the dyad. But the dyad proved unsatisfactory, and they moved to the triad. This was the period of the emphasis upon the nuclear family. Then with the recognition of the importance of extended kin and the social context of the family, the unit shifted to an even larger ecological network.

With each of these steps both researchers and therapists sought an appropriate social model. Group theory based upon artificial groups seemed to be of no use since it did not involve habitual behavior among intimates with a history and future together. Role theory was popular with some investigators, but others thought it was too much a characterization of individual positions and could not deal with sequences between people. Other investigators tried information theory, or explored the language of symbolic logic, or experimented with games theory or learning theory. The most consistently popular model was a systems theory derived from cybernetics. This model could deal with interacting elements responding to one another in a self-corrective way, which is the way family members seemed to behave. Communications terminology began to be part of the language of this field as it was of other social sciences, and slow-motion films of family behavior were analyzed for body movement communication as well as linguistic and verbal behavior. Yet at the end of the decade no particular theoretical model was accepted by all the various investigators and therapists in the field. This lack of consensus might have been because they came from different professional backgrounds, or it might have been because the investigators worked in different geographic areas and some had not even met each other. Everyone talked about the family, but in a mixture of tongues.

Despite these difficulties, by the 1960's, the early pioneers had established a secure enough beachhead for family therapy and research so that others could follow them. The family view had been either ignored or opposed by the general psychiatric field, but it was beginning to be taken up in the larger cities and even some universities. Quite a bit of observational family research literature was developing, but little was being written about family therapy technique. Often the therapists knew how to treat a family but did not know how to describe what they had done for the printed page.

It now seems apparent that the 1960's was the period when family therapy and research left the pioneering stage, consolidated a body of knowledge and technique, and began to intrude seriously in the general clinical field. Since it takes about twenty years for an idea to enter a university, the decade 1960-1970 brought about the introduction of family concepts to the clinical programs of many departments of psychiatry, psychology, and social work. Generally, it is the younger generation of clinicians who have become interested in family therapy, particularly psychiatric residents and graduate students in psychology. In many parts of the country such students are treating families while their teachers have no experience to help them. This generation of students seems less interested in esoteric explorations of pathology and more concerned with what can be done. Family therapy appeals to them because it is an action-oriented form of treatment.

The entrance of family therapy ideas in the respectable psychiatric arena had consequences which were not anticipated. We have begun to realize, for example, that the status and function of the disciplines in the helping professions is based on the idea that the individual is the focus of diagnosis and treatment. When the unit of treatment shifts from the individual to the family, the disciplines become undisciplined and no one quite knows what profession should be looked on as an authority on what is wrong and what should be done. The change is particularly painful to psychiatrists, who have had higher status for many years because the medical model was the basis for individual diagnosis.

Another problem which is both practical and theoretical has been the change in the definition of the family. By the beginning of the 1960's, many family therapists were widening their focus to include not only the nuclear family but also the extended kin in family treatment. Later in the 1960's the unit of treatment broadened still more. The "family" language began to be applied to all systems with a history and a future, whether blood relatives, business staffs, or political systems. In relation to family therapy, the context of the family began to be taken into account, so that at times the unit of treatment was a larger ecological one yielding network descriptions and network therapy. Some family therapists realized that they had been talking about a family in isolation much as they had once talked about the isolated individual. Now a wider area of concern is being considered, partly because of the explosive force of community problems and the needs of mental health centers, which are responsible for a wider group than the family, and partly as the result of a systems orientation, which inevitably forces an awareness of the influence of context. Over this brief ten-year period we have already developed a generation gap, with the older family therapist talking about "pure" and "deep" family therapy of the single family and the younger family therapist talking about treating ecological systems.

Also in the 1960's the conditioning therapists began to move to join the family therapists. From setting up reinforcement schedules with individuals, a few conditioners began to program parents to reinforce the behavior of their children differently. This brought them into the family therapy field. One curious difference between conditioners and family therapists is the unit focused upon. Unlike psychodynamic therapists, conditioners have moved from the individual to the dyad, but they do not think in larger units. Learning theory has only a dyadic framework. Conditioners do not describe a child in a triangle with his parents or in terms of his larger ecology. They think of the way the mother reinforces the child and the way the father does, but they do not describe the conflict between the parents about the child.

Attempts at formal training in family therapy also began in the 1960's. This brought questions, such as "What ideas about the family are relevant to therapy?" and "How can an experienced family therapist teach what he knows how to do but has difficulty in describing?" When it is recognized that family therapy is not a method of treatment but a new orientation to the human dilemma, it is clear that any number of methods might be taught and used. With experience, family therapists often shift from a method approach and become more problem oriented, adapting what they do to the problem that has come in the door. Since students like to have a "method" which they can learn, family therapy is difficult for them to grasp. They must absorb a new orientation which is different from the one taught them in school, and they must learn a problem approach which can only be learned from experience with different problems.

Aside from such practical difficulties, a diverse conglomeration of ideas in the field continues; the 1960's did not bring about more certainty over what body of theories would achieve primacy. In the discourse among family therapists, concepts drawn from communication theory, ethology, anthropology, sociology, and learning theory occur as frequently as traditional psychological concepts. Everyone hesitates to construct a new language.

The mystery of what causes change has been only slightly clarified. Many new therapists beginning to treat families could abandon the idea that transference interpretations or insight into unconscious processes cause change. (Often they abandoned these concepts without realizing that this could also mean abandoning the theory of repression.) But as former individual therapists began treating families, they learned that some experienced family therapists were even doubting that helping family members understand how they deal with each other is related to change. It is beginning to be argued by many family therapists that talking to family members about understanding each other is necessary because something must be talked about and families expect this form of discussion, but that change really comes about through interactional processes set off when a therapist intervenes actively and directively in particular ways in a family system, and quite independently of the awareness of the participants about how they have been behaving.

Research in the 1960's explored different types of families, which resulted in more uncertainty about whether a typology of families is possible. Rather than establishing a typology, the trend is toward greater appreciation of stages of family development as a crucial factor in the development of symptomatology. Differences between families are being examined in terms of family crisis points rather than just in terms of type of family. With this emphasis, there is increasing awareness of the relationship between the ecological context of the family and the way the family members respond to one another. To explain what is happening in a family, the context of treatment, whether hospital involvement or the intrusion of multiple helpers quarreling over territory in the family, is becoming a necessary part of the description. Family diagnosis now includes the therapist, or the researcher, since family members are evidently not only responding to each other but also, simultaneously, to the situation in which they are observed. Some family therapists now argue more confidently that a "type" of family does not produce a "type" of patient, but that a disturbance in a family at a certain stage *plus* an external intervention combine to produce the symptomatic behavior apparent in one or more family members. For example, adolescent schizophrenia can be seen as a product of a stage of family life, when the child is disengaging from his parents, *and* a particular kind of outside intervention, which brings about a failure in successful disengagement and therefore strange behavior.

Perhaps one of the major discoveries of the 1960's was that of the importance of treating families at a moment of crisis, since structural changes are most easily brought about in crisis. If a treatment program subdues and stabilizes the family, change is more difficult. The leisurely pace of information-gathering diagnostic interviews, long-term expectations of the therapist, or the use of drugs and hospitalization to calm the atmosphere is being seen as a handicap to effective treatment. To change a stabilized, miserable situation and create space for individual growth of family members, the therapist often must induce a crisis which creates instability. When hospitals are involved in the stabilization process, this is hardly possible.

Another important struggle for the field of family therapy has been the necessity of preventing the distortion of family therapy ideas as they become more widely accepted. Now that family therapy is becoming respectable and is being taken up by the establishment, it is apparent that much which has been gained can be lost. A new idea about treatment which is introduced into a traditional psychiatric department in a university not infrequently is transformed to look remarkably like an old idea. The current attempt to save psychoanalysis by broadening its concepts to include a family view may have an effect on family therapy similar to that of the air pollution of a large city on a fresh breeze. Watching what is done to family therapy in a number of psychiatric departments and social work schools, one sees a grand confusion of individual and family concepts and goals of treatment. Often such places seem to take up family therapy not because of a concern for effective treatment, but rather because they see that the medical model is being abandoned by therapists in the field and are trying to catch up, or because their funds for training require them to emphasize community work, where the family approach is more relevant than traditional individual therapy. Perhaps the community endeavors might save some of the family ideas even when they have been put through the political process in a university or a psychiatric network in a large city. In time, social work schools might even give up training their clinicians to be psychoanalysts and teach them something about changing the family and the community, as some nursing schools are now doing.

The family view poses a difficult digestive problem for the established institutions training clinicians, particularly the traditional inpatient centers. Having tremendous personal and financial investments in psychodynamic theory and practice, the staff cannot be expected to like the idea that family therapy represents a discontinuous change in basic premises about treatment and requires acceptance of new ideas and new forms of therapeutic intervention. If this is so, they will have wasted years of training in a diagnostic system that is not relevant to therapy. It seems more reasonable to believe that family therapy is really a variation on something Freud proposed, to argue that family systems are easily explained by more sophisticated ego theory, and to pretend that family problems can be resolved with transference interpretations. The need to salvage the past and defend status positions forces such institutions to exclude and dilute what is new in the field and to obscure the important issues.

Let me offer an example of how different the family view is from the traditional psychiatric posture in an inpatient institution. Rather than emphasize the average state hospital, which is often a custodial dustbin run by people with no knowledge of therapy, let us take an inpatient unit in a university psychiatry department. Such places have a large staff, considerable funds, and supposedly sufficient knowledge of therapy to be accredited to train young psychiatrists. I have visited many such places recently, and an example from one of them illustrates how discontinuous the family, or ecological, view is from the psychiatric orientation still being perpetuated in the better universities.

A young man had been hospitalized because he was possibly schizophrenic, was acting helpless, was involved in a dependent homosexual relationship, had severe anxiety spells, was possibly suicidal, and had dropped out of graduate school before completing his academic requirements. It was generally agreed by the staff that he should be hospitalized for two or three years and receive intensive individual psychoanalytically oriented therapy. This therapy would transform him and he would return to society as a mature, responsible individual —the goal described in the case protocol. Despite the fact that this institution had never reported, or even examined, whether such treatment of similar cases ever produced mature, responsible individuals, everyone assumed this was the proper treatment. Because the staff was up to date, they also recommended that the young man's parents be placed in a parents' group, apparently thinking this would help in the treatment. There was no theory or rationale of how this would help. From a traditional psychiatric view, what was being offered was the treatment of choice and it was fortunate that the patient's family could afford the great expense of the best psychiatric treatment.

According to the family orientation that has developed these last two decades, this traditional treatment program is absolutely contraindicated. It is based on an ideology which assumes that the patient's problem is internal and his social situation is secondary. The family view adopts quite the opposite view—the young man's problem is his social situation and his internal dynamics are a response to that situation. These two points of view represent a discontinuous change in thinking about human problems and how to change them.

From the family therapy view, the kind of treatment recommended above should fail. (There is increasing evidence that it does; the cure rate of long-term psychoanalytically oriented therapy in inpatient institutions has not matched the record of spontaneous remission.) The logic of the family view derives from the idea that a person is responding to his social situation, which must change before he can change. If the artificial environment in which a person is placed not only encourages psychopathology but includes factors which prevent change, the problem is compounded for a patient. The goal of treatment was to change the young man to a mature, responsible individual. Yet the treatment placed him in an artificial hospital situation where such a response was not possible. To be mature and responsible, one must make decisions about how to deal with large and small events in daily life. In the hospital, the young man is not required, and does not have the opportunity, to support himself as a responsible person must. Nor can he continue his academic education to prepare to support himself. He is not responsible even for elementary decisions; he does not have to decide when to get up in the morning, what to eat at mealtime, when to have mealtimes, or when to go to bed at night. These daily events are all decided for him, along with all his other activities, by people supposedly helping him to learn to be mature. He does not have to, nor can he, choose the friends he will associate with, as other people do, because they are chosen by the hospital. He does not have to work out the problem of courtship behavior with other young people, either male or female, because sexual behavior on the ward is forbidden (or defined as acting out). He does not have to, nor can he, keep up with his peers in a rapidly changing contemporary society; each day in the hospital he is falling behind his contemporaries in the real world.

Perhaps most important is the enforced dependency. Young people usually achieve independence and maturity when they support themselves and are no longer financially dependent upon their parents. This is a major step toward emotional independence and maturity. By the nature of hospitalization, the young man is tied more tightly in a dependency relationship to his parents. His father and mother must pay several thousand dollars a month for his hospitalization and treatment, making a financial sacrifice and so increasing his obligation to them as well as his dependency upon them. Whatever benefit he receives in the hospital he must owe to them (while the hospital staff often imply that he should reject his parents because they treat him badly). Should the young man become fond of his individual therapist and establish a "deep" relationship with him, there is the constant threat that his parents will deprive him of that friend by cutting off the money for his treatment. In this way the movement toward closeness with someone outside the family—which is normally a move toward independence from the family—is done in a setting which drives the young man toward more dependence upon his parents.

The parents in this case were to be seen separately from the young man in a parents group, where they apparently pass the time of day with other parents who have hospitalized children. There is no therapeutic intervention to resolve the entanglements of child and parents as they attempt to disengage from each other. In fact the total structure of the treatment situation forces financial entanglement whether the young man and parents like it or not. Within this peculiar, dependent setting, the staff encourages the young man to be more responsible and condemns him if he behaves childishly. Viewed from the family, or ecological, orientation, this is a Kafka-like treatment situation in which the goals of therapy cannot be achieved because of the nature of the social system set up to achieve them.

If a family therapist is brought into this situation as a consultant, what advice can he offer? No information is given him which he can use to understand the case; psychological tests or interviews with the individual patient provide little of use, and there is no data on how the parents and patient behave with each other. Besides having no information to help him understand the problem, the family therapist consultant cannot see how this kind of hospital situation could bring about change. If he suggests that the patient be immediately discharged and treated within his natural social setting, the hospital staff will inevitably protest that the patient might do something disastrous. The argument is offered that hospitalization saves the patient's life because he might commit suicide (even though hospitalization does not prevent suicide and sometimes does not even delay it). The problem is compounded when a virtue is made of interminable treatment by insisting that the patient should be hospitalized for two or three years no matter how he responds because that will be "deeper" therapy. If a family therapist attempts to work within this setting, he must either change his ideas so that they are palatable to the establishment or he must produce a change in the orientation of the entire staff of the hospital and the resident training program as well as in the patient's family.

The fact that traditional psychiatry has no way other than hospitalization to treat a difficult young man like the one described is a serious defect. What makes the problem worse is the fact that it is almost impossible for psychiatrists to innovate other modes of treatment, even if they acknowledged that hospitalization is a failure, because young psychiatrists are being trained within this kind of setting. Since they do not learn other modes of therapy for difficult young people, they must logically end up recommending hospitalization even if they suspect that such treatment is not usually successful. Within such a treatment structure, young psychiatrists learn to focus upon fantasies and to ignore the real world. They think in terms of crazy individuals rather than crazy situations. Such learning today is likely to make them ineffective therapists in the clinics and practices where they will face real life problems when they finish training. They get no experience in crisis treatment, since hospitalization stabilizes crisis, and they learn nothing about working with families. Despite (or because of) their thorough knowledge of diagnosis, their ability to estimate ego strength, their concern with organicity, and their understanding of the myths of etiology, they are handicapped when they attempt therapy. The young patient will also be handicapped when he leaves the hospital to face his real problems because he will carry the stigma of being a former mental patient along with his other unsolved social dilemmas.

Experienced family therapists often find themselves opposing a structure in which there are large financial investments, and debating with hospital staffs about psychodynamic concepts they had found irrelevant to therapy many years ago. It is becoming evident that the more respectable the field of family therapy becomes, the more problems it will meet. To maintain the diversity of ideas of family therapy, as well as their integrity, as they are absorbed and transformed by the establishment will be an increasingly difficult task. As I look back, the work seemed easier when the family field was more ignored and less popular. Looking forward, I experience a curious uncertainty about what will happen to family therapy technique and theory in the decades to come.

2

Conjoint Family Therapy: Some Considerations on Theory, Technique, and Results

DON D. JACKSON
JOHN H. WEAKLAND

The paper presented here is a product of the Family Therapy in Schizophrenia Project of the Palo Alto Medical Research Foundation, and thus reflects the ideas and experience of the entire project staff and associated therapists. In it we should like primarily to report some observations based on this particular experiment in conjoint family therapy with schizophrenics—that is, in treating the identified patient and other members of his family together as a functioning natural group. We shall have little to say about the work of others, except by way of acknowledging and illustrating a growing trend toward this form of treatment. There is still only a limited amount of such work being done, and less published, so perhaps the best way to introduce something that is bound to be somewhat new and strange is to have the reader accompany us on our

Reprinted with permission of the authors and publisher from *Psychiatry* 24:30-45, 1961.

This investigation, directed by Gregory Bateson, was supported by Mental Health Project Grant OM-324 from the National Institute of Mental Health, U. S. Public Health Service, by the Veterans Administration Hospital, Palo Alto, and by the Mental Research Institute, Palo Alto Medical Research Foundation, Palo Alto, California.

13

own voyage of exploration and discovery, in part. As we go, we shall also attempt to formulate more systematically what we ourselves have been learning along the way.

Our research group stumbled onto conjoint family therapy by accident, or at least tangentially. In 1954 we wished to view the schizophrenic patient communicating and behaving in his natural habitat, which was not the hospital, and we inevitably turned to the family as the proper milieu in which to view his interactions. Our thinking in this direction was spurred by experiences with relatives in our private practice, by chance home visits made in connection with schizophrenics we had in individual therapy, and by stories we heard from various staff members at the Veterans Administration Hospital about their encounters with families.

In order to study the patient directly in relation to his parents and siblings, it was necessary to bring them together and, more important, to observe them together over a period of time. An answer to this practical problem seemed to lie in interviewing the schizophrenic patients and their family members as family groups, a procedure which would provide data for us (especially since all our interviews are recorded) and some therapeutic help for them. In setting up this work, we had no clear plans for family treatment, nor did we know at the time that family therapy was going on elsewhere. However, our experience soon demonstrated that, once one begins to talk directly with these families with a schizophrenic member, there is rapid development of pressures to treat them. Situations arise in which it is important to consider them from a therapeutic point of view, both to keep some control of the family's tendencies to involve the interviewer in their problem and to help them with their increasingly evident difficulties. So our own work in family therapy began.

Against this background, however, it is interesting to note that, as has happened repeatedly in the history of science, similar developments were occurring about simultaneously elsewhere, and in retrospect a rationale for this broad development, and a pertinent need to which it is a response, can be outlined rather clearly.

As we have been increasingly involved in studying and working with families over the past five years, we have been surprised to come upon various other people who have independently gotten into similar work. Some of these—for instance, Lyman Wynne and his co-workers, Murray Bowen and his group (both originally at N.I.M.H.), and Ivan Boszormenyi-Nagy and his associates in Philadelphia—have like ourselves been most interested in schizophrenia. Others have been interested in a range of psychiatric problems, like Nathan Ackerman in New York, Kalman Gyarfas and Virginia Satir in Chicago, John Bell of the U. S. Public Health Service, and Eugene MacDanald in Galveston; while still others have been primarily interested in another particular problem, as in Charles Fulweiler's work with the families of delinquents in Alameda County, California. But all share a basic orientation toward understanding and treating the family as a unitary system.

Some of the background of this development is clear enough. Ever since Freud's early work, the fact that the patient's family is important has been recognized at least conceptually. But practically, this fact has been dealt with mainly by segregating the patient and therapist and excluding all relatives from contact with the patient's treatment. An important and increasing exception to this practice, however, has been in the treatment of child patients; here at least the mother has become more and more an object of therapy also. Yet this leaves some problems hanging—for example, what to do about the father—and raises new ones about the need for time and for adequate communication between therapists if parents and child are not seen by the same therapist. Similar problems arise in the treatment of marital partners. Meanwhile, there are serious practical problems attending individual treatment that are made especially evident in the case of hospitalized schizophrenics. On the one hand, hospital personnel frequently experience difficulties in necessary dealings with relatives, sometimes in being unable to get together with the relatives effectively when necessary and sometimes in being unable to get the relatives off their backs. On the other hand, when patients are successfully helped in relative isolation in the hospital, their return to the family too often is marked by upsets—of the parents, or of the patient, who then relapses, or of both.

The essential point to be gleaned from all these matters of common knowledge is that treatment of a psychiatric patient *necessarily* involves dealing with members of his family, and with family relationships, either directly or indirectly. Clearly, even setting up a rule of excluding the family from the therapy involves handling these matters, and drastically, though perhaps simply. The question at issue, then, is not *whether* the members of a patient's family are to be dealt with, but *how* they are to be dealt with. This paper is concerned with describing our work with conjoint family treatment as a means of dealing with this problem in the case of schizophrenic patients particularly.

THEORETICAL BACKGROUND

To understand our attempts at treating these families and formulating our treatment approach, it is necessary to understand the theory under which we labor, since our present practices and present conceptions have both developed out of the interplay of some very broad original orientations and our groping attempts at treatment of actual families.

At the outset of our program of work with families of schizophrenics our two main concepts were (1) the double bind [1] and (2) family homeostasis.[2] The concept of family homeostasis arose from observations that psychotherapeutic efforts with one member of a family might be hindered by the behavior of other members, or that another member might become disturbed as the member in treatment improved. These observations, in connection with existing ideas about homeostatic systems generally, suggested that a family forms such a dynamic steady-state system; the characters of the members and the nature of their inter-action—including any identified patient and his sick behavior—are such as to maintain a status quo typical of the family, and to react toward the restoration of this status quo in the event of any change, such as is proposed by the treatment of any member.

The double bind concept is grounded in our most basic conception about communication as the chief means of human interaction and influence: that in actual human communication a single and simple message never occurs, but that communication always and necessarily involves a multiplicity of messages, of different levels, at once. These may be conveyed via various channels such as words, tone, and facial expressions, or by the variety of meanings and references of any verbal message in relation to its possible contexts. The relationships among these related messages may be very complex. No two messages, at different levels of communication, can be just the same; however, they may be similar or different, congruent or incongruent. Difference and incongruity appear fundamental to the richness of human communication, as when certain combinations of words and tone define styles of expression, such as irony or humor; however, they also appear fundamental to the origin and character of much psychopathology, as in the symptom "inappropriate affect," considered as an evident incongruence between words and tone or expression. Further, the use of double level messages seems increasingly central to therapy in ways we shall mention later.

The double bind concept refers to a pattern of pairs or sets of messages, at different levels, which are closely related but sharply incongruent, occurring together with other messages which by concealment, denial, or other means seriously hinder the recipient from clearly noticing the incongruence and handling it effectively, as by commenting on it. Instead, he is influenced toward incompatible behavioral responses while enjoined not even to notice either influence or incompatibility. We believe that, within an important relationship, where messages cannot merely be ignored or avoided, the combination of extensive experience of such communication being uttered and the recipient's learning to participate by accepting incongruence without question can be productive of schizophrenic behavior.

It is not hard to note that these two main concepts are both concerned with the description and specification of interaction among actual persons, by various means of communication, at a level of directly observable behavior. This focus implies further an emphasis on what is real and on what is current and continuing to occur. Taken together, these emphases define a broad "communicational" and transactional orientation to the study, understanding, and treatment of human behavior—including that special class most interesting to psychiatrists, symptomatic behavior. This orientation, while related to earlier work, especially Sullivan's, and currently increasing in acceptance, still is considerably different from the strong traditional orientation of psychiatry emphasizing the individual patient and constructs about the unreal or unobservable: fantasies or misperceptions of reality; past, mainly childhood, experience; and intrapsychic organization and content.

In brief, we are much more concerned with influence, interaction, and interrelation between people, immediately observable in the present, than with individual, internal, imaginary, and infantile matters. It is worth making this difference in basic orientation explicit, since to do so helps clarify the nature of our main specific concepts, indicates some important connections between them, and provides a background essential for understanding our whole therapeutic approach--what we do and what we do not do, especially some of our differences from other therapeutic concepts and practices.

The family homeostasis and double bind concepts, with some expansion and modification,[3] continue to be of major significance in our family work. Since these ideas have not always been clearly understood by others, particularly the importance of difference in levels of messages, some more concrete discussion of them seems to be in order here. Some of our critics have felt that the double bind situation is essentially an either-or situation, a damned-if-you-do and damned-if-you-don't predicament, or merely a complicated way of describing ambivalence.[4] The double bind situation is all of these things. But it is more. As an illustration, take the predicament of an innocent person who undergoes a lie detector test. It is common practice in such tests to invoke a standard situation for the establishment of a base line. One such situation is to have the subject draw a card from a deck, look at it, and replace it. He is then told not to reveal which card he drew even should the examiner guess it. When the card drawn is guessed and the subject answers, "No," the squiggles on the tape reveal how much he reacts to a lie. However, a theory merely invoking guilt over the telling of a lie fails to account for some of the complexities in the situation. Most subjects in this situation cannot be confident of innocence because a person cannot know a priori what his body will do and thus the subject's literal innocence is no protection against the context being one in which the power rests in the hands of the examiner. Since the examiner has asked him to lie, is this really a "lie" or is it not the truth—that is, a correct perception of what it takes to make the machine work? The double level situation renders the subject especially vulnerable because if he denies what he totally perceives, he has put into play a self-deception that does not come equipped with clear boundaries. Suppose at the completion of the test the examiner stated to the subject, "You have been lying." Could the subject be sure that the examiner was referring only to his deliberate "cooperative" lie? Could he be sure that he is not a person who is in a chronic state of not processing all the data available to him and thus subject to self-deception?

THE THERAPEUTIC PROCESS—
ARRANGEMENTS AND TECHNIQUES

"The family" we are talking about in practice usually consists of father, mother, and patient. They are seen together once a week for sixty to ninety minutes in a room equipped with a microphone for tape recording and a one-way window for occasional observation and supervision. The meetings may be conducted more frequently than once a week when indicated, but time limitations have not made this possible on a regular basis and it does not seem essential. Any combination of the basic group's members may be seen as outside necessity— such as trips or illnesses—dictates, or if the therapist feels it is technically wise. We used to be fairly rigid about meeting only if all members could be present. Now, although the general emphasis remains on the whole group, there is variation on this among our several therapists.

The status of the patient's siblings remained obscure for some time and is still only partially settled. We have found them reluctant to be drawn into a potentially unpleasant situation. In retrospect, it appears that we attributed more health to them than they had in fact, and unconsciously went along with their characteristic defense: "This is a situation I am not involved in." For example:

The younger brother of a chronic schizophrenic was visiting this country on vacation from his European job. The therapist had anticipated his arrival by getting him to agree to three family sessions during his visit, since it appeared likely that he would not be available again during the course of therapy. At the first session, the brother appeared to be everything his parents claimed he was and everything the patient was not. During this session, he maintained a pleasant aloofness and claimed amnesia for any events that the therapist felt had been important in the patient's life. At the end of this session, his mother stated that she knew he would be happy to return, but the therapist, discouraged, made it clear that he realized this was a great imposition on the brother's limited time and, without realizing it, left an excellent opportunity for the brother to back out. However, he did return for the next session, and the several days he had spent with his parents brought to the fore more data than could have been hoped for. He expressed genuine regret at the end of the third session that he could not continue to participate in the family meetings and stated that his life abroad probably protected him from a crack-up.

Currently, we have no hesitation about trying to include one or more siblings in the family sessions if they are living with the parents. If they have established other residences, we generally limit the contact to occasional meetings, usually for our own data needs.

Given this basic group of at least three persons, what is the therapist's orientation toward them and his goal? In other words, how does he envisage the therapeutic process and how does he structure the situation for the group?

When we started to try family therapy in treating schizophrenia, we assumed from our previous work that the identified patient was on the receiving end of double binds from a parent or parents, and we knew that we needed the parents' cooperation, about which we were uncertain, at least to the extent that they keep coming for a period of time. Accordingly, our initial efforts were crude attempts to protect the patient from his parents and to impress the parents with how much help we might derive from the data that they might furnish about the patient. It rather quickly dawned on us, however, that, first, the patient was not a delicate violet and was quite capable of upsetting his parents and blocking the therapist's ambitions, and, second, the parents were unhappy people who potentially could benefit from psychotherapy.

By now, the ten or so therapists involved in the schizophrenia project appear to be reasonably uniform in their impressions as to why they and the family are in the room. All of the therapists, while still inexperienced, were patient-oriented, but they quickly achieved the realization that the three persons confronting them are bound together in a mutually destructive way and that the primary symptom presented by all three is a crippling entanglement that from the surface is apparent only in the patient. The parents initially try to preserve this surface view, and hence every initial session is replete with remarks about poor X and his unfortunate illness. Once, however, they respond to the lure of the therapist's curiosity about them, the brittle surface cracks and the utter desolation that can only be experienced by two people living together in apartness begins to ooze from below. It is at this point that the therapist's humane interest can still save the day. It is at this point no longer enough that the parents come for the patient's sake. An abbreviated but typical sequence in early family sessions is as follows:

The patient is a 30-year-old man with some five years of hospital experience who is currently living at home. The parents are disturbed with his inactivity, sloppiness, and delusions. Their attempts to push him into activity or to get him out of the house boomerang and result in unpleasantness not only between them and the patient but sometimes between the parents themselves. In the initial interview, the patient is hugely sloppy, quiet, and makes a point of not appearing involved. The parents are careful to point out their own attainments in contrast to the patient's many faults, which of course are labeled sickness, and there is a sticky back-and-forth exchange between them and the therapist over the details of therapy time—the frequency of sessions and so on.

During the second session, the parents have been thinking about the patient's illness and recall anecdotes from the past having to do with outside events or acts of God that they suggest may have caused it. Typically the schools and school-teachers are mentioned as culprits. In this session, the patient demonstrates some of his symptoms with obvious encouragement from the parents.

During the third session, the therapist expresses curiosity about the parents, their background, how they met, and their early marriage. He introduces these topics deliberately, at the suggestion of his supervisor. Although the parents start out initially to report factually, there appears to be more tension in the air. Finally, well along in the session, the mother says to the father, "Why don't you tell the doctor about New York?" Her reference is to a not completely estimable escapade on the father's part, and he responds with an unhappy but gallant attempt to face the music. But the focus does not stay on the parents and off the patient for long. In the course of recounting this episode, it is stated that the patient was living with the father temporarily. This is quite correct, but largely irrelevant. The son was only about ten at the time and his staying in one city with the father temporarily, while the mother remained in another, was the parents' arrangement and indeed one related to their problem being discussed. But once the son is mentioned, the parents are soon off again on his difficulties and the father is off the hook.

During the fourth session, the therapist attempts to clarify the experience alluded to in the previous session and to discuss further some aspects of the parents' marriage. During this session, the patient appears interested and laughs heartily on several occasions when the father is willing to make himself the butt of a particular story. There is more of a feeling that, however unhappy they are, these people do share something together.

In the next session, the father appears alone. The mother is said to be down with some vague illness, and the patient is waiting in the car. The father has come in only to tell the therapist that they won't be arriving that evening. However, he stays to chat and, to the therapist's surprise, writes on a matchbook cover (presumably so it won't be overheard by the tape recorder) that he and his wife are having terrible fights. He then retrieves and destroys the matchbook cover. The father is almost totally unable to break down and to allow the therapist to sympathize with him over his marital discord; nevertheless, a breach has been made, and subsequent sessions reveal that the mother was not ill but that there had been a family quarrel before the session and she had refused to come. This leads to further consideration of their difficulties as well as those of the patient.

This example illustrates some of the typical characteristics of our families and typical responses they show to the situation posed by initially entering into therapy together. We may explicitly summarize some of these before going on to list and illustrate certain standard initial moves we have developed to deal with the problems these features pose, and then to consider the further course of therapy similarly.

In most of the families we have seen, perhaps especially in middle-class ones, the mother appears as the prime mover about therapy, with the emphasis on her concern for her child; many mothers also appear as "lay experts" on schizophrenia and its treatment on the basis of long experience with their child's illness, often plus reading up on the subject. In some cases the father is more in the foreground, but on closer inspection he seems usually to be so largely as a spokesman or front man for the mother. Often it is found that the father is physically absent from the family a lot, as by being very much occupied with his business. In fact, in many of the families it seems that the members hardly ever get together except in the therapy room, although they have little independent life as individuals either.

The father and mother both center their initial discussion on the subject of their child, especially on his illness; this might seem natural in the circumstances, except that this focus is extreme while at the same time it often centers on minor aspects of the illness, such as details of the patient's dress and manners. The parents are able to get together and agree fairly well when the patient's illness is thus the topic of discussion, although they may both speak of this in a disjointed or incongruent way—that is, at one moment they may insist that the patient is too sick to be held responsible for anything, and the next complain in extreme ways about his irresponsible misbehavior, making this abrupt transition without giving the cues or structuring that ordinarily accompany such a shift. Yet this area of agreement stands out, especially as it soon becomes evident that these two people can agree very little on any other matter. The patient, meanwhile, is appearing helpless and hopeless, yet by withdrawal or acting up is influencing everyone and upsetting the therapy situation in part. It is thus very easy to see from these early sessions why observers without further experience would naturally tend to draw big distinctions between the "sick" patient and the "well" parents and siblings. Yet on closer and more extended contact with these families, we have been struck by the observation not only that the parents also have considerable personal difficulties, but that their difficulties are apt to be fundamentally like those the patient exhibits via his symptomatology.[5]

A number of problems connected with these characteristics tend to arise very quickly in the therapy. The parents keep their discussion centered on the patient, and by this avoid talking of themselves and their relationship. The patient often helps them in this by some kind of overt "goofing up" or going too far, which aids in keeping him labeled as *the* patient; this may occur especially at points when the parents do happen to approach some topic that is hot for them, and so strongly that even the therapist is likely to turn on the patient, away from the parents, without quite noticing what he is doing.

If the therapist does attempt to put the focus on the family, or to define the parents as equally patients with their child, certain other difficulties are expectable. Either the mother or the father may move to involve the therapist in individual and private communication, by phone calls or before or after the family session. Fathers tend to avoid involvement in the family therapy by distancing devices, sometimes actual absences from meetings, sometimes withdrawal by silence, or intellectualization under the label of "objectivity." Mothers seem to feel more guilty about their possible relationship to the child's illness, and they tend to be correspondingly active in one way or another. In some cases there is danger that the mother will be so concerned as to terminate therapy very rapidly once the "family therapy" idea really is clear. In others, sessions may continue but be dominated by the mother, who may take over the therapist's position by endorsing everything he says, by being more expert and scientific than he, usually with biological and chemical theories of schizophrenia which deny her guilt, or even in a few cases by taking blame on herself so strongly and indiscriminately that examining actual family interactions again is badly hampered. Indeed, such examination is difficult at best, since it is a real project to get clarity about anything with these families; the statements of the various members do not agree, and each tends to be vague and shifting, or to bury everything in details, or both. Of particular importance is the fact that the family members present their behavior in terms of responses to outside situations, so that it is difficult even for the therapist to keep in mind and in view how much they are responding to each other, and to begin to clarify this with them.

Framing of the Therapy

If such typical initial problems are not dealt with adequately, they are likely to become acute or chronic, ending the therapy quickly or leading into a repetitious stalemate similar to the family's usual circle of interactions, only with the therapist drawn in as one more player in this game with no winners. On the other hand, effective dealing with these initial problems is correspondingly valuable. As we see it, "patient management" in family therapy, which includes management of all the family members involved in the therapeutic situation, is a central part of therapy, and by no means only superficial in its effects. Thus, the standard procedures we have evolved to utilize in the initial family sessions represent much more than merely a means of avoiding limited particular difficulties. They involve a framing of the therapy as a whole, a setting up of continuing broad standards and expectations. Also, the means by which the therapist does this framing are illustrative of much about our overall technical orientation and practice.

In the initial session, the therapist customarily expresses a philosophy of "We are here to work together on better understanding one another so that you all can get more out of your family life." Such a statement implies that the parents are as much involved in the family unhappiness, specified or unspecified, as the patient, and also that they equally have something to gain from therapy. This replaces our former tendency to open the initial interview by asking what they would like to get out of the sessions, an approach that resulted in the standard answer, "Nothing is wrong except poor Bill," or whoever the identified patient happened to be. Such mention of "working on understanding" also implicitly focuses on communication as deeply involved in their difficult relationships and as a means of therapy. There are similar implications in our usual handling of the problem of private communication. Formerly, it was customary for the therapist to receive a phone call from one or both parents during the early weeks of therapy asking if the patient shouldn't be put on tranquilizers or shouldn't be getting more exercise, and so on. Then the therapist would feel awkward about bringing this up at the next family meeting and awkward if he did not bring it up because it implied a conspiracy with one or the other of the parents. Now, in the initial session, the therapist casually announces that all parties are privileged to all information about contacts with the therapist, and, like most rules that are brought up matter of factly, this is accepted.

Alternatively, the therapist may sometimes handle similar matters less by implication and more by making fairly explicit statements, while attaching to these a prefabricated framing interpretation. For example, he may state that all families develop habitual patterns of communication, including some avoidances by which the family members protect each other, and therefore part of the therapist's job is to clarify these patterns and avoidances when they stand in the way of resolving important blocks between the family members; it is the therapist's responsibility to them all—while treating them impartially, although naturally each of them will feel at times he is not doing so—not to let the solution of such problems be missed even by such protective tendencies. Thus the family is given credit for their good intentions, while the therapist's position of stirring things up at times is defined as a positive duty for their benefit. Also the therapist will point out that they must have some important relationship with each other, regardless of their difficulties, since they have stayed together for a long time; in addition, they really know each other better than anyone else, including the therapist, can, and thus they are the best possible therapists for each other. This framing places responsibility for helpful participation on all the family members equally, which both calls on the more withdrawn ones to take more part and undercuts the usual tendency of some one family member to take over the situation from the therapist.

The members of our group also tend to be active in similar ways in connection with many of the more specific issues that arise initially. For example, we commonly avoid some dreary time-wasting by politely interrupting the parents' attempts to focus exclusively on the patient's illness. In addition, we tend to discipline the patient if he attempts to utilize the "I am the sick one, so I am not responsible" ploy, as the following example shows.

The therapist was questioning the parents in the initial session about their living. The mother was uneasy, apparently about her alcoholism, which had not yet been disclosed. At this point, the schizophrenic son broke in to announce how much he had benefited from shock therapy in the hospital. Immediately both parents discussed this with him, and the father asked if he wished more. The mother stated that maybe he needed tranquilizers, and then thought to ask him if he was currently taking them, to which the patient replied, "No." At this juncture, the therapist broke in to ask the patient in a rather commanding tone, "Bob, you're not on shock therapy now? Right?" The patient replied that he was not. The therapist added, "And you said you were not on drugs." Again the patient acknowledged that this was true. The therapist continued, "So it's fortunate then that you are *you* this morning here with us. In other words, you and mom and dad and I are all responsible for what we say and *that makes it easier to understand each other.*"

The patient's rescue operations that dig his own hole deeper are usually an issue in the first few minutes of the initial session. The therapist's criticism or irritation at these attempts implies not only that this kind of thing is not acceptable but also that the patient can do better. This attitude is in contrast to that of the parents, who usually will drop whatever they are engaged in and follow up the patient's intervention like a hound dog in pursuit. (However, an alternative approach that is sometimes feasible is to accept this line of joint interest in the patient's symptoms but to press the inquiry in such a way as to include more of the family circumstances surrounding symptomatic behavior and their relevance to it.) Another matter that comes up in the first session is the question of what to do if someone in the family is absent from one of the sessions. It may seem to be borrowing trouble to anticipate such a happening, but experience has taught us that the multitudinous excuses proffered for someone's not appearing would delight a sage truant officer. It seems more efficacious to announce to the family that there will be times when they do not wish to come and that such absence is a rather powerful lever to use against the therapist and against family members, or to announce that they are likely to feel reluctant to come just when important progress is occurring. Such announcements also emphasize our philosophy that family members do have a great effect on each other and that there is no such thing as not commenting even if the "No comment" is attempted through silence or through a nonappearance.

In summary, a few principal means that the therapist may use—separately, jointly, or alternatively, according to taste and circumstances—in handling the typical problems arising at the start of family therapy might be listed as follows. First, there is a certain place for being very clear, direct, and explicit. This is comparatively limited, applying mostly to practical details such as the schedule of meetings; unless the therapist is quite clear and definite, even such a simple matter can set off a long, inconclusive discussion. Second comes the making of certain matter-of-fact statements whereby the important messages are conveyed implicitly. Third comes the making of statements about some aspect of the therapy which are accompanied by some comment that serves to anticipate and disarm resistance—for example, "I intend to be impartial, though each of you will surely doubt that I am at times." This may be carried all the way to an "inversion of meaning" statement such as "There will be times, just as real progress is being made, when you will feel like not coming to the meetings."

From the discussion so far it must now be evident that active intervention in and management of family interaction has an important place in our initial work, and, indeed, this holds true of the further course of family therapy also. This active orientation, however, grew out of our experience and was not a predisposition except that experience in treating individual schizophrenics presses one toward an active and varied style of therapy. Nevertheless, in beginning our work with families, we were concerned lest activity on the part of the therapist would obscure family operations and dim the light of our research. Actually, it has been so difficult to keep the sicker families involved, to produce shifts and not mere repetitions of the standard patterns characteristic of any one family, that we are no longer so concerned about the therapist remaining a flyspeck by his own design and efforts, and more concerned with his avoiding being put into such a useless position by the family.

If it is kept in mind that families have horizontal as well as vertical layers, then the pattern of response to the therapist's intervention can simply be viewed as a further unfolding of the range of this particular family's transactions. By vertical, we mean going back in time; by horizontal, we mean layers of complexity of communications or, as they might be called, layers of defense in concentric circles. One of the things that the tyro therapist must experience is that he will have to deal with the same problem over and over again in different forms and guises, as the following example suggests.

Initially, the father of a paranoid patient complained to the therapist of his son's obesity and requested a diet for him. He and his wife expressed futility about "doing anything with him." They occasionally took action of an interesting sort, considering their son's suspicious nature; for example, the father sneaked out early one morning to tell the milkman that he was to ignore any requests for ice cream. The therapist held fast to his recommendation that the patient would change himself when he was ready, and several sessions later the patient announced that he had lost some weight. As the therapist tried to congratulate him, the mother cut in to discuss her own weight problem, and the father topped her by recounting a rather bizarre episode in which he was found unconscious and taken to a hospital in peril of his life.

This sequence was characteristic for this family. The patient's statements tended to be ignored or rationalized away, the mother usually sounded a serious note about something, and the father topped it by telling something on himself which, while dramatic, inevitably made him out to be slightly foolish. A kind of closure was usually attained at the end of these sequences by the father, mother, and son all chuckling slightly at the father's expense. This sort of closed sequence, however, constitutes the sort of pathological family homeostasis that it is the therapist's business and duty to alter.

Further Technical Means

As family therapy proceeds, we are ordinarily not much concerned with the topics and content of the family discussions, except perhaps when there is evident talking of one matter to avoid something else. Indeed, it may be valuable at times to shift the discussion from a hot topic to a less important one involving the same sort of family alignment and interaction, in the hope that the nature of the interaction can better be seen and some revision inaugurated while dealing with a more minor matter.

Such alteration of self-reinforcing and mutually destructive networks of interaction is the most general goal of our work with families, and our emphasis correspondingly is on means of influencing these patterns rather than on examining their content, or even on describing the pattern as such.

Our experience with this kind of repetitive pattern is that pointing it out to the family does little good. However, its meaning, intent, or focus can be shifted by the therapist's intervention, and after a series of such interventions, the pattern loses some of its highly stereotyped repetitiousness. Various means may be essayed in relation to this formidable task, several of which have already been mentioned. Implication is a powerful tool in the therapist's hands, but making explicit what the family members communicate only implicitly can be equally important. Framing or interpretation of messages—in a communicational, not psychoanalytic, sense of interpretation—is most important, and occurs in many varieties: the therapist may frame his own message, and, equally important, he may reframe and reinterpret the messages of family members. By this means, the positive side of difficult of provocative behavior in the family can be shown, sense made out of craziness, and congruence out of incongruence. Such inverting is a powerful lever for change. Certain sorts of dualistic positive-and-negative messages also are important, such as criticism administered with personal attention for easier swallowing or a strong comment given in a mild tone; in this sort of "quiet bombshell" there is an evident similarity between our communicational orientation and more orthodox psychiatric thought and practice.

We may also give advice. However, our aim in advising is not to tell family members the proper thing to do; rather it is to enable them to accept interest, advice, and help, for they ordinarily are so defensive as to disqualify and reject whatever is offered, even if they have been demanding it. If we can present a little advice in an acceptable way, in accepting it from us as experts, they take a first step toward accepting from each other.

The giving of some rather specific instructions as a technique in therapy illuminates this area still further. We do not expect to achieve change directly by giving instructions on how to behave, and we ordinarily avoid doing so, especially on matters of obvious practical importance—although this is where our advice and instructions are most likely to be solicited. Instead, we are apt to choose an apparently minor matter—which still will be involved in some significant pattern of interaction—and give an instruction to do A, expecting that the person, from our knowledge of his reactions, will in fact do B, which will cause change C in a family relationship. An example may clarify this complicated but significant situation:

The mother of a 15-year-old schizophrenic boy was a very managing woman, taking over everything from her nearly mute son, her rather quiet husband, and also from the struggling therapist. Yet she was very unhappy and anxious. Finally she was able to say one day that she was upset because she felt that her husband was distant; she couldn't get in close touch with him. Yet she felt wrong if she reacted to this, even if only by becoming silently upset. The main emphasis was on the problem of feeling wrong uncontrollably, even when she thought she had some just cause for distress. The therapist then suggested that she could act to resolve this problem of feeling wrong, if she seriously wanted to, by following a simple instruction. After a pause, she agreed. The therapist's instruction was that, during the following week, she should deliberately do something that she considered wrong. The only conditions imposed were that the wrong was not to be a really serious one and was to involve some other family member in some way; other than that, she should choose the action. During the next session, she revealed that the daring deed she had committed was sub-scribing to a book club.

The members of the research group laughed as they heard this section on the tape, thinking how constricted she was to commit such a minor sort of sin. How-ever, they had failed to appreciate the limitations placed on the range of action in this family, because the father, who in the session heard for the first time what she had done, angrily disapproved. Although his reasons were a bit obscure, they appeared to concern the expense involved. In fact, since this was not great, and money was used by the father as a means of control, the mother's independence seems more important. From this episode, the therapist and the group as a whole learned a little more about why this woman had to breathe her sick son's every breath. The fact that she was severely controlling did not mean that she was not similarly controlled by herself and her husband. And if control is that severe, then even the small change of behavior, change of evaluation, and change in relationship with her husband that this act represented, though initiated by the therapist's instruction, may be correspondingly significant.

FAMILY PATHOLOGY AND THERAPY:
A THEORETICAL SUMMARY

Perhaps we can now utilize the preceding material to attempt a more con-densed and general statement of our ideas on the pathology of these families and its treatment. Even though such a theoretical statement is bound to be over-simplified and incomplete at this stage of our knowledge, it will provide a basis for some comparison between our theoretical and therapeutic slants and those of other workers.

Summing up very broadly, then, it appears that these families of schizo-phrenics are enmeshed in a pathological but very strong homeostatic system of family interaction. That is, regardless of their past history—although that might be enlightening—they are *at present* interacting in ways that are unsatisfying and painful to all, provocative of gross symptomatology in at least one, and yet powerfully self-reinforcing. Their overt behavior may appear varied or even chaotic, but beneath this a pervasive and persistent pattern can be discerned, and one that is quite resistant even to outside therapeutic efforts at change.

How and why is this so? On what basis may such homeostasis be clarified and understood? We may at least begin to do so by using further our basic concepts of the double bind and the still broader concept of the necessary multiplicity of messages, of different levels, in all communication. These ideas, which were helpful in understanding the occurrence of schizophrenic behavior, are also helpful in attacking the more fundamental problem level: why does pathological behavior or organization persist, even under pressure to change? We have not solved this problem, but we can state a few leading ideas. First, the double bind pattern itself tends to be circular and interactive in a self-perpetuating way, even though we may speak of it carelessly as if it were a one-way matter, with a "binder" acting on a "victim." Actually, if A sends incongruent messages to B, B is very likely to respond with a correspondingly incongruent set of messages in reply. The one main difference likely to exist between their communications only serves to intensify the vicious circularity: if the incongruence between A's messages is concealed and B falls in with this, then the incongruence in B's reply is apt to be correspondingly *exaggerated,* the typical case for schizophrenic utterance. This in turn influences A toward further incongruence, even more concealed or denied, and so on. In three-party situations,[6] essentially the same process may occur. If A and B are parents giving incongruent messages to C, their child, C is likely to respond in a disturbed way with markedly incongruent messages and ones likely to have some reference to the family relationships; at this A and B are very likely to insist more strongly that there are no differences in what they think and say, rather than admitting differences, as we have described earlier.

Second, the existence of a multiplicity of messages obviously offers great possibilities for interaction among family members in which nothing is ever clarified because *both* agreement and disagreement can be avoided. It is possible, with incongruent messages, to agree with another person, yet not agree, by agreeing at one level of message yet disagreeing at another or indicating that it is not really the speaker who is agreeing. And similarly with disagreement; this also can be no-yet-yes. We find that members of families in which there is a schizophrenic are likely to communicate largely by remarks we may call "disqualifying"—that is, they effectively negate what someone else has said, only in an indirect way, so that statements are not really met. This sort of communication and its paralyzing effects have been particularly striking in some standard interviews that we have given experimentally, since these interviews focused on family organization, leadership, and planning, first by asking the family members to plan something they would like to do together, and then by inquiring who was in charge of the family.

This sort of problem may be seen from a somewhat different angle by considering the two sorts of families of schizophrenics discriminated by Lidz [7]: one (skew families), in which harmony is conveyed overtly but with covert persistent disagreement; the other (schism families), in which there is constant overt scrapping yet the family members somehow remain together for many years. Both may be seen as types of pathological organization whose stability is related to the existence of such incongruent double messages about family relationships plus the avoidance of recognition and acknowledgment of such incongruence by family members.

Any move toward change or therapy, finally, immediately encounters difficulties similar to those just mentioned. The members of these families have long been adept at using incongruent messages. Thus, if some change in behavior or family organization is proposed, what is more likely than that it will be met with agreement that is not agreement, with disagreement that is not disagreement, with agreement from one member and disagreement from another, while they insist they are together on the matter, and so on? If a specific change can be brought about in the behavior of some member, it is likely to be negated by a shifting of the general context, by the same person or another: "Yes, my husband is behaving better to me now, but of course that's just because you told him to, not that he cares any more about me." Or a more general shift may be negated by a specific change, or the two parents may both change at once so that they remain on opposite sides of whatever fence divided them, even if reversed from their original stands. All this also throws light on why description or labeling of family behavior is usually ineffective, even where the members themselves appear to grasp it; thus we are more concerned with altering interaction than with "insight."

In other words, these families have a tremendous aptitude for "plus ça change, plus c'est la même chose." It appears increasingly clear to us as we work with them that to be effective we must meet them on their own ground, though with different orientation—toward positive change instead of defensive maintenance of a sick system. That is, the therapist must himself employ dual or multiple messages involving such incongruences as will serve to come to grips with the whole complexity of the messages of the family members he must deal with. A reconsideration of the techniques we have mentioned earlier shows readily enough that for many this is already explicitly so, and it is implicit for most of the others. That is, we have been concerned with using explicit statements that convey concealed and unexpected implicit meanings as well, with using content messages joined with framing statements, with giving instructions whose carrying out will constitute a further message. We have spoken of this elsewhere, perhaps too narrowly, as the "therapeutic double bind"; the broad principle described here, of using multiple—and often incongruent—messages therapeutically, is what needs recognition, and then further investigation.

OURSELVES AND OTHERS: FAMILY
THERAPY AS A COMMUNICABLE DISEASE

Except for political rallies, baseball games, and burlesque shows, it is difficult to imagine a situation more capable of arousing enthusiasm among therapists than conjoint family therapy. It is not completely clear to us why this should be, but it does make us cautious about accepting new adherents and we do attempt to review our work with the limited objectivity available to us.

There is little question that exposure to conjoint family therapy alters the psychotherapeutic approach of the exposed, both in his private and research work. Most of those engaged in our family therapy research project have private practices on a part-time basis. It is fascinating and predictable to note that their psychotherapeutic approach undergoes at least the following changes:

1. The therapist will become more "active" in individual therapy, especially in suggesting the meaning of other people's behavior vis-à-vis the patient.

2. The therapist will be less interested in diagnosis or the accepted dynamic formulations; he will tend, rather, to describe his patients in terms of an interlocking milieu, consisting mainly of the immediate family situation, but drawing also upon the wider family context and sometimes including ethnic or subcultural factors.

3. The therapist will greatly increase the number of couples he treats, mostly in the conjoint situation. We believe it is rare for our therapists not to have met the spouses of all their patients.

These tendencies, in other words, parallel several distinctive emphases in the orientation of our family therapy: activity of the therapist rather than passive listening, more concern for alteration of behavior than for "insight," more intense focus on the present than on the past, and more attention to interaction than to intrapersonal experience.

Perhaps two brief examples will illustrate how the family therapy bug affects its victim:

Example A. A catatonic young woman was discharged from a Midwestern state hospital because her parents were moving to California. She was referred to one of us for recommendations as to local hospital care. Although the patient was mute and stiff, she appeared evanescently pleased by the suggestion that if she and her parents were willing to start family therapy, we could see how it would work out to have her live at home, with a practical nurse assisting the mother during the daytime. She has remained out of the hospital now for two years and appears to be functioning fairly adequately. Previous to our family work, it would have been unthinkable that such a catatonic patient who did not appear to be in good contact would not be hospitalized.

Example B. On an emergency home visit, one of us met a 60-year-old woman who had made a mild suicidal gesture. She appeared to be in a typical agitated depression, and the question seemed to be where to hospitalize her and whether it should be in an institution where she would receive electroshock therapy. After speaking to her for a few minutes, the psychiatrist asked her daughter with whom she was living to join them, and he noted that, despite a smiling cooperative kindliness, not all was well between daughter and mother. When this was touched on, the daughter mentioned that she had her husband and her own 17-year-old daughter to worry about and perhaps her mother's attitude was a little bit too much. The mother sparked noticeably at this and implied that the daughter didn't have a complete romance with her husband and had in fact invited the mother to live with her partially on this account. The patient was not sent to a hospital but was seen in conjoint therapy with her daughter, son-in-law, and granddaughter. After a very brief time, the blocked communication in the family had noticeably improved and the mother decided she would like to live by herself. In retrospect, it seemed fairly certain that getting the patient's daughter involved after a few minutes of the initial visit, and the orientation of the therapist, altered what would have been fairly standard psychiatric disposition.

Transference, Countertransference, and Interaction

Many analysts have had strong doubts about the idea of family therapy, which are often put on transference and countertransference grounds. Thus the terms "transference and countertransference" are troublesome unless it is kept in mind that they refer strictly to aspects of a very special situation—psychoanalysis. We have no doubt that our therapists have feelings about the family members and vice versa; on the other hand, no clarity is achieved if we label such states of mind transference and countertransference. There are several reasons for this:

Transference is a manifestation related to the inactivity prescribed for standard psychoanalytic treatment. The patient, on the basis of minimal cues, creates a framework and embroiders it with past personal references. In conjoint psychotherapy, there is a good deal of activity, even if the therapist is only acting as a traffic cop. If skillfully managed, the interaction is largely among family members and not with the therapist. Thus we would consider the proper intervention when a wife is chopping her husband to ribbons not to be "Look what you're doing to the poor man," but to ask *him* if she always shows her attachment to him in this way. The wife will be fascinated awaiting his reply and will be busy with her rebuttal.

That is, with so much interaction among the family members and active therapeutic focus on this, there is no emergence of standard transference phenomena. What we do see can better be labeled parataxic distortions, since the data consist of discrete examples of expectations on the part of a family member that the therapist does or does not fulfill. Some of these instances even seem to be a combination of ignorance and misinformation as to what one can legitimately expect of a therapist, while others appear to result from explanatory concepts that the person brought with him into therapy, such as, "All men are . . . ."

It is difficult to explain the difference between these phenomena in individual and family therapy unless one has observed or participated in both forms of psychotherapy. A statement by a family member which, if it occurred in an individual psychotherapeutic session, may be labeled evidence of transference can have a very different meaning in family therapy. Thus, a comment by the wife that the therapist is the only one who has ever understood her is apt to be an expression of dissatisfaction with her husband, a pointing out of a direction he should take, and before the therapist can label this himself as father transference the husband's reaction will have to be dealt with, plus one of the children, plus the wife's reaction to her husband's reaction, and so on.

The same difficulties apply to countertransference. If the therapist is active, he becomes aware of his feelings partially through the kind of action he takes, and often not until a supervisory session. An experienced, fairly secure therapist may change the direction of a beginning feeling in himself by taking an action opposite to the feeling. For example, if he finds himself irritated by the mother's quietly nagging, martyred tone, he may turn to the father and ask what he experienced in himself during the time when the wife was speaking. On the surface, it would appear that the therapist simply passes the buck to the father and that this technique might be a fairly destructive one. On the other hand, if it is kept in mind that the father has been having thoughts for years about his wife's attitude, and that now is his chance to express them with the support of another male present, a different face is put on the situation. By the time the husband has made his comments, the therapist may then be in a mood to reaccept the wife and to help find out what she has to complain about. Such interlocking transactions are part of the ordinary family life and have been referred to in papers on everything from pecking order to role playing.

RESULTS

We are not yet in a position to support any claim that family therapy is better or worse than the more usual methods of treating schizophrenics. Insufficient time has elapsed, and unusual and difficult problems of evaluation are posed by our interest not only in the identified patient but in the parents and siblings and especially in the functioning of the family as a whole, while means for evaluation at this level are largely lacking in psychiatry at present. Thus it is appropriate that the emphasis in this paper has been on our ideas and methods; we have pointed out that family therapy differs from individual therapy, in ways we have tried to outline, and that this difference helps to shape a new orientation in the therapist. We may, however, end by discussing briefly the inconclusive yet promising results of our therapeutic efforts so far.

Various studies have shown that prognosis for recovery from schizophrenia is importantly related to the history of the illness—that is, its duration, amount of hospitalization and other treatment without success, and so on. Therefore, our evaluative scheme for family therapy, with reference to the identified patients, is based on comparing the level of their social adaptation, before family therapy and currently, against the background of information on the prior history of their illness. On this basis, our cases can hardly be considered other than difficult ones. We have worked with eighteen families so far. Of the identified schizophrenic patients in these families, eleven were males ranging in age from 13 to 41, and seven were females ranging in age from 14 to 34. Of these eighteen, six had been originally diagnosed as schizophrenic between 10 and 16 years ago, four between 5 and 10 years ago, and eight less than 5 years ago. Perhaps four of these eight were first seen by us as fairly new or acute cases, but fourteen of our eighteen patients could be labeled as already chronic cases when we first saw them. Some had been diagnosed in early childhood, as young as 3 years; the maximum age at first diagnosis was 25. Eleven of these patients had been hospitalized at some time, from a minimum of 2 months up to 6 years maximum, the average being 3 to 4 years. Of the seven patients never hospitalized, probably three or four were clinically sick enough to justify hospitalization and had avoided it only because they were so young or had such passive-withdrawing symptomatology that their behavior could still be tolerated or handled within the home.

Information on prior treatment other than hospitalization, although it is certainly not complete, shows that at least seven patients had received EST and one insulin shock, eight had had tranquilizing drugs, and twelve had received individual psychotherapy ranging from a minimum of three sessions to a maximum of 9 years of intermittent examination and treatment. In several cases family members—usually the mother—had also had some individual psychotherapy. In only four instances, all young persons and fresh cases, had there been no therapy before family treatment was started.

At the time of writing, our families had been seen, usually on a once-weekly basis for an hour or an hour and a half, from a minimum of 3 months up to 41 months in one case, the average being about 12 months. Most of our families are still in treatment, although four terminated therapy against our advice.

There were seven patients hospitalized at the outset of family therapy. Of these, one is still in the hospital, three are living at home and able to go out unaccompanied, one is living at home but working, one is living alone and caring for her child though still financially dependent on the parents, and one is living alone, working part-time but financially dependent on her parents. Thus, six of these seven have shown a noticeable improvement in terms of social adaptation and independence. Of the remaining patients, nine were young persons, mostly never hospitalized, who were living with parents and restricted to the home or, if going out, not productive—that is, not working or doing badly in school. All but two of these improved in such degree as starting to school again, changing from failure to passing, starting to work, or at least starting to go out unaccompanied, as did the two remaining patients who had previously been confined to their homes after release from hospitalization.

It is still more difficult to characterize results with the parents and siblings, and with the family as a whole. But, very broadly, it can be said that the other family members generally have improved, though less noticeably than the identified patients. More than half of the fathers were judged improved by their therapists, with the rest showing no distinct change. The picture for the mothers was similar except for two cases where it was judged that the mother was worse. And limited data on siblings showed about evenly divided improvement and no change, excepting again one sibling judged worse.

Finally, though it often appeared a severe course of treatment, all of our therapists seem to have been helped, without exception.

NOTES AND REFERENCES

1. Bateson, G., Jackson, D. D., Haley, J., and Weakland, J. H., "Toward a Theory of Schizophrenia," *Behav. Sci.* 1:251-264, 1956.
2. Jackson, D. D.: "The Question of Family Homeostasis," *Psychiat. Quart.,* Suppl., 31:79-90, 1959.
3. For instance, Weakland, J. H., "The 'Double Bind' Hypothesis of Schizophrenia and Three-Party Interaction," in Jackson, D. D. (Ed.), *The Etiology of Schizophrenia,* New York, Basic Books, 1960, pp. 373-388.
4. Despite our previous discussion of the "illusion of alternatives" in Weakland, J. H., and Jackson, D. D., "Patient and Therapist Observations on the Circumstances of a Schizophrenic Episode," *A. M. A. Arch. Neurol. Psychiat.* 79:554-574, 1958.
5. Jackson, D. D., and Weakland, J. H., "Schizophrenic Symptoms and Family Interaction," *A. M. A. Arch. Gen. Psychiat.* 1:618-621, 1959.
6. Discussed in Weakland, J. H., note 3.
7. Lidz, T., and Fleck, S., "Schizophrenia, Human Integration, and the Role of Family," in Jackson, D. D. (Ed.), *The Etiology of Schizophrenia,* New York, Basic Books, 1960, pp. 323-345. For other references and more extensive discussion, see Weakland, J. H., note 3, pp. 380-382.

3

Multiple Impact Therapy: An Experiment

AGNES RITCHIE

The Youth Development Project, a unit of the Neuropsychiatric Department of the University of Texas Medical Branch at Galveston, came into existence about 1952 to provide a specialized service of therapy and counseling for teen-agers and their families; to offer to medical students, nursing students, residents, and members of related professions an opportunity to study the adolescent and his problems and to learn some techniques of treating them; and—by no means least—to develop and test new ideas, new theories, new techniques of helping. In short, the functions of the Youth Development Project include service, teaching, and research.

Since the Medical Branch serves the entire state of Texas, patients may be

Reprinted with permission of the author and publisher from *Social Work* 5:16-21, 1960.

This paper is a report of a demonstration project of the Neuropsychiatric Department of the University of Texas Medical Branch at Galveston, Texas, partially supported in its pilot year by a grant from the Hogg Foundation for Mental Health and at present supported in part by a Mental Health Project Grant from the National Institute of Mental Health, U. S. Public Health Service.

referred from any of the 254 counties in the state. The staff and medical consultants of the Youth Development Project faced repeatedly the frustration of having to recommend long-time therapy and counseling for adolescent patients and their families who lived in communities where such treatment was not available within a fifty-mile radius—if they could afford it, which many could not. The wish and need to offer help and hope to some of these troubled adolescents and families, many of whom were desperate, was at least as strong a factor as any other in the development of the *multiple impact therapy.*

Multiple impact therapy (referred to familiarly within our agency as MIT) is a brief, usually two-day, intensive study and treatment of a family in crisis by a guidance clinic team.[1] In our project the team includes a psychiatrist, clinical psychologist who is also research director, a psychiatric social worker, and a resident clinical psychologist. The multiple impact therapy team has the benefit of regular consultation and supervision of senior staff members of the Department of Neurology and Psychiatry, as well as opportunity for consultation with Medical Branch staff and personnel. The team devotes full time, six or seven hours a day for two (sometimes two and a half) days, to one family. Families come to the clinic frequently from a considerable distance, anywhere from 50 to 450 miles, sometimes viewing the trip to Galveston as their last hope.

The multiple impact therapy plan is based on two assumptions. First, that individuals and families facing a crisis are stimulated to mobilize strength and resources to meet it, and that they are more receptive to interpretations, more likely to be flexible in attitude, than at other times. The second assumpion is that in any type of psychotherapy there is likely to be faster and more dramatic change in the early stages of treatment, and that under long-range treatment later change and improvement is more gradual— is a deepening and strengthening of the initial movement, during the first few hours or weeks, toward improved health or adjustment.

The procedures are quite flexible, but consist essentially of an initial family-team conference, followed by a series of individual interviews, joint interviews (two patients with one or more therapists, or two therapists with one or more patients), and overlapping interviews—all these procedures being interrupted by formal and informal team conferences. The family, also, is advised to talk together, to share thoughts, ideas, insights, and feelings, both about themselves and about the clinic experience and the clinic team. Psychological tests are given the adolescent during the first afternoon, and results are shared, in a general way, with the parents and the adolescent, usually early on the second day. The two-day contact terminates with a final family-team conference, sometimes with the adolescent present but sometimes not, and it is in this last conference that "the back-home problem" is discussed in terms of specific recommendations and that insights gained during the preceding day and a half are applied to behavior and situations that can be anticipated. This whole project at present is primarily research and demonstration; the family is told of the plan for a follow-up conference six months later, and they understand that this is primarily for the benefit of the research team, to evaluate results of our work with the family, although they are also assured that additional consultation or service from us is available to them either at the end of six months or earlier if a new crisis arises.

An important feature of multiple impact therapy procedures is the overlapping interview, in which a team member who has been talking privately with a family member terminates his interview and joins another conference, either alone or accompanied by the person he has been seeing. One or the other of the team gives a brief summary of the conference up to this point. This summary not only informs the newcomer but gives the patient an opportunity for critique of the therapist on the accuracy and interpretation of what has gone on between them and of the work with the family. Differences of opinion or of interpretation between two parents, or between parent and child, are sometimes aired and resolved in these overlapping interviews.

Differences of opinion or interpretation between team members are also brought out and discussed fully in the family's presence. In some families this freedom in the team to disagree—sometimes with heat, but with no decrease in mutual respect or ability to work together effectively and to remain friendly—has tremendous impact on the family; they are exposed to a demonstration rather than an exhortation to express feelings as well as thoughts. Sometimes they are invited to participate in the discussion, which conveys our confidence that they are not so fragile that they cannot bear to disagree with us or with each other. Frequently differences are not resolved, and we comment, explicitly, that there is frequently room for different interpretations and methods of handling problems, and we express confidence in the individual's or family's ability to find their own answers and solutions. In a few instances, where communication within the family is so poor that no interchange occurs, the team members may present deliberately different versions or interpretations of some material that has been presented, each arguing for the validity of his point of view, with the patients being invited to participate, even to take sides.

PROCEDURES

The procedures for our multiple impact therapy are generally as follows: the clinical team meets together before the family arrives and reviews briefly the information already available about the nominal patient, the family, and the situation. This information may have been furnished by the referring person or agency (such as the family doctor, the John Sealy Hospital or outpatient clinic, a school, or a social agency), or the applicants may have been seen previously by our clinic staff for brief screening interviews. In the initial team conference there is usually some speculation about family dynamics and the genesis of the presenting problem, and some tentative plans are made for distribution of labor among the team during the first day, or at least the first morning of the contract.

The family has been advised to arrive at the clinic at 9:30 in the morning, and at about that time they are invited to meet with the team in a conference room. The initial family-team conference is usually planned to last about an hour, during which time a great deal may happen. First there are introductions all around, and the family's attention is called to the tape-recording equipment; in suggesting seating arrangements both the distance and the position of each person in relation to microphones is considered, as well as separate chairs for family members (so that they will not sit together on the couch and run the risk of feeling that they are huddled together against an imposing array of "experts").

After a very few moments spent in amenities and in getting settled, the family is invited to explain the problem to us or—since they know we already know why they are there—to bring us up to date on the current situation. Almost invariably one family member will act as spokesman initially, and we encourage participation from the others; all our questions and comments to encourage participation are worded in a way calculated to convey respect for the feelings and opinions of each member of the family, and to convey our recognition, sometimes verbalized, that the behavior of each, whatever it may have been, must have "made sense" at the time if viewed in the light of interpersonal relationships and attitudes, or in terms of the total situation.[2] For example, when parent or parents describe the patient in terms of his difference from another child who is, for example, more obedient or respectful, or more industrious, one of us will usually address a question or comment to the adolescent about sibling relationships, e.g., "Your brother seems to know how to get you in bad with your folks. What do you do to get him in bad?" Or to the woman who cashed rubber checks on her husband's bank account, "It looks like you just had to see if your husband would stand by you!" Or perhaps we would say to her husband at that point, "Mrs. S seems to trust you enough to know that you would protect her!" Interpretation and even speculation by the team are begun very early, usually in the opening conference. For example, when the chief complaint is school phobia, questions about the problem are couched in terms of the child's "fear to leave home," with verbalized speculation by team members about conscious or unconscious fears the child may have as to what might happen at home in his absence. The theory of the oedipal conflict and its application to the family problem and the crisis are presented usually in simple nontechnical words.

INDIVIDUAL INTERVIEWS

Not infrequently there is more communication between family members and more sharing of feelings both positive and negative in the initial conference than has occurred in the family for many years, if ever. However, unaccustomed as most families are to this free communication, considerable tension is built up from things none feel free to say before the others. Usually after about an hour one team member will suggest that we separate into individual sessions, and each team member invites a family member to accompany him to a private office. Although pairing off at this point is extremely flexible, most commonly the psychiatrist will see the adolescent patient after the initial conference, the social worker (who in our team is a woman) interviews the mother, the psychologist interviews the father, and the second psychologist interviews any other participant; it may be another child in the family, or a close relative who lives in or near the home and is an important person in the child's environment, or a referring person (social worker, probation officer, school counselor) who for one reason or another has accompanied the family to the clinic. When only the adolescent and two parents are with us, the fourth team member may participate in one of the individual interviews—may conceivably visit from office to office, permitting more use of the overlapping summary technique described—or may withdraw for the balance of the first morning.

The individual interview with the adolescent gives the child an opportunity to receive undivided attention from the doctor, to "present his case" and his side of any argument, and to ventilate his feelings more freely than he could in his parents' presence; at the same time it gives the psychiatrist an opportunity to form a diagnostic impression of the patient. If it was not mentioned in the earlier group meeting, the patient is told about psychological tests that will be given him after lunch, and any anxiety or resistance about this can be handled immediately. Individual interviews with adolescents are shorter than with adults, and the staff member who has seen the boy usually calls by phone for permission to join an interview with one or the other parent.

These initial individual interviews with the parents are frequently used by them to ventilate grievances and present defenses and rationalizations, each for his or her behavior and attitude toward spouse, patient, and community.

GATHERING INFORMATION

There is very little history taking as such, but relevant family history, developmental history of the adolescent nominal patient, of the other children, and of parents themselves, is usually brought out in these sessions, as this information, in the parent's mind, is pertinent to the problem or as explanation or defense of his own attitude, behavior, and so on. The therapist soon has an opportunity, either in an overlapping session immediately following the interview or in a later joint session, to review relevant history briefly, integrating it into history or rationalizations presented by other members of the family and/or condensing or rephrasing information in an interpretive way.

The family is advised at the end of the morning to share as freely as they can with each other any ideas, insights, or reactions they have had during the morning, and are told that the team, also, will confer during lunch, sharing information and ideas with each other, so that work can be continued together during the afternoon. This same recommendation is made to the family at the end of the day, and some of the most dramatic improvements in communication between family members, and especially between parents, occur away from the office.

During the afternoon of the first day the adolescent is usually given a battery of psychological tests. Parents are seen individually at first in what we call cross-ventilation interviews, in that the team member who has seen the father in the morning now sees the mother, and vice versa. By this time each team member has some fairly clear-cut impression of the strengths and weaknesses of each parent; the one who has seen the mother for an hour or more has some appreciation of what father "has to put up with." Discrepancies and distortions not uncovered in overlapping sessions during the morning come to light as the team confers during and after lunch, and during subsequent sessions cloudy areas are clarified, not only by team but also by patients.

Probably the dominant leitmotif of the team's activity with the family is the emphasis on each member's role in the family: the delineation and spelling out of the appropriate role of father, of mother, of child. In most of the twenty-six families seen during the past twelve months, mothers have been—with a depressing uniformity—preoccupied with motherhood and the fathers frequently preoccupied with job or with hobby, sometimes to the point of being psychologically excluded from the family, more than one father has seemed and has felt more like a roomer or boarder than a husband and father. Many mothers have defensively protested about their endless efforts to be a "good mother" and have offered (much too readily) to accept full responsibility, even guilt, for the children's difficulties. Both directly and indirectly we have encouraged parents to rediscover each other, to seek and share adult interests, companionship, and recreation with each other and with their peers. We attempt to build up the father's confidence, and his wife's, in his ability to function as the head of the house. We point out to the mother and to her husband her feminine attractiveness (actual or potential) and express concern that she is denying herself adult feminine satisfactions in life, giving them up to live in a children's world. The unconscious emotional exploitation of children by parents who are no longer giving and receiving tenderness and emotional satisfaction from each other and the obstacles this places in the maturation of the children are frankly presented in simple, nontechnical language as a common phenomenon occurring in many families, and the applications made as this operates in the particular family.

The second day is an accelerated version of the previous day, usually starting with a brief team-family conference, followed by individual and joint sessions. The decisions as to who sees whom and in what combinations are based on evaluations as to relationships established between a family member and a team member or on the team's judgment as to the effectiveness of certain special attributes or attitudes of individual team members. Overlapping interviews are more freely used on the second day, and by this time the rewards of freer communication are sufficiently appreciated by the family members so that usually no objection is raised to sharing with each other newly discovered insights. This disintegration of the usual confidentiality, with the knowledge and approval of the confider, seems to be a criterion of the family's trust in the team and increased trust and confidence in each other.

The final conference, which occurs during the last hour or two of the second day, has been described earlier and is usually devoted to discussion of the "back-home problem," with much more active participation by both parents than in the opening session.

TENTATIVE EVALUATION

A wide range of presenting problems and types of crises have been treated by these methods during the past ten months. These have included chronic runaways, delinquent acting-out behavior, school failure and school phobia, homosexual behavior and other sexual deviations, and so on. In fact, the diagnostic categories have included the range from adjustment reactions through the schizophrenias. Six-month follow-up evaluations have been done on all twelve families seen during the pilot study and on seven families of the current series, with quite promising findings. Institutionalization of the adolescent, either in a correctional school, a mental hospital, or some other residential facility, seemed imminent and inevitable in many cases, but has been avoided (or at least postponed) in all but two instances. This is a very gross measure of success, but repeat psychological tests and professional evaluations of change or improvement in various areas of individual and family adjustment indicate that the effectiveness of this type of treatment for the limited number of families seen so far is as great (statistically) as the longer type of conventional therapy. It should be mentioned that as many professional manhours of time are invested in each family we have seen as in six months or more of one-hour-a-week appointments in conventional, individual therapy. A three- or four-member team devoting six or seven hours a day for two days represents between thirty-six and fifty hours of interviewing and conferring, without counting preliminary correspondence and/or conferring, recording, and the like.

Among the twenty-six cases studied during the past year, two families in which the crisis centered around a preadolescent child were included successfully, and it seems evident that the multiple impact therapy procedures are equally applicable to this kind of family. In six of these twenty-six families the crisis situation was the return of the adolescent to the home and community following a period of institutional care in a training school or a psychiatric hospital. These youths had the benefit, of course, of the training and treatment services of the institutions, but prognosis for satisfactory adjustment in the home environment was considered poor in each case; by this is meant that the physicians and agencies who referred these cases to the Youth Development Project expressed the opinion that the adolescent patients would quickly regress to the earlier deviant and antisocial behavior which precipitated their removal from home and community. In the four of these six families in which formal follow-up evaluations have been made this has not happened. On the other hand, family structure has been strengthened, parents are more supportive, each of the other, and more accepting and more realistically firm with the children, and after a period of testing these new strengths and the new limits imposed by parents, the adolescent nominal patients have been able gradually to settle down into reasonably acceptable and appropriate behavior patterns.

Children's institutions and placement agencies have long recognized that planning for discharge is at least as important and in many ways more difficult than initial planning and preparation for placement. Ideally, discharge planning is a part of the work with child and family throughout placement, but frequently this is impractical or sporadic. If an adaptation of multiple impact therapy can be used as part of discharge planning, this will be a valuable tool for many types of institutions.

Much study remains to be done before the possibilities and the limitations of this approach can be clearly understood and described. Originally developed to meet a particular problem in a rather specialized clinic, multiple impact therapy procedures have already proved flexible and adaptable for use in several different settings and in the treatment of a variety of individual and family problems. Several outpatient clinics have expressed an interest in planning for demonstration or use of multiple impact therapy in their own agencies, and indeed have experimented successfully with these techniques, or with a modification of the procedure adapted to their own agency needs and staff resources. Our experience to date has indicated that this type of procedure will prove a valuable addition to the therapeutic tools of guidance clinics, hospitals, residential treatment centers, and so forth, as well as a teaching device of merit in the training of mental health workers.

ACKNOWLEDGMENTS

Acknowledgment is made for participation in all phases of the project to its directors, Harold A. Goolishian, Ph.D., and Eugene C. McDanald, M.D., and to the other basic team members: Robert MacGregor, Ph.D., research director, Franklin P. Schuster, M.D., psychiatrist, and Cullen Mancuso, M.A., Resident in psychology.

NOTES AND REFERENCES

1. Brief descriptions of the psychotherapeutic procedures from the standpoint of their personal experiences with them have been given by Dr. Goolishian before the American Orthopsychiatric Association in San Francisco, March, 1959; by Dr. MacGregor before the Southwestern Psychological Association in Topeka, May, 1959; and by Dr. Schuster before the American Psychiatric Association in Philadelphia, April, 1959. Agnes Ritchie also presented a description of the procedures at a meeting of the San Jacinto Chapter of the National Association of Social Workers in February, 1959.
2. MacGregor, R., "Multiple Impact Psychotherapy with Families," paper read at Southwestern Psychological Association, Topeka, May, 1959.

4

On the Nature and Sources of the Psychiatrist's Experience with the Family of the Schizophrenic

LESLIE SCHAFFER

LYMAN C. WYNNE

JULIANA DAY

IRVING M. RYCKOFF

ALEXANDER HALPERIN

Our intention in this paper is twofold. We wish first of all to describe some experiences regularly encountered in the course of psychotherapeutic work with schizophrenic patients together with their families. Second, we intend to discuss the nature and sources of these experiences in terms of the light that may be thrown on the latent culture of the family and thus on the shaping of characteristically schizophrenic experience. This paper, undertaken in the course of a program of research primarily concerned with the familial context of mental disorder, may be understood as a kind of stocktaking. In an attempt to formulate an approach to the understanding of mental disorder as an ailment of the family organization, it will focus specifically on one element of the ailment—namely, the disorder of thought which has, since Bleuler, been considered one of the fundamental symptoms of the schizophrenic state.

Early in our work with families with at least one schizophrenic member, we noticed that the therapist's experience was singularly different from that with

Reprinted with the permission of author and publisher from *Psychiatry* 25:32-45, 1962.

families in which other kinds of mental disorder were present.[1] The difference was not simply one of more intense and pervasive anxiety, although it included this; it was a difference that was readily, even vividly, sensed, but which remained elusive of definition and always apparently just beyond grasp. The experience tended informally to be reflected in the use of words such as maddening, enraging, bewildering, and exhausting; it was all of these and yet more than and different from all of them. To begin with, the whole matter seemed an incidental nuisance which interfered with carrying out the task as we then conceived of it, and this tendency to dissociation is germane to that follows here. We found ourselves tempted to set the experience aside and become occupied with matters such as the spoken content of the hour or a variety of technical problems related to the novelty of the setting—matters which did not so completely reduce us to a state of inarticulate bafflement. In this paper we wish to reverse this tendency; we shall focus on the experience as a major finding and discuss its implications for the pathology of the family, setting aside the innumerable other problems associated either with the nature of schizophrenic disorder or with the technical problems of attempting to treat the family as a group. We will touch on some aspects of the setting in which the observations were made, but will not otherwise be concerned with problems of therapeutic technique.

THE CONTEXT OF OBSERVATION

In the setting of a research hospital, we have chosen to work with families in which the patient—the focus of the presenting complaint—is a person in the late teens or early twenties, sufficiently disturbed or disabled so that hospital care and management are required. The family therapy group consists minimally of the person defined as the patient, both parents, and two psychotherapists. Optimally, the group might include everyone significantly involved in the situation within which the disorder came about—all those immediately participant in the shared dilemma, impasse, or crisis of which the illness may be regarded as one manifest aspect, although by no means the only important one.

The family's presenting definition of which member is the sick one may be most plausible, and more than adequately supported by the behavior of the one labeled in this way. In the case of psychosis, the definition may be compelling to the point where there has seemed to be no question about the necessity for hospital care. However, we do not take this as meaning that the definition must be accepted literally and exclusively as *merely* the natural consequence of illness. The definition may be among the consequences of illness, but is not necessarily simply that. To act exclusively on the family's conception and to base the entire strategy of treatment and thought on this, may, we propose, serve to reinforce the structure of the family and thus help to perpetuate the form of the matrix within which, say, schizophrenic patterns of adaptation have developed and tend to endure. Thus while it may be found essential to admit one member of the family to the hospital—the one who has somehow come to be manifestly ill—it is at least equally necessary to remain alert to questions unlikely to arise within the family, questions, for example, about the genesis of the situation within which this person, rather than another, has become ill, and about the functional value of the illness for the family as a group.

From the standpoint we have adopted as potentially useful and enlightening, the family is the analogue of the patient or the group in more conventional psychiatric theory and practice and the setting of family therapy is conceived of and used both as the means and the object of collaborative investigation. The work begins with the provisional acceptance of, and interest in, the family's conception of what (and who) ails them, and with a contractual agreement that the family will, together with the patient, participate in the work on a regular and continuing basis. The group meets twice each week for periods of an hour; the patient (a term to be understood here as invariably contained within quotation marks) may or may not be seen concurrently in individual psychotherapy.

To a considerable extent, the model for the setting as we have conceived it was derived from that of the psychoanalytic situation, at least with reference to the participation and goals of the therapists. Their initial goal is the provision of a stable setting within which the family group process may unfold as spontaneously as possible, in whatever way it will, within the limits of the setting. These limits begin to be defined during an introductory period of mutual appraisal and orientation, roughly comparable to a trial analysis.

The therapists' long-range goal, and the major emphasis they present, is that of discovering as much as possible of the dimensions and sources of the current predicament. The task is proposed as a joint undertaking, in which it may be possible that the family's concerns, however presented, and the therapists' investigative interests will coincide sufficiently for the work to be mutually rewarding. Advice is generally restricted to the invitation that the members of the group notice whatever thoughts they may have during the sessions, and get them said. The overt participation of the therapists is otherwise confined to comment, and, in its broadest sense, interpretation—the last a matter which we shall presently discuss in some detail.

The mere fact of number invites comparison with the more conventional forms of analytic group therapy, but certain gross structural differences are immediately apparent. Group therapy commonly includes a number of persons, ordinarily strangers to one another, who come together regularly in a situation which is characterized, among other things, by its discontinuity from the rest of their lives.

In the beginning of their work together, they are unlikely to be preoccupied with complaints about one another or to share an absorption with the distribution of blame within the group. With such notable exceptions as treatment groups made up of prisoners or mothers of schizophrenic patients, the participants are likely to arrive having formally acknowledged their roles as patients, however conflictually so. A degree of privacy attends their dealings with one another, and their joint explorations of tensions and relationships emergent within the group. While the group has an evolving natural history of its own, it remains, in a sense, wholly synthetic, an artifact, its past dating back only to an arbitrary point in time and with no future as a community. As with the psychoanalytic situation, these synthetic discontinuities facilitate going beyond conventional limits of that which is made explicit: the unique limitations provide the opportunity for a continuing expansion of self-disclosure.

In contrast to this, in family therapy at least three persons are present who have a long natural history as a more or less established and ongoing social system: for at least one of them—more if siblings are present—the history is life-long. There is commonly the assumption that they will have some kind of future together—a future which, in the families of schizophrenic persons, is characteristically defined nostalgically in terms of a return to the idealized prepsychotic state of affairs. The discontinuities stressed above are absent, save with regard to the therapists, and the family's association together continues between sessions. We will not do more than mention the complexity of the structure: superimposed upon the more or less durable—and durably conflictful—structure of the family group is the role structure of the therapy group, and there is commonly considerable ambiguity within the family concerning the roles of parents and siblings. These matters aside, the task of the group is fundamentally that described by Bion for one kind of group therapy—"the study of intra-group tension." [2]

While the model for the setting of family therapy is derived from psychoanalysis, there are important differences, aside from number, in the two settings—differences which also distinguish family therapy from group therapy and have in part been suggested in our discussion of the artificial discontinuity of the latter. In psychoanalysis, it may be an unpredicted—though not necessarily unpredictable—misfortune if transference expectations are in fact fulfilled by one or the other of the involved pair, or if the analyst and his patient happen to share similar patterns of dissociation. In family therapy, one may rely with considerable confidence on the presence of such sharing within the family. Indeed, the survival of the family in its established form may be understood as a function of the sharing and the reciprocal fulfillment of role expectations or wishes. In addition, the shape of the family organization may be regarded as a function of those collusively maintained and highly restrictive barriers to novelty of experience and change previously characterized as a "rubber fence." [3]

To state this in a slightly different fashion, the situation of family therapy includes three or more persons who may have unwittingly conspired to make certain aspects of the "transference" real and lasting. This reality of the transference is constantly being reaffirmed, and thus a variety of resistances have been built into the structure of the group which serve to preclude change, and which permit neither genuine separation nor meeting. Patterns of dissociation have become institutionalized, and may be maintained by stereotyped models of role complementarity established over very long periods of time.[4] The dissociated phenomena are predominantly externalized, and reciprocally so; thus positions regarded by the family members as inevitably opposed and irreconcilable are stably represented in the role structure of the family.

This may be illustrated by allusion to the family of a young schizophrenic man whom we will call Fred, who will be discussed in more detail later.

Fred was distinguished, *inter alia,* by a certain grandiose arrogance which was entirely in keeping with a major dissociated aspect of the structure of expectation shared within the family. Thus this aspect of Fred was unattended within the family and conspicuously absent from the parents' many complaints about him. His father repeatedly insisted that Fred could, if he chose, control his behavior and change or "mature" simply by some effort of will. The father's insistence in this respect was nicely matched by his conviction, frequently expressed in complaints and pleas, that the psychiatrists could, were they only willing to do so, change Fred's behavior. The father presented himself in the group as totally impotent in this regard, and he often commented that his own contribution to the work was empty and meaningless—"just words." It was, however, clear enough that he never renounced his belief that, perhaps by a continued display of impotence, he might persuade or manipulate the omnipotent mother somehow to realize his wishes.

Some of Fred's behavior might thus be understood as an attempt to fulfill this component of the father's demands. The mother acted as though convinced of her omnipotence. Her participation in the group was for a considerable time marked by a paralyzing caution, and she eventually provided some clarification of this and confirmation of her feeling of omnipotence—by revealing, in a strikingly matter-of-fact fashion, that she was afraid she might unduly influence Fred and "put ideas into his head" if she permitted herself to speak freely in his presence.

Thus, the therapists find themselves confronted with a highly elaborate, and for the most part covert, concealed, or denied, *folie à famille,* but one of style rather than, or in addition to, that of manifest content, in terms of which *folie à deux* has been classically described. On the other hand, the emergence of both shared and unshared patterned distortions in the family's dealings with the therapists is comparable to the emergence of distortions in the psychoanalytic situation, providing opportunities for new experience and analysis.

THE THERAPISTS' EXPERIENCE AND THE CULTURE OF THE FAMILY

Without reference to problems of etiology, of what is cause and what consequence, we shall try to describe some aspects of the culture of the families of concern here. Our interest is in the shared and institutionalized values and practices which distinguish these families from others, setting apart in the world and making them—not only for the psychotherapist—extremely difficult both of access and egress. Our description is based in part on our observations of the families, but more importantly on observations of our own experiences as participants in the group sessions—these experiences providing inklings of what it has been like to be members of these families.

We begin by noting that it is generally peculiarly unpleasant to spend an hour in the company of the family of a schizophrenic, and that the quality of the experience seems strangely different from that in work with other kinds of families, although the latter may be hardly less arduous at times. One is likely to emerge from a session at least somewhat less confident of the integrity of one's senses, to say nothing of the value of previously—and sometimes subsequently—held beliefs and conceptions concerning psychiatry. The difficulty of defining the unpleasant effect seems simply to aggravate the effect—which, incidentally, is reproduced to a considerable degree in a group listening to a recording of a session. In attempting to grasp something of the nature and source of this sometimes quite uncanny experience,[5] we may first of all consider some of the less damaging aspects of the encounter which undoubtedly contribute to the overall effect.

Prominent among a variety of discernible deprivations is denial,[6] whose impact is heightened in these contexts by the sharing and mutual reinforcement already noted. The therapist is more likely defensively to discount the extent and reality of the denial than to exaggerate them, and in these situations he may unwittingly support the pathological structure of the family in a variety of ways. He may fall in with the denial, in effect, by his tacit agreement not to notice certain kinds of events or categories of experience; since denial is a quietly cumulative process, this may occur without his noticing his collusive participation. He may not notice, or not take seriously, the other's denial, and this denial of denial may be evident, for example, in the style and content of descriptive account. The therapist may comment, for instance, on the "unwillingness" of one of the family to acknowledge what he "really knows." The therapist thereby fails to conceive of the conspicuous absence of recognition, much as if he failed to conceive of a scotoma or a negative hallucination. The denial of denial may occasionally be manifest in the insistent confrontation of the other, or sometimes in shouting at him. Such denial is nicely comparable to saying that a person who experiences auditory hallucinations only imagines, and does not really hear, that to which he responds so vividly. When one kind of denial is countered by something approximating its mirror image, when each is blind to the other's blindness, it is hardly surprising that communication disintegrates quite rapidly and the procession grinds to an uneasy halt without anyone's immediately realizing quite what is happening.

One may from time to time become disconcertingly aware of something utterly crazy going on during the session, while the family continues to behave as though this were not so. The absence of any indication that, from the family's point of view, anything unusual is happening invites the assumption of familiarity. The "something utterly crazy" may include the practically simultaneous presence of gross and apparently quite explicit contradictions, which are simply not heard as such. The contradictory sequences lead into a resumption of the familiar impasse which is, in its turn, enveloped in denial. For example:

In a session which was not unusual for this family, the mother of Mary, who was severely schizophrenic and much of the time demurely paranoid, openly dismissed the therapists as lunatics. Her manner was almost disarmingly affectionate, thus both augmenting and obscuring the murderous character of the assault: they were obviously harmless, well-meaning, and even amiable lunatics, but to take them at all seriously was patently absurd. Both the therapists in this group were men, and the mother had frequently made her position (or something of her position) abundantly clear to anyone who listened to her—a category which seldom included herself—that men were inherently unreliable and abandonment by them was inevitable. Thus the fact that they were also childlike, ineffectual, and stupid was perhaps less than tragically consequential. It was within the framework of this position, and in the immediate context of the comments about the lunacy of the therapists, that the mother angrily reproached her daughter for "not really wanting to get well," since otherwise she would trust the doctors and confide in them.

The father of this family spent a great deal of time delivering weighty and protracted homilies to his wife and daughter. The tone of his remarks was generally kindly and detached, condescending and moralistic; their content included pedantic reminders of why they were present, platitudes about maintaining a "positive outlook," injunctions about facing the truth, no matter how unpleasant it might be, and repeated eulogies of the virtues of the analysis of motive and meaning. His decidedly pompous air neatly complemented his wife's uniformly depreciating fondness. He invariably agreed with anything that was said by either of the therapists, and, as invariably, the character of his agreement, as this was reflected in restatement, was—conspicuously outside of his awareness—one of elusive parody, partly in its grave solemnity. He dealt with his daughter's intense distrust by gently lecturing her on the need to rely on others. While it was clear, he said, that untrustworthy persons existed, the majority were decent enough human beings, and her distrust was "just a part of her illness" which she should try to put out of mind. At the same time he maintained a constant vigilance over the therapists, watching them closely during the sessions. He often interrupted his wife, scolding her for having interrupted Mary. He would sometimes sternly reprimand her for failing sincerely to acknowledge the fact that Mary was seriously ill, but otherwise seldom failed to refer to this as anything but "her little nervous trouble."

During one session, Mary launched into a diatribe about her roommate's selfish appropriation of their bathroom and utter lack of consideration for others, which she judged as outrageous. Mary was immediately condemned by her mother for appalling selfishness "which is not like you" and for "not appreciating that this girl is sick—otherwise why on earth do you imagine that she is in the hospital!" After rudely rebuking his wife for her lack of understanding and sympathy, the father turned to Mary and went on patiently to explain that the other girl was "not very well" and that Mary should really try to be more tolerant.

Quite regularly, the therapists' attempts to reflect sequences of this order and bring them into view resulted in the wholesale denial of the foregoing intricate maze of more discreet denials and projections—projections which seldom failed to describe quite accurately some aspect of whichever family member served as the target.[7] The response to the intervention was as though it were merely an accusation, and this, in its turn, was denied. Some of this may be clarified by the clinical examples which follow.

In Fred's family, which was somewhat less pathologically organized than Mary's, the presenting complaint centered around his behavior. Fred's appearance on entering the hospital was bizarrely out of keeping with that of his apparently conservative, upper-middle-class parents. He seemed an arrogant, eccentric, highly mannered young man. His ostentatiously disgusting throat clearing and spitting were very embarrassing to his parents, notably the father, whose obvious, though unacknowledged, mortification was routinely enhanced by Fred's stereotyped and sardonic apology. Fred habitually chewed antiseptic throat lozenges and had on several occasions been taken to ear, nose, and throat specialists with consequences neither enlightening nor alleviating.

Initially Fred presented himself, in a faintly bored fashion, as devoted to a developing career of alienation and failure, much of his behavior superficially reflecting a slavish opposition to every value that his father expressly held dear, including success, punctuality, respect for his elders, and the desirability of being "an average person" who gets along with others. For the first year or so of the work, the parents were regularly early for the sessions, while Fred was punctually fourteen minutes late. His father was much preoccupied with what he conceived to be Fred's careless disregard for time, totally denying the fastidious punctuality contained in Fred's tardiness. After failing in his freshman year in college, some three or four years earlier, Fred had spent a great many of his waking hours in movies, often seeing films through several times in succession. Later on, having been somehow persuaded to work, he had found a job as an usher in a movie theater.

Fred's mother was reserved to the point of seeming virtually characterless—a quality which also seemed to lie beneath the empty conventionality of Mary's father. It was evident that she was chronically depressed, and just as evident that the depression was denied. The therapists' reflection of what they heard as the occasional eloquent communication of her sense of apathy, futility, and despair was always a source of mild surprise to her. On one occasion she was moved to make it clear, quite categorically, that "as far as I am concerned, I don't see how it is possible to feel hopeless as long as there's a straw to cling to." "The word pessimism," she asserted almost vigorously, "is not included in my dictionary." During an experiment in the use of painting, she produced a drably somber landscape, suggestive of bleakness and isolation, whose flat monotony was broken only by some shading of the grays and browns—and by a quite incongruous rainbow.

One striking regularity of her participation in the family sessions was her response to any departure of Fred's from the style of "illness." When, for example, Fred began to talk about returning to college, she would wonder aloud whether "diseases like Fred's could cause brain damage" or whether "in view of what you might call his slow progress, it might be worth considering shock treatment or lobotomy"—hastening to add that, of course this was only a thought. Responses of this kind were conspicuously absent when Fred was withdrawn and inactive, bizarrely psychotic, or apparently confined to a stereotyped negativism. The father's responses to Fred's behavior were similar in style. After many months in which Fred's spoken participation in the group was restricted to fragmentary and highly enigmatic comment, the patient began to share something of his experience with increasing coherence and directness. Following something of this kind, the father would often complain about the difficulty of persuading Fred to talk and participate more actively in the hours, and would wonder aloud whether the therapists might do something toward that end. Later in the work, when the parents began to engage themselves more actively with the therapists, Fred would intervene in such a way as to bring this to a halt.

As the work went along the father complained with mounting bitterness that the therapists provided neither guidance nor leadership. At the same time he contemptuously dismissed everything that was said as "just plain imaginary"— his rather stark euphemism for "crazy." The reflected idea that he was complaining, or that he felt in some way abandoned, elicited an identical response. A review of the extended sequence (in effect, the therapists' uneasy opposition to the snowballing denial) was again wholly dismissed save as further evidence that the therapists irresponsibly distorted everything he said. During one session, the father spent most of the hour amplifying and refining many of his previous statements of intense ambivalence toward the psychiatrists. He said, among other things, that they sadistically withheld much that would relieve the family's plight with Fred, and he commented sarcastically on "the men of science" who were insanely suspicious of every little thing that happened, and whose stupid preoccupation with making mountains out of molehills simply advertised their pathetic lack of any true sense of proportion. Their only contribution to these "farcial" sessions was to make an already intolerable situation worse. When the therapists reflected some of this, in order to make sure that they had understood him correctly, it became clear that he had not heard himself in this way, but had heard simply the reaffirmation of his high regard for the psychiatrists.

He continued, "Now you gentlemen should know by now that Mrs. R and I have nothing but the highest respect for you and your profession, otherwise why would we waste our time and yours coming out here all the time? If I felt in any way contemptuous of you, the way *you say* I do—and you used the word, I didn't— then I wouldn't be able to come, and anyway I wouldn't say so, because it wouldn't be polite. I don't see what's to be gained by dragging personalities into this—I think that's rude. I wasn't brought up that way and neither was Fred. I've always tried to keep these, er, conversations on the highest possible level, and I think the record will bear me out on that."

During the first year or so of the work, the therapists' efforts to acknowledge something of what they imagined to be the immediate affective experience of any member of the family were treated as malevolent intrusions. It seemed clear that it was other than customary for the family members so to acknowledge each other. No matter how vividly implied was, say, the experience of grief, despair, loneliness, or rage, the response—if any—within the family was reliably confined, literally and concretely, to the manifest content of the statement.

One vivid example occurred in a session in the second year of the work. The mother had consistently been withdrawn and somewhat apathetic, seeming to bear out her reputation within the family (as well as with herself) as infinitely patient, tolerant, and unemotional. Early in the hour, she spoke of a dream of the previous night, and her associations to this included a magazine article that she had read the evening before which had to do with the treatment of schizophrenia. She had been struck by the author's comments on the relationship between early recognition of illness and the outcome of treatment. As she talked, it became apparent that she was becoming increasingly disturbed. She recalled an event prior to their having recognized that anything was wrong with Fred. He had been learning to type, and one afternoon she had picked him up after class so that they could drive home together. On the way, he had turned to her and asked, "What do you do if your brain doesn't work?" She now thought that had she not simply dismissed this as meaningless perhaps things might have turned out differently. As she talked, she became increasingly distressed, until finally she burst into intense grief, self-accusation, and anguished, despairing tears, which continued uninterrupted until her son, when she spoke of typing classes, said in a dry, pedantic fashion, "Not typing classes, Mother, typing *school*."

The impact of extended sequences of this order was strangely unnerving, often prompting the therapists' intervention, which, in turn, again provoked denial. During the sessions, the therapists often missed, or dismissed as incredible, the fact that neither of the involved pair was aware of implication, whether in the self or in the other. Fred's father was sometimes tearful during the sessions, but his tears meant only that he was "naturally emotional"; the fact that they occurred only at certain times, within clearly identifiable contexts, was wholly "meaningless" to him. Fred's responses to what the therapists intended to be confirming or acknowledging interventions were usually murderously sarcastic, their impact heightened by his customary blandness of expression. From time to time he would mimic the accent or manner of one or the other therapist, occasionally provoking a sharp reproof from the father for his lack of respect for the doctors "who are doing their best to help you"—a somewhat elaborate instance of the manifold and denied contradictions.

The isolation, containment, obscuring, and denial of affective experience in Mary's family were similar in form. The family members, except for the father, tended to express themselves more stormily, and even dramatically at times, yet they consistently denied the authenticity of experience, in much the same way that Fred's father denied the authenticity of his own tears and Fred denied the authenticity of the therapists' responses to him. Mary's disruptive rage, which occurred regularly at times of separation and reunion, was dismissed by her mother simply as a "childish tantrum" or "hysterics," and both parents brushed off the mother's periodic access of intense grief as her "being upset" because Mary was in the hospital—a matter of no consequence, since any mother would be upset to see her child ill. The idea that "You don't really feel that way" or "That isn't really you" was a routine ingredient in the family's dealings with each other, often stated as explicitly as that. The father insisted on "keeping to the facts," on their dispassionate discussion and "analysis"—again the denial of the authenticity of sentiment, since emotions were not facts.

THE THERAPISTS' PARTICIPATION

We have referred, most broadly, to three characteristics of exchanges within these families: the extravagance of manifest contradiction, the quietly savage destruction of meaning and intent, and the routine elimination of a very broad spectrum of felt experience, all of which are repeated in the family's dealings with the therapists. It is clear that none of these exchanges is, in itself, uniquely confined to families which include a person manifesting schizophrenic disorder. We have yet to encounter any particular response within these families which we have not observed from time to time in our dealings with other people, schizophrenic or not. It must be emphasized, however, that these are regular and familiar ingredients in the culture of these families, rather than occasional departures at times of severe stress. Furthermore, the form and substance of these exchanges are blanketed by the shared denial which we have described.

Under conditions of this order, intensity, and regularity, the therapists will do a great deal of work in the service of their own survival, such as the unwitting collusion in denial and the denial of denial which have already been mentioned. Our intention now is to move toward a more general rubric of defense or counterresistance, which would also include the denial of the irrational and of concrete thinking. Having stressed that exchanges within the family are characterized by the extreme reduction of experience, as in the denial of implication and overtone, we wish now to attend to the mirror image of this phenomenon manifest in the therapists' interventions within these sessions.

These varieties of counterresistance are likely to interefere with, if not altogether exclude, the possibility of discovering and sharing a major aspect of the family's experience—that of fragmentation. On the other hand, if the therapist analyzes the counterresistance, then something of the experience of fragmentation is revealed, and he is thus able, however tentatively and indirectly, to grasp such previously neglected components of the culture and structure of the family group.

The psychiatrists introduce into the situation a variety of attitudes and beliefs, more or less durably organized. Their conception of the situation, implied in description and participation, is fashioned out of those relatively implicit and taken-for-granted categories and assumptions which, in a sense, define the nature of their experience, and which have both limitations of that which can be grasped and a characteristic style of formulation. It is by virtue of the limitations of grasp that experience is capable of organization, both limitations and style of organization being conceived of as a function of acculturation, personal and professional.

We wish to call attention to one specific and shared psychiatric attitude which serves in a curious way to illuminate what we have come to consider a crucial component of the culture of the family. This psychiatric attitude is so highly valued that stating it seems at first to be merely underlining the perfectly obvious: regardless of appearances, human situations make sense. This attitude and its value are reflected in such everyday matters as the psychiatrist's intuitive alertness to relatively undisclosed meaning, to the implications of otherwise unremarkable statements, or to the overtones of transference in the apparently casual remark.

Transcending commitments to particular theories, preferences for conceptual models, and attachments to particular methods, the psychiatrist is frankly and profoundly committed to the idea of pattern and relation, and thus to the discovery and confirmation of meaning, for himself both as a person and as an investigator, and—as a therapist—for his patient. As a pattern maker, the psychiatrist is at one with the poet and the artist, the philosopher and the mathematician, and the historian and the scientist, regardless of cultural context, time, and place, prevailing ideological fashion and allegiance, choice of expressive medium, or field of inquiry. While certain kinds of pattern may be experienced as congenial and enlightening, or as alien, misleading, and incomprehensible, the idea of pattern is, in itself, seldom if ever contested. The familiar dialectic is that of opposition between one and another variety of pattern and commitment to pattern. That it is possible to imagine the wholly unpatterned is at least questionable, although paradoxically the pattern of poetic allusion may serve to suggest something of this. It is generally regarded as characteristically human to experience pleasure in the discovery or creation of meaning, and to feel anything from a vague sense of discomfort to something approximately panic in its absence.

. . . the negation of familiar meaning may . . . usher us into the presence of nothingness. Sartre's "Nausée" contains the classic description of this process. It is a generalization of the technique for rendering a word incomprehensible by repeating it a number of times. You say "table, table, table . . ." until the word becomes a mere meaningless sound. You can destroy meaning wholesale by reducing everything to its uninterpreted particulars. By paralyzing our urge to subordinate one thing to another, we can eliminate all subsidiary awareness of things in terms of others and create an atomized, totally depersonalized universe. In it the pebble in your hand, the saliva in your mouth and the word in your ear all become external, absurd and hostile items. This universe is the counterpart of the cosmic vision, with despair taking the place of hope. It is the logical outcome of utterly distrusting our participation in holding our beliefs. Left strictly to itself, that is what the world is like. . . . Fragmentation alone can . . . be trusted; only an aggregate of fragments can carry a meaning that is wholly ineffable and protected thereby against self-doubt.[8]

Within psychoanalysis, the principle of psychic determinism is a fundamental and unchallenged assumption, whose value is nicely reflected in the style of Brenner's statement from his *Elementary Textbook:*

The sense of this principle is that in the mind, as in physical nature about us, nothing happens by chance, or in a random way. . . . Events in our mental lives that may seem to be random and unrelated are only apparently so. In fact, mental phenomena are no more capable of such a lack of causal connection with what preceded them than are physical ones. Discontinuity in this sense does not exist in mental life.
The understanding and application of this principle is essential for a proper

orientation in the study of human psychology as well in its normal and in its pathological aspects. If we do understand it and apply it correctly, we shall never dismiss any psychic phenomenon as meaningless or accidental. We shall always ask ourselves, in relation to any such phenomenon in which we are interested: "What caused it? Why did it happen so?" We ask ourselves these questions because we are confident that an answer to them exists.[9]

This, then, reflects something of the psychiatrist's position. Within the limits of the context, including his own limitations, the psychiatrist listens reflectively to what constitutes, from his point of view, associations. His listening is guided sometimes by conflictful forces more or less outside of awareness, and sometimes by the appearance of tentative hypotheses which he entertains or discards for the time being, as the situation unfolds and more information becomes available. His interest is in sorting out something of what is going on in a situation which seems much of the time fragmented and incoherent. He notices such matters as the impact of one or another series of events on the group, and is sometimes curious about his own responses, implicit or explicit, which may appear unheralded and seem at first quite unrelated to anything he notices happening within the group.

Now all of this, as a hypothetical statement of the therapist's participation, and at best a crudely reductive approximation of his position, seems unremarkable enough, particularly as this kind of covert behavior is episodic and unobtrusive— that is to say, not so preoccupying that the therapist is no longer *there*.[10] Paradoxically, however, it seems that, within these contexts, this attitude and its derived operations, notably interpretation, may in at least one very important way be inappropriate and misleading, largely defensive in function and resulting in the therapist's selectively missing the *subjective experience* of meaninglessness. One may note parenthetically that, where everything is meaningful, the idea of meaning becomes simply tautological. To the extent that he insists on meaning and urgently seeks pattern, a crucial component of the family's experience—that of fragmentation—disappears from view. The fundamental guiding assumption of the family is the negative counterpart of the psychiatrist's: broadly stated, it is that nothing has anything to do with anyhing else—that everything means, if it means anything at all, only one thing. This assumption, in the tradition of extreme reduction which is illustrated in concrete thinking, is shared and insisted upon, but both the assumption and its sharing are denied, and the denial is wholly consonant with this cultural imperative.

Earlier we referred briefly to those aspects of the family culture which pertain to the shared denial of a very broad span of affective experience, without going into either the meaning of the experience or the function of the denial. We noted that when denial is no longer tenable, and expression overwhelmingly obtrusive, then its authenticity is characteristically denied. In the families with which we have worked, interventions primarily concerned with the simple clarification and articulation of sentiment are generally unwelcome. Such interventions are, in a sense, violations of the family culture, and yet they are relatively minor infractions compared with those which suggest meaning, especially those which propose the relevance of sentiment over and above its mere existence as an isolated event.

Even more grave is the interpretive comment, where the violation may be of such magnitude that the comment actually seems to be without meaning *within the family group*. We refer to something very different from the more familiar fate of interpretations in, say, the analysis of neurotic patients. Matters of transference aside (and this is not to dismiss them, but to avoid a complexity which will obscure what we are concerned with here), in the latter situation the analyst and his patient are, to a degree, concerned with particular forms and meanings. In general, the analyst may take for granted some sharing of the general structure of thought and values between his patient and himself. In the situations with which we are concerned here, this seems hardly the case at all. The possibility of authentic relation and meaning are precluded by the cultural imperatives operating within the family boundaries: it is the structure of the interpretive comment which is alien, so that its specific content is beside the point. In other words, it is not specific kinds of meaning, particular aspects of relationship, or certain forms of experience which are repressed, but rather a superordinate and more fundamental category of experience and thought, which includes the idea of relation, meaning, continuity, and coherence.

We use the term interpretation here to cover a wide range of comment, distinguished from other kinds of intervention in that it is primarily concerned with continuity and relation.[11] Such a comment seeks to bring into view, say, the relation between experience and event, past and present: it may point toward similarities where only differences and the absence of relation have been noted. The comment may touch on familiar resemblances between persons who see themselves only as strangers having nothing in common. It may be observed that we are not concerned here with "deep" interpretations, or with comments which seek to decode the obscurely symbolic, but rather with interventions which have as their purpose the bridging of what are regarded (correctly or incorrectly) as the smaller and more immediate gaps in experience. The comment is thus most likely to refer to the here and now situation, or to the immediate past, since the last session. It often simply underlines associations already made. Without reference to the therapeutic and technical problems involved, we may briefly illustrate the characteristic fate of interpretive comments in the two families already mentioned.

In Mary's family, any interpretation offered to the mother had a somewhat stereotyped reception. She often missed what had been said: she hadn't realized, she would say, that the therapist was speaking to her—perhaps he would like to say it again. Her busy adoption of a posture of earnest attention would quietly reinforce what might have been, until then, a merely fleeting sense of dismay within the therapist. The moment had now passed and was utterly beyond recall, but, often after a sigh, the therapist would repeat his comment, sometimes louder and more deliberately. She would restate it slowly and carefully (in much the way that one might, with enormous caution, taste some wholly alien food in deference to one's host) and then say something to the effect that, well, that was certainly very interesting, but she didn't see what it had to do with anything. On other occasions, she would respond to the therapist's comments by turning to her daughter and saying, in an affectionately bantering and flirtatious style, "Mary, dear, don't you just love the way Dr. X talks!" The father's stereotyped and empty agreement had an essentially similar impact, and the consequence of these exchanges was generally, once again, the familiar impasse.

In Fred's family, in which the gulf was less extensive than in Mary's family, the father's response to interpretive comments was the most readily defined. He would confine himself to such matters as pointing out some error of syntax in the therapist's statement, questioning his pronunciation, or demanding the precise definition of a particular word, torn out of the context of the comment. Sometimes he would offer a caricatured legalistic rebuttal of the therapist's reflection of a statement, based on the fact that the therapist had introduced a new word rather than using that previously employed by himself or the family—for instance, "anger" instead of "irritation." Thus he automatically disqualified the comment from further consideration. When the therapist noted a sequence in the father's statements and repeated these statements verbatim, the father would say that undoubtedly the therapists were experts in this business of "subconsciousness" but, for himself, he wouldn't know about such matters. The denial of meaning in such instances seems essentially comparable to the denial of authenticity of feeling.

It happens then, quite reliably, that interpretations are rejected, not only with respect to their content, but also with respect to their form and intent. The rejection, the inability to hear them or to tolerate their existence, does not refer only to particular kinds of meanings, or merely to specific forms of relatedness, but seems to have to do with the general nature of the comment, its structure and its intent. Whether an interpretation is valid or not, how it is phrased, and how it is timed are of little or no consequence: if the sound of a language is intolerable, what is said in that language and precisely how it is phrased are of no moment at all.

The psychiatrist, in his efforts to introduce the idea of relation and continuity, violates the culture of the family. In just the same way, the family's responses—the systematic destruction of meaning and the denial of authenticity —are experienced by the psychiatrist as acts of extreme violence. The exchanges —which have very little to do with conversation—both among the family members and between them and the psychiatrists, are essentially characterized by the mutual failure or inability to understand, tolerate, or confirm the other's experience. The psychiatrist's dread of meaninglessness and fragmentation, manifest in his search for coherence and pattern, and sometimes in his insistent bombardment of the family with interpretations, is countered by the family's shared dread of meaning and relation, manifest in the systematic destruction of meaning, the routine elimination of implication, and the insistence on fragmentation of experience.

To recapitulate, from the regularity of experiences of this kind, it seems possible to posit a general principle about subjective experience within the family—namely, that within its boundaries (as within the selves composing the family) nothing has a meaningful relation to anything else. The governing assumption of the absence of relation and continuity is reflected in a variety of rules which are reminiscent of those of the primary process. Just as the assumption of the principle of psychic determinism shapes the listening of the analyst, or, more generally, as commitment to theory shapes experience and perception, so this guiding principle *prohibits* the shaping of the subjective experience of the family members, virtually precluding coherence of experience and the development of a genuine sense of identity. The principle of fragmentation and its derived rules are shared and insisted upon within the family, and at the same time the principle is denied. The denial of meaning and relation is entirely consonant with the culture of the family, just as the denial of discontinuity and of the irrational is wholly in keeping with the culture of the psychiatrist.

Thus in Fred's family, the father's pedantic insistence on the use of particular words served to exclude intrusive overtones, and to practically eliminate one potential channel for the emergence of implication—which was treated as dangerous rather than enriching. Within the family boundaries, there were—as if by fiat—neither implications nor ambiguity of statement or purpose. There was a shared insistence on the absence of historical continuity. Insofar as meaning was permitted at all, what was said meant simply what was said, literally and concretely, no more than that and nothing else but that. The denial of conceptual relationship went hand in hand with the denial of emotional relationship and affective experience. Regardless of the appearance of explicitness, the rules are denied—the culture does not recognize or permit pattern; what is ordered is the absence of order.

We have confined ourselves here to a consideration of some aspects of the *latent* culture of these families. For the sake of clarity and economy of presentation, we have neglected—among many other matters—the manifest culture of the family, the manifold disguises and the sometimes grotesque counterfeits of meaning and relation. One variety of the counterfeit of meaning is the paranoid formulation, which, from the point of view we have been interested in exploring, may be understood as a defense against fragmentation. In the paranoid formulation, instead of the extreme reduction of experience in concrete thinking and the denial of relation, both conceptual and emotional, there is an effort to salvage or create an opposite state of affairs, manifest in subjective, coherent certainty, although the coherence is often a virtual travesty of meaning. Here, nothing is without relevance, and the facts, say, that a knife and fork touch as they are laid on the table, that an ashtray contains cigarette stubs of varying lengths, and that the sum of the digits in the date is twenty are vital data of increasingly cosmic significance—candidates for inclusion in a grand and comprehensive paranoid theory.

We have sought here to describe some characteristic patterns of behavior in groups composed of schizophrenic patients and their parents, patterns which emerge regularly in the ways in which the family members deal with the psychiatrists. We have discussed some aspects of the psychiatrists' experience, and some of the ways in which they find themselves responding to these families. From this we have derived some propositions regarding the latent culture of the family, notably the institutionalization of fragmentation of associations and concrete thinking, traditionally regarded both an essence and product of disease, which can perhaps, like other cultural phenomena, be regarded as learned behavior.

In attempting to make statements about these situations, we have again and again found ourselves confronted with paradoxes. We have, for example, been trying to describe some aspects of a culture for which our own categories are curiously inappropriate, and have suggested something which seems on the face of it contradictory—namely, the implicit ordering of disorder and the patterning of incoherence and absence of pattern. A related paradox is encountered in the clinical aspects of the work: to the extent that the therapist confidently grasps meaning within the group, he is, at that moment, conspicuously out of touch with the experience of the family at its current stage of organization. The use of the term *organization* in this last sentence, as well as previous references to *structure* and *culture* in remarks about the family *group,* is again illustrative of this dilemma. From where the psychiatrist stands, the descriptions seem to us appropriate and useful; from the vantage point of the family members, whose experience we are interested in understanding, they are quite inappropriate and even without meaning. Early in this paper, we referred to the peculiar quality of the therapist's emotional experience within these situations. While readily sensed, it was by no means readily defined and seemed strangely resistant to articulate grasp. To the extent that we have succeeded in conveying some of these paradoxes, it will be apparent that the experience lies outside the realm of that which may be defined, and that the effort to put this into words is one further instance of the kind of counterresistance with which we have been concerned—but not *only* counterresistance.

ACKNOWLEDGMENT

We wish gratefully to acknowledge Dr. Robert A. Cohen's contribution to the final formulations presented here.

NOTES AND REFERENCES

1. For purposes of comparison and contrast, we have been working under similar conditions with the families of persons manifesting a variety of other psychiatric syndromes. These have included affective reactions, obsessional and hysterical character disorders, delinquency, and ulcerative colitis.
2. Quoted by Rickman, J., in "The Role and Future of Psychotherapy within Psychiatry," *J. Ment. Sci.* 96:181-189, 1950.
3. See Wynne, L. C., Ryckoff, I. M., Day, J., and Hirsch, S. I., "Pseudo-Mutuality in the Family Relations of Schizophrenics," *Psychiatry* 21:205-220, 1958.
4. See Ryckoff, I. M., Day, J., and Wynne, L. C., "Maintenance of Stereotyped Roles in the Families of Schizophrenics," *A. M. A. Arch. Gen. Phychiat.* 1:93-98, 1959.
5. See various comments of Sullivan regarding *uncanny* emotion, for example: ". . . the not-me component of personality, the source of the tension in inter-personal fields elsewhere described as the experience of uncanny emotions—awe, dread, loathing, and horror—felt components of the most strongly disjunctive force of which we have knowledge" (Sullivan, H. S., *The Interpersonal Theory of Psychiatry,* New York, Norton, 1953, p. 371 n.)
6. The impact of denial, or more generally of the reliable absence of confirmation in interpersonal relations, has only occasionally provoked psychiatric comment. Polanyi has touched on this matter with respect to the arts. "We are shocked by the offer of an unfamiliar system purporting to be meaningful. When the public is pressed to enter the new framework so as to discover its meaning, their bewilderment turns into indignation. They are outraged by the respect paid to what seems to them deserving of contempt and angry at the implied contempt for their own standards of excellence." He goes on to allude to the scenes of violence in response to the exhibitions of the early impressionists in Paris and to the first performances of works of Stravinsky and Wagner. "*In such conflicts the two sides are actually fighting for their lives, or at least part of their lives. For in the existence of each there is an area which can be kept in being only by denying reality to an area in the*

existence of the other. And such a denial is a shock to the conviction of the other and an attack against his being, to the extent to which he lives in this conviction." (The italics are ours.) See Polanyi, M., *Personal Knowledge,* London, Routledge and Kegan Paul, 1958, pp. 200-201. L. H. Farber's paper, "The Therapeutic Despair," *Psychiatry* 21:7-20, 1958, is also pertinent. It seems to us highly probable that the patterns of denial we are describing— particularly the denial of relation and meaning—represent a primary failure or incapacity, rather than the loss of a capacity formerly developed, and are analogous to primary repression as distinct from secondary repression, or repression proper. Thus the family is confronted with the task of discovering meaning and relation rather than recovering them.

7. See Searles, H. F., "The Schizophrenic's Vulnerability to the Therapist's Unconscious Processes," *J. Nerv. Ment. Dis.* 127:247-262, 1957.

8. See Polanyi, M., note 6, pp. 199-200.

9. Brenner, C., *An Elementary Texbook of Psycho-analysis,* New York, Doubleday-Anchor, 1957, p. 2. Also relevant to this theme are some findings, as yet unpublished, of Alex Bavelas, mentioned by Parloff, M. B., and Rubinstein, E. A., in "Research Problems in Psychotherapy" (pp. 276-293, in *Research in Psychotherapy,* edited by Rubinstein and Parloff, Washington, D.C., American Psychological Association, 1959). Bavelas presented a series of subjects with randomly selected information and found that almost all of them insisted that the information was patterned and were able to deduce systematic relationships from the data. When the subjects were told of the random nature of the data, they refused to believe this and persisted in their beliefs regarding the accuracy of their formulations. Farber has alluded to this problem: "A dimension of terror is added to our existence, as we learn to live with the insane possibility —which is, after all, one of the facts of madness—that meaning itself can be the mirage. To avoid this insanity, we grasp at every possibility of meaning as though it were the staunchest fact." (See Farber, L. H., note 6, p. 17.)

10. It is our impression that some therapists with the families of schizophrenics ward off the impact of the family culture and the resultant subjective experience of fragmentation by maintaining a high degree of emotional detachment and preoccupation with technique. Such detachment is, in our opinion, an instance of work done in the service of the therapist's survival, understandable, and at times necessary, but greatly limiting the depth of his view of the family's experience—and his own.

11. This use of the term *interpretation* is in some ways broader than that prevailing in psychoanalytic writings. The psychoanalytic interpretation would be, however, subsumed under this category of intervention. The majority of the kinds of interpretive comments referred to in this paper would be described by Lowenstein as preparations for interpretation, rather than interpretations proper. As we understand the idea, the essence of interpretation lies in its goal, namely that of bringing into relation or reintegrating that which has undergone dissociation—or facilitating growth in the sense of developing new integrations of experience (that is, the discovery rather than the recovery of meaning). Compare Lowenstein, R. M., "The Problem of Interpretation," *Psychonal. Quart.* 20:1-14, 1951, and Bibring, E., "Psychoanalysis and the Dynamic Psychotherapies," *J. Amer. Psychoanal. Ass.* 2:745-770, 1954.

5

Indirect Hypnotic Therapy of a Bedwetting Couple

MILTON H. ERICKSON

A young couple in their early 20's, much in love, married for a year, and close friends of several of the writer's medical students at that time, sought psychiatric help. Their problem was one in common—lifelong enuresis. During their fifteen-month courtship, neither had the courage to tell the other about the habitual enuresis. Their wedding night had been marked, after consummation of the marriage, by a feeling of horrible dread and then resigned desperation, followed by sleep. The next morning each was silently and profoundly grateful to the other for the unbelievable forbearance shown in making no comment about the wet bed.

This same silent ignoring of the wet bed continued to be manifested each morning for over nine months. The effect was an ever-increasing feeling of love and regard for each other because of the sympathetic silence shown.

Then one morning (neither could remember who made the remark) the

Reprinted with permission of author and publisher from *The Journal of Clinical and Experimental Hypnosis* 2:171-174, 1954.

comment was made that they really ought to have a baby to sleep with them so that it could be blamed for the wet bed. This led at once to the astonishing discovery for each that the other was enuretic and that each had felt solely responsible. While they were greatly relieved by this discovery, their enuresis persisted.

After a few more months, discreet inquiry of the medical students by the couple disclosed that the writer was a psychiatrist and a hypnotist and probably knew something about enuresis. Accordingly, they sought an appointment, expressed an unwillingness to be hypnotized and an incapacity to meet the financial obligations of therapy, but earnestly asked if they could be given help.

They were informed that they would be accepted as patients on a purely experimental basis and that their obligation would be either to benefit or to assume full financial responsibility for the time given them. To this they agreed. (This reversal of "cure me or I won't pay" is often most effective in experimental therapy).

They were then told that the absolute requisite for therapeutic benefits would lie in their unquestioning and unfailing obedience to the instructions given to them. This they promised.

The experimental therapeutic procedure was outlined to them, to their amazement and horror, in the following fashion:

You are both very religious, and you have both given me a promise you will keep. You have a transportation problem that makes it difficult to see me regularly for therapy. Your financial situation makes it practically impossible for you to see me frequently.

You are to receive experimental therapy, and you are obligated absolutely either to benefit or to pay me whatever fee I deem reasonable. Should you benefit, the success of my therapy will be my return for my effort and your gain. Should you not benefit, all I will receive for my effort is a fee and that will be a double loss to you but no more than an informative disappointment to me.

This is what you are to do: Each evening you are to take fluids freely. Two hours before you go to bed, lock the bathroom door after drinking a glass of water. At bedtime, get into your pajamas and then kneel side by side on the bed, facing your pillows, and deliberately, intentionally, and jointly wet the bed. This may be hard to do, but you must do it. Then lie down and go to sleep, knowing full well that the wetting of the bed is over and done with for the night, that nothing can really make it noticeably wetter.

Do this every night, no matter how much you hate it—you have promised though you did not know what the promise entailed, but you are obligated. Do it every night for two weeks, that is, until Sunday the 17th. On Sunday night, you may take a rest from this task. You may that night lie down and go to sleep in a dry bed.

On Monday morning, the 18th, you will arise, throw back the covers, look at the bed. *Only as you see a wet bed, then and only then* will you realize that there will be before you another three weeks of kneeling and wetting the bed.

You have your instructions. There is to be no discussion and no debating between you about this, just silence. There is to be only obedience, and you will then give me a full and amazing account. Goodby!

Five weeks later, they entered the office, amused, chagrined, embarrassed, greatly pleased, but puzzled and uncertain about the writer's possible attitude and intentions.

They had been most obedient. The first night had been one of torture. They had had to kneel for over an hour before they could urinate. Succeeding nights were desperately dreaded. Each night they looked forward with an increasing intensity of desire to lie down and sleep in a dry bed on Sunday the 17th.

On the morning of Monday the 18th, they awakened at the alarm and were amazed to find the bed still dry. Both started to speak and immediately remembered the admonition of silence.

That night, in their pajamas, they looked at the bed, at each other, started to speak but again remembered the instructions about silence. Impulsively they "sneaked" into bed, turned off the reading light, wondering why they had not deliberately wet the bed but at the same time enjoying the comfort of a dry bed.

On Tuesday morning, the bed was again dry. That night and thereafter, Monday night's behavior had been repeated.

Having completed their report, they waited uncertainly for the writer's comments. They were immediately reminded that they had been told that they would give an "amazing account" in five weeks' time. Now they knew that they had, and that the writer was tremendously pleased, *and would continue to be pleased,* so what more could be asked?

After some minutes of carefully guided, desultory conversation, they were dismissed with the apparently irrelevant statement that *the next month was May.*

About the middle of May, they dropped in "spontaneously" to greet the writer and to report "incidentally" that everything was fine.

A year later, they introduced the writer to their infant son, amusedly stating that once more they could have a wet bed but only when they wished and it would be just "a cute little spot."

Hesitantly, they asked if the writer had employed hypnosis on them. They were answered with the statement that their own honesty and sincerity in doing what was necessary to help themselves entitled them to full credit for what had been accomplished.

To understand this case report, it might be well to keep in mind the small child's frequent demonstration of the right to self-determination. For example, the child rebelling against the afternoon nap fights sleep vigorously despite fatigue and will repeatedly get out of the crib. If each time the child is gently placed back in the crib, it will often suddenly demonstrate its right by climbing out and immediately climbing back and falling asleep comfortably.

Concerning the evasive reply given to the patients about the use of hypnosis, by which they were compelled to assume fully their own responsibilities, the fact remains that the entire procedure was based upon an indirect use of hypnosis. The instructions were so worded as to compel without demanding the intent attention of the unconscious. The calculated vagueness of some of the instructions forced their unconscious minds to assume responsibility for their behavior. Consciously they could only wonder about their inexplicable situations, while they responded to it with corrective, unconscious reactions. Paradoxically, they were compelled by the nature of the instructions and the manner in which these were given to make a "free, spontaneous choice" of behavior and to act upon it in the right way without knowing that they had done so.

Favoring the therapeutic result was the prestige of the writer as a psychiatrist and a hypnotist well spoken of by their friends, the medical students. This undoubtedly rendered them unusually ready to accept indirect, hypnotic suggestion.

The rationale of the therapy may be stated briefly. Both patients had a distressing, lifelong pattern of wetting the bed every night. For nine long months, both suffered intensely from an obvious but unacknowledged guilt. For another three months, they found their situation still unchanged.

Under therapy, during a subjectively never-ending two weeks, by their own actions, they acquired a lifetime supply of wet beds. Each wet bed compelled them to want desperately to lie down and sleep in a dry bed. When that opportunity came, they utilized it fully. Then, the next evening, understanding unconsciously but not consciously the instructions given them, they used their bed-wetting guilt to "sneak" into and enjoy a dry bed, a guilty pleasure they continued to enjoy for three weeks.

The uncertainty, doubt, and guilt over their behavior vanished upon discovery at the second interview that they had really been obedient by being able to give the "full and amazing account." Yet, unnoticeably to them, the therapist's influence was vaguely but effectively continued by the seemingly irrelevant mention of the month of May.

Their final step was then to bring into reality a completely satisfactory solution of their own devising, a baby, the solution they had mentioned, and mention of which had led to an open acknowledgment of enuresis to each other. Then, at a symbolic level, they dismissed the writer as a therapist by introducing him to the infant, who, in turn, represented a happy and controllable solution to their problem. This they almost literally verbalized directly by their amused comment about having a wet bed any time they wished and that it would be only a pleasing thing of adult and parental significance.

6

Conjoint Family Therapy in the Inpatient Setting

EDWIN L. RABINER
HANS MOLINSKI
ALEXANDER GRALNICK

In recent years the subject and practice of family therapy has commanded increasing attention in psychiatry. The major work thus far has been done in the field of research with families placed in a hospital setting, together with the primary patient,[1] or with ambulatory patients and their families.[2] In most instances primary patients have been children or adolescents. In addition, a number of papers have been devoted to efforts directed at understanding [3] and treating the relatives of inpatients in order to aid the therapeutic task with the primary patient and to make his future life with them more tolerable.[4-6]

Little work has been reported concerning treatment by joint interview of members of the family together with the psychotic inpatient. The present paper is a preliminary report of our experience with this conjoint family therapy approach in the inpatient setting. (The term conjoint is borrowed from Jackson.[7, 8]) To some extent it is the logical evolution both of some of our

Reprinted with permission of authors and publisher from *American Journal of Psychotherapy* 16:618-631, 1962.

former work and of the nature of our treatment facilities, already described in previous papers.[9, 10] Primary patients in our series range in age from adolescence to the sixties.

FAMILY INVOLVEMENT IN THE INPATIENT TREATMENT PROCESS

It is increasingly accepted that one cannot hope to do too well with the psychotic, particularly schizophrenic inpatient, with the aid of the one-to-one psychotherapeutic relationship alone, analytically oriented or otherwise. Schizophrenia is an isolating process that destroys the patient's judgment and makes him a trial to others. It is a crippling disease which frustrates and exhausts the best of therapists who attempt its resolution purely on their own. Those who would adjust to and help the schizophrenic must therefore care for him a great deal. As such, the family unit, often made up of the very individuals who have abetted the schizophrenic's retreat from reality, has a vital role to play. The family's empathic support or lack of it through the long, costly, and trying treatment process crucially affects its outcome. Failure to acknowledge this has, perhaps, all too often led us to rely upon the one-to-one psychotherapeutic relationship, only to find that our own stores of love, understanding, and personal ministration are inadequate to the task, especially since our own families have prior claim to them.

It is a striking fact that, when one immerses himself in the treatment of psychotic inpatients and sees their family members frequently, one develops feelings of sympathy for the family. This is not to say that less positive attitudes do not also present themselves. Usually, however, one does find oneself assuming responsibility for the welfare of family members as well as for the patient. It is likely that this "countertransference phenomenon," if it may be called that, has been an important motor force in the evolution of family therapy. It is clear that changes in the primary patient, along with decisions one makes for him or helps him make for himself, impinge upon the family group with effects one must take into account.

The major task of the inpatient center is to bring the patient to a level permitting return to the community or family for further ambulatory care. Put another way, pathology must be reduced or circumscribed to a point that makes life in extramural society feasible. For the schizophrenic, with his social mobility frozen by his pathology, this means making life in the biologic family unit feasible.

Central to our own quest of this goal has been the planned replication in the inpatient setting of specific structural elements and interactional demands characteristic of family life. In this regard fellow patients and hospital personnel are viewed as surrogate family members. The patient lives in a new, therapeutically controlled social field upon which family conflicts are replayed. His life experience in it, as well as the psychotherapeutic utilization of observations of his life style in relation to it, have, we feel, contributed significantly to our effectiveness in achieving this major task.

All too often, however, we have seen hard-won gains in relation to the "intramural family" dissipate themselves toward the end of hospitalization as they are tested against increasing exposure to the vicissitudes of life in the untreated family to which the patient must return. In effect, in many instances, it has appeared insufficient to attempt to create within the inpatient setting an environment patterned on healthy family interaction conducive to individual growth and repair without extending these efforts into the actual family unit.

Other factors derived from the extent of the schizophrenic's interpersonal disability further substantiate the importance of intensive work with the families of such patients. We know that there is a universal tendency in the human personality to persevere in wresting from its primary frustraters a greater measure of gratification. Whether conceptualized in the context of Freud's "repetition compulsion" or Silverberg's concept of "transference," [11] every individual seeks to recreate unsatisfactory situations in order to resolve them better. For the personality sufficiently intact to form new relationships, the potential exists for repair of self-esteem in the new relationships. For many schizophrenics, however, the old battles must be fought on the same battleground with the same frustraters. In the face of this, the schizophrenic's helplessness to alter family members' response toward him gives rise to profound despair. If this despair is to be mitigated, the patient needs an active ally to shift the balance of power. When he works in isolation with the patient, the therapist's chances of shifting the tide of battle are perhaps no better than those of the manager in the corner of the outclassed boxer.

The concept of schizophrenic regression which has led to the equating of the schizophrenic and the child has been criticized for reasons having to do with the differences between the two. Yet there is a striking similarity in the helplessness of both to communicate feelings directly rather than by acting out in a fashion that is incomprehensible to family members and merely serves to alienate them.

In the therapy of children in a similar plight, therapists have long since responded to needs implicit in the situation for (1) active intervention to shift the balance of power away from the omnipotent parent, and (2) facilitation of communication between patient and family. In the parallel therapy of children and their parents, the therapist plays both roles, setting limits for parents and interpreting to them the meaning of the primary patient's behavioral communications. In the treatment of adults, however, we have tended to avoid the contamination of the relationship that might result from direct contact between therapist and family members. For the schizophrenic inpatient this sacrosanct position of the one-to-one psychotherapeutic relationship seems hardly justified by the results achieved with it, especially since it blocks a frontal approach to the problem of the schizophrenic's obligatory dependency upon family members who need help in adequately responding. That degree of accommodation to family members, therefore, where the patient cannot make, despite our best treatment efforts, requires direct intervention in the family situation.

To date such intervention on the part of inpatient centers has taken the following forms: (1) casework interview, usually by someone other than the therapist of the primary patient; (2) referral for psychotherapy, usually to a therapist having little or no contact with the treatment center; (3) parallel interview of family members by the therapist of the primary patient.

Conjoint family therapy as a fourth technique of family intervention seems to us most specifically addressed to the assessment and alteration of family interaction. It alone permits direct observation of patterns of family interaction. Thus it minimizes the misperceptions implicit in the secondhand reporting of family transactions. It avoids the interposition of an additional relay station (caseworker or other therapist) with its possibilities of introducing further distortion and widening the gulf. It affords the therapist the greatest opportunity to observe and confront the family with its interactional distortions.

THE CONJOINT FAMILY PROCESS

A number of workers with a variety of theoretical orientations, have written on this subject. Common to all these orientations has been the primary aim of structuring the interview situation so as to encourage a maximum interplay between family members, with the therapist serving (1) decode veiled communications, and (2) to provide role clarification for the involved family members while protecting the participating individuals against joint assault through the transient shifting of his support as the process unfolds. In this setting the aim is to foster a feeling of cooperative effort toward more gratifying family life, to clarify the mutual needs and expectations of each family member, to explore the self-defeating ways in which these needs are currently being sought and to elucidate, wherever possible, the historical determinants of individual patterns of self-defeat, making the provocative behavior of each more comprehensible to the other until it can be beneficially altered.

TACTICAL ADVANTAGES IN THE INPATIENT SETTING

It is a common experience to find that in precisely those instances where the need to alter family members' pathology is most crucial to the outcome of therapy with the primary patient, the severity of pathology either makes the family member refractory to treatment referral or precipitates acting out. Guilt feelings about having brought the patient to the hospital, and about having contributed to the primary patient's illness, are often intensified by a direct treatment recommendation to the family member. This may lead to a family member's acting out so as to sabotage the primary patient's treatment opportunity. On the other hand, the proposal on the patient's behalf of joint meetings of the family with the patient and therapist is far less likely to arouse defensiveness. Under the face-saving illusion of being a "co-therapist" (which will be dealt with later in the conjoint therapy) we have found family members to be generally enthusiastic in their response to this proposal. Furthermore, inclusion in the patient's active treatment tangibly conveys to the family members an appreciation of their true significance in the patient's life and prospects. This feeling of inclusion reinforces positive and constructive motivations in the family member. It contrasts with the guilt-reinforcing effect frequently seen to result from the traditional practice of barring active participation of the family in the treatment effort.

Frequently, the schizophrenic patient, in his great anxiety at being hospitalized, cut off from symbiotic gratification, fearful of losing what little social identity he may have possessed, and convinced that things cannot be changed anyway, sees no other way open to him but illness. This circumstance manifests itself as "a lack of motivation," seemingly "insurmountable defensiveness," and "bad judgment." He wants nothing but release from the hospital without regard to whether he is ready or not. He may be assisted in his wish by the family's own needs. At times the relatives' needs may be even more instrumental to an untimely departure than his own tremendous anxiety and hopelessness. This "lack of motivation" so typical of him, or lack of objectivity, or both, so typical of his family, tends to deprive him of the treatment that is available. The schizophrenic often needs the firm guidance of his family, who should not permit him to bolt from treatment. Clearly the need for prompt engagement of the family in rehabilitative efforts is of vital importance in establishing and maintaining the treatment situation. In this regard the conjoint setting offers families a number of constructive opportunities, in addition to evidence from us of their importance to the patient's prospects, and the guilt-mollifying feeling of participation. First, it affords the family access to the patient under carefully controlled circumstances at a time when unsupervised contacts might lead to further injury to the patient and reciprocal acting out by family and patient. Furthermore, patent manifestations of the patient's continuing pathology can be either directly observed by them or subsequently elucidated by the therapist. Distortions feeding their mutual anxieties can be minimized and promptly dealt with since all data are directly available to all participants, including the therapist. Direct witnessing of the therapist's competence and interest in the family do much to foster positive attitudes on the part of the family toward the inpatient center.

Conjoint family therapy also provides important tactical advantages for the patient. Feelings of isolation from the family are mitigated by the frequent contacts with them which might be contraindicated for him if unsupervised. Of great importance, we think, is the contribution such meetings can make toward mitigating the pervasive sense of hopelessness described above. Because the schizophrenic process results in withdrawal from reality-bound, constructive efforts to deal with overwhelming interpersonal anxieties, primarily involving family figures who remain everlastingly important, it creates an abiding sense of hopelessness. In our view this often limits development of the psychotherapeutic relationship with the schizophrenic, who in effect says, "I need to believe that if I give the world a second chance things will be better for me. In the absence of evidence of this I will cling to my illness for what little comfort it affords me." In the face of such hopelessness, some therapists have devoted years of their time to attempts at proving via sustained accepting relationships with patients that the world deserves a second chance.

We have seen, in instances like the case illustrations below, a dramatic melting of this frozen hopelessness come about after a series of conjoint therapy sessions. We have attributed this to the following factors:

1. "If the therapist dares to stand up to the omnipotent parent perhaps he or she is less formidable than I believed."

2. "If the therapist can make him or her understand me perhaps I can too," and conversely, "if the therapist cannot understand [that is, double bind], no wonder I can't."

3. "If he or she (family member) can accept without falling apart or viciously retaliating, the therapist's criticism (confrontations, interpretations), then maybe I, too, can risk self-assertion."

4. Spontaneous remarks by relatives, for example, "I never looked at it that way before," as well as shifts in family alliances, no matter how transient, create the impression that change is possible.

Further unique potentialities of the conjoint treatment setting work to the advantage of the treatment staff. In the inpatient setting, one is often confronted with the difficult task of having to help a patient to decide between moving toward or moving away from family members. Prognosis for sustaining even a marginal extramural existence, as well as for further growth, is often directly contingent upon the family's ability to accept changes in the patient and to alter its attitudes and interactional patterns in response to these changes. Traditionally, the impact upon the patient of increasing exposure to family members toward the end of a hospitalization has been the sole means of prognostically assaying these factors. All too often, by the time trouble signs appear on visits, the patient or his family, or both, have taken the bit in their teeth and consider the patient to be on convalescent status, so that the opportunity for further work is lost. We have found conjoint family therapy to provide an excellent predictive basis with regard to the stresses to which return to the family setting will expose the patient. Since this information can be gathered in an exclusively intramural hospital setting as a part of treatment, rather than on weekend visits as a part of convalescent extramural reintegration into family life, the reins are more likely to remain in the therapist's hands.

Thus far we have spoken primarily of the potentialities of the conjoint family treatment situation for solidly establishing and maintaining the treatment situation of the primary inpatient. Perhaps of even greater significance are its potentialities for the long pull, the total rehabilitative program.

The needs and expectations of patient and family members of each other can be interpreted in parallel interviews. The conjoint setting, however, has the decisive advantage of having all the raw data of aberrant communication and perception vividly available to all participants. Under these circumstances the therapist's decoding of ambivalent and veiled communication becomes a potent generator of insight, especially since the involved parties are present to confirm dramatically such translations. Several examples of this phenomenon are given below.

Case Histories

Case 1. J. R., a 21-year-old, single schizophrenic girl had lived in a symbiotic relationship to her mother, which isolated both of them from the father and sister. The father and sister had simply resigned themselves to their exclusion, playing along in their helplessness to change it, in order to get what little gratification they could from both of them. Typical of this symbiosis was the patient's custom, upon returning home after a date, of getting into bed with her mother, to the father's chagrin, and recounting the most intimate details of the evening. The patient's gratification in this symbiosis existed alongside of the simultaneous protestation that mother violated her privacy and would not let her grow up.

Progress made in the patient's individual psychotherapy was repeatedly vitiated by the mother's coercive maneuvers in response to the patient's efforts to maintain a separate identity. The therapist's repeated attempts in parallel interviews over a six-month period failed completely to bring to the mother's awareness the nature of her growth-restricting activity. On several occasions these attempts were followed by calls from the father pressuring for the patient's early discharge.

During the fourth conjoint session (thirteenth hospital month), in relation to a question about expressing her feelings to her parents, the patient said, "My mother speaks to me as if I were one of her friends." The mother smiled and seemed pleased. Aware of the veiled meaning of this communication, the therapist said, "J. means to say that you treat her as a contemporary and not as a daughter, which is confusing and upsetting to her." With this the patient beamed her approval at the therapist. The father brought confirmatory material and, for the first time, in response to this momentary weakening of the alliance, expressed his feeling of being left out. The mother began to sense currents of deeper meaning in her relationship to her daughter and for the first time realized the implications of the many previous confrontations attempted by the therapist in his one-to-one interviews with her.

Case 2. P. L., a 29-year-old single male schizophrenic, utilizing obsessive-compulsive defensive maneuvers to control otherwise unmanageable angry feelings toward others for perceived slights, was seen in joint interview with his mother after lengthy preparation via parallel sessions. She asked, "Do you want to see me next visiting day?" The therapist knew that he wanted to see her and was angry that she did not put her wish to see him in more affirmative terms. He also knew that she desperately wished to see the patient but wanted some prior commitment from the patient lest she go too far out on the proverbial limb. The patient was about to react violently to her question which he experienced as another rejection of him. Rather than risk letting them go on to work it out with much heat and some risk of their being driven further apart, the therapist elucidated these dynamics, bringing dramatic awareness of the similar fear of rejection underlying their mutual response to each other.

In our experience, the process of decoding of communication, initially performed primarily by the therapist, rarely fails to excite the interest of all participants, motivating them toward more conscious efforts to decode for themselves. In effect, the conjoint treatment process provides a valuable educative or retraining experience which, in time, makes it decreasingly necessary for a therapist to serve as a communication bridge. Where family members are reasonably pliable, this experience of "really listening" and communicating more directly may suffice to turn the tide in favor of the patient's continued extramural adjustment following discharge.

Often, however, it is necessary to regard the family's conjoint treatment experience in the hospital as the first step in their ongoing treatment, which needs to continue following discharge of the primary patient. In such instances we have seen the hospital family treatment experience serve in good stead in overcoming resistances of family members to an ongoing treatment situation for them. The following case is illustrative of such a result.

Case 3. S., a 22-year-old relapsing catatonic schizophrenic whose hospitalization was precipitated by an attempt to move away from her psychotic family through attendance at an out-of-town college, had devoted her whole life to magical maneuvers designed to lift mother and brother from psychosis under the grandiose, dependency-denying delusion that she alone could save them. At the same time she felt a painful loss of personal identity in her dedication to save them, and hated her mother for being enslaved by her. It became clear during her hospitalization that the extent of her ego disability precluded in the foreseeable future a life independent of her family, leaving only chronic hospitalization as an alternative to returning to this destructive family field. Although the patient's father had for many years been in psychotherapy for recurrent depressions, the mother had stubbornly resisted all efforts to get her to seek help despite the fact that for ten years she had urged her withdrawn schizophrenic son to enter therapy. The father died during the patient's hospitalization. Thereafter, mother and son were constantly at each other's throat over the management of the apartment house left to them by the father. A further complication, when the hospital staff contemplated the patient's return home, lay in her continued erotic feelings for her brother. There had been overt sexual encounters between the patient and her brother subsequent to which they had completely ignored and avoided each other.

During the eighth hospital month, after attempts to get mother and brother into therapy had failed, conjoint family therapy "to help the patient" was begun on a once-a-week basis. The patient was seen twice weekly by the therapist in the intervals between the joint interviews. During the ensuing four months, the mother's need, heightened by her husband's death, to snatch the patient from the hospital for her own symbiotic gratification was controlled. The patient and her brother began to communicate again. The initial screaming at each other by mother and brother gave way to more controlled and meaningful communication under the therapist's steadying influence. The mother began for the first time to make such spontaneous statements as "maybe it isn't so good for S. to sleep in my bedroom." The patient gained the courage to assert tentatively her individuality to her mother, and began to feel that saving her mother was a burden shared by the therapist and therefore not exclusively hers. The possibility that something could be done about their long-frozen despair with each other other gave new hope to all three. Family tensions, though far from resolved, diminished to a point that made the patient's discharge feasible. All three enthusiastically accepted a referral for ambulatory family therapy.

PREPARATION FOR CONJOINT FAMILY
THERAPY IN THE INPATIENT SETTING

Some of the considerations entering into the selection of cases for conjoint family therapy have already been alluded to. Actually, we find ourselves hard put to state categorically a set of indications for its use. We consider it to be indicated, at least on a trial basis, when:

1. Current or anticipated tensions between patient and family significantly affect the patient's intramural or potential extramural adjustment.

2. We have gained a sufficient knowledge of the strengths and weaknesses of the primary patient and family members to form judgments in the following areas:

(a) The defensive necessities underlying the role played by each member of the family are not so fixed and desperate as to lead to decompensation upon conjoint exploration of them.

(b) There exist unfulfilled mutual needs of family members and patient to relate to each other in a more gratifying way.

(c) The reactions of all parties to the initial stress of joint family interview within predictable limits will be manageable by the therapist in his supportive and protective role toward each.

(d) The primary patient has developed a sufficient positive transference to the therapist so that inquiry into the determinants of his own behavior in the joint setting is possible without jeopardizing the existing rapport between patient and therapist.

3. The involved family members can arrange to come to the hospital at least once a week.

Having on these grounds decided to attempt conjoint family therapy, we have pursued the following procedure. The therapist waits for an appropriate cue, such as the patient's mention of some feeling about a situation that has transpired with family members during a visit or phone call which reflects a communication disturbance between the parties involved. He suggests to the patient that communication problems such as this might be resolved by frank discussion between the parties involved in the presence of the therapist. If the patient seems willing and not unduly anxious at the prospect, the therapist sees the family, elicits their impressions and feelings about the particular exchange, and presents the patient's point of view. Several interviews may be necessary before the patient is brought in. Should the patient seem unduly fearful about such a meeting, this fear is specifically examined in individual psychotherapy until, assured of the therapist's support, and aware of the irrational determinants of the fear, the patient seems willing.

The joint session is arranged and enjoined by the therapist in the following fashion. "We've arranged to get together here to see if frank discussion of some of your feelings about each other can be helpful to you. As I've explained to you individually, such discussion is not easy. It can be most helpful, however, if you can try to listen and feel along with each other as you talk, although we all have a tendency to be most open to our own feelings and viewpoints. It might be well to begin with the recent incident that we've discussed individually."

Thus having launched conjoint family therapy, the therapist begins his role in it as interpreter, arbiter, and protector, pointing out in the early phases evidence of problems in empathy and meaningful communication between the parties as they unfold. Conjoint interviews are held on a once-a-week basis. The primary patient is seen twice a week, and transactions of the joint interview, with particular emphasis on the patient's contributions, are minutely discussed. Analagous reactions in the patient's "intramural family" process are mustered by the therapist in studying with the patient his role in the conjoint setting. Family members are seen without the patient, when indicated, between successive joint interviews. Joint interviews may be temporarily abandoned when they appear too stressful for the parties involved, to be resumed after further individual interviews have resolved the intercurrent crisis.

GOALS OF CONJOINT FAMILY THERAPY IN THE INPATIENT SETTING

We have already described some of the partial aims one may seek with this technique in the inpatient rehabilitative setting in contrast to other practices of family therapy which may deal more totally with reconstructive phenomena. In general, such goals are broadly divisible into five categories:

A. Preserving the patient's treatment opportunity.

B. Improving the conditions for the primary patient's hospital treatment.

C. Facilitating family acceptance of long-range treatment goals along with such environmental alterations as may be expedient for the primary patient. This may include treatment placement for family members.

D. The synergistic use of the biologic and intramural family process for the working through of the primary patient's salient patterns of self-defeat.

E. Favorably altering family communication patterns where the patient's postdischarge residence with the family is either mandatory or expedient so that further treatment on an outpatient basis becomes feasible.

Which one or combination of goals is appropriate, must, of course, be individually determined. These goals run the gamut from mere environmental manipulation and education to reconstruction of communication and family interaction patterns, and at another level from repressive to uncovering. Just as in individual psychotherapy, where personality reconstruction, though always desirable, is not always feasible, so too, achieving goals in categories D and E, though probably conducive to the best prognosis, is not always attainable or appropriate to the inpatient setting, when this setting is viewed as a locus for only a part of the total treatment process.

TECHNICAL PROBLEMS

In our thinking and discussions about the conjoint family process in the inpatient setting, much interest centered on the management of the therapists' countertransference. In their high degree of commitment to family therapy, our therapists mirrored those described by Jackson and Weakland,[8] lending further credence to their notion that once one tries it, one is "hooked." Because it works? Perhaps. But this can be tested only by valid outcome studies for which adequate controls would be hard to devise. There is, however, also room to believe that therapists' enthusiasm for this technique may have countertransference determinants. Surely there are few situations that lend themselves more readily to exploitation by the therapists' grandiose strivings. In contrast to the one-to-one psychotherapy model, the therapist must be active. He is forced to regulate verbal traffic in the context of his own value judgments as to what kinds of contributions and by whom will best serve the interests of the process. He is inexorably cast in the role of arbiter, mediator, and judge, carrying the hopes of all participants for acceptance and corroboration under circumstances where the vested interests of all may conflict. The investment of each in these conflicting interests is by virtue of the long history of prior relatedness and conflict between family members far greater than that with which the group therapist must work.

The therapist is apt to see the primary patient as his chief responsibility. Yet it is unlikely that in all cases the primary patient's need for the therapist's support will exceed that of other family members. To whatever extent the therapist carries into the conjoint situation from the one-to-one treatment frame of reference loyalty to the patient rather than to the family unit, he runs the risk of jeopardizing all treatment goals. He must fight a continuing battle against antipathy toward family members who "have brought this suffering upon my patient." He must avoid responding to multiple seductions as well as those inherent in his own omnipotent strivings, which constantly beckon him to bludgeon refractory participants into change and compliance with his own notions of how the process should proceed. He must avoid subtly coercing the primary patient in his individual sessions with him to exclude other areas of his total day-to-day experience for the sake of exalting the therapist's skill in managing family members during conjoint sessions. He must avoid inconsistencies in his attitudes toward the individuals involved as he moves from the conjoint situation to parallel meetings with them. He must avoid countertransference behavior deriving from his own unresolved family problems.

The conjoint situation is highly charged for all its participants. Its high life proximity reduces tolerance for error. And yet the likelihood of countertransference errors of commission is geometrically increased over individual psychotherapy or parallel treatment where the therapist may wear different cloaks in his separate roles with the various individuals involved.

Because the stakes are high and the risk considerable, the decision to employ conjoint interviews is a crucial one, demanding keen clinical judgment on the part of the therapist. On several occasions we have seen the enthusiasm of therapists for this procedure compromise their clinical judgment, leading to an antitherapeutic reestablishment of symbiotic ties or disturbances of the therapists' rapport with the primary patient, or both. To avoid such unfavorable results, it is of paramount importance that (1) the therapist be fully aware of his own motivations in recommending this procedure, and (2) the primary patient and family members be adequately prepared for it.

REFERENCES

1. Bowen, M., "The Family as the Unit of Study and Treatment," *Amer. J. Orthopsychiat.* 31:1, 1961.
2. Ackerman, N., and Behrens, M., "The Family Group and Family Therapy," in Masserman, J. H., and Moreno, J. L. (Eds.), *Technique of Psychotherapy,* New York, Grune & Stratton, 1958.
3. Gralnick, A., "The Carrington Family—A Psychiatric and Social Study Illustrating the Psychosis of Association or Folie à Deux," *Psychiat. Quart.* 17:2, 1943.
4. Lefebvre, P., et al., "The Role of the Relative in a Psychotherapeutic Program," *J. Canad. Psychiat. Ass.* 3:110, 1958.
5. Gralnick, A., "The Family in Psychotherapy," in Masserman, J. H. (Ed.), *Individual and Familial Dynamics,* New York, Grune & Stratton, 1959.
6. Gralnick, A., "Relation of the Family to a Psychotherapeutic In Patient Program," *Int. J. Soc. Psychiat.* 5:131, 1959.
7. Jackson, D., "Family Interaction, Homeostasis and Some Implications for Conjoint Family Psychotherapy," in Masserman, J. H. (Ed.), *Individual and Familial Dynamics,* New York, Grune & Stratton, 1959.
8. Jackson, D., and Weakland, J., "Conjoint Family Therapy," *Psychiatry,* Suppl., 24:2 1961.
9. Gralnick, A., and D'Elia, F., "Role of the Patient in Therapeutic Community: Patient-Participation," *Amer. J. Psychother.* 15:63, 1961.
10. Gralnick, A., "Family Psychotherapy: General and Specific Consideration," *Amer. J. Orthopsychiat.* 32:515-526, 1962.
11. Silverberg, W. V., *Childhood Experience and Personal Destiny: A Psychoanalytic Theory of Neurosis.* New York, Springer, 1952.

7

Multiple Family Therapy:
Further Developments

H. PETER LAQUEUR
HARRY A. LABURT
EUGENE MORONG

Working as a psychiatrist in charge of an active treatment and research unit for schizophrenic patients in a large mental hospital since 1951, I (H. P. L.) soon became convinced of the necessity of integrating the patient's family in the treatment plan if optimal benefits from hospitalization were to be gained for the patient.

In *individual psychotherapy* the patient is isolated from actual family contact in the therapeutic setting in order to examine and understand himself better. The patient's relationships to significant family figures are therapeutically examined solely as intrapsychic events. If successful, individual therapy deepens the patient's insight into his motivation but frequently leaves him somewhat unconcerned about other people until a full resolution of his more important conflict areas has been achieved.

Peer group psychotherapy broadens the therapeutic setting by including

Reprinted with the permission of authors and publisher from *The International Journal of Social Psychiatry,* Congress Issue, 1964, pp. 70-80.

examination of actual relationships between peers. It can make individual patients more perceptive of the needs of their fellow men, at the same time deepening their insight into their own motivation.

A combination of peer group psychotherapy and individual psychotherapy under favorable circumstances can assure a harmonious progress in understanding both in the intrapersonal motivational and the interpersonal area. There is, however, a tendency to retain specific blind spots in the understanding of the behavior of those persons closest to the patient in life, i.e., his parents, siblings, marital partner, or children.

Therapeutic gains made by patients in individual and peer group psychotherapy in the hospital often are dissipated by renewed contact with the family. Discharge from the hospital to the home is often followed by readmission to the hospital, and even after weekend visits at home or ward visits by the family we see an exacerbation of the schizophrenic symptoms in the patient. It would seem that through the renewed contact with the family the patient or ex-patient again becomes involved in using his schizophrenic symptoms to perpetuate a system of living that maintains the family unity at the expense of his own mental health.

Another problem in a large mental hospital is the apparent desertion of some patients by their families and the overdemanding, support-seeking behavior of other families. In many families both attitudes are present at the same time in a characteristic pattern of rejection and oversupport, suggesting family ambivalences that must ultimately be resolved.

All these observations led me to organize the ward as a therapeutic community [7] in which the patients' families were integrated in the treatment plan. From 1951 to 1960 the ward had only seventeen to thirty-five patients on insulin coma therapy.[8] The patients and their families met with me regularly every Sunday in joint sessions of $1\frac{1}{2}$ to 2 hours. In 1960 the unit was expanded into a hundred bed active treatment and research unit. The greater number of people changed the atmosphere of these weekly joint patient-family-doctor meetings. The former intimacy and therapeutic value were lost, and the meetings became almost exclusively didactic and administrative. Although these Sunday meetings are being continued, their main function today is the preparation of the families of newly admitted patients for integration into the treatment plan.

We then organized smaller groups composed of four or five patients with their families (parents of patients and, in some instances, siblings and spouses) which meet weekly for a $1\frac{1}{4}$- to $1\frac{1}{2}$-hour group psychotherapy session with a therapist and an observer during the entire period of hospitalization of the patient.

Thus *multiple family therapy* [10] (previously called conjoint family therapy [9]) was born.

This paper sums up the experiences gained by our group of therapists and observers over a period of $2\frac{1}{2}$ years in approximately 1200 multiple family therapy sessions with more than 100 families.

THE SETTING

The setting for the work described is a hundred-bed active treatment and research unit in a large state hospital (Creedmoor State Hospital, Queens Village) within the city limits of New York. Most of our patients are schizophrenic adolescents and young adults of both sexes. Approximately half of them receive insulin coma therapy and the other half receive electroconvulsive and/or chemotherapy. The entire unit is organized as a therapeutic community. The families of our patients are organized in a very active family committee (Auxiliary Council 40, named after Building 40 of the hospital which houses our unit).[8] This organization participates through committee representatives in staff meetings and ward operations and also raises funds for supplementing furnishings of the ward and services of the hospital.

The permanent staff of the unit consists of myself, as the psychiatrist in charge of the ward, a senior resident psychiatrist (E. M.), two head nurses, two staff nurses, and twenty attendants.

OBJECTIVES OF MULTIPLE FAMILY
THERAPY

Communication in the family of the schizophrenic patient is usually very poor and sometimes almost nonexistent. Patients often say, "There is no use talking to my parents; they don't understand," and the parents say the same thing about their child.

Our aim is twofold: *improvement of communication* between all members of the family, and achievement of *better understanding of the reasons for their disturbing behavior* toward each other.

In the older forms of psychotherapy one worker talks with the patient and another with the relatives, and then the two therapists communicate with each other. This can lead to misunderstanding and distortion, and often contributes little to better communication and clarification within the family.

It also has been observed that schizophrenic patients in peer group psychotherapy sometimes tend to produce a great deal of narcissistic soliloquy and vague abstract statements reflecting disinterest in the group and difficulty in establishing meaningful relatedness with other group members. These observations are consonant with the classical theory of schizophrenia, which sees autistic communication as a dominant symptom of the schizophrenias.

In contrast, these same patients in multiple family therapy sessions in the presence of their families tend to display high motivation, interest in the group, and disturbed but rich communication. This seemingly ununderstandable, disturbed communication, when seen by an observer in the total communication system of the family, "makes sense," as Boszormenyi-Nagy,[2] among others, pointed out, because the *reciprocal* responses of the patient's family are observed at the same time.

One logical development based on these observations was group therapy with individual families, as advocated by Midelfort,[11] Ackerman,[1] Jackson and Weakland,[5] Haley,[3, 4] and others.

However, this direct confrontation of the hospitalized schizophrenic patient with his most intimate opponents in life, his family, often mobilizes strong defensive and protective mechanisms, such as denial, avoidance, and resistance, and can tend to increase intellectualization in all members of the family.

Bringing four or five families, including the hospitalized patients, together in a group with the therapist (multiple family therapy), affords the families an opportunity to learn from each other indirectly, through analogy, indirect interpretation, mimicking, and identification. The members of a family observe what happens to other families and apply part of that knowledge to their own case. They see themselves as in a mirror in an atmosphere that is more permissive than is the case when only one family is the center of attention at all times. One of our therapists coined the very apt phrase, "A sheltered workshop in family communication," to describe the atmosphere of these multiple family therapy meetings.

In our experience such indirect approaches as are possible in multiple family therapy usually lead to improvement of communication within the family and better understanding of the reasons for the patient's, as well as the other family members', behavior much more rapidly than other methods of psychotherapy.

RATIONALE FOR MULTIPLE FAMILY THERAPY

Clinicians had long resisted family group therapy that included the patient on the grounds that both the patient's and the family's unwholesome defenses would be reinforced and that existing communication between family members would further deteriorate. This hypothesis was suggested, perhaps, by the recognition that the patient became sick within the family setting and that distance between the patient and his immediate environment was therefore necessary.

Multiple family therapy, however, is founded on the concept that the family relationships, in which the illness emerged, can and should be changed in order to hasten recovery of the patient and improve his prospects after release from the hospital.

We work with the hypothesis that in normal development primary objects of attachment or rejection are gradually replaced by secondary ones, and that the normally developing child learns to transfer energies from the inner circle of primary objects (mother, father, siblings) to a gradually widening circle of outside figures and tasks, learning at the same time to accept failures and cope with them. The *neurotic* goes, at least partially, through this process, but with great suffering, because he unconsciously wants to maintain his close relationships, particularly the pathological symbiotic ones, with the inner circle and yet, at the same time, wants to have good object relationships in the outside world. His fear of giving up the primary shelter expresses itself in neurotic symptoms.

The *young schizophrenic,* hypothetically, never really succeeds in transferring the energies of early symbiotic relationships to external objects. Instead of forming new relationships with figures in the outside world and of solving problems, he flees into autistic primitive wish fulfillment. This system becomes clearly understandable only when the psychotic patient's behavior is observed simultaneously with the often bizarre symbiotic reaction pattern of the persons in his inner circle who usually, unless provided with psychiatric help, are unable to surrender their pathological responses and to allow the patient to learn a new and more useful way of coping with life.

Symbiosis is ultimately expressed in mutual, reciprocal control, exerted by the patient and his family. Commonly, patients exert greatest control over their parents by maintaining dependence and passivity through highly varied means. This, incidentally, suggests one of the reasons for the motivation of the family to participate in treatment: to alleviate anxiety by closing the reciprocal gap left by the patient's removal to the hospital. Thus, not only the patient but also the nonhospitalized parent may be viewed as engaged in an active identification struggle.

If we then see the schizophrenic patient's main problem as a conflict between his struggle to reach differentiation as an individual and his need for symbiotic attachment to primary family objects, we can understand how multiple family therapy provides a unique situation in which to resolve this conflict.

The presence of other families and other hospitalized patients seems to allow the patient to engage in the struggle toward increasing self-differentiation and independence. Patients and parents tend to re-create in the multiple family therapy sessions primitive, long-standing family situations and conflicts; thus a patient may identify with a member of another family on a given occasion and learn by analogy with much less anxiety than usually is associated with such learning. The same holds true for the patient's relatives.

The multiple family therapy situations also provides support and opportunity to patients as well as parents for new interpersonal relations. The patient experiences new interpersonal relations with other than his own parents, and these parent-surrogates are less threatening to him than his own primary family had been. His relatives may have similar experiences; these experiences are gratifying to the patients and families as they change. Such gratifying experiences would be much less likely to occur if the patient were to attempt to change within the family context alone (either in single family therapy, or in individual therapy) since he would be met with more intense and more frequent rejection by the family than in the multiple family therapy situation.

The multiple family paradigm thus is a situation in which family relationships are pooled, so to speak, providing a wider opportunity for trying out adaptive behavior and new role relationships. The resources of all family members tend to be exploited more successfully when several families are treated together in one group than when each family is treated as a separate entity.

THE GROUPS

Participation in multiple family therapy is voluntary. At present, approximately seventy patients and their families (either father, mother, and siblings or husband/wife respectively) participate in such groups.

The groups meet once a week for $1\frac{1}{4}$ to $1\frac{1}{2}$ hours with a therapist and an observer who may occasionally act as co-therapist. The team of therapists consists of myself, the senior resident psychiatrist, and ten clinical psychologists of the Psychology Department of the hospital. The observers are two psychiatric nurses, two interns in psychology, and one sociologist.

At first, we selected families with supposedly similar problems to form a group; one of the first groups, for instance, consisted of five unmarried young adults and adolescents with their parents. Later on, such selection became administratively impossible because as one family left the group when the patient was discharged from the hospital it had to be replaced by another family whose patient had recently been admitted to the ward. Furthermore, families must be placed in a group that meets at an hour convenient for them.

We found, however, that a certain selectivity in the composition of groups is necessary. An imbalance of sex in the composition of the patients in a group may tend to inhibit and block participation in the group interaction by the outnumbered sex. In a group of four male patients and one female patient with their relatives, the female patient clearly showed this. When, after discharge of one male patient, a female patient replaced him, the first female patient opened up and seemed more at ease. Lack of an opportunity to identify with another patient of her sex in the group inhibited this female patient so that she could not fully participate. In another instance, a group of three male patients and one female patient with their families showed a similar picture. When by coincidence in one session all three male patients were absent, although their relatives were present, the female patient opened up and participated as she had never done before.

A group of all patients of the same sex with their relatives functions better than one with the imbalance of sexes, as described before, but, of course, something is inevitably lost. The male patients in such a group are not confronted with the real relationships and the resultant real problems of a female patient with her relatives, and this part of life remains in fantasy for them; vice versa if the group consists of female patients only.

We have no objection to mixing married couples, of whom one marital partner is the hospitalized patient, with single patients with their parents. The objection that the most important problems of married couples will be of sexual character and that the single patients in the group will inhibit the married ones from discussing their sexual problems is, in our experience, not valid. The single young adults of our times are usually very well informed on sexual matters and also have problems in this area, so that they feel on common ground with young married couples.

The question of how many members of a family should be admitted to the group is a difficult one and must be dealt with on an individual basis. Ideally no limit should be set to the number of relatives who want to come. In practice, however, one must guard against the relatives—and sometimes even "friends of the family"—who only come out of curiosity. Especially in the case of the "friend of the family," we have found it advisable to ask specifically what the family or the patient who proposes his admittance to the group think he can contribute to the elucidation or solution of the patient's and his family's problems, and also to make sure that none of the other patients and families objects to the admittance of a stranger. We have learned from experience that some patients and families feel the presence of someone not directly related to the participants of the group as an intrusion into their privacy.

The preference for the number of families that should compose a group seems to vary with the individual therapist. Some therapists find four the ideal number of families and think that three families are not enough because several members may fail to attend a session and then the group may become too small, while five to six families may become too large a group for fruitful interaction. Other therapists do not object to a maximum of six families in a group. It will, of course, ultimately depend on how many members of each family attend.

TECHNIQUE

In a therapy room, assigned for the purpose, the group members seat themselves in a circle. The therapist and the observer assume casual positions, rarely twice in the same spots. In a newly formed group families usually sit together, sometimes with the patient between the parents, sometimes next to the father or mother. Later on some families seem to loosen up, some fathers sitting together, some patients mixing in with other families, etc. The therapist does not influence the seating arrangements.

All therapists working with families, even individual families, agree that in this setting the therapist must be more active than in peer group psychotherapy sessions. This is even more so when several families are combined into a group. In the beginning, the therapist's frequent intervention is necessary to promote interaction between members of the group and to prevent some families from using the time for "family visits," i.e., sitting together and whispering among themselves, thereby invalidating the group purpose of the session.

Some therapists leave the choice of topic for discussion to the group; others may suggest a topic. In multiple family therapy sessions lively communication occurs much faster than in peer group therapy, and the therapist will more often have to deal with a mild free-for-all than with dullness or silences.

The therapist will attempt to focus on basic messages that patients and their relatives send to each other. Time is short (usually one year at most). There is no time to get involved in peripheral communication. Luckily, psychotics work in basic values. Patients and relatives are helped by the therapist to focus on basic messages. These messages are sometimes multiple (double bind). The therapist sets an example by not getting caught up emotionally, nor becoming involved in an intellectual pro and con in these communications. He becomes a model of "proper distance," not responding to guilt inflections with guilt or to exaggerated dependency reactions with either too much distance or closeness. If successful at this task, the therapist becomes a model for parents to identify with, as well as for the patient who perceives him dealing with his parents with proper distance.

Focusing on repetitive communications may lead to the production of primary fantasies possessed by one or both parties caught in a symbiotic relationship. The therapist will then attempt to expose these fantasies and explore them with the group. One example of such a fantasy is: "My daughter cannot survive without my sacrificial concern; on the other hand my death will cause her to get well." The symbiosis is seen as necessary for the daughter's existence, and on the other hand the end of symbiosis is proclaimed as the only possible solution to the daughter's condition. As the primary fantasies derive from continuous focusing on basic messages, parents and patients begin to test out behavioral options or alternatives, taking a lead from their identification with the therapist's responses. Sacrifice may change to aggressiveness, and this in turn may lead to detachment. A new response is being tested.

The therapist must develop his technique of cutting through peripheral webs and getting rapidly down to basic messages. He must be alert to and understand basic messages; otherwise therapy sessions will go off on unimportant tangents. Great elasticity and creativity are demanded of the therapist. Complicated therapeutic interactions are going on at all times, and a rigid technique may not come to grips with all that is going on in group interactions.

The use of dreams in multiple family therapy may produce more spontaneous group interaction and invite projection on a safe level. Basic problems are communicated with pictorial vividness.

A certain emphasis on discipline and self-control will be advisable. Extremely permissive attitudes toward individual unruliness defeat the purposes of the group. On the other hand, overemphasis on rules and group behavior may ultimately destroy individual benefits and impede the gaining of insight by participants. The therapist must have a variety of techniques quickly available: on the one hand, he must keep the group from superficial intellectualizing, ruminative monopolizing of a subject, shallow display of wittiness or hostility; on the other, he must also avert excessive probing that might embarrass group members who may not yet be ready for disclosures desirable at a later stage. Like the conductor of an orchestra, the good therapist will strengthen some individuals and hold back others so as to obtain a balanced session.

Essentially three levels of observation are necessary for an adequate description of events in a multiple family therapy session:

1. *Phenomenological description* referring to the concrete statements and actions which occurred in an event.

2. *Communication description,* which focuses on the *mode* of communication, be it direct, or unconscious, via gesture, movement, intonation, or otherwise.

3. *Psychodynamic description* reflecting intrapsychic processes, i.e., affective and experiential factors evidenced in the present behavior of each individual.

This framework helps to clarify the multidimensional, often simultaneous communications occurring in every session.

Much of the success of multiple family therapy will depend on the awareness and skill of the therapist in distinguishing the levels on which the patient and his family communicate and on which they are being reached.

MECHANISMS OPERATING IN MULTIPLE
FAMILY THERAPY

Denial, blocking, and *projection* occur in individual members of the group in much the same way as in other forms of therapy. Also as in other forms of group therapy, *displacement* is used quite often. Patients seem to express poorly veiled hostility toward their relatives by displacing it to the therapist, frequently in the form of criticism of the ward administration. This precedes any sustained direct expression of hostility by patients toward their relatives. As direct communication of aggressive or hostile meaning between patients and relatives increases, criticism and hostility toward the therapist diminish.

Identification occurs on different levels. Parents frequently identify with authority figures, such as hospital authorities, judges, policemen. Patients (children) identify with the underdog in the persons of rebellious figures within the institution or of fellow patients.

At times almost complete identification of a patient with a parent becomes visible. A 17-year-old girl says that she eats, hoping that her mother will become fat; that instead of creating something, she wants to destroy or hurt her mother; that sometimes she feels she *is* her mother. No interpretation on the part of the therapist is required; the statements are clear to everyone.

Identical family configurations give rise to something that might be called *identification constellation.* In a group containing four young female patients and their mothers (three of the mothers widowed for many years, and one divorced since the patient was four years old), an extremely rapid identification of the four patients with each other and of the four mothers with each other was observed.

Characteristic of multiple family therapy is the simultaneous presence of many authority figures, although not all of the same degree of authority. The therapist will have the highest authority value; the observer may rank next to him; while the respective heads of the families (father or mother or husband), in accordance with their performance in the group, represent more or less strong authority figures. This setting affords a unique opportunity to work through fully and immediately the *relationships between patients and authority figures* by means of a comparatively nonthreatening process of understanding through analogy and example. Transference feelings toward the therapist in the role of parent-surrogate may transiently efface the parent-child hierarchy and diminish the parents' authoritarian status with the patient, thereby encouraging the latter to behave more independently and to be more "daring" in multiple family therapy than he would otherwise be.

A *reversal of roles* is frequently observed. Parents act like a begging child, while the child plays a stern, demanding, domineering parent.

SIGNIFICANT DEVELOPMENTS AND
MOVEMENTS IN MULTIPLE
FAMILY THERAPY

In the beginning, identification according to the role in the family easily takes place. Most parents show empathy and understanding for each other; most patients identify with each other or show empathy for their problems in dependency and rebellion. Within six to eight sessions, the *relatives begin to emerge as patients.* "A slight nervous breakdown at some time in the past" is admitted by a parent, and at this signal many others usually come forward with problems of their own, past or present. The "we are well, they are sick" attitude, so often found in relatives when patients are admitted to the hospital, breaks down as a myth. The longer the group continues, the less distinct become the partitions between patients and family.

As the group progresses, quiet members will *gradually open up.* Indirect communication—speaking *of* a person to the group—will change to direct communication—speaking *to* the person—and this latter mode of communication is usually better tolerated by the patient who finds it easier to express his own feelings about something said *to* him than about something said *of* him to the group.

As the group gains in understanding of the significance of interaction, it progresses from seeing a patient's behavior only as a *symptom* to perceiving it as an interaction between the patient and his relatives.

SUPERVISION

All therapists and observers meet once a week in conference with the chief psychologist of the hospital and myself to exchange detailed experiences and critically explore interactions in the group.

The single most important problem the therapist must deal with is countertransference. The multiple family therapy situation is filled with persons of all ages, and if the therapist has significant residual problems with his own parents, siblings, or children he will unconsciously permit "favoritism" or foster suppression of one or another member of the group. The therapist must function as participant-observer in the group. His perception of group processes can thus be only fractional.

In this context the observer is important in perceiving the therapist's countertransference reactions. He will discuss his observations with the therapist after group sessions and his written record also provides the basis for the exchange of experiences in the supervisory meetings.

Detailed analysis of taped sessions can also broaden the therapist's understanding of the events in the group and facilitate the discovery of new material as well as disclose countertransference patterns. A great deal, however, happens on a nonverbal level not recorded by the tape. If more funds were available, filming of the group sessions from several angles simultaneously, and through one-way observation windows, might be tried. For the time being, note-taking by a trained observer, describing purely phenomenologically what he thinks he sees happening in the room, together with the tape recording, gives the therapist a reasonably complete audiovisual record of the session.

RESULTS

It is too early to report statistically significant results. In a self-evaluation of eighty treated families, 67 per cent reported definite improvement of communication and mutual understanding between the patient and other family members, 21 per cent were doubtful about the results, and the rest were negative in their answer. In an evaluation by the therapist, 46 per cent of the families were described as improved to a marked degree, 32 per cent as showing some improvement, and the rest as unimproved.

Our clinical impression is that few patients and relatives fail to make at least some gains in communication and understanding. It may be significant that we receive many requests for continuation of multiple family therapy after discharge of the patient from the hospital, a request we never have for peer group psychotherapy. It would seem that multiple family therapy fills a definite need.

SUBJECTS FOR FUTURE STUDIES

We must develop measures for recording changes in attitude of patients and relatives occurring in the course of multiple family therapy, both in interpersonal and intrapersonal terms. Also a follow-up study of all patients and their families after completion of multiple family therapy and discharge of the patient from the hospital in terms of family adjustment is planned.

By standardizing matters for observation in therapy sessions, such as seating arrangements, critical incidents, mutual support or aggression, frequency with which members of the group use certain types of communication, etc., we will attempt to develop a technique for training observers.

So far our most extensive experience with multiple family therapy is with schizophrenic patients in the hospital setting and only one of us (E. M.) has gained very limited experience in a private office setting. We will now begin to study the possibility of applying this form of psychotherapy to phobic and compulsive neuroses or more generalized maladjustments and character disorders, alcoholism, addictions, etc.

It will be of special interest to us to discuss our experiences with our English friends, who seem to be generally more open to all family therapy approaches, as well as with our colleagues from other parts of the world where strong hierarchical family structures have been maintained and family therapy therefore has run into more resistance. It would seem to us that deficiencies in intrafamilial communication must be faced everywhere if patients are to return to an environment that is more conducive to mental health and development.

ACKNOWLEDGMENTS

The authors are indebted to Leon Goldberg, Ph.D., Chief Psychologist, Creedmoor State Hospital, and his staff, in particular Stuart Marcus, M.A., and Kay Greenbaum, M.A., who assisted with the theoretical plan for this work and the preparation of this paper.

Valuable help was also obtained through discussion with M. Ralph Kaufman, M.D., Director, Department of Psychiatry, Institute of Psychiatry, The Mount Sinai Hospital, New York City.

This study was supported by grants from The Manfred Sakel Foundation, and from Auxiliary Council 40.

REFERENCES

1. Ackerman, N. W., *The Psychodynamics of Family Life,* New York, Basic Books, 1958.
2. Boszormenyi-Nagy, I., and Framo, J. L., "Family Concept of Hospital Treatment of Schizophrenia," in Masserman, J. H. (Ed.), *Current Psychiatric Therapies,* Vol. II, New York, Grune & Stratton, 1962.
3. Haley, J., "Whither Family Therapy?" *Family Process,* 1(1):69-100, March, 1962.
4. Haley, J.: "Family Experiments: A New Type of Experimentation," *Family Process,* 1(2):265-293, September, 1962.
5. Jackson, D. D., and Weakland, J. H., "Conjoint Family Therapy," *Psychiatry,* Suppl., 24(2):30-45, May, 1961.
6. Laqueur, H. P., and LaBurt, H. A., "Coma Therapy with Multiple Insulin Doses," *J. Neuropsychiat.* 1(3):135-147, 1960.
7. Laqueur, H. P., and LaBurt, H. A., "The Therapeutic Community on a Modern Insulin Ward," *J. Neuropsychiat.* 3(3):139-149, 1962.
8. Laqueur, H. P., and LaBurt, H. A., "Family Organization on a Modern State Hospital Ward," *Ment. Hyg.* 48:544-551, 1964.

9. Laqueur, H. P., and LaBurt, H. A., "Conjoint Family Group Therapy: A New Approach," presented at Annual Meeting of American Psychiatric Association, St. Louis, Mo., May 8, 1963.
10. Laqueur, H. P., LaBurt, H. A., and Morong, E., "Multiple Family Therapy," in Masserman, J. H. (Ed.), *Current Psychiatric Therapies,* Vol. IV, New York, Grune & Stratton, 1964.
11. Midelfort, C. F., *The Family in Psychotherapy,* New York, McGraw-Hill, 1957.

8

Some Guidelines for Exploratory Conjoint Family Therapy

LYMAN C. WYNNE

In this paper I shall consider some of the circumstances under which psychotherapeutic work with family units seen conjointly may be especially useful or may be inadvisable or impractical. I approach this problem with an investigative spirit, not with the intent of making doctrinaire pronouncements. I do not regard the method of family therapy as a psychiatric panacea—not as applicable to all

This paper is an updated (1970) revision of "Some Guidelines for Exploratory Family Therapy," from *Psychotherapeutica Schizophrenia, Third International Symposium, Lausanne, 1964,* Basel 'and New York, Karger, 1965, pp. 24-31, which in turn was extracted from a longer paper by Dr. Wynne, "Some Indications and Contra-Indications for Exploratory Family Therapy," in Boszormenyi-Nagy, I., and Framo, J. L., *Intensive Family Therapy: Theoretical and Practical Aspects, with Special Reference to Schizophrenia,* New York, Harper & Row, 1965. It is published with permission of the author and both publishers.

The paper is not intended to be a comprehensive statement of the author's views about all the varieties of therapeutic work with families which he himself uses and recommends for others; for example, family crisis therapy is not included within the scope of this paper, but appears to be very useful indeed under certain circumstances.

varieties of psychiatric difficulties—but as a valuable ingredient in a comprehensive psychiatric repertory.

A terminological distinction should be made immediately: between family therapy as a method and family therapy as an orientation. A family orientation is possible—and desirable—with a great diversity of specific treatment approaches. For example, a therapist may see only one family member at a time, but nevertheless give special attention to the family context and thus indirectly treat the family as a whole. In recent years, especially since 1965, a number of therapists who use a family orientation have referred to any of their work as family therapy, even when they see only one family member at a time face-to-face. My usage in this paper is narrower but, hopefuly, less confusing. Although family relationships are highly relevant to any psychotherapeutic effort, even after other family members are far removed by geography or death, I am mainly concerned here with the special circumstance when two or more family members actually meet together (conjointly) with the therapist.

As the term implies, exploratory family therapy may move in a variety of directions. The goals and the details of the procedures followed evolve from the nature of the interaction and experience of the family with the therapist and, preferably, are minimally predetermined, before the therapeutic transactions have begun. The immediate, ongoing transactions of the family members with one another and with the therapist are regarded as the most significant data to be explored, understood, and altered. Exploratory family therapy is problem oriented, not technique oriented. That is, the particular techniques of intervention are chosen by the therapist on the basis of the actual presenting problems which unfold over time. (Of course, as I shall stress later, his interventions are also limited by what his experience and skill permits of him.) Exploratory therapy can be contrasted, for example, with any variety of therapy in which a particular form of intervention is attempted, no matter what the presenting problem may be. Exploratory therapy also contrasts with therapy in which the number of sessions has been limited by advance plan, for example, to four or six sessions, regardless of the therapeutic outcome at the end of this designated number of sessions. Exploratory therapy may be prolonged, but it also may be fairly brief, depending upon the nature of the difficulties which present themselves. Further, the term exploratory implies that the therapist and the family are involved together in efforts to consider alternative modes of family life. Thus, the therapist's interventions to facilitate changes in how the family relates, communicates, and organizes its values and style of living may be quite different from one family to the next.

As a broad, preliminary generalization, exploratory conjoint family therapy may be indicated for the clarification and resolution of any structured intrafamilial relationship difficulty. In using the term relationship difficulty, I refer to problems in the transactional patterns, in the reciprocal interaction, amongst family members, to which each person is contributing, either collusively or openly. Ideally, for such therapy to proceed most easily and effectively, a central part of each family member's life should be absorbed in wrestling with, fending off, or coping with the shared problem.

PROCEDURE FOR SETTING UP
EXPLORATORY FAMILY THERAPY

Such shared involvement in family relationship difficulties is best evaluated in a series of conjoint sessions conducted on a trial basis, during which alternative approaches can be considered. However, even during the referral process there may be preliminary indications that difficulties exist in the family relationships for which exploratory family therapy will turn out to be useful. Sometimes the referral comes about explicitly because family members are disturbed by, worried about, or angrily involved with a family member whom they feel should be in treatment. They thus manifest their own involvement at the same time that the complaint is focused on one family member. More and more frequently, two or more family members present themselves simultaneously as having difficulties with one another. In our therapy program at the National Institute of Mental Health, we have found that it is quite workable simply to say to an individual family member calling for an appointment that we have found it useful to meet first with the whole family together. If the individual protests that the other family members will not come or that someone will not be able to speak freely in the presence of the others, it is often sufficient to repeat, "The way I work is to have a meeting with the family together at the beginning," or to add, "I'd like you all to come in, and then we may meet in various combinations if that seems like a good idea."

In those families in which family members have paranoid suspicions toward one another and in families in which secrecy about treatment intentions is a manifestation of the relationship difficulty in the family, having individual sessions initially without the knowledge of the other family members may crystallize a split of this family member from the others. At best, it may be difficult later on to make a shift to a family treatment approach if the therapist has appeared to establish a special relationship or alignment with an individul family member.

Such alignments of the therapist with an individual family member and splitting off of this individual from the rest of the family is, I believe, a common cause of disrupted individual psychotherapy. This is especially obvious if other family members have the power to cut off financial support for the therapy or direct power to take the patient out of a hospital or out of treatment, but more subtle, indirect forms of sabotage of individual therapy by other family members are much more common, I suspect, than is generally realized. Many patients who simply "stop coming" to individual psychotherapy are unable to tolerate the split from other family members which an intense individual psychotherapeutic or psychoanalytic relation often involves. This difficulty especially arises for patients who are highly dependent, and especially if they are living at home or are about to return home from a mental hospital. Thus, a solid orientation to the family as a whole can be an important aid in establishing and sustaining psychotherapeutic work for many family relationship difficulties.

During the initial family interview, with the family actually together, the distress which all of the family members feel may be vividly apparent. The therapist then can appropriately make a general comment such as, "There seem to be some problems here which are troubling and distressing to all of you." He may go on to identify tentatively what some of these shared difficulties are and suggest that further joint sessions may be useful to clarify and deal with these aspects of the problem, at the same time that the work with individual family members is planned. Sometimes, even in the conjoint sessions, one or more family members may at first appear indifferent or unaffected. Others may come to the initial conjoint sessions with reluctant grumbles or compliant lip service. The literal content of these initial forms of interaction may be misleading. If the therapist goes ahead with an exploratory family approach on a trial basis, he may find that the apearance of indifference or grumbling belies a deep involvement.

One way for the therapist to begin to explore such initial behavior is to wonder if this person may be expressing the unspoken feelings or wishes of other family members as well as his own. In effect, the therapist raises the question whether the grumbling, compliance, silence, or whatever, serves a purpose or function for the family as a whole. For example, it may represent a style of warding off or of encompassing the "outsider" therapist. This inquiry may lead into consideration of feelings and difficulties family members have about making relationships which go across family psychological boundaries. Then too, the therapist may observe that the interaction between himself and a family member is also manifest between family members as an aspect of intrafamilial relationship difficulties.

If the family members actually become involved in working in conjoint treatment on their problems together, this appears to be a better criterion of shared involvement than their verbal avowals or disavowals. Certain family members may continue to assert for months or even years, whenever they are anxious, that the problem, as they see it, resides only in the individuality of some other family member, and that they are only coming out of a wish to help this person. Yet, behaviorally, these same family members may be vigorous participants and speak, when more relaxed, of the value and meaningfulness of the family therapy both for themselves as individuals and for their family.

Thus, exploratory family therapy by no means is indicated only when all the family members acknowledge verbally their personal motivation for the treatment. The expectation of such acknowledgment by a family therapist is certain to arouse defensiveness and is contrary to the view that, during the conjoint family sessions, "the patient" is the family, not any individual.

In general, it seems unfruitful to try to embark upon exploratory family therapy if the evaluative conjoint sessions indicate that the presenting problem does not have current emotional and behavioral meaning and consequences for the family members. For example, there is not sufficient basis for active exploratory family therapy if some of the family members have merely politely narrated historical facts about the problem. Difficulties in current family relationships or interaction, as revealed in the conjoint sessions themselves, serve as a springboard for exploratory family therapy.

The intent in exploratory family therapy is to establish a treatment setting within which the kind of communication and relatedness that has been troublesome to the family can take place in the presence of the therapist, who then has the opportunity to interview in such a way that the family can develop alternative, less disturbing relationships. It is usually necessary and desirable that disturbing instances of communication take place in the therapy itself before they become recognizable as part of a recurring pattern. Many or most recurrent interaction patterns are unnoticed by the participants who are caught up in them. This applies especially to nonverbal exchanges and to the sequences in which interaction takes place. No one in a family is apt to be aware of a recurrent pattern in which, for example, the mother becomes confusingly disorganized and takes over the center of attention immediately after father and daughter have been exchanging reciprocally solicitous glances. Here the therapist or therapists add a new ingredient by being able from time to time to step back from, and to comment upon, the interaction patterns.

Exploratory family therapy, especially if prolonged and intensive, is usually facilitated by the provision of a stably structured treatment setup. This includes a schedule of regular appointments with regularly expectable participants. With some (though not necessarily all) families such arrangements help develop a therapeutic culture, in which the conjoint sessions gradually become a safe place and time to express directly and verbally feelings which have otherwise been blocked or displaced or which have erupted into destructive action.

Especially in the early phases of exploratory family therapy, much of the therapist's activity necessarily consists of helping the family to notice their immediate, ongoing behavior, to become aware of the sequences and patterns into which this behavior falls. As a therapeutic technique, this activity of the therapist is not interpretation in the psychoanalytic sense but clarification. As in psychoanalysis, the therapist's comments may bring into consciousness that which has been out of awareness, but in family therapy the focus is more on the unnoticed but observable rather than on the unnoticed but inferable.

Inferences about links between present and past events may usefully be expressed by the family therapist on certain occasions, especially in late stages of therapy. However, the special opportunity of exploratory family therapy is to make maximal use of directly observable interactional data and the immediate impact of the interaction. Here I include the impact upon the therapist's own subject experience as he comes into contact with the varied facets of the family. With most families, discussion of the past is an intellectualized exercise unless considerable work has first been done in noticing and understanding current experience and interaction within the sessions themselves.

In summary, then, difficulties in *current* family interaction or relationships as revealed in the conjoint sessions themselves, serve as a broad but clear indication, and a lively springboard, for exploratory family therapy.

EXAMPLES OF INDICATIONS

Without attempting to make a comprehensive inventory, I shall describe here a number of problems for which exploratory conjoint family therapy seems especially suited. These problems are not mutually exclusive but tend to be found in combinations with varying emphases in different families.

Adolescent Separation Problems

In our family therapy program at the N.I.M.H., special attention has been given to the problems of families in which an adolescent member was referred as the presenting patient. These difficulties are seen as "separation" problems:

(a) Rebellious, often delinquent, moves by the adolescent to establish himself apart from his family and its value system.

(b) Failures to separate, later in adolescence, at a time usually regarded as necessary or appropriate in this culture, sometimes with an intense relationship between the adolescent and one parent (and a complaint about this relationship coming from the other parent).

(c) Identity crises, including acute schizophrenic episodes and many other forms of turmoil, often occurring at the time of the first major separation from the intrafamilial environment, such as going away to college or running away earlier in adolescence.

Traditionally, these various problems are regarded as indications for individual psychotherapy with the adolescent, sometimes with diagnostic or supportive sessions with the parents conducted separately from those with the adolescent. When the adolescent is primarily involved in clarifying the meaning of his own experience and when his parents currently are not deeply enmeshed with him, individual therapy with the adolescent does seem to me a reasonable and appropriate part of a treatment program. However, a series of conjoint family sessions is, in my view, nearly always useful in order to consider directly the extent to which the parents share in the adolescent's ambivalence and confusion about his separating from them and his going ahead with new extrafamilial roles. More often than not, in my experience, the parents are suffering as deeply as, or more deeply than, the adolescent from their conflicted feelings about these changes. Even if conjoint therapy is not long continued, exploratory conjoint sessions may assist in distinguishing those problems which have an active, continuing residue chiefly in one family member (for which individual therapy may be more suitable) from those problems in which the difficullties continue to be reciprocally shared. It is in the latter situation that exploratory conjoint family therapy appears to me to be especially indicated.

The Trading of Dissociation

There is a large and important group of family problems for which conjoint family therapy is indicated in which the intrafamilial problems are complementary and interlocking. This significant kind of problem is so complex that here it can appropriately be discussed only by way of illustration. The general form of these problems is the following: Each person sees himself as having a specific limited difficulty which he feels derives from another family member and which he announces can only be alleviated by the other family member. While the claims appear to have some basis in fact, the person about whom they are made does not recognize the possibility that he himself makes any contribution to the problem. However, this other family member may be highly perceptive about corresponding difficulties which are similarly unacknowledged (dissociated) by the first, or by still anothr family member. Thus there is an intricate network of perceptions about others and dissociations about oneself in which each person locates the totality of a particular quality or feeling in another family member. Each person perceives one or more of the others in a starkly negative preambivalent light and experiences himself in a similar but reciprocal fashion, with the same abhorred quality in himself dissociated out of his awareness. What is distinctive about this pattern, and therapeutically difficult, is the trading of dissociations: the fixed view that each person has of the other is unconsciously exchanged for a fixed view of himself held by the other. The interlocking result is similar to the system of reciprocal role expectations which sociologists have described in intrafamilial relationship. However, here I refer to a system or organization of deeply unconscious processes, an organization which provides a means for each individual to cope with otherwise intolerable ideas and feelings.

The psychodynamic mechanisms operative here have been described under a variety of headings—projective identification (Bion, 1957; Klein, 1946), externalization (Brodey, 1959), etc. In the present connection, I wish to emphasize especially the ways in which the involvement may be shared by the whole family, is organized in a "social subsystem" (Parsons and Bales, 1955), and is to a degree enduringly established.

It should be stressed that the reciprocal and shared trading of dissociations serves both to keep out of each individual's awareness of himself the dreaded qualities and ideas and to retain these qualities within his purview—at a fixed distance from his ego. The individual's fear that the dissociated experience might become unmanageable is thus reduced, but at the same time the problem is perpetuated, especially insofar as the interactional process helps make this a real and abiding part of the other person's behavior.

The trading of dissociations means that each person deals most focally with that in the other which the other cannot acknowledge. Thus, there can be no meeting, no confirmation, no mutuality, no shared validation of feelings or experience. Here we have, of course, an aspect of schizoid and schizophrenic experience—or, more accurately, failure of experience.

To give a clinical example of one family described highly schematically, the father, mother, and son each had dissociated into unawareness his or her own intensely destructive feelings for the others but were keenly perceptive of the evidence for such feelings in the others. The father saw himself as having frustration but no real animosity toward his son, who was a caricature of the occupational failure which the father struggled to avoid feeling himself to be. However, the son and mother were acutely aware of the angry contempt contained in the criticism which the father heaped upon the son, which the father regarded as helpful concern and advice.

The son, in turn, was blandly casual, at the time treatment began, about his academic and occupational failures with which his father was so preoccupied. However, the son sharply noted numerous indications that the father felt, but could not acknowledge, despair and failure about his own career. The mother, in turn, saw the father and son as dependent, helpless squabbling boys needing her to manage the most minute responsibilities for them. When she brought up in family therapy one plan after another for them, they accepted her decisions quietly but nevertheless spoke of her activities as meaningless busywork. They failed to see their very real dependency on her, but belittled her feelings of loneliness and emptiness, feelings which she dissociated until family therapy made it possible for her to recognize them.

Collective Cognitive Chaos and Erratic Distancing

Exploratory family therapy also seems indicated with the families of those schizophrenics who manifest bizarre, disruptive intrusions of so-called "primary process" thinking. These families commonly manifest what can be called *collective cognitive chaos,* or, as Dr. Margaret Thaler Singer and I have described it in another connection, *transactional thought disorder* (Waynne and Singer, 1963a). From still another vantage point, Schaffer et al. (1962) have described the subculture of these families as having an "institutionalization of fragmentation" of deep psychodynamic significance for each of the family members and for the family as a social subsystem.

In these families each person's individual statements, apart from the transactional context, may appear sufficiently normal so that one would not ordinarily question the rationality of specific, isolated statements. However, the overall transactional sequence may be utterly bizarre, disjointed, fragmented. Even when the parents are psychotic to some degree, the overall transactional disorder in these families often exceeds the severity of the individual parental disorder. This discrepancy between individual parental disorder and transactional family disorder can be grasped only with the greatest difficulty from individual diagnostic or therapeutic contacts with the family members. A number of clinical illustrations of this phenomenon have been described in previous publications (Wynne, 1961; Schaffer et al., 1962; Wynne and Singer, 1963a).

All the family members seem caught up in this chaotic communication, which is the symptom of their familial pathology. They chronically have been unable to step back from this chaos, comment on it, or interrupt it in any useful fashion. Here the family therapist has a useful function to perform. As he gradually begins to grasp the nature and impact of these kinds of problem, his capacity to intervene actively is a matter of the greatest importance and complexity. Exploratory family therapy is the only means available, so far as I can see, for observing and treating the shared aspects of familial cognitive chaos.

In family problems, as well as otherwise, cognitive and communicative difficulties go hand in hand with difficulties in emotional distancing (Wynne and Singer, 1963a; Singer and Wynne, 1964). Families with chaotic thinking and communication characteristically have highly erratic, unstable styles of relating and of establishing proper distance with one another. At one moment they are remote and emotionally detached, and the next intrusive or engulfing. The cognitive focal distance appropriate for a given task or communication thus shifts bewilderingly; blurred and fragmented thinking is inevitably associated with erratic distancing.

In principle, the family therapist's role can be, from time to time, to intervene, forcibly if necessary, and to assist the family in focusing upon specific issues, upon what was said and meant in a particular exchange. Thus, he may gradually help create a new model or pattern for thinking, communicating, and establishing appropriate distance or closeness.

Fixed Distancing, with Eruptive Threats and Episodes

In other families for whom exploratory family therapy is indicated the presenting problem is not erratic distancing but a relentless, deadening fixity of distance in relationships and a perseveratively rigid manner of organizing thoughts and perceptions. Whimsical, poignant, anxious, angry, and simply narrative accounts are all likely to be viewed in these families from the same fixed vantage point.

For example, in one family, a son was manifesting increasingly explosive restlessness and anger during a family session and expressed these feelings, while looking at the wall clock, by making a ten-second countdown ending in a loud "Blast off!" His mother, with characteristic literal mindedness and detachment from direct encounters with her son, turned to the therapist and said: "I don't understand why Tommy has always been interested in clocks."

The members of these families regularly suffer from a shared sense of being unable to reach one another on any sort of human, feeling level. Each family member is painfully aware of his own need and wish for relatedness, but each feels that the others block and do not allow intimacy or affection. They are on the one hand inextricably caught up with one another, yet on the other are unable either to separate or to develop mutuality (Wynne et al., 1958). They appear to be held apart at more or less fixed psychological distance.

CONDITIONS LIMITING THE ADVISABILITY OR PRACTICALITY OF EXPLORATORY CONJOINT FAMILY THERAPY

For exploratory family therapy there is an analogous array of considerations which should be evaluated in order to decide whether this form of treatment is indicated on a practicable basis in a specific situation. Three varieties of such considerations will be discussed here: (1) the physical and psychological availability for treatment of the appropriate family constellation; (2) the phase of the overall psychotherapeutic process in which conjoint family therapy is undertaken; and (3) the characteristics of the therapists who are available for conjoint family therapy.

Family Constellation Available for Therapy

A very special and significant problem in exploratory family therapy is to ascertain who the patient is, that is, who constitutes the relevant family group that should be brought into treatment. Should married offspring and their spouses be included? Grandparents? Preadolescent offspring? If a key family member can, or will, attend only irregularly or not at all, should a conjoint family aproach be undertaken without this family member?

As I have already implied, the most important consideration in selecting and maintaining an appropriate constellation of family members for exploratory family therapy is that they have a network of continuing, emotionally significant relationships with one another. This network or system of relationships, however malfunctioning and troublesome, is holding these people together in a pattern of reciprocal obligations and expectations. The family therapist thus endeavors to establish a relationship not with an individual nor with an aggregate of individuals, but with an interpersonal organization having both a history together and potentialities of a future together. In Parsonian sociologic terms (Parsons and Bales, 1955), the treatment relationship is with the social subsystem.

The special characteristics of a family constellation in treatment can be illuminated by a comparison with conventional group therapy. The differences are striking. Too often, in my opinion, family therapy is regarded as a variant form of group therapy, as reflected, for example, in the unfortunate term family group therapy, presumably because of the superficial similarity of numbers of individuals meeting together. Family therapy, when carried out on an exploratory level, has distinctive features which are obscured by regarding it as a form of group therapy.

First of all, the motivation which brings family members into conjoint therapy is quite different. Family members are not necessarily aware of individual motivation for personal change, but, rather, agree and want to meet with their family because they are entangled in a web of troublesome relationships with them. Group therapy participants, in contrast, usually have never even seen the other group members before and agree to meet together because of a wish for personal change. Later, the situation may be reversed as a result of treatment: family members may discover personal dissatisfactions and the wish to change aspects of themselves, not just of others; group therapy participants may develop an emotional investment and entanglement in the group structure. However, the criteria for selecting participants are very different. Personalized motivation for change is a bonus in selecting family therapy participants, while it ordinarily is a precondition for getting individuals to begin to come to group therapy.

This distinction perhaps makes clearer the importance of the previously mentioned stricture that family therapy participants be emotionally invested and entangled with one another, not just interested in the family constellation from a detached or intellectual standpoint. This shared entanglement is the functional equivalent in family therapy of the individual inner distress which gives impetus to individual psychotherapy and conventional group therapy.

A second, closely related distinction between the kind of constellation treated in family therapy and in conventional group therapy lies in the historical continuity of the family social organization and the discontinuity of the group therapy constellation. In those families which are appropriately treated with exploratory conjoint therapy there is a deeply unconscious basis for a shared family ideology and set of values which may have become more or less idiosyncratic for the particular family as a subculture. In this respect, individual psychotherapy and family therapy are rather close to each other. Both the individual psychotherapist and the family therapist are presented with a historically established ongoing unit (individual therapy) or system personality (family social organization).

In conventional group therapy, in contrast, the therapist can only endeavor to create such a system. The group therapy system which is created in the course of therapeutic interaction cannot have, and perhaps should not have, the historical continuity and depth of reciprocal expectations which have naturally arisen as the family nurtures and infuses its characteristics into the cognitive and emotional bones, the ego structure, of at least some of its members—the offspring.

It may be helpful to describe here an example of a family in which historical continuity and current emotional entanglement did not exist and, therefore, for whom exploratory family therapy was contraindicated. In this family the husband's illness with a brain tumor apparently had precipitated an acute schizophrenic episode in the wife. She had been married for a number of years and had a couple of children; she was mainly involved emotionally with her family of marriage rather than with her family of origin. A staff member who wanted to work with an acute schizophrenic in family therapy set up family therapy sessions with this woman and her parents. However, she no longer had a really meaningful system of relationships with her parents, even though the three of them complied with the request that they meet together. This arrangement was not useful therapeutically; in fact it was a disturbing distraction to getting around to more useful, more specifically indicated individual therapy with the wife. It represents a situation in which, in retrospect, I feel that family therapy was inadvisable.

In selecting the appropriate family constellation for exploratory family therapy, it is important not to be bound by literal and legalistic definitions of the family. Although those persons who live in the same household together are most commonly the appropriate constellation to see together, the possibility of exceptions should be considered in the preliminary evaluative phase of the work with every family. Sometimes grandparents, spouses of offspring, and other members of the extended family are active participants in the current family dilemma, whereas in other instances members of the nuclear family, such as very young offspring and married offspring who live elsewhere, may not be centrally involved in the family impasse which is the focus of treatment.

Thus, my suggestion is that the constellation of persons seen in family therapy be those who are functionally linked together, within discernible psychological boundaries. These persons are not necessarily limited to the nuclear family (parents and their immediate offspring). This point is especially important in those cultural groups in which extended family and nonfamilial social networks are prominent and significant.

Phase of the Psychotherapeutic Process

One of the conditions affecting whether exploratory family therapy is indicated in a specific instance is the phase of the psychotherapeutic process which admits of passage through a series of phases, in which first one problem area and then another comes into focus. For example, one focus for individual therapy with an adolescent may involve the details of sexual experimentation, which could not usefully be discussed with his parents and siblings. Another focus may be a confused power struggle permeating all of a family's relationships. As various foci of these kind come into view, long-range changes in the nature of the presenting problem and the nature of the emotional organization of the individual family members and the family as a whole may make appropriate a shift of main focus from family therapy to individual therapy or the reverse. These shifts, if carefully considered, need not involve the random, haphazard changes in treatment arrangements which, as I have suggested above, may prevent the development of therapeutic trust.

An example of long-range shifts depending on the phase of treatment occurred in the work with a family in which I participated (Schaffer et al., 1962). In this family the parents and two sons, aged 23 and 21, were seen together. The parents were in constant conflict and had come to the kind of impasse I have called pseudohostility (Wynne, 1961). This constitutes a shared defense or ruse against recognizing or experiencing potential tenderness, affection, or sexual attraction. For twenty-five years this couple had been talking about getting a divorce but had never gotten around to it. The elder son, who was the presenting patient, was constantly involved in negotiating between the parents and in rescuing the marriage. This left him in constant turmoil, with a melange of obsessional, schizophrenic, and depressive symptoms. Previously, he had started individual psychotherapy three times without being able to make effective use of it.

In conjoint therapy with this family we noticed and were able to comment upon the way that every time the parents began to quarrel, or later, to express positive feelings, they turned away from each other to the elder son. Reciprocally, he actively interceded with pithy attacks on one or the other until their quarrel or incipient lovemaking was temporarily disrupted. Despite the regularity with which this interaction pattern was manifest, none of the family members had been aware of it and could not have described it verbally in individual therapy.

In passing, it is of interest that the elder son was literally conceived in order to fill this mediating role between the parents. Within a year after the parents were married, the mother felt that the marriage was going to break up. The husband had been previously married and divorced without having children. In a deliberate effort to hold the marriage together, the wife omitted the use of a contraceptive and became pregnant. The elder son was in effect a child savior. Only after extended therapy was he able to relinquish this gratifying but anguished role and were the parents able to attenuate their need for him.

The younger son in this family had not been so caught up in this conflict. His role differed. Although he was a quite emotionally isolated young man, his problems were not predominantly intrafamilial relationship problems. Soon after the family therapy began he went away to college, was married, and dropped out of the family picture.

Over a period of about two and one-half years the family interaction gradually changed, and the conjoint family therapy was combined with various other approaches. The elder son began to stand apart from the parental struggle, and, at the same time, the parents were occasionally talking to each other rather than only about each other. However, these changes did not stabilize until several other levels of interaction, long-standing in the family life, made their appearance in the conjoint therapy. If the son failed to intervene actively, the tempo and intensity of the parental quarrel characteristically heightened, at which point the son diverted their attention in another fashion. He would stretch out horizontally with a profoundly aggrieved facial expression, a combination of rage, paralyzed withdrawal, and ostentatious boredom. The parents, who had long familiarity with this behavior, would become preoccupied with stably divergent interpretations of its cause. At any rate, their quarrel again shifted focus from each other to the son.

Although the son was inclined to describe himself as the hapless victim of the parental struggle, his behavior, as the therapists noted, had a distinct element of actively sharing in, and contributing to, the struggle. He acknowledged considerable perplexity about his involvement, and, when the therapist proposed that he explore his personal distress more fully in individual therapy (with another therapist), he readily agreed.

He entered psychoanalytic therapy on a four times a week basis. As he gradually focused more and more on his personal problems, the family sessions increasingly were concerned with the marital problems of the parents. First, however, another family interaction pattern made its appearance, once again a long-standing pattern. When the son quietly but clearly was becoming more involved in extrafamilial interests, his mother became alternately furious and depressed. She attacked him for being disinterested in her, not caring about her any more, and so on. At first he retreated from his outside interests and again spent more time at home.

Eventually, however, it was apparent that the son was no longer really a part of this family's emotional organization in the same sense that he had been originally. He was dating a girl regularly in spite of his mother's objections. He was succeeding in his college work, which he had not been able to do previously despite high intellectual capacity.

As he went ahead with his individual therapy and his own life and as the parents became more intensely and directly involved with each other, the therapy changed its focus. After these changes in the kind of problem and the kind of family psychological constellation were fully apparent, the conjoint sessions were discontinued. Marital therapy with the two parents took its place, and the son went ahead with his individual therapy, which was completed with a very satisfactory result.

In the course of time, the mother, who was rather more reflective than the father, began to notice that some of her sources of difficulty with her husband stemmed from her early life experience with her father and from her identification with her mother, who had been in a rather similar marriage. The intensity of involvement in the marital struggle attenuated. She said she would like to have some individual therapy because she would like to work more intensively on problems which did not directly involve her husband. Although some of these things had been dealt with in the family sessions, it now did seem as if the focus of emotional tension had shifted. We arranged for individual therapy for the wife, and eventually all the conjoint sessions were discontinued.

Here then, was a situation in which family therapy seemed to be highly indicated during a particular phase of the overall treatment process in which the family members were very caught up with one another. Individual therapy, attempted previously but unsuccessfully with the son, appeared to be facilitated by the conjoint therapy. The mother would never have considered the possibility of individual therapy for herself without the experience of family therapy first. Throughout, it should be noted, a family orientation was maintained as a frame of reference even when the family members were only seen individually.

This example should not be taken to mean that the facilitation of individual therapy is a primary criterion of successful family therapy. This outcome may be appropriate for certain families, but for others altered behavior, increased understanding, or reduction of tension in the family relationships may usefully occur without individual therapy for anyone.

Kind of Available Therapists

Finally, I shall discuss the very important issue of the kind of therapists available for exploratory family therapy. The absence of certain characteristics and skills in the family therapist imposes limitations on and sometimes contradications to the use of exploratory family therapy. Even though a family problem exists for which family therapy would be indicated under ideal circumstances, this approach may not be indicated under actual conditions, including the unavailability of a suitable family therapist, as well as the unavailability of the appropriate family constellation during a suitable psychotherapeutic phase.

The Therapist's Self-Awareness. Whenever work with a particular family continues over a prolonged period, an especially high level of self-awareness in the therapist is desirable. Through unconscious or deliberate selection of particular kinds of individual patients and avoidance of others, a psychotherapist can systematically avoid persons in roles which give him especial countertransference difficulties. For example, a therapist who has not fully resolved his problems with authority figures may omit older males from his practice. However, in his relationship to the constellation of persons seen in family therapy, the therapist cannot so easily bypass partially unresolved problems stemming from his own family experience. He must retain the capacity to be empathic with each of the family members and still be able to step back and reflect on the nature of the overall transactions.

Either overidentification with a particular family member or a failure to appreciate, understand, and empathize with individuals in a particular family role may create difficulties. The therapist new to family therapy often feels in an impossible double bind with conflicting demands from the various family members and from his expectations of himself. Some therapists seem to deal with these experiences by becoming more tightly constricted in the expression of their feelings and in the reflective utilization of their fantasies; other therapists, however, do manage to regain confidence in their own resiliency and that of the family, even in the face of these emotional dilemmas.

Gradually there has been a diminution of an earlier tendency in family studies and family therapy to perceive offspring as primarily vicitimized by their parents. Clearly, as an abiding, constricted perception, this view involved an overidentification with the offspring and a failure to grasp the nature of the reciprocal processes in family relations.

Sustained Interest of the Therapist. A practical problem of some importance in therapy with highly disturbed families is that the tasks of maintaining alert self-observation and of simultaneously observing the very complex transactions in the therapy are emotionally wearing and exhausting. As with therapists working intensively with individual schizophrenics, there tends to be a fairly high attrition rate of therapists who are willing to continue with this kind of professional activity. At least part of the problem is a matter of the amount of energy that a therapist is willing to expend over long periods. Special interest in work of this kind, especially with regard to research objectives, may be necessary to sustain the activity with highly disturbed families over long periods.

In addition, it is not easy to develop a workable orientation to families as units (social subsystems). Many therapists conduct family therapy in a manner which suggest that they continue to be primarily concerned with the individual presenting patient or, sometimes, some other individual family member. In effect, they do individual therapy in a family setting. Although at certain times it is desirable to direct most of the verbal attention to a particular family member, the therapist who is doing family therapy of the sort I have been describing will retain an underlying alertness to the nonverbal reactions of the other family members and will be considering in the back of his mind how the individual material fits into the overall family patterns. An orientation to families as units is, I believe, not so much a matter of the skill of the therapist as of his set, his way of thinking about therapy and human relationships. It should be acknowledged that some therapists are primarily oriented to intrapsychic issues and to the dyadic patient-therapist relation. Conjoint family therapy conducted by therapists who cannot, or do not wish to, shift from this traditional set will not capitalize upon the full potential of the conjoint treatment situation.

Active, Limit-Setting Capacities of the Therapist. A third characteristic of therapists which is more important in family therapy than in individual therapy is that the therapist needs to be comfortable with the aggressive, active, limit-setting aspects of his role. Hoedemaker (1960) has written a very valuable paper on this subject in which he has contended that an intrinsic aspect of even the classical psychoanalytic situation is the limit-setting function of the analyst. Ordinarily, with well-acculturated neurotics who know what to expect of the analytic setup, very little overt limit-setting needs to be done. With acting-out, borderline, psychotic patients, more activity is required of the therapist. In family therapy, the necessity of activity by the therapist is regularly a problem. The therapist who is apprehensive about setting limits and defining conditions for the therapy is going to have even more difficulty in working with families than with individuals.

In some instances the family social system is so tightly organized and integrated that the therapist finds himself treated as an outsider who may have difficulty making entry into this system. This situation is somewhat analogous to the treatment of ego-syntonic character disorders; comparably, some families present what might be called *family-syntonic disorders.* Especially with such families, activity of the family therapist is a necessary stimulus to change. Family therapy, like the psychoanalysis of individual characters disorder, requires special orientation to the opening up of closed-off issues.

Because many families will continue talking, with one another, even though the therapist does nothing, it is easy for the family therapist to be passive and even to rationalize a belief that his inactivity is desirable. Repetitious talking or squabbling can be a means of avoiding reflective therapeutic work. The mere fact that a family is willing to keep coming and keep talking does not necessarily mean that this is therapeutically useful. With those families which are all too highly patterned in their use of homeostatic mechanisms, the therapist who "lets the family work out their own problems" will be confronted by a staggering monotony and failure to change.

Capacity of the Therapist for Restraint. Activity by the therapist, of course, should not be confused with acting out. The temptations and pressures to be indiscriminately active are often even greater than in other forms of therapy. Sometimes this takes the form of giving poorly considered advice, sometimes laying down reckless ultimatums, and sometimes badgering one or other family member endlessly.

A more subtle and more common form of this difficulty is the use of premature interventions. A great deal of observable dynamic material is often very impressive to the family therapist. It is easy for him to assume that the family members are noticing at least some of what is going on. The family therapist needs to use all of his empathic capacities to understand the form in which the various family members are experiencing what is going on so that he does not leap ahead in ways which either are simply confusing to them or which provoke heightened defensive operations. A problem in family therapy is that the material, both verbal and nonverbal, which is available for clarification and interpretation, rapidly outdistances what the family members are ready to allow into their awareness. In individual therapy the data known to the therapist accumulate at a pace more nearly that which the patient can assimilate.

Finally, I would like to state that it appears easy to exaggerate the possible hazards in family therapy. The likelihood of bringing about drastic or precipitous changes unintentionally is actually extremely small. Examples which

I have heard cited of major changes occurring as a consequence of family interaction turn out to be actually a repetition of a long-standing family pattern, new only to the therapist, or involve gross errors in the treatment approach, especially excessive passivity on the part of the therapist and a prior failure to establish a treatment plan. In family therapy, as an individual psychotherapy and psychoanalysis, the appearance of symptoms in the treatment situation is necessary and appropriate. The important consideration is whether a treatment structure has been set up for containing and working with the symptoms. This has obviously not been done when therapists and family become alarmed and drop the conjoint family approach as soon as significant psychopathology emerges, either in the form of symptoms or resistance.

I have been far more impressed with the difficulty of bringing about genuine and lasting change in family patterns than in the dangers of unintentionally disorganizing them. Inept comments may make various family members angry or upset, and the therapist and the family members may become quite uncomfortable, but this is not the same as bringing about lasting change. The homeostatic, self-regulatory capacities of families as social subsystems, especially if one is actually meeting with the whole family rather than a piece of it, are very considerable. Indeed, *families have a staggering capacity to remain the same.* Hence, the caution which persists in some centers about trying out family therapy approaches may reflect in part an underestimation of the strength of patterning in human relationships.

Individual psychotherapy and psychoanalysis, conventional group psychotherapy, and conjoint family therapy each have distinctive kinds of patient-therapist relationships, leading to distinctive problems, goals, and indications. I have attempted here to summarize my current views, subject to revision, of some of the issues pertinent to an appraisal of the place of exploratory family therapy in the psychiatric repertory.

REFERENCES

Bion, W., "Differentiation of the Psychotic from the Non-Psychotic Personalities," *Int. J. Psychoanal.* 38:266-276, 1957.

Brodey, W. M., "Some Family Operations and Schizophrenia," *Arch. Gen. Psychiat.* 1:379-402, 1959.

Hoedemaker, E. D., "Psycho-analytic Technique and Ego Modification," *Int. J. Psychoanal.* 41:34-46, 1960.

Klein, M., "Notes on Some Schizoid Mechanisms." *Int. J. Psychoanal.* 27:99-110, 1946.

Parsons, T., and Bales, R., *Family, Socialization Interaction Process,* New York, Free Press, 1955.

Schaffer, L., Wynne, L. C., Day, J., Ryckoff, I. M., and Halperin, A., "On the Nature and Sources of the Psychiatrists' Experience with the Family of the Schizophrenic," *Psychiatry* 25:32-43, 1962.

Singer, M. T., and Wynne, L. C., "Thought Disorder and Family Relations of Schizophrenics, III, Projective Test Methodology," *Arch. Gen. Psychiat.* 12:187-212, 1965.

Wynne, L. C., Ryckoff, I. M., Day, J., and Hirsch, S. I., "Pseudomutuality in the Family Relations of Schizophrenics," *Psychiatry* 21:205-220, 1958.

Wynne, L. C., "The Study of Intrafamilial Alignments and Splits in Exploratory Family Therapy," in Ackerman, N. W., Beatman, F. L., and Sherman, S. N. (Eds.), *Exploring the Base for Family Therapy*, New York, Family Service Association of America, 1961, pp. 91-115.

Wynne, L. C., and Singer, M. T., "Thought Disorder and Family Relations of Schizophrenics, I, A Research Strategy," *Arch. Gen. Psychiat.* 9:191-198, 1963.

Wynne, L. C., and Singer, M. T., "Thought Disorder and Family Relations of Schizophrenics, II, A Classification of Forms of Thinking," *Arch. Gen. Psychiat.* 9:199-206, 1963.

9

Ethical Issues in Family Group Therapy

GEORGE H. GROSSER
NORMAN L. PAUL

The development of family group therapy as a therapeutic and research technique has been associated with a variety of approaches. Current interest concerning the indications, the composition of family groups, and the formal aspects of the treatment setting are juxtaposed with questions and concerns about procedure and ethical considerations. This scene is somewhat reminiscent of questions raised around the turn of the century concerning the ethics of individual psychotherapy. Just as that form called for a considerable departure from the established doctor-patient relationship of that day, conjoint patient-family therapy finds itself in an analogous situation today. By conjoint patient-family therapy, we mean a technique of family group therapy in which the two or more members present are related by either blood or by marriage. In comparing the current ethical quandaries with those of sixty years ago, we note that at that time there were qualms concerning the revelation of sexual

Reprinted with permission of authors and publisher from *American Journal of Orthopsychiatry* 34:875-885, 1964.

material. Freud himself, when confronted with the question about insisting on truthful disclosure of such material by the patient, stated, "But in this, it is asserted, lies the danger both for the individual and society. A doctor, I hear it being said, has no right to intrude upon his patients' sexual secrets and grossly injure their modesty (especially with women patients) by an interrogation of this sort. His clumsy hand can only ruin family happiness, offend the innocence of young people and encroach upon the authority of parents; and where adults are concerned he will come to share uncomfortable knowledge and destroy his own relations to his patients." [2] The only difference is that the ethical considerations then were raised by the public and nonpsychiatric physicians, whereas today such questions about family therapy are raised by psychiatrists, especially those who are oriented toward individual psychotherapy or psychoanalysis. However, it serves no purpose to point the finger or polemicize, and it is more fruitful to focus on and deal with the current ethical realities, acknowledging that these critics, who successfully wrestled with similar ethical questions about individual therapy yesterday, prepared the ground for our current efforts.

At this point, we will consider the following frequently expressed concerns about conjoint patient-family therapy, discussing each of them in the light of the objections as we perceive them.

All ethical questions raised to date stem basically from two areas of concern, each of which covers maxims rooted in the history of Judeo-Christian heritage and traditional professional ethics. That family solidarity and inviolability of the family are strongly emphasized in the ethical teachings of the Old and New Testaments need not be belabored here. That going beyond the confines of Western culture, such systems as those of Confucius or Buddha similarly emphasize the proprieties of intrafamilial conduct.

Among the concerns of these ethical systems, of particular relevance here are the forms of respect demanded by spouses and the values of filial piety enjoined to the children. Of further relevance here is the extremely strong interdiction of any form of intrafamilial hostility or violence. This is the source of separate categories of criminal offenses designated in a nomenclature for patricide, matricide, and fratricide; parenthetically, the only other two forms of homicide so singled out are regicide and infanticide—both rooted in the family concept. It is therefore not surprising that objections in the name of family solidarity and authority should be raised when the practice of conjoint patient-family therapy comes under discussion. The aspects deemed particularly objectionable seem to be the following:

1. The disclosure of hatred and other negative affects by either parents or children to one another. This becomes more of a problem in the presence of a stranger, i.e., the therapist.

2. The disclosure of parental failures leading to the dethronement and lessened respect of the parents in the eyes of the children present.

3. The disclosure of personal details in the sexual area.

If the above ethical considerations ultimately refer to social value orientations, a second group of concerns arises from professional ethics, rooted more in the technical requirements for the adequate performance of a given role, i.e., that of the healer. This role, as Parsons [4] aptly put it, requires a variety of relational features between patient and therapist which are designed to safeguard and facilitate the following areas of interaction:

1. They must provide the climate for an honest disclosure of symptoms of dysfunction.

2. They must provide safety for the patient against the misuse of this revealed knowledge by the physician in the latter's self-interest.

Furthermore, they must protect the physician against an involvement in the patient's personal affairs except for those restricted areas necessary for the technical conduct of the therapy. The code of professional ethics, which encompasses these among other features, has evolved as part of the evolution of the medical specialty and was incorporated into the practice of psychiatry by broadening the area of confidentiality to include not only specific symptoms but also practically all details of the patient's personal life. In view of this enlargement of the physician's knowledge of the patient and his life circumstances, the problem of confidentiality has become a central focus around which many attitudes and anxieties converge. To make psychiatric treatment effective, it was held earlier that confidence by the physician definitely excluded any disclosure about the patient's problems to anyone, including members of his immediate family who were regarded to be a major etiological determinant of the patient's problems.

Freud's [1] attitudes towards patients' relatives suggested not only an uncompromising exclusion of their presence but at times he went so far as to indicate that a patient's dependence on "anyone else in the essential relations of his life" (p. 460) constituted a contraindication for the undertaking of psychoanalytic treatment. In another passage, Freud compared the relatives' involvement to an undesirable intrusion in a surgical procedure: "Ask yourselves now how many of these operations would turn out successfully if they had to take place in the presence of all the members of the patient's family, who would stick their noses into the field of the operation and exclaim aloud at every incision" (p. 459). He further stated in the same paragraph, "No kind of explanations make any impression on the patient's relatives; they cannot be induced to keep at a distance from the whole business, and one cannot make common cause with them because of the risk of losing the confidence of the patient, who—quite rightly, moreover—expects the person in whom he has put his trust to take his side."

It may be justifiably retorted that current psychiatric practice, especially with psychotic patients, has modified its technique to the point where the aid of relatives is often actively enlisted. It is now held by many practitioners, such as Frieda Fromm-Reichmann,[3] that with the proper safeguards, family members may be spoken with in separate interviews by the patient's therapist, provided the patient has initially consented to this procedure.

In the evolution of the conjoint patient-family therapy setting with patient and his relatives physically present, there remain the concerns of potential effect and danger of this confrontation, which is replete with all the anxieties rooted in past interactions. In the objections to this setting, there exists a residue of both anxieties and ambivalence not only related to violation of the patient's confidentiality, but also about what to do with the relatives' natural concerns of guilt, curiosities, and rivalrous feelings towards both the patient and therapist. An additional concern is whether family members will be able to cope with the feelings aroused in each other once the therapeutic hour is over and the therapist is absent.

The related ethical problem alluded to by Freud also is felt to be of great importance and can be rephrased in this way: The patient is the primary concern of the therapist and the contract is with him; the other family members are, from the point of view of traditional therapeutic technique, a secondary concern whose adjustment problems are not regarded as part of the therapeutic contract. The question therefore arises in conjoint patient-family therapy: "Whose interest is the therapist ethically bound to serve, especially when confronted with issues of intrafamilial conflict?"

At this point, we shall sketch what we consider to be the goals of conjoint patient-family therapy. Ethical considerations of this procedure cannot be fruitfully discussed without reference to the means and specific goals of this therapeutic approach. They are:

1. To broaden the range of appreciation of both ego-alien and ego-syntonic affects and related fantasies among family members through shared emotional release and exposure.

2. To broaden the capacity for reality testing and consensual validation as a check on projections and distortions by having different members review the same event from their respective points of view. This serves to increase the individual's ability to tolerate differences in perception, ambiguities, and uncertainties, and to appreciate, respect, and tolerate needs of other family members as well as one's own as they relate to differences in perception.

3. To accept the existence of illness, deviance, and differences as they exist within the family circle.

4. To free up and relate relevant unconscious material to present-day intra-familial problems.

5. To encourage each family member to develop a greater capacity for empathic, observing ego functioning in tolerating anxiety with related affects and fantasies.

6. The ability to increase frustration tolerance when confronting disappointments and loss.

7. From the foregoing, to assist in providing for mutual accommodation and adjustment of role relationships in accordance with newly perceived appreciation of reciprocal needs, perceptions, and feelings. This fosters simultaneously the development of ego identity, and both independence and interdependence among family members.

8. To facilitate object relationships outside the family unit by neutralizing fixation-related symbiotic patterns as they exist within the family circle.

9. Finally, to prepare for termination by working through the issues related to the loss of the therapist.

At this point, returning to the ethical questions, we must now consider those effects of conjoint patient-family therapy which are held to be deleterious for the family unit. Thus, in practice, it is a fact that an essential ingredient of conjoint patient-family therapy is the disclosure of negative feelings and attitudes of one family member to another. This violates the ethical maxim that family members at all times love and respect one another. It is felt that, by such disclosure, respect of family members for each other would be destroyed and the family would be rent asunder.

It is also feared by some that the hostility expressed in the conjoint patient-family therapy setting may lead to uncontrollable acting-out behavior with, at the least, verbal recriminations and, at the worst, acts of violence in the intervals between sessions. Parenthetically such incidents reported by other investigators have come to our attention.

We agree that if conjoint patient-family therapy would merely consist of a cathartic ventilation of negative feelings, the feared breakup of a family might very well be the result. What makes the difference? First, we must take issue with the objection that negative affects are new to family members. Every practitioner knows the opposite to be true, not only from experience with his patients, but also from his own personal life. Family members act out their hostilities in one way or another and thus are in many, if not most, cases, aware of being either the bearer or the recipient of such feelings. The shock of this experience in family therapy is therefore not so much the revelation of the existence of these feelings, but rather the actual speaking and hearing of such feelings in the presence of a stranger, i.e., therapist. To draw an analogy, this experience can be likened to a person who, though well familiar with certain four-letter scatological words, finds himself somewhat stunned when he picks up a novel and sees them staring at him in bold print. Here, as in the conjoint patient-family therapy setting, he finds himself suddenly stripped of the social facade and must come to recognize the reality of the communicated feeling, which he had attempted to deny.

It is naturally the therapist's task here to see to it that such negative feelings do not lead either to assaultive behavior (which should go without saying), verbal brickbats, or premature termination. Part of the required skill of the family therapist is to facilitate the neutralization of negative affects by harking to an emphatic frame of reference, at the same time using the expression of such feelings for beginning interpretation of the realities of ambivalence. Seen in this light, then, the ethical issue of threat to family solidarity disappears since in practice the solidarity of the family is more likely to be enhanced or transformed when based on more honest and mutually emphatic understanding. This solidarity tends to increase since conjoint patient-family therapy not only evokes negative affects but, what is more crucial, leads to the shared recognition and expression of positive affects.

What has been said about family solidarity applies to family authority. Here the objection is raised that the parents lose their authority and respect of their children through disclosure of failures, mistakes, and weaknesses. What is, in effect, lost, is parental authority based on pure status ascendancy without recognition of the personal worth of both parents and children. Here, too, parental respect can be compromised if the therapist fails to help family members to adopt a more emphatic frame of reference. We have found it of therapeutic importance in many families to shake the patient's primitive beliefs in the parents' omnipotence by first preparing the patient and family members for this, focusing on the gains to be acquired by loss of the aura of omnipotence. (We obviously are not advocating that family members of very young age be included in conjoint patient-family sessions if matters disclosed will either not be understood or be inappropriate for their ears, i.e., parental discussion of sexual problems.)

That the parents' self-esteem could be permanently damaged through disclosure of their failures and mistakes also does not accord with our experience. Rather, parents find themselves, often for the first time, relieved of a sense of guilt or inadequacy for which they carried both a heavy burden of defense and compensation. Thus both patient and parents (and even siblings) learn to tolerate and accept anxieties related to failures and disappointments in others and themselves. They also learn to look at each other as adults with compassion for each other's humanity.

It is the responsibility of the therapist at the time conjoint patient-family therapy is contemplated, as during a diagnostic evaluation, to make clear to all involved what the experience will entail. The therapist cannot leave it to the imagination of even the most intelligent and seemingly sophisticated family groups. He must point out that this experience, though associated with dis-agreeable and disquieting moments, has the long-term goal of a genuine emphatic mutuality with resolution of long-standing conflicts. Thus the family doesn't come unprepared, but is provided with information as to what to expect in terms of gratifications and stresses. Finally, even under these circumstances, the therapist must invite the family members to express both positive and negative attitudes toward this form of treatment so that stressful feelings about the procedure can be continually worked through.

As for the behavior of family members toward each other between sessions, our experience led us to recognize that, in all cases where acrimonious family arguments were reported, they were repetitious of behavior which antedated family therapy by years. In only one instance out of forty families studied has it come to our attention that family members refused to talk to one another after the commencement of a course of eight family therapy sessions. As time elapsed, a guarded relationship was reestablished similar to that which prevailed before the family meetings. Even in this case, it is felt that if treatment had continued such a rift could have been healed and relationships could have developed on a more mature level.

A fundamental consideration here is the timing of the introduction of conjoint patient-family therapy. If individual therapy had preceded the beginning of family meetings by more than a year or two, such defensive hostility against the supposed therapist-patient alliance is built up that the introduction of other family members, especially parents, creates major difficulties. This forces the therapist first to unite, as it were, the two camps, if such is possible, before further constructive work can be undertaken. This problem of a time lag between individual and family therapy is most conspicuous in families with very seriously disturbed members such as schizophrenic children and adults. Unfortunately, it is also most frequent in those families that family therapy is not considered until several years of individual psychotherapy have passed and not brought about sustained results.

To summarize our point of view thus far, we feel that the ethical objections to conjoint patient-family therapy, on the grounds of destroying the family units or dealing a serious blow to the self-esteem of family members, are not warranted. Our reasons are that feared effects from this type of family therapy are not inherent in this mode of therapy but can be readily avoided by proper and judicious handling of the family situations and appropriate therapeutic skill in the therapist. We, furthermore, believe that no more rifts would result from the inherent nature of this form of therapy than from individual psychotherapy.

At this juncture, we turn to the second area of ethical concerns, that of reconciling conjoint patient-family therapy with some aspects of the code of professional ethics. Here the question of confidence and disclosure of various kinds of material which is taboo in front of family members of both sexes is a major concern. We therefore will focus on only two questions: can individual confidentiality be shared with the rest of the family group, and who is to be regarded as the patient, the individual or the family?

We have already indicated that conjoint patient-family therapy cannot be undertaken without consultation with all family members to be involved. Family members should be assured and, if need be, reassured of the confidentiality of any matter disclosed during the therapy towards any outsider. This includes safeguards for their own anonymity as well as that of the patient. Thus, the principles of professional ethics are extended to the total family unit.

What if one family member does not wish to divulge material to a spouse or other family members, though he is willing to share it with his psychotherapist? The role of the therapist here is clear; he is obligated to respect his patient's wishes. However, this does not preclude working through some of the implications or resistances of such disclosure. In most cases where this has been accomplished, the family member in question is able to bring up at his own discretion the material which previously was regarded as highly sensitive. Crucial in such situations is the therapist's skill in recognizing the motivation for such secrecy; more often than not, the material is not the charged issue, but rather the patient's wish to be special in having a secret with the therapist.

Of greater controversial nature is the second question concerning the contract and the responsibility of the therapist. It has been argued that in individual psychotherapy the code of professional ethics clearly delineates the physician's responsibility, and, although he is committed to help the patient to deal effectively with his family members, he must regard the patient as his sole responsibility, and this at times requires that he side with his patient in areas of family conflict. This is true even though the therapist may recognize that the therapeutic success on the part of his patient may be associated with the behavioral deterioration of a family member, or may involve a divorce, or complete dissociation from the family circle.

What are the ethical principles involved in conjoint patient-family therapy? Who is the primary object of the physician's responsibility? With whom is the therapeutic contract made, and, since it is likely that there is disturbance in family members other than the patient, how should these related problems be evaluated with respect to those of the patient in terms of priority, urgency, and gravity? In our discussion of this complicated ethical and technical issue, we shall separate two types of family situations: one in which the patient is clearly defined by his disorganized behavior and comes to the attention of the therapist first, usually in quest of individual treatment; the second is one in which two or more persons, either in a marital relationship or a parent-child relationship, come to the attention of a psychiatrist without clear differentiation as to who is labeled as the patient.

We are aware of the fact that this distinction at times may be artificial, but for practical purposes it is useful to make it here. We feel that the ethical dilemma which often is posed as to whether the patient or the whole family is the object of responsibility is inappropriate. In the first case, where there is a patient with a diagnosed mental illness, treatment is of course undertaken primarily to help the patient. In these cases, where family therapy is contemplated it is essential that treatment be viewed as a commitment shared by other family members with the therapist. This means that agreement for pursuit of this program must be obtained from both patient and his family members. The latter must assume their part of the contract, failing which the program cannot be continued. The reasoning here is that if the patient either has not made substantial progress or, in the opinion of the physican, is not likely to make substantial progress unless his family is included in conjoint patient-family therapy, the physician has a responsibility to relate this to both the patient and his family.

Two other issues deserve discussion here. One relates to the concurrent deterioration of a family member when a patient appears to be improving in either individual psychotherapy or conjoint patient-family therapy. This phenomenon has been observed by us and other investigators and is regarded as indeed a difficult and challenging situation. While temporary deterioration of family relationships and transitory appearance of anxiety, nervousness, and psychosomatic symptoms in one family member or other will invariably occur when a fixed family equilibrium begins to disintegrate, this need not cause great alarm. We believe that this occurs in individual psychotherapy as well, often unobserved by the therapist. The family therapist has the advantage of both witnessing and handling such problems supportively, recognizing that increasing ambivalence about altering family role structure is the primary source of such phenomena. Particular difficulties can arise when more serious pathology emerges. This, too, is likely to occur in individual or conjoint patient-family therapy if a family member has been excessively dependent on the patient who now is moving towards more stable independence. The particular forms of this psychopathology can be that of a moderately severe to a severe depressive reaction or the appearance of profound withdrawal, distortion, or paranoid episodes. Here the family therapist is obligated to make a referral for concurrent individual psychiatric treatment. It is also necessary before beginning conjoint patient-family therapy to inquire whether any family member, other than the patient, has ever suffered from severe emotional disturbance. At this time the doctor can evaluate the advisability of including this family member without concurrent individual psychotherapy. Our experience has been that, with marked improvement in the patient, especially a psychotic patient, severe dormant problems are likely to emerge in at least one of the other family members, whether in family therapy or not. We regard it as an advantage to such a vulnerable family member and to the family unit that such decompensatory situations are both anticipated and promptly dealt with when they occur.

Other conflicts of interest between the patient and family members may arise, such as financial problems and living, occupational, and business arrangements. In these cases the therapist is obligated to help the family assess all sides of the controversy at hand, which usually will enable them to make an appropriate choice. In all such instances one must strive for clear understanding and appraisal of the realities involved. It must be clear that the family therapist cannot make decisions which are clearly the responsibility of the family itself, including the patient.

This brings up one final point about conflicts of values and interest. Both the family group and the patient will at times try to use the therapist as an ally or an enforcer of their own values, beliefs, and attitudes. One must be cautious at all times so that inappropriate responses by the therapist do not occur. These cautions cannot be repeated often enough, as the quality of countertransference may incline the therapist either to rebel with the patient against his parents or, contrariwise, to identify with the parents against the patient or his sibling.

As for the case where no labeled individual patient is referred at the outset of therapy, i.e., a husband and wife or a parent and child, and where it is clearly recognized that the basic problem is that of interpersonal friction with shifting ego boundaries, the therapist from the outset should clarify his position of nonalignment. He has to make it clear that he considers all parties equally in need of assistance and that each one has contributed to the creation and persistence of the family problem. In this case, if the therapist wishes to use conjoint patient-family therapy in association with individual treatment, he should see both parties individually and jointly.

In summary, we have attempted to review and clarify a few of the most frequently expressed ethical concerns in the area of conjoint patient-family therapy which to date have not found adequate discussion. These concern primarily the supposed incompatibility of this form of treatment with family solidarity and professional ethics. We have tried to show that many ethical objections to family therapy are not in disagreement with basic ethical principles held by both the culture and the profession. We feel that such ethical concerns may mask two things: first, the anxiety attending innovative therapeutic procedures possibly associated with the realization of dormant ambivalence about current therapeusis, and second, some countertransference issues of therapist vis-à-vis the patient and the therapist's own family background.

As far as anxiety about innovation is concerned, this is a generally observable phenomenon not confined to the psychiatric profession. We can only hope that the restlessness and the search for new therapeutic approaches will carry the day as it has with other forms of therapy. Our hope is founded on the belief that reality testing of the outcomes of family therapy will be the determinant as to whether this form of treatment has any merit.

As far as the issue of the therapist's feelings in the family therapy setting is concerned, he is in a position analogous to that of the family members present. Just as they have to disclose publicly their previously hidden actions, feelings, and failures, he has to demonstrate his therapeutic skill with the family as his public. This is undoubtedly a situation for which hitherto little opportunity or training has been provided. Such a setting is obviously fraught with multiple countertransference issues which tax the therapist, principally because they remind him of his own family setting, with parental figures and siblings present. The continuing recognition of and reaction to these countertransference tendencies increase the emotional load on the therapist beyond that generally experienced in psychotherapy. It is understandable that under these circumstances the wish not to have family members present can be disguised by ethical objections to their presence lest such family members suffer from the effects of family therapy.

REFERENCES

1. Freud, S., "Analytic Therapy," in Strachey, J. (Ed.), *The Complete Psychological Works of Sigmund Freud,* Vol. 16, London, England, Hogarth Press, 1963, p. 460.
2. Freud, S., "Sexuality in the Aetiology of the Neuroses," in Strachey, J. (Ed.), *The Complete Psychological Works of Sigmund Freud,* Vol. 3, London, England, Hogarth Press, 1962, p. 263.
3. Fromm-Reichmann, F., *Principles of Intensive Psychotherapy,* Chicago, University of Chicago Press, 1950, p. 220.
4. Parsons, T., "The Social System," in *Social Structure and Dynamic Process: The Case of Modern Medical Practice,* New York, Free Press, 1951, pp. 428-479.

IO

The Family as a Treatment Unit

VIRGINIA M. SATIR

Using the family as a treatment unit in therapy seems to be the inevitable out-come of experience and research in which new knowledge about human be-havior has suggested different approaches to the meaning and causation of behavior and consequently made different treatment procedures possible. (For further discussion of this idea, see Ackerman et al., 1961.)

Treating the family as a unit means having all family members present at the same time in the same place with a single therapist or with male and female cotherapists. The whole family is then viewed and treated as a system originally developed by the male and female adults who were the "architects" of the family.

The symptom of any family member at a given time is seen as a comment on a dysfunctional family system. The wearer of the symptom, the identified patient, is seen as signaling distortion, denial, and/or frustration of growth.

Reprinted with the permission of author and publisher from *Confinia Psychiatrica* 8:37-42, 1965.

Simultaneously, he is signaling the presence of pain, discomfort, or trouble in his survival figures. (Survival figures are those people who have provided and continue to provide nurture, economic support, and directing functions for him.) The major treatment tool in family therapy is the application of concepts and procedures relating to interaction and communication.

To begin to look at a family system, one can remind oneself that each member of any family is unavoidably committed to the system of his family, if only because that is where he had his beginnings. If the system is an open one, he can use it for his growth. He continues to move in and eventually out of his family system as his maturity develops. Then he himself becomes an architect in developing a further branch of the system, interacting with other people in other situations.

To exist as an open system, the family needs rules which allow it to meet changes openly, directly, clearly, and appropriately. Ability for expansion and reshaping is needed for three kinds of changes that inevitably occur because of the nature of life and living. These are:

1. Changes within the individual members, for example, *changes which occur between birth and maturity in the use and perception of authority, independence, sexuality, and productivity.*

2. Changes between family members; for example, *between adults and a child from birth to maturity, between husband and wife before they have a child and after the coming of a child, the illness or injury of one or the advancing age of both husband and wife.*

3. Changes which are demanded by social environment, for example, *war, a new job, school, neighborhood, or country, or new laws.*

If the family system is a closed one, the family will handle these inevitable changes by attempting to maintain the status quo, and thus by denying or distorting the change. This creates a discrepancy between the presence of change and the acknowledgment of change, and presents a dilemma which must be dealt with before life and relationships can continue.

Because change must be coped with, a family system which does not have functional ways to assimilate it will have dysfunctional ways. Generally speaking, a system which has rules requiring that the present be seen in terms of the past will be dysfunctional. If the rules of the system can be changed to meet the present, it will become functional. The dysfunctional family, when confronted with change, produces symptoms.

The precursors to what we call symptoms, to modern clinical entities, are the physically ill person, the witch, the pauper, the idiot, and the criminal. It was not until relatively recently that it was recognized that all of these entities had something in common. Family therapy is concerned with all of them.

Initially the treatment of behavior problems—of deviant behavior—centered around the person wearing the symptom. This was true until the advent of child guidance clinics, where the mother was seen along with the child who wore the symptom. Fathers were not discovered until relatively recently in the child guidance clinics. Some time later, marital counseling or marital therapy including both husband and wife was initiated.

Now we have ideas about family therapy which include people as individuals and in their respective roles: marital, parental, filial, and sibling. Furthermore, we see that the conclusions drawn from experience in the family of origin are connected with the selection of spouse and with the blueprint for child-rearing practices. The symptom is regarded as a report about the individual wearing it, about his family, and about the rules of the family system; and to understand the symptom, one must understand not only the symptom wearer but also his family and the family system.

This means that a symptom such as psychosis in either parent indicates dysfunction in the marital relationship as well as in child-rearing practices. By the same token, symptoms in a child indicate dysfunction in the marital relationship. Thus by seeing the whole family together we can serve both treatment and preventative functions.

We believe that by observing and learning to understand communication in a family we can discover the rules that govern each individual's behavior. The family system has rules about (1) self and manifestation of self, or "how I may report," (2) self and expectation of other, or "what I may expect from you," and (3) self and the use of the world outside of the family, or "how I may go outside the family." Family members are not necessarily aware of these rules. We believe the rules are shaped by interactional experience and acquired as each person attempts to survive, grow, get close to others, and produce.

Because each person comes into the world without a blueprint for interacting in these ways, he must develop it as he grows from birth. The beginning of this blueprint will of necessity be shaped by those who surround him. These are the adults who attempt to insure his survival—through nurture and economic support, through directing his actions, and through providing a model for what he can become.

Most adults have little notion about their importance as models for a child. They behave as though the child sees and hears only that which he is directed to see and hear. If the way in which adults behave with each other and with the outside world and the way in which the child is asked to behave are incongruent, the child will perceive this. Because the child is confined by the rules about what he may report, by his inability to judge, and by his lack of a complete enough set of reporting symbols, the adult is deluded into believing that he is successfully labeling what the child sees and hears. The parent believes, in other words, that the child does not see or hear that which the parent does not directly direct him to see and hear. We believe that children's symptoms are a distorted but obvious comment on the discrepancies which they have experienced or are experiencing. The child cannot grow if he must deal with important discrepancies upon which he may not comment openly. Clues to the nature of the discrepancies may be found in the way the family communicates.

We approach the analysis of communication by observing and understanding the *means* of communication—the giving, receiving, and checking out of meaning with another as it is revealed through the use of words, the tone and pace of voice, facial expressions, and body tonus and position. Then we look at the outcome: what actually happens in the communication process, and what kinds of joint decisions or understanding occur.

Next, we examine certain processes to shed light on how these outcomes evolved. We ask: (1) how is the uniqueness and individuality of each person manifested? (2) how are decisions made? and (3) how is differentness reacted? In other words, we are attempting to discern the rules for: (1) manifesting self and validating to the other uniqueness and individuality, (2) making decisions, and (3) acknowledging the presence of, reacting to, and using differentness.

Our goals in therapy are also related to this analysis of family communication. We attempt to make three changes in the family system. First, each member of the family should be able to report congruently, completely, and obviously on what he sees and hears, feels and thinks, about himself and other, in the presence of others. Second, each person should be addressed and related to in terms of his uniqueness, so that decisions are made in terms of exploration and negotiation rather than in terms of power. Third, differentness must be openly acknowledged and used for growth.

When these changes are achieved, communication within the family will lead to appropriate outcomes. Appropriate outcomes are decisions and behavior which fit the age, ability, and role of the individuals, which fit the role contracts and the context involved, and which further the common goals of the family.

I would like to give you a simple example of the relationship between communication rules and behavior. Suppose that right now you are committed to taking back a report of what I have to say, but you can't get my meaning. And you have rules that you can't ask about my meaning, for fear of *exposing* you or me (making a conclusion of badness, sickness, stupidity, or craziness about you or me). If these conditions are present, you will probably lay blame somewhere —there will be three places to point your finger: to yourself, to me, or to the situation.

You will undergo some form of personal discomfort; you will feel anxiety, hostility toward me, and helplessness toward the situation (anxiety, "I am no good"; hostility, "You are not good"; helplessness; "I am little and weak"). You will probably experience all three feelings, roughly in that order—anxiety, hostility, and helplessness. They will have been occasioned by the fact that you could not keep your *commitment* to yourself. And your inability to keep your commitment to yourself will have been caused by your *rules* about what kind of questions you can ask.

If you have rules which permit you to risk exposure and seek clarity, in the presence of confusion or lack of clarity, you can save yourself these feelings of anxiety, hostility, and helplessness. *Risk* requires a perception of your ability to survive in the face of pain, anger, and hurt in another and the perception that the other will not die from his experience of being pained, angered, and/or hurt, (pain, "I am injured"; anger, "You injured me "; and hurt, "I don't count").

A direct question is often regarded as a risk runner. The infrequent use of direct questions is one of the signals of inability to communicate in a troubled family; another is the infrequent use of first names.

It should be clear by now that I believe that human beings are continually searching to make things fit. Lack of success in making things fit becomes manifested in symptoms. Inability to explore by asking direct questions and making accurate reports does not stop the search; it only makes the search come out in a confused, indirect, or unclear way, which may show up in symptoms or inappropriate outcomes.

Thus the analysis of a symptom starts with an analysis of communication and a documentary of the outcome. Then comes the exploration of the family system, which makes explicit the rules for maintaining the system and points out the individual processes which implement these rules.

In summary, family therapy centers around the application of concepts of interaction and deals with the present rules and processes of individuals by exploring the family system. Theories relating behavior to interactional process are far from new. Freud used this idea in his treatment of little Hans; Sullivan, Moreno, Ackerman, Lidz, Fleck, Bowen, Bateson, Jackson, and Berne—to mention a few—have used interactional concepts to understand human behavior. At present, theories of human behavior which include interactional phenomena are more widely embraced and are getting to be better understood. Using the family as a treatment unit is a further way to both use and develop the theory.

REFERENCES

Ackerman, N., Beatman, F., and Sherman, S. W. (Eds.), *Exploring the Base for Family Therapy,* New York, Family Service Association, 1961.

Brodey, W. M., Bowen, N. M., Dysinger, G., and Basamania, B., "Some Family Operations of Schizophrenia: A Study of Five Hospitalized Families Each with a Schizophrenic Member." *A. M. A. Arch Gen. Psychiat.* 1:379-402, 1959.

Jackson, D. D. (Ed.), *Etiology of Schizophrenia,* New York, Basic Books, 1960.

MacGregor, R., Ritchie, A. M., Serrano, A. C., and Schuster, F. P., Jr., *Multiple Impact Therapy with Families,* New York, McGraw-Hill, 1964.

Overton, A., and Tinker, K. H., *Casework Notebook,* St. Paul, Minn., Family Centered Project, 1959.

Satir, V., *Conjoint Family Therapy,* Palo Alto, Calif., Science and Behavior Books, 1964.

I I

Experiential Family Therapy

WALTER KEMPLER

Experiential family therapy is a psychotherapeutic approach to the treatment of emotionally disturbed individuals within the framework of the family. Its core is experiential exploration of the "what and how" of "I and thou" in the "here and now." A fundamental of such an approach is the acceptance of the vital importance of the immediate, the present, the whole, not to exclude perspective but to establish a central point to which that perspective can be readily related.

The family framework, has, of course, always been implicitly and explicitly recognized, as has, in remoter context, the social, economic, ethnic, and national status of the individual. But many therapists have assumed, until recently, that treatment could proceed only—or at least more beneficially—with a temporary physical divorce of the patient from his familial surroundings during the therapeutic interviews.

Individual therapy had and has its subjective advantages; however, in many

Reprinted with permission of author and publisher from *The International Journal of Group Psychotherapy* 15:57-71, 1965.

instances these are overbalanced by the benefits of an approach which brings together the family group with the therapist. Therapeutic sessions are inevitably artificial in arrangement and atmosphere. Individual sessions dignify the patient with peculiar importance, exemplified by the entire attention of the therapist, while at the same time removing him from the ordinary actions and counter-actions of his daily life. The few hours of the week spent with the psychiatrist are far outweighed, in duration at least, by the many hours spent with the family. It is the case of the sand in *Alice:*

> "If seven maids with seven mops
> Swept it for half a year,
> Do you suppose," the Walrus said,
> "That they could get it clear?"
> "I doubt it," said the Carpenter,
> And shed a bitter tear.

Just too much sand and not enough mops.

Experiential family therapy is particularly well suited to individuals who are captive to family, whether by virtue of age (children) or inclination (adults who identify their problems as interpersonal). However, it is not limited to these categories, but has been used successfully in treatment of individuals, couples, and groups whose needs have not been so manifest. No diagnostic classification is contraindicated, and family participants include many who would otherwise have never seen a psychotherapist.

Most of us who have begun to approach psychotherapy within the context of the family unit rather than by following the traditional method of separating an individual from his intimate environment have come to it by way of the family who presents us with a disturbed child as the identified patient. The success of the family technique in these instances led to an exploration of other applications for the "family" approach to treatment. Any two persons who feel strongly about preserving a relationship and who blame the existence or course of that relationship for their personal discomforts may be considered eligible, that is, childless couples need not be deprived.

I have been confronted by patients whose complaints were of interpersonal rather than intrapsychic discomfort. By the end of the interview, it was apparent that the individual's personality was what we typically call a character disorder with little anxiety or capacity for introspection. Psychiatric literature generally reports such individuals as difficult to treat, and personal experience has tended to confirm this. With the concept of family pathology, I have been able to accept these patients' starting point of an interpersonal rather than an intra-personal construction of their problems, and have suggested that the irritant party, usually a spouse, be included, since the problem is posed as existing between two people. (It would not be reasonable to send one lung to one hospital and the other to another for treatment of pneumonia. Once resistance to this is acknowledged as the therapist's rather than the patient's, a profitable beginning has been made.)

The approach is an experiential or phenomenological one characterized by exploration, experiment, and spontaneity. By spontaneity I mean allowing sub-surface material to emerge whenever possible from myself and the people I sit with. It means encouraging an atmosphere in which the underlying flow of affect toward or away from each other is welcomed as part of our verbal ex-change. I encourage this atmosphere by doing it, being it, and sometimes by exploring verbally my difficulty in doing it, never by talking about (broadcasting or announcing) this desired atmosphere. In exploring and experimenting, no topic is taboo from our right to toy with it, tease it apart, or try it on for size. However, spontaneity is not license for manifest irrelevances or abstract dis-cussion, no matter how tempting, which are, of course, resistances on the part of the therapist or the patient. The approach is predicated on the assumption that in the room, within the accepted setting, the family members and the therapist have needs which will emerge. These needs may come out as thoughts fully or partially expressed, feelings subtly indicated or vehemently vented, changes of posture, gesticulations, or perhaps fantasies which develop in the mind of the individual and are not shared with the group.

To the expression of these needs, adequate or, more likely, halting reactions occur: comfort, antagonism, worry, detachment, horror, disgust, resentment, indifference, pleasure, and so on, endlessly. Sensitivity to these evidences of human interaction is encouraged, and attention is directed to the use to which awareness of them is put. This applies to therapist and patient alike. If I become aware of being bored, I will consider my boredom and most likely mention it. If I get the idea that all the verbiage spoken by one of the group to another could be summarized in the statement "I want your unqualified approval of my behavior," I may suggest that this member experiment by trying out this state-ment with the other person.

This therapy is kept vital by constant attention to our differences. Awareness in this sense always includes who is doing what to whom and how it is perceived by others. Awareness means action. When an active (total behavioral response, not merely verbal agreement or abstract discussion) response is absent, I ask, as the lighthouse keeper did who awoke when his light failed, "What wasn't that?" The inactive response then comes to the foreground. I judge the effectiveness of what I do by direct observation of altered behavior and peripheral cue comments of outside experiences. If there is a discrepancy between the two, I am likely to comment on it. If behavior is being altered merely to please me and I sense this, I will introduce my thought for their perusal. If I am not aware of this, then so be it, until such time as the resentment they are likely to feel comes to the awareness of one or both of us. Then we will attend it. I say likely rather than inevitably since sometimes their altered behavior, although motivated primarily by a desire to please, is sufficiently rewarding to preclude any concern with revenge. A goal I have for others is behavior predicated on pleasing themselves. This may or may not be achieved. The decision does not rest with me.

My aim is to utilize these family sessions as a meaningful experience and to encourage the participants to engage themselves likewise, not as spectators or aloof commentators, but as vitally concerned combatants. It is still a process of pointing up and ferreting out resistances, as we have traditionally formulated, but the orientation here considers the patients as resisting awareness of themselves and involvement in their current world, wherever they may find themselves.

I am interested in coming to know the persons I am with. To this end, I am interested in the what and how of their behavior primarily; my concern with the verbal content is almost exclusively in this perspective. The verbal content or subject matter per se is for me the launching equipment to be jettisoned as soon as possible in favor of a free flight of self-awareness and of self-expression, literally, direct expression of self in the atmosphere of another. By responding to the what and how, a more intense and vital interaction ensues. This is something which not all people can accept at all times. I find myself diluting the intensity by concentrating on verbalizations when my patient reveals to me as a total response, not just verbally, that he cannot tolerate the intensity. This may become the next thing we discuss.

In such a give-and-take, an exploration of the differences in our perceptions of ourselves and others and an examination of what we do or do not do with this awareness takes place. But it does not take place in the isolation of introspection. It occurs in an atmosphere of human, familial, and immediate concern which makes a crucial contribution to movement in therapy.

In terms of the familiar concept of transference, this technique of family group therapy does not foster regressive phenomena in relation to the therapist, only for the patient to be confronted at some later "suitable" time with the reality of who the therapist is and what he is as distinguished from the images projected upon him. Experiential family group therapy presents a constant exposure of transference phenomena whenever experienced in the psychotherapy sessions. From the outset, I discourage the fabrication of a stylized or stereotyped image labeled "therapist" or "doctor." "I am whatever I happen to be" is, of course, an oversimplification, but it suggests rough approximation with a status I think essential to this therapy. The family group not only has the opportunity to know this, but should any of them at any point contaminate my identity with, for instance, a projection of a parent as that parent appeared to them earlier in life, this would become the focus of my attention.

Members of the group have the same privilege of offering, or insisting upon, what they feel is a more accurate personal image. In this atmosphere the therapist often feels most keenly the therapeutic aspects of the experience. By being, so nearly as possible, a total person, rather than by playing the role of therapist, the atmosphere encourages all members to participate more fully as total personalities. Such resistances of functioning as may occur in this atmosphere may also become the focus of attention in our group.

At this point, or perhaps earlier, the question may be raised, "Are such techniques a short-cut?" If a short-cut means to bypass some of the unpleasant moments which seem to me inherent in developing awareness and change, the answer is no. If it means abbreviating the number of hours in treatment, the answer is yes.

The conjoint family therapy structure further contributes to this in several ways. First, it identifies the patient as the family rather than any single member of it. This modification of structure immediately confronts many resistances other than that of the one who has been identified as the patient. In one family, the father, a policeman, brought in his "delinquent" son, identifying the boy as the patient. The essence of the father's attitude toward his son was: I don't want you to be a delinquent and I try to prevent it by showing you criminals so you can see what they are and how they have become so, and by insisting you do not break rules and then overlooking it when you do." When this attitude was examined in the family sessions, all family members assisted in deterring this delinquent-provoking behavior. Had I seen the boy alone, with the family continuing to identify the problem as solely that of the son's behavior, this hidden domestic pressure would have been a tremendous force in thwarting any efforts the boy and I could make by ourselves.

A second way in which family therapy works to shorten the course of behavioral change is when one member of the family begins to modify self-defeating behavior. Often, another family member, fearful of change or "needing" the other member's self-defeating behavior, resists this change, and, when this happens within the purview of the group, it immediately commands attention. In individual therapy, these manipulations by others often go unnoticed by the patient (and consequently the therapist) for long periods.

A third way in which family therapy favorably affects the course of psychotherapy is in the empathic response. To witness another member of the family exposing, for instance, some fear or anxiety in preference to a defensive pose of bravado, usually elicits a new response from the observer. The others suddenly see through the defensiveness and respond with compassion and understanding as they feel less threatened. Another important contribution is the developing awareness by momentarily silent members that they are not the sole cause of each others' problems. As projections are lifted off spouses and children, all members have greater freedom to seek new ways of responding. It provides a rapid method for disentangling interlocking psychopathology.

I have seen patients alter in a manner they and those around them considered more satisfactory when they changed from one therapist to another, both of whom I have felt to be competent. In part, this may be due to different therapists' evoking different responses, not necessarily through the application of differing techniques but simply by the impingement of their differing personalities. Family members have the effect both of serving as unique stimuli to the patient and responding uniquely to the patient's behavior.

When a family member calls for an appointment and identifies a problem as familial or primarily involving another family member, I press hard to have the other members join in the initial interview. If a child is involved, the entire family is asked to come in. During the course of family therapy, individual sessions are avoided. From experience, I find individual sessions unnecessary, manipulative, and, most of all, tending to be destructive for the requesting member. When confronted with the most popular mechanism: "I have something to say which I can't say in front of the others," in keeping with this approach, I suggest that they simply make this statement to "the others" during the session. These "secret data," important as the implications are, can be left unstressed, and attention drawn to what the protagonist is doing and what responses the others make to this stimulus. Again, the what and how of the current behavior preempts the verbal content.

Response to my suggestion is rarely compliance; more likely, an attempt at evasion is made: "But it's you I want to say it to." To my, "Why me?" they may answer, "Because you would understand and they won't." "Tell this to them." If they answer, "I can't," I retort, "Then tell *that* to them." If the point is reached where I get a flat, "No!" I stop pressing and wait for subsequent phenomena, either a comment from a family member about what has happened or a shifting of the focus of attention to some other matter. This is an important moment in this type of therapy. It would be easy to yield to temptation and utilize this opportunity for all kinds of explanations and interpretations, such as: "This individual has put me in the same position as the family members, of being unable to understand him, because I do not comply with his request," or, "He has had a verbal battle with me, and in the process of coming to me for help has refused that help in order to win the battle of the moment." But this would not only be fruitless, it would also thwart his opportunity to evaluate the exchange on his own terms, at his own speed, as well as interfering with the chance for other members of the family to respond to the maneuver. The only interjection I might make at this point would be an observation on some nonverbal expression in the room, such as a rejecting grimace on the part of another member during the exchange.

The relevance of this approach is that this family has come to me for help. One member says he has something to say to me, that is, that I am the focus of his attention. It is apparent to me that his world does not really include me but uses me merely as a rescuer in an attempt to avoid experiencing something with the other members who are the primary figures in his life at the moment. This person is trying to tell the others that he is unable to talk to them. It seems easier for many of us to tell a stranger that we like them than to tell an intimate that we do not like them. This becomes the crucial observation. As part of the therapeutic technique, I continue to refuse to accept a positive comment to me as a substitute for a negative one to a primary person in the individual's life.

Sometimes the would- be escapist complies, turning to another family member and saying, "I don't really expect you to understand me. You never do. You always twist things around." To this the other member responds with, "I don't know what in hell you're talking about. You are the one who doesn't understand, not me." I wait. The principals are involved and I now retire, to return at the next impasse. I want the first party to point out the live demonstration by the second of what he was saying. I want the second to say more about his anger toward the first. I want them to do this for themselves. So I wait. What is likely to happen is that the first reverts back to his original posture and either looks helplessly at me or sits dejectedly, staring at the floor. The second also sits silently. Now I may reenter and have my say. To the first member: "Your partner proves your point and you respond by collapsing and fleeing." And to the second member: "You seemed so angry." Now I wait and see who does what to whom next and how it is done. Hopefully, one of them will respond to my comments and begin a fruitful exchange with the other. Should they start to speak to me instead, I will again encourage, in some way, their self-awareness and involvement with each other.

It is difficult to spell out what I would specifically say or do. It depends on what I sense would be appropriate to everyone's needs as I know them at that moment, including my own. I am unable to describe all the variables that comprise my intuitive behavior. The principles enunciated in this paper are admittedly primitive and crude, but they are the only way I know at present to begin.

Structure and technique are often overlapping. Three principles I use in the structuring of interviews are certainly to be considered aspects of the technique, and the category in which they may be placed depends solely on application. If they are a precondition of the interview, we can call them structure; if they are part of the verbal interplay, they become aspects of technique. For me, they were aspects of technique originally but have now become a part of structure in most instances; I have eliminated them as operational obstacles by confronting them directly when they occur. These three principles are: no interruptions, no questions, no gossip. Interruptions, if not picked up by other members of the group, are pointed out by me. I say, "You interrupted," and to the others, "You permitted the interruption." Those interrupted are no less responsible than those who do the interrupting. When it persists, I point out that interruptions are inefficient, wasteful, and a destructive mechanism better excluded. Should they continue, I become a principal and proclaim, often with considerable affect, that they have come to me for help and persistently ignore what help I can offer.

Questions are communication media for obtaining information. Socially, they are used for many other purposes, for among other things, establishing superficial, and avoiding more personal, contact. It is the rare exemplar who will not give a person the time of day. The person can pick a category ("What do you think of the weather?") without making a commitment or assuming any responsibility. But on the assumption that an individual comes to treatment seeking knowledge of himself, the questions have little place. On rare occasions, a point of information is legitimately sought but more often questioning is a maneuver to obscure or evade. Whatever words the therapist actually employs, questions are met with some such request as: "Please convert that into a statement starting with the word 'I'."

Gossiping describes any remark made *about* rather than *to* the other person. It is a popular method of escape from immediate pressure. Consonant with the technique, if a remark is directed to the therapist about another member of the family, the therapist urges that it be redirected to the involved subject. Should the gossiper refuse, the therapist suggests the refusal itself be directed to the other member.

Clearly, the tendency of both patient and therapist is to escape from the here and now experience, Therapists know the patients' techniques well, and readily detect and label them as resistances. We are less familiar with our own. Common resistances used by therapists are immersion in historical data, raising "why" questions which send both patient and therapist scurrying off into the world of abstract thought, and encouraging exploration of circumstances which are not immediate and are of questionable theoretical pertinence.

The alacrity with which patients bring out samples from their vast storehouses of memories reveals their feeling of safety with these samples and preference for living in this world of talking-aboutness. It is not so easy to elicit their responses to the here and now, including their feelings toward the therapist and what is going on. A preference for talking-about material from earlier in the same session has been observed to represent avoidance of more painful immediate material.

Here is what happened at the start of a first interview with a mother, father, and their two daughters, aged 8 and 14. There was no history elicited. Whatever it was, it would be reflected in their current behavior, and this was enough; there was no need to go into the past. The only contact and information I had prior to this interview was a call from the mother who complained about the behavior of the 14-year-old daughter, expressing the fear the she was becoming a "juvenile delinquent," citing stealing the family car, poor schoolwork, ditching school, and going with the wrong crowd of kids who were having wild parties where petting was the obvious and primary activity. The mother wanted an appointment to tell me more before I saw the daughter. I assured her it would not be necessary to prime me ahead of time and offered an appointment time when *all* members of the family could come together.

The family looked conventional enough. The 14-year-old's rather disheveled appearance was in contrast to the rest of the family's neat attire. The mother was particularly well-groomed, and sat alert, upright, and attentive. The father's face was expressionless. The 8-year-old smiled at me. The 14-year-old slouched in her chair, looking off into the distance. The mother alternately glanced at the 14-year-old and at me. No one spoke. The pressure was clearly mounting in the mother, and it was apparent that the entire family supported her wish to be the spokesman. Finally, she opened with, "As I told you on the phone, we're having sort of a problem with our daughter. I don't know quite where to begin." There was a silence.

"I don't know where to begin either," I said.

"Something happened to Milly [as I shall call her] in the seventh grade that I think is important for her to tell you about."

She was gossiping to me about her daughter, so I remarked, "Perhaps this is something you could discuss with Milly herself."

She turned to the girl. "Milly, why don't you tell the doctor about the incident in the seventh grade?"

Milly replied to this with a grunt and a negative headshake. The mother persisted, repeating the question, adding, "I think it's very important. Why don't you tell the doctor?" The mother's intent smile was slightly strained; she looked at me, probably for encouragement, and then went back to prodding Milly to reveal what had happened. After she had made several fruitless tries, I made two observations to the mother. I remarked that she was trying to get her daughter to talk about herself when she, the mother, was apparently unwilling to reveal herself, that although she was speaking she was not speaking of herself or what she wanted, but instead had put the responsibility on the daughter by way of the repeated question which kept herself free of direct involvement. I also noted aloud that she apparently had not heard her daughter refuse, since she kept repeating the same question.

The mother quickly responded, "Oh, no, you misunderstand, Doctor. She knew what I meant. We communicate with each other very well. She knows exactly how I feel and I know how she feels, and we are able to talk together freely all the time." Then she reflected a moment and said, "I didn't mean to put her on the spot; I just thought it important that she tell you about the incident. Well, I suppose I could talk about myself."

I began to feel that the mother was playing a game of I've-got-a-secret in collaboration with her daughter. She would not reveal something she felt was important; neither would Milly. What they were doing to each other and to me at the moment was of greater interest than the ostensible purpose of the session. I waited in the silence for the next move; no one else in the family seemed to have any inclination to say anything.

The mother became restive in her chair and somewhat faltering in her speech as she said, "I . . . I guess I could say some things about myself. I don't know just where to begin. I don't know what you want me to talk about. I wasn't prepared to talk about myself. My mind was on Milly and her problems. It didn't occur to me to talk about myself. . . ." I alluded to her behavior, mentioning her restlessness and the hesitancy in her speech, and suggested that she appeared uncomfortable. "I *am* uncomfortable," she said.

Moving from her verbal communication to her total communication, I suggested she discuss her discomfort. "I suppose I hesitate to speak about myself in front of the children. It's rather uncomfortable. Probably I want them to see me as strong and knowing what I'm doing." She laughed nervously. This was gossiping, and her statement was not really for all of us. Since she was speaking of her feelings in relations to her children, I suggested she direct her comments to them. She looked somewhat startled, turned to the 14-year-old, stared at her for a moment, and burst into tears. After her crying had subsided, she said to Milly, "I guess I don't want you to know how inadequate I feel as a mother. I've even thought now and then that you might be better off if you had a mother who knew what she was doing. I feel so inadequate. I don't know why I try so hard to keep this from you. I guess I'm afraid you won't have any respect for me." Mother and daughter confronted each other in searching silence. The mother went on, "This must be why I expect so much from you. If you become the perfect daughter, you reassure me that I'm a good mother. That must be why I expect so much." By now Milly was also crying. Father and the 8-year-old sat quietly.

The mother kept on talking. She spoke to Milly about recent incidents in which conflict between them had been most painful for the mother. As she went on, her tone and demeanor gradually shifted from the kindly parent to the didactic lecturer. The content changed from admission of her own inadequacy to complaints of her daughter's shortcomings and the need for both of them to turn over a new leaf. Milly stopped crying. Father and the 8-year-old still sat silent and motionless. I did not.

When making observations during an interaction, it is often useful to make comparable comments to both parties, giving each the opportunity to hear an observer's view of their separate behaviors, so I mentioned to the mother the change in her attitude and the content of what she was saying, and observed to the daughter that she had stopped crying and had turned away again to stare blankly into space without answering her mother. Milly looked at me and exclaimed exasperatedly, "She does this all the time." This was gossiping, so I suggested she tell this to her mother, further suggesting that she comment to her how she felt about this. This was an attempt on my part to get her to make verbal the exasperation so evident in her expression. Milly complied to the extent that she said wryly to her mother, "You know you do this all the time."

The mother's response was to override her daughter's comment with another lecture beginning with a typical dismissal comment: "Yes, but. . . ." I remarked to the mother that she was lecturing again and had ignored her daughter's words. The mother looked perplexed, saying, "I must do this all the time. I've never been conscious of it before. I don't know what to do about it though; I can't seem to stop it." I suggested she tell this to Milly. She did. Milly answered, "Why don't you just listen to me once in a while? When you come into my room, and I ask you to leave, you always refuse. Why don't you just go out?"

Before I had time to interrupt—and it would have been an interruption—to suggest to Milly that she convert her questions into more meaningful statements about her wishes and feelings, the mother answered, "I can't do that. I have to finish what I'm saying first. Or do I? Maybe I'm just lecturing there too." The mother looked thoughtful, and then she and Milly smiled at each other. I, too, felt pleased. I felt that a point of healthy contact had been made between them which they had acknowledged. For me, it represented a point of closure, and I now became aware of all four members again.

There was another silence, and I found myself wondering where the father stood in all this, so I turned to him: "You haven't said a word." He smiled, and answered, "I never say much." The mother remarked to me, "He's never said much. It's only recently that he's begun to participate in the family at all. Milly said the other day that it has been only lately that she really felt she had a father." Milly nodded confirmation. The father remained impassive. I was aware that the mother was being his spokesman and he was permitting it, but I chose to focus on a softer issue at this time: the content of the mother's statement. I asked him whether he had been aware of this reaction from his daughter. "No, this is the first I've heard of it, although I know I haven't been too close to the rest of the family. It's getting better now, I believe."

The mother hastened to agree with him. Now I pointed out to the mother her part as spokesman for the father, and to the father his passive acceptance of this. The mother smiled and said to me, "I'm the talker and will speak for anybody who will let me. He doesn't mind." Her husband nodded, saying, "It's all right with me." There was no apparent conflict here, at least not at the moment. My thoughts moved to Milly's relationship with her father and I pointed out to him that he hadn't responded directly to her observation. He began to repeat that he was now more involved with the family, "I understand," I said, "but I'm wondering what you felt when you heard what your daughter said."

He looked puzzled at first. "I suppose I feel sorry."

"You suppose?"

After a moment he said, "No. I *am* sorry she feels this way." He had now clarified his current sentiments toward Milly, had permitted himself to examine them, but telling them to me was gossip. I suggested he state them directly to her. He turned to Milly. "I'm sorry you felt this way. I suppose I knew it, but just didn't want to see it. As your mother says, I've been around a lot more lately, and I'm going to try to be around even more. Okay?" Milly nodded.

The mother smiled, and said to me, "That's a lot of talking for him." Before having her direct her remark to its appropriate target, I asked her how she felt about his unusual loquacity. "I like it," she said to him.

At the conclusion of the hour, as they were leaving, the mother said to me cheerfully, "I boasted how well we talked to each other, but we've probably talked more to each other in this hour than in the past couple of years."

This family terminated treatment after six weekly interviews. During that time the daughter's acting out had stopped and the entire family agreed that Milly's behavior and relationship with the family had changed remarkably for the better; the 8-year-old participated actively in parts of two sessions, appeared quite healthy, and identified mildly with her older sister in condemning the mother's dominance. ("When I ask you to help me with an arithmetic problem, you do all of them for me.") Mother's steamrolling and discussion of Father's seeming excessive sensitivity and tendency to withdraw from the family were the two central themes of our six sessions, although many other aspects of child and parental and therapist behavior had our attention.

This family was seen about a year ago. I called recently to inquire about their current status. The mother was the only one home. The following is an excerpt from the conversation:

THERAPIST: I'm wondering if you would venture an opinion on the sessions that we had. Do you feel they were of any help?

MOTHER: I would say yes, but it was too superficial, you know, just six sessions, when you have chronic behavior that's been going on for thirty years. What are six hours? It almost just scratches so lightly.

THERAPIST: Yes, well, that is what I am trying to evaluate. I am also wondering about the children; do you think it was of any benefit to them, or to the family in general?

MOTHER: I think it helped Milly quite a bit. Before we went to you, Milly thought she was some sort of delinquent kid, you know, and I think after our experience with you she realized more that she was part of a group and there was a mother who was a steamroller and so maybe she wasn't this scary kid she thought she was. That was of great value.

THERAPIST: One of the things I recall that we talked about in our meetings was some of the relationship, or lack of relationship, between Milly and father. I'm wondering if since that time there has been any change in that? I recall your revealing for the first time a statement Milly made to you that she felt sometimes she really didn't have a father.

MOTHER: Well, now, apparently there have been tremendous changes. At this point I would say that Milly and her Dad have a lovely loving relationship and that they are very important to each other, and there's a great deal of interaction and your comments sound like they are almost not the same two people. I have more respect for my husband, which may be related.

This is not a case report of a successful analysis of an entire family in a single hour or in six hours using the techniques of experiential family therapy. But it describes a not atypical initial visit and is submitted mainly to transmit some flavor of the approach. This paper presents an approach to psychotherapy with the structure of the family. The goal is fuller awareness of self in the world with others, with the implicit corollary that, coupled with the inherent drive in all of us for a more satisfying and efficient existence, achievement of this end is possible.

The approach is oriented to an exploration of the resistances to experience within the psychotherapy session itself. Gossiping, interrupting, and questioning are popular diversionary tactics used by patients. Seeking historical data and genetic derivatives are common diversions from the therapeutic goal employed by the therapist.

12

Conflict-Resolution Family Therapy

SALVADOR MINUCHIN

In basic science the interrelatedness between technique and theory and the way in which their development is mutually affected is clear. The development of new instruments expands our understanding of a particular universe, requiring new theories to explain the new facts, or a new theory evokes the development of new techniques that allow refined exploration of its implications. This has not been, until recently, the course of psychoanalytic and psychotherapeutic theory and technique, wherein a large body of theory has been accompanied by limited exploration in the development of new techniques in therapy. My own recent experience, however, with a population of multiproblem families has forced me to turn to the exploration of new therapeutic techniques, one of which I shall describe here.

For the last five years, I have been working, at Wiltwyck School for Boys, with families who produce delinquent children.[1] These families are in the low socioeconomic group—most of them on public welfare rolls; and only 25 per-

Reprinted with permission of author and publisher from *Psychiatry* 28:278-286, 1965.

cent of them are intact in the middle-class sense. Some of them are composed of one or more transient males or a transient mother; others are made up of a mother, her children, and the children of her adolescent or young adult daughters; aunts are in maternal roles as frequently as are older siblings, and so on.

Psychologically these people are impoverished, rather than complex; their areas of experience are limited. Family themes are restricted, with emphasis on aggression, helplessness, abandonment, and nurturance. Role organization around family themes is narrow and stereotyped, and family members adhere rigidly to one another's expectations. Communication involves an unusually large amount of disconnected monologue, meaning being most often expressed through paraverbal channels. Since family members find it difficult to carry subject matter through to some conclusion, exchange of information is faulty. Interaction centers on the here and now, and transactions among members can shift abruptly from a highpitched emotional charge to passive disengagement. Consequently, these families are relatively helpless in the face of interpersonal tension, with very few tools for conflict resolution.

In spite of their needs, multiproblem families have traditionally refused therapeutic approaches, and it has been necessary to search for approaches more adequate to this special population. At present there are at Wiltwyck sixty families in treatment, and our staff has been experimenting with a variety of techniques for working with them.[2] The technique to be described here has been used for the last year with fifteen families at Floyd Patterson House.[3] Because this technique, *conflict-resolution family therapy,* is still being explored, there are too few cases in long-range therapy for complete evaluation of its effects. Yet even at this stage it seems to be a promising new tool in the armamentarium of therapeutic techniques.

An explanation of the underlying theoretical assumptions of conflict-resolution family therapy is an essential first step in my description of the actual technique.

For the human being it is economical to develop certain short-cuts in the organization of experience—namely, generalizations that allow such a cataloging of experiences that one need not always repeat anew the total process of perceiving and apprehending what has already been experienced. Although these generalizations may lead to distortions of individual situations, they compensate for such distortions by increasing one's speed in organizing responses to new situations. Clearly, this blunts the familiar; people lose their ability to perceive not only nuances in known situations but also new elements embedded in familiar experience.

The blunting of one's experience by mere familiarity is, of course, a complex phenomenon; it becomes infinitely more so within the immediate family.

After all, the family insures the predictability of interaction among its members through precisely this process of generalization, which has been explained differently by different schools of thought. There is agreement, nonetheless, that people do develop patterns of interpersonal responses and that knowledge of these patterns allows the therapist to predict with relative certainty the direction of behavior in similar circumstances. The more anxious a person is— the more his reactions tend to be affective only—the narrower and more predictable will be his range of interpersonal responses. A neurotic person, then, may be defined as one who in conflictual areas sees almost no alternative modalities of response, perceiving people along a narrow range of stereotyped categories, and with very few roles available for interpersonal relationships. A neurotic person will play the part of Falstaff, say, even when a situation calls for Romeo or Othello.

Psychoanalytic schools emphasize that developmental processes in the midst of the family during a person's earliest years orient him to a particular way of experiencing life; he then tends to handle new experiences through this set, modifying them if necessary, to make them fit his available molds. Implicit in this interpretation of human development is the idea that new learning can be handicapped by an overlearning of the previous experiential set, to the point that, for the neurotic person, new learning does not occur in emotionally charged areas.

Among the psychoanalytic schools, the existential movement holds that therapy should help the patient "find himself," rather than "strive" for success, achievement, or even understanding. The Zen Buddhist model of "interpretation," which creates an experience disregarding the intellectual understanding of the situation, has fascinated many existential analysts. In a similar vein, the modern theater has moved toward a theater of "experience." Playwrights of the "theater of the absurd" [4] have broken away from the plot, to experiment in creating an emotional experience in the audience. Familiar concepts are treated in such unusual ways as to shock the observer into recognizing—emotionally and cognitively—and experiencing anew something that has become stereotyped. Such a shock reaction to the familiar obliges the observer to encompass the concept in an emotional, rather than a logical, way. The meaning of recognition in this sense is "cognition again" with the emotional connotation of the encounter.

Because experience, especially within the multiproblem family, tends to be cognitively undifferentiated and emotionally blunted, a therapeutic method is needed through which learning anew from familiar experience can be fostered in these patients. The existential analysts and the playwrights of the theater of the absurd provide a clue to a means for helping multiproblem families encounter their own life and surroundings with new eyes. It is my view that the foregoing is relevant for psychotherapy in general; nevertheless, it seems particularly significant for the development of psychotherapeutic techniques for the multiproblem family.

In their interactions, members of these families seem to move from one extreme, enmeshment, to the other, abandonment. At the enmeshment pole, family transactions are characterized by a fast tempo of interpersonal exchange; multiproblem families tend to resolve tensions by action because of their paucity of mediating processes between impulse and action. The resulting style of interpersonal relationship has a high degree of mutual enmeshment and fast shifts in both focus of transaction and affective tone. At the abandonment pole, family members seem oblivious to the effects of their actions on one another. Monologues, parallel play, and a variety of maneuvers of psychological and physical abandonment characterize this modality.

Neither extreme of interaction facilitates a differentiated experience of family transactions. Awareness of personal impingement and interpersonal causality remains global. A technique of family therapy adapted to this population must therefore *actively* frame interpersonal transactions around clearly *focused* issues and *direct* the attention of the participants to the nature of their mutual impingement. It could then foster among family members the capacity to observe interpersonal causality, as a stepping-stone for achieving change.

The technique of task-oriented family therapy directs family members to participate in familiar tasks under conditions that are different from, and sometimes the opposite of, their usual patterns of response. The family is seen once a week for one hour, usually by one therapist, sometimes by co-therapists. The majority of the fifteen families had already undergone some variation of family therapy for from six months to as long as two years prior to their introduction to this approach.[5]

The procedure during the session is as follows. The therapist first meets with the whole family. During this initial period, he observes the free development of interaction among family members, deriving from this a diagnostic picture of transactional patterns. He then makes explicit the unstated forces ruling the transaction. He selects one area of conflict between some members of the family and addresses himself to these members, pointing out the nature of the conflict and their usual pattern in dealing with it. He points also to the pain-producing characteristics of this pattern. The therapist then instructs the family members involved to continue dealing with this conflict, but now he suggests that the interaction should occur within a different emotional context—for example, if the family members are involved in competitive interaction, he suggests cooperation.

The therapist then asks the other members of the family to join him behind a one-way mirror where they can act as observers of the family subgroup transaction. The members of the family involved in the conflict remain alone in the original room, while the therapist directs and assists the rest of the family in their observations, so that they become more discriminating in their perception of a familiar transaction. Usually the participant family members begin, at some point, to relate according to their former patterns and contrary to the instructions of the therapist. The therapist may then instruct one of the observer family members to enter the room and try to change the situation toward the growth-encouraging lines that they have previously discussed.

If this new transaction follows the usual pattern, the therapist allows the process to develop, and then he may send another family member back into the room, or enter himself, to help the family members consolidate their understanding of what has happened. He points out the way in which the process has developed, and how their usual patterns of transaction inhibit the possibility of developing new patterns of interaction that can bring more satisfaction to the members. In this way, in a session lasting one hour, the exploration of one area of conflict may involve four or five different subgroupings within the family, the various members alternating between the roles of participant and observer.

As a partial example of this process, I shall describe a session with a family composed of a man whose self-derogatory image and feelings of isolation were expressed in an autocratic, critical relationship with his spouse and children; a woman whose dependency and helplessness were reflected in an explicit acceptance of her husband's dominance and an implicit coalition with the older son, encouraging him in a continuous rebellion against his father; and their two sons, aged 14 and 12, who, caught between the mother's overprotectiveness and the father's domineering demands, projected their confused identity in the home arena as well as in school through blind attack on their "pursuers."

During the session, the therapist pointed out to the father that his attack on the older son was accompanied by an explicit statement that he was helping his son, as well as by a less audible and more jumbled message indicating the father's pain about his own helplessness. The therapist pointed out to the 14-year-old son that, although he seemed to want paternal acceptance, he could not trust that it would be forthcoming, and he was continuously engaged in provoking his father and rendering him helpless, thus intensifying his father's negative and critical responses toward him as his only way of remaining a worthwhile adult. The therapist then directed the father and son to continue dealing with the issue in conflict, but gave them instructions on the modalities in which interaction should occur. He suggested that the father should find positive areas in his son that he could highlight, and that the son should talk in such a way as to elicit his father's support.

In the observation room, the therapist, the wife, and the younger son observed how the father and older son, after a feeble attempt to become engaged along the lines suggested by the therapist, again became involved in a power operation. The mother expressed her impatience with her husband's "preaching" and his rigid behavior, while the younger son pointed out that his father wanted to teach his brother something worthwhile. The wife expressed her feeling of wanting to be in the other room to stop the onslaught.

The therapist then pointed out to the wife how she and her husband were fighting through their son, leaving the father and son isolated from each other and robbing them of all possibilities of developing a mutually satisfactory relationship. Her tendency was to empathize with the attacked child, label her husband the aggressor, and so intervene that she and her husband became involved in a heated argument, which "freed" and isolated the son. The therapist suggested to the wife that she should now go into the room and try to help her husband to support their son. Some minutes later, the husband and wife were blaming each other, and the older son was isolated. After the process developed, the therapist intervened and helped the family members to reexamine their interactional patterns. In the next session, under similar conditions, the wife left the room, saying that since she could not remain without intervening between the father and son, at least she could remove herself and go to the observation room where she could not interfere.[6]

In general, the family members organize into supplementary and complementary subsystems which interrelate in ways that either hinder or enhance problem solving.

The therapist's work in a session entails the following: (1) diagnosing family structure in relation to a salient conflict and recurrent interactions that impede the observing and problem-solving capacities of the participants; (2) assigning participant roles to family members centrally involved in the conflict, and removing other family members from the situation; (3) instructing the participant members in new and unfamiliar ways of dealing with the conflict; (4) actively guiding the removed participants into the observer's role; (5) identifying the kinds and forms of interpersonal and intrapersonal obstacles that emerge as the new problem-solving participation is attempted, and making inferences as to the defensive systems, both interpersonal and intrapersonal, that block new growth; and (6) helping family members progressively integrate the observing role into their active participation in conflicting interaction.

There is a theoretical rationale for this type of therapy. In the first place, to become aware of one's manner of functioning one must observe one's own actions. The ability to introspect—reflexive observation—develops in the child through his incorporation of the vigilant parental control and his need to tell the parental figures what happens to him. This subjective process of observing myself and what I am doing involves, in the words of David Rioch:

. . . [a need] to abstract myself, as it were, from any commitment in interaction in order to be aware of it. In the state of commitment [to another person] I have no sense of "I" and all other sensations become only guides, useful or not useful in directing the course of the interacting system of which I am part.

. . . [In the process of personal commitment] we "open our controls," as it were, to the messages from our vis-à-vis, *committing* ourselves to the involvement, and . . . we expect and receive responses adequate to maintain the dialogue. . . .

. . . one does not—indeed, cannot—"make observations" [when one is committed in personal involvement, but] . . . successively one interacts and successively one "abstracts oneself," as it were, from the involvement retrospectively *recreating* a concept of what, at least in part, *must have happened.*[7]

Acting as a participant observer, in effect, entails a paradox: to become an observer, one must stop participating, yet while one is participating, one cannot observe his participation because of the process of commitment. This paradox has been a problem for effective psychotherapy. Existential therapists are trying to help the patient to experience without concerning himself with observing the new experience, whereas therapists generally have been trying to bring about an intellectually integrated interpretation and, at the same time, to maximize the affective experience of the process. Ackerman has experimented with showing family patients films of their own sessions.[8] Other workers help families listen to tape recordings of their sessions.[9] All such therapeutic devices aim at maximizing a person's ability to observe without handicapping his ability to participate. The use of tasks also capitalizes on this principle, but the observation is of an "unfolding" process; moreover, it provides an artificial barrier against the strong habitual reaction of the patients. The one-way mirror maintains the emotional impact of interpersonal experiences, while it does not provide an opportunity for impulsory discharge. The most serious problem with acting-out families is that they are unskilled in introspection—in observing and evaluating their own actions—and require a therapy that centers on ways of making this process more available to them.

The questions, then, are these: How can the patient be helped to observe his own actions within the family without, at the same time, stopping his participation or devitalizing his experience? How can introspection be introduced at the moment of interaction? The answers to these questions may be best provided by considering what happens, first, to the observing members of the family, and then to the participating members.

The observer can see the family conflict while he has no responsibility for participating. The one-way mirror acts as a semiporous membrane. The observer is still very much caught in the interaction. He is, as it were, still sitting in the other room in the empty chair, but he is, simultaneously, aware that his role has changed. Although he cannot influence what is happening to the participant members, he continues to be subjected to the impingement of their behavior. His impulse to react with action, which is generally characteristic of the families described here, can be said to bounce against the mirror; thus it is delayed and, with the help of the therapist's questions, is channeled into verbal forms. The therapist, sitting near him, now engages him in a completely new function: he is invited to join the therapist in the observation of the participant members' interaction. His role has changed from that of participant to that of observer, although he continues to feel involved in the interaction. With this change in role, there is a change in his relationship to the therapist, with whom he has become, in a sense, a peer in the observation.

This change from participant to observer is certainly not automatic. Parents and children of multiproblem families frequently respond to cognitive affective stress by defensive maneuvers of fast engagement. Interpersonal proximity is a time-honored way of escaping from conflict. A child caught stealing, for example, refuses exploration by attacking his sibling for not "minding his own business"; a mother's awareness of her helplessness is usually blocked by her multiple and erratic control maneuvers. Some mothers, when asked to observe the therapy of their children for a number of sessions, responded with increased anxiety in the observation room: the level of noise, the inability of the children to keep to the subject, the power operations that characterize their daily behavior—all had a powerful impact on the mothers *as if they were perceiving these things for the first time.* "It's too emotional to observe," said Mrs. G., who had spent two years in conventional family therapy. To counter the use of fast engagement as a defensive maneuver that blocks differentiated perception of interaction, part of the procedure is for the parents, at some point in therapy, to remain in the observation room with another therapist for a number of sessions.

An example of the difficulty in assuming the observer role is the A. family, who came to therapy because the older daughter was delinquent. The family was composed of a mother, her two adolescent daughters by a former liaison, and her present husband, who was older and less educated than she was. The daughters complained that their stepfather was autocratic and punishing and did not listen to or understand them. The stepfather complained about the loose behavior of American teen-agers and the lack of filial respect; the mother interpreted her daughters and her husband to each other. It became clear that the family structure was organized around at least two subsystems—the three females, and the husband and wife—and that the husband felt excluded from the first subsystem as well as from the parental function. When he was asked to observe the three females of his family in the observation room, he continued to engage polemically with his two daughters even though he was aware that they could not hear him, and only after repeated efforts by the therapist could he disengage himself and become an observer.

The separation of one member from the system can sometimes highlight processes that would not otherwise appear. For example, the B family, which has been in treatment for six months, consists of the grandmother, the mother, and her five children. Three of the children are delinquent, and the mother has been suicidal at various times, with a history of three hospitalizations. The grandmother has assumed all parental roles and relegated the mother to the role of older sibling. When the grandmother was asked to observe through the one-way mirror how the family functioned in her absence, she became impatient when one of the children began to drum on a chair while the mother was talking with another child, and told the therapist that she would have stopped it right there. Some minutes later, the mother addressed herself to the child by engaging him with a question about his schooling, stopping his disruptive behavior. The therapist could then point out to the grandmother how her always being two minutes ahead of her daughter left her daughter unemployed as a mother.

In considering what happens to the participant members, it is well to remember that certain transactions between them have become automatic. For example, a characteristic pattern may be that a wife asks for help in an indirect way, which brings the husband's response of resentful help. Perceiving his response as controlling, she then refuses to accept help. This, in turn, gives him a sense of helplessness about relating to her, followed by anger toward her. Such behavior can occur again and again in an automatically triggered sequence. The conversation between them may seem altogether unrelated to what is being transacted nonverbally. Though help is asked for and offered, the tension lies in the pitch of the voice, the posture of the body, the muscles of the face. This transaction becomes automatic, and the participants find themselves in their usual conflicting positions, unaware of how they got there. When it is suggested in the task situation that the wife ask for help in a direct form and that the husband respond to her request without his usual controlling attitude, their participation is being demanded in a strange modality—in a new form that minimizes the possibility of automatic responses and increases the awareness of participation. Their assignment is conducted in a situation of induced stress because they are aware that the rest of the family is observing them. *A consciousness of being observed is an intermediary step in the process of introspection.* The participant observes in himself what he assumes the unseen observer is focusing on. This sense of being observed brings the observer's role indirectly to the participant members as well. When people fail to operate along the lines of the assignment, there is a heightened awareness of the handicapping nature of the usual patterns of interaction, and certain patterns that have been ego syntonic are seen as ego dystonic. For example, while the mother is in the observation room, the children are asked to "talk to each other, one at a time, without 'ranking,' and looking for positives in each other." After the initial increase in noise that always accompanies this task, some of the siblings will take the lead in organizing the interaction, and when there is disruptive behavior, or when a sibling is derogatorily labeled—and this is very frequent—some of the children will attempt to reinforce the task by pointing at the mirror, stating that they should do better because their mother and the therapist are observing them.

Thus distance is established from an automatic process by introducing awareness of the process itself—a psychological function ordinarily almost unused among these multiproblem families. The observer becomes, as it were, internalized, and the process of introspection is fostered.

At some point in therapy, the family members begin to respond with new nuances in their interactions. Because such changes first occur in a clumsy and hesitant way, the other members often fail to take them into account. It is then the function of the therapist to point out the new behavior. Unfortunately, therapists are often unskilled in perceiving new behavior that may first manifest itself largely in formal ways—a deference to another person's speech, a slight change in the tone of voice, a hesitancy before entering into the automatic response— and they must learn the art of spotting and supporting these new developments. Eventually the observing family members also reward the participants, and this is more significant for the crystallization of the change than is the therapist's support. When a change occurs and the family members solve a conflict in a new and different way, the reward lies in the actual resolution of the conflict, the mastering of the new pattern of interaction—even though it may be only temporary—and the emotional support of the family as a group.

Implicit in this technique of family therapy is the idea that people can learn not only from a clear awareness of their neurotic conflicts but also by the mastery of alternative solutions to conflicts. The therapist must keep in mind that in order to produce change he must be alert not only to the areas of conflict and the ways in which the patients' character structures affect or handicap growth, but also to the possibility of increasing the patients' sense of mastery by offering them alternative ways of functioning and help in perceiving alternative solutions to conflicts. It is not uncommon to see a patient in psychoanalysis who, after having incorporated a thorough knowledge of the nature of his dynamics and the antecedents for his neurotic functioning, rejects old patterns of response, but nonetheless remains handicapped when it comes to selecting new ways of experimenting in life.

Devising the strategies of task assignment in conflict-resolution family therapy requires a clear understanding of individual dynamics and how these are manifested in family transactions, as well as in the family's patterns of communication. These strategies must be flexible, continuously responding to the changes the family is undergoing. At this point it should be emphasized that when an interaction in an unfamiliar modality is sought, the attempt is not to break a habit by the simple formula of creating another; the vivid awareness of hidden patterns and underlying motivations is being increased at the same time that experience is offered in alternative ways of attacking a problem.

The role of the therapist in this technique is both more and less central than in traditional family therapy. He is somewhat like the director of a play, asking the family members to try to comply with his instructions, pressuring them to seek other than their usual repertoire of interaction, demanding that they fulfill his expectations. He also plays his traditional role, interpreting underlying dynamics and teaching the family a new experiential language. In the observation room he gives direction to the perceptions of the observing members; he also acts as the connecting link when a new member comes to the observation room, filling him in on what has been going on. At the same time, because the family members are themselves participants and observers, and even in a sense therapists, when they return to the therapy room to help the other family members correct their faulty transactions, the therapist's role is partially decentralized. When he is in the observation room, the participant family members are alone in the other room tackling the conflicting transactions by themselves; they are actually trying out in the therapeutic sessions, without the help of the therapist, new modalities of mutual interaction.

One final word of caution: Conflict-resolution family therapy in the hands of an inexperienced therapist can lend itself to an authoritarian display of power and an artificial manipulation of people. The only road for the development of meaningful tasks is a deep understanding of family dynamics.

In conclusion, for the last year at Wiltwyck School for Boys the conflict-resolution technique has been used as a therapeutic focus, in combination with the three-stage technique [10] and with conventional family therapy, and the clinical results with the conflict-resolution technique have been encouraging. Families that have been in treatment for a year and longer respond to the introduction of conflict-resolution tasks with a sharpening of awareness of their dynamics; sessions become more focused; children's participation increases, and the level of noise so prevalent in these families' interactions decreases; and concentration on one issue and verbalization around this issue, framed by the task, become central. Also, the therapist's verbalization diminishes. Through failures in reaching multi-problem families, the therapist as well as the social scientist has focused attention on the special characteristics of this population and on the need for developing therapeutic techniques that take these characteristics into account. [11] The significance of conflict-resolution family therapy for the low socioeconomic population lies in the following: It presents usual interaction framed as interpersonal problems and suggests that these problems have concrete solutions in the interpersonal realm; the tasks are clearly structured, deal with familiar situations, are focused in the here and now, and compel family members to search for solutions through interaction among themselves; and the division of a large family into subgroups

—participants and observers—facilitates the differentiation of the transactions in family subunits, which are usually hidden in the erratic and multiple stimulation of the larger group. Having the nonparticipating members observe the interaction keeps the total family involved; and observation through the one-way mirror maintains the impact of the familiar impingement, delays or eliminates the discharge of the habitual response, and channels the impulse into verbal forms.

NOTES AND REFERENCES

1. Because as yet there is no system of diagnosis in the area of family therapy, there is no precise term to delineate this particular group of families. Throughout this paper, therefore, I refer to them as "multiproblem families," with the awareness that this term is purely descriptive and does not carry dynamic meaning.
2. Minuchin, S., Auerswald, E. H., King, C. H., and Rabinowitz, C., "The Study and Treatment of Families That Produce Multiple Acting-Out Boys," *Amer. J. Orthopsychiat.* 34:125-133, 1964.
3. This is a halfway residence house of Wiltwyck School.
4. Esslin, M., *The Theatre of the Absurd,* New York, Doubleday, 1961.
5. We have also explored the effects of this approach on a number of middle-class families.
6. I am aware that such a verbal description of an active intervening technique as this creates the impression of a controlling therapist dictating the movements of the patients as though they were objects. In the actual setting, however, there is the same quality of emotional commitment and human contact between family and therapist that characterizes other forms of therapy.
7. Rioch, D. M., "Communication in the Laboratory and Communication in the Clinic," *Psychiatry* 26:209-221 (215, 212-213), 1963.
8. Ackerman, N., "Emergence of Family Psychotherapy on the Present Scene," in Stein, M. I., *Contemporary Psychotherapy,* New York, Free Press, 1961, p. 229.
9. Paul, N., "Effects on Family Members of Playback of Their Own Previously Recorded Conjoint Therapy Material," presented at the American Psychiatric Association Regional Research Conference on Family Structure, Dynamics, and Therapy, Galveston, Texas, February 26-27, 1965.
10. See Minuchin, S., et al., note 2.
11. Riessman, F., in *Some Suggestions Concerning Psychotherapy with Blue-Collar Patients,* New York, Mobilization for Youth, 1962 (mimeographed), has contrasted the expectations of low-income culture with the typical emphases of psychotherapy. Thus, for example, the expectations of the low-income culture emphasize: desire for authority and direction; preference for work and action (with talk deprecated); desire for structure and organization; focus on the present; emphasis on the family and group; problem focus; desire for simple, concrete, objectively demonstrable explanations; desire for less intense relationships and preference for informal friendliness, respect, and sympathetic,

nonpatronizing understanding. On the other hand, the typical therapeutic emphasis is on: do it yourself, change yourself, assume responsibility; introspection, thought-centeredness, word focus; an unstructured, permissive approach; stress on the past; self-focus; stress on resistance and transference; symbolic, often circuitous interpretations and explanations; intensive transference and countertransference. See also Bernstein, B., "Social Class and Linguistic Development: A Theory of Social Learning," in Halsey, A. H., Floud, J., and Anderson, C. A. (Eds.), *Education, Economy, and Society,* New York, Free Press, 1961.

13

The Use of Family Theory
in Clinical Practice

MURRAY BOWEN

In little more than one decade, family psychiatry has evolved from the relative unknown to a position of recognized importance on the psychiatric scene. The term family therapy, or some variation of it, is known to the informed lay person. What is the origin and current status of the family movement? I believe it is a movement, which I shall attempt to convey in this paper. Since there is disagreement even among leaders of the family movement about some of the critical theoretical and therapeutic issues, any attempt to explain or describe the family movement will represent the bias and viewpoint of the author. In this paper I shall present some of my ideas about circumstances that gave rise to the family movement and some ideas about the current status and future potential of the movement. The main body of the paper will be a presentation of my own theoretical orientation, which provides a blueprint for the clinical use of family psychotherapy.

Reprinted with permission of author and publisher from *Comprehensive Psychiatry* 7:345-374, 1966.

I believe that the family movement began in the early and mid-1950's and that it grew out of an effort to find more effective treatment methods for the more severe emotional problems. In a broad sense, I believe it developed as an extension of psychoanalysis, which had finally achieved general acceptance as a treatment method during the 1930's. Psychoanalysis provided useful concepts and procedures for the mass need of World War II, and a new era in psychiatry began. Within the course of a few years psychiatry became a hopeful, promising specialty for thousands of young physicians. Membership in the American Psychiatric Association increased from 3684 in 1945 to 8534 in 1955. Psychoanalytic theory had explanations for the total range of emotional problems, but standard psychoanalytic treatment techniques were not effective with the more severe emotional problems. Eager young psychiatrists began experimenting with numerous variations in the treatment method. I believe the study of the family was one of these new areas of interest.

There are those who say the family movement is not new and that it goes back twenty-five years or more. There is some evidence to support the thesis that current family emphasis evolved slowly as the early psychoanalytic formulations about the family were put into clinical practice. In 1909 Freud reported the treatment of "Little Hans," [1] in which he worked with the father instead of the child. In 1921 Flugel published his well-known book, *The Psycho-analytic Study of the Family*.[2] There was the development of child analysis and the beginning of the child guidance movement in which it became standard procedure for a social worker or second therapist to work with parents in addition to the primary psychotherapy with the child. Later, the child guidance principles were adapted to work with adults, both in inpatient and outpatient settings, in which a social worker or second therapist worked with relatives to supplement the primary psychotherapy with the patient. With these early theoretical and clinical awarenesses of the importance of the family, there is accuracy to the statement that family is not new. However, I believe that the current family direction is sufficiently important, new, and different to be viewed as a movement. I shall review some of the theoretical and clinical issues that seem important in this development.

Psychoanalytic theory was formulated from a detailed study of the individual patient. Concepts about the family were derived more from the patient's perceptions than from direct observation of the family. From this theoretical position, the focus was on the patient and the family was outside the immediate field of theoretical and therapeutic interest. Individual theory was built on a medical model with its concepts of etiology, the diagnosis of pathology in the patient, and treatment of the sickness in the individual. Also inherent in the model are the subtle implications that the patient is the helpless victim of a disease or malevolent forces outside his control. A conceptual dilemma was posed when the most important person in a patient's life was considered to be the cause of his illness, and pathogenic to him. Psychiatrists were aware that the model did not quite fit, and there were attempts to tone down the implicit starkness of the concepts, but the basic model remained. For instance, the concept of the unconscious postulated that the parent could be unconsciously hurtful while trying to help the child. This was different from what it would be if the hurt had been intentional or an irresponsible act of omission, but it still left the parent pathogenic. There were efforts to modify diagnostic labels and there were even suggestions that labels be discarded, but a *patient* requires a *diagnosis* for his *illness* and psychiatry still operates with a medical model.

One of the most significant developments in the family movement, which distinguishes it from previous family work, is a change in the basic treatment process. Since the beginning of psychoanalysis, the analysis and resolution of the transference has been viewed as the primary therapeutic force for the treatment of emotional illness. Though modified by different schools, the therapeutic relationship is the basic therapeutic modality used by most psychiatrists. The confidential, personal, and private nature of the relationship is considered essential for good therapy. Over the years there have been methods, rules, and even laws to guard this privacy. Since the beginning of the child guidance movement there have been efforts to involve the family in treatment, but the therapeutic patient-therapist relationship was protected against intrusion and the family assigned secondary importance. Among those who initiated the current family movement were psychiatrists who, in addition to the patient's dilemma, began to pay more attention to the family side of the problem.

I believe the current family movement was started by several different investigators, each working independently, who began with either a theoretical or clinical notion that the family was important. As the focus shifted from the individual to the family, each was confronted with the dilemma of describing and conceptualizing the family relationship system. Individual theory did not have a conceptual model for a relationship system. Each investigator was on his own in conceptualizing his observations. One of the interesting developments has been the way investigators first conceptualized the system and the ways these concepts have been modified in the past ten years. There were terms for the distortion and rigidity, the reciprocal functioning, and the interlocking, binding, stuck togetherness of the system. The following illustrates some of the terms used by a few of the early investigators. Lidz and Fleck used the concept schism and skew,[3] and Wynne and his co-workers used the concept pseudomutuality.[4] Ackerman, one of the earliest workers in the field, presented a conceptual model in his 1956 paper, "Interlocking Pathology in Family Relationships." [5] He also developed a therapeutic method which he calls family therapy, which might be described as observing, demonstrating, and interpreting the interlocking to the family as it occurs in the family sessions. Jackson and his co-workers used a different model with the concept of the double bind.[6] As I perceived his original position, he used communication theory to account for the relationship system and individual theory to account for functioning in the individual. His conjoint family therapy, which I interpret as the joining of individuals in family therapy, would be consistent with his conceptual scheme. I conceived of a preexisting emotional stuck-togetherness, the undifferentiated family ego mass, and developed a therapeutic method for which I have used the term family psychotherapy, which is designed to help individuals differentiate themselves from the mass. Other investigators used a spectrum of slightly different terms to describe and conceptualize the same family phenomenon. As the years pass, the original concepts tend to be less different.

CURRENT STATUS AND POSSIBLE FUTURE OF THE FAMILY MOVEMENT

The family movement is currently in what I have called a healthy, unstructured state of chaos. The early investigators arrived at family therapy after preliminary clinical investigation and research. There may have been one exception to this general statement, recounted by Bell,[7] one of the earliest workers in the field. He misinterpreted a statement about psychotherapy for the family, following which he worked out his own plan to begin seeing family members together. After the idea of family therapy was introduced, the number of family therapists began to multiply each year. Most went directly into family therapy from their orientation in individual theory. Group therapists modified group therapy for work with families. As a result, the term family therapy is being used to refer to such a variety of different methods, procedures, and techniques that the term is meaningless without further description or definition. I consider this healthy, because once a therapist begins seeing multiple family members together, he is confronted with new clinical phenomena not explained by individual theory, he finds that many previous concepts have become superfluous, and he is forced to find new theoretical concepts and new therapeutic techniques. The increasing number of family conferences become forums for discussion of experiences and acquiring new ways to conceptualize the family phenomenon.

A high percentage of therapists are using the term family to designate therapy methods in which two or more generations (usually parents and children) attend the sessions together, the term marital therapy when two spouses are seen together, and individual therapy when only one family member is seen by the therapist. The one most widely held concept of family therapy, both within the profession and by the public, is that of entire families (usually parents and children) meeting together with the therapist while the family acquires the ability to verbalize and communicate thoughts and feelings to each other, with the therapist sitting alongside to facilitate the process and to make observations and interpretations. This I have called family group therapy. In my experience, this can be amazingly effective as a short-term process for improving family communication. Even a slight improvement in communication can produce dramatic shifts in the feeling system, and even a period of exhilaration. I have not been able to use this as a long-term method for resolving underlying problems.

Although the family movement may continue to focus on therapy for many years to come, I believe the greatest contribution of family will come from the theoretical. I think the family movement rests on solid ground, that we have hardly scratched the surface in family research, and that family will grow in importance with each passing generation. The study of the family provides a completely new order of theoretical models for thinking about man and his relationship to nature and the universe. Man's family is a *system* which I believe follows the laws of natural systems. I believe knowledge about the family system may provide the pathway for getting beyond static concepts and into the functional concepts of systems. I believe that family can provide answers to the medical model dilemma of psychiatry, that family concepts may eventually become the basis for a new and different theory about emotional illness, and that this in turn will make its contribution to medical science and practice.

THEORETICAL AND CLINICAL ORIENTATION OF THE AUTHOR

The primary goal of this presentation is to describe a specific theoretical and therapeutic system in which family theory serves as a blueprint for the therapist in doing family psychotherapy and also as a useful theoretical framework for a variety of clinical problems. A family orientation is so different from the familiar individual orientation that it has to be experienced to be appreciated. It is difficult for a person who thinks in terms of individual theory, and who has not had clinical experience with families, to hear family concepts. Some are better able to hear abstract theoretical ideas while others hear simple clinical examples. The first part of this section is designed as a bridge between individual and family orientations. To provide a variety of bridges, it will include a spectrum of clinical observations, broad abstract ideas, theoretical concepts, and some of my experiences as I shifted from an individual to a family frame of reference.

My family experience covers twelve years and over 10,000 hours of observing families in family psychotherapy. For the first five years of family practice I also did some individual psychotherapy and I had a few patients in psychoanalysis. The term family psychotherapy was reserved for the process when two or more family members were seen together. The technical effort was to analyze the already existing emotional process between the family members and toward keeping myself emotionally disengaged, which I called staying out of the transference. This will be discussed later. During those years I used the term individual psychotherapy for the process when only one family person was seen. I had not dealt with my own emotional functioning sufficiently nor developed techniques to avoid a transference, and there was the either-or distinction between family and individual psychotherapy. I considered it *family* when the emotional process could be contained within the family, and *individual* when this was not possible. During those years, another evolutionary process was taking place. After having spent thousands of hours sitting with families, it became increasingly impossible to see a single person without seeing his total family sitting like phantoms alongside him. This perception of one person as a segment of the larger family system had governed the way I thought about and responded to the individual, and it had changed my basic approach to psychotherapy. For the past seven years my practice has been devoted entirely to family psychotherapy, although about one-third of the hours are spent with only one member of a family. The volume of clinical experience has been in private practice, where an average clinical load of forty families are seen with a maximum of thirty hours per week. In past years only a few families have been seen more than once a week, and an increasing number do as well with less frequent appointments. It has been difficult to communicate the notion of avoiding a transference and family psychotherapy with only one family member. It is my hope that this can be better clarified in this paper.

A number of facets of the human phenomenon come into view in observing family members together that are obscured with any composite of individual interviews. Any person who exposes himself to daily observations of families as they relate to and interact with each other is confronted with a whole new world of clinical data that do not fit individual conceptual models. I use the terms relate to and interact with because these are a few of the inadequate terms that have been used to describe the family phenomenon. Actually, family members are *being,* and *doing,* and *acting,* and *interacting,* and *transacting,* and *communicating,* and *pretending,* and *posturing* in such a variety of ways that structure and order are hard to see. There is something wrong with any single term that has been used. To this point, family research has gone toward selecting certain areas for detailed, controlled study. In 1957 one of my research associates did a study called "The Action Dialogue in an Intense Relationship," [8] which was an attempt to blank out words and do a coherent dialogue from one period of gross action between a mother and daughter. Birdwhistell and Scheflen [9,10] have made a significant contribution in their precise definition of kinesics, a body language system, automatic in all relationships. One of the popular areas for study has been communication, which on the simplest level is verbal communication. There have been the linguistic studies and the different communications that are conveyed by nuances in tone of voice, inflection, and ways of speaking—communications that each person learns in infancy and uses without knowing he knows it. Bateson and Jackson and co-workers, from analysis of verbal communication, developed their concept of the double bind, which has to do with conflicting messages in the same statement. There is also the area of nonverbal communication and extrasensory perception which operates with fair accuracy in some families. There is an advantage in using terms such as communication or transactional system in that each lends itself to more precise research analysis. The disadvantage is in the narrowness of the concept and the necessity of using a broad interpretation of the concept. For instance, under communication theory it becomes necessary to assume the full range of verbal, action, nonverbal, extrasensory, and feeling communication, plus other modalities such as a visceral response in one family member to anxiety or a mood shift in another. However one approaches the family, each investigator has to choose his own way of conceptualizing the family phenomenon.

One striking group of clinical patterns, present to some degree in all families, will provide a brief view of the family relationship system. These follow the general pattern of the family process that diagnoses, classifies, and assigns characteristics to certain family members. Observations may prove reasonably consistent, periodically consistent, or inconsistent with the family pronouncements about the situation. The family projection process by which a family problem is transmitted to one family member by years of nagging pronouncements, and then fixed there with a diagnosis, has been discussed in detail in another paper.[11] Family assignments that overvalue are as unrealistic as those that devalue, though the ones that devalue are more likely to come within the province of the psychiatrist. The diagnosed one may resist the family pronouncement and precipitate a family debate; or he may alternately resist and accept; or he may invite it, at which time the assigned characteristic becomes an operational *fact*. Family debates on subjects such as rejection, love, and hostility will force the therapist to reevaluate his own use of such terms. As I see rejection, it is one of the most useful mechanisms for maintaining equilibrium in a relationship system. It goes on constantly between people, usually unmentioned. At one point in the family process someone makes a fuss about rejection and the debate starts. At a point when rejection is present throughout the family, the one who claims rejection is usually more rejecting of the other, rather than the obverse being true. Positive statements about the presence or absence of love, with reactions and counterreactions, can occupy the scene while there is no objective evidence of change in love within the family. Whatever love *is*, it is factual that many family members react strongly to statements about it. The misuse and overuse of the concept hostility is another in the same category. The same can apply to terms such as masculine, feminine, aggressive, passive, homosexual, and alcoholic.

The use of the term alcoholic provides a good example. In one family, two generations of descendants referred to a grandfather as alcoholic. He had been successful and fairly responsible except to his wife, who was a very anxious woman. He found reason to stay away from her, and he did drink moderately. The wife's label was accepted by the children and transmitted to the grandchildren. A recent consultation with another family illustrates another aspect of the problem. A wife had presented the details of her husband's alcoholism. I asked for the husband's view of the problem. He agreed he had a real drinking problem. When asked how much he drank, he flared with, "Listen, Buster! When I tell you I have a drinking problem, I mean it!" When asked how many days he had lost from work because of drinking, he said, "One! But I really hung one on that time." It can be grossly inaccurate to assign *fact* to statements such as, "He was an alcoholic." It can be accurate and also convey a *fact* about the relationship system if such statements are heard as, "One family member *said* another was an alcoholic." This applies to the entire spectrum of terms used in the family relationship system.

I would like to present the concept of the family as a system. For the moment I shall not attempt to say what kind of system. There is no single word or term that would be accurate without further qualification, and qualification would distort the *system* concept. The family *is* a system in that a change in one part of the system is followed by compensatory change in other parts of the system. I prefer to think of the family as a variety of systems and subsystems. Systems function at all levels of efficiency from optimum functioning to total dysfunction and failure. It is necessary also to think in terms of overfunction, which can range from compensated overfunction to decompensated overfunction. An example of this would be the tachycardia (overfunctioning heart) of an athlete in strenuous physical activity to tachycardia that precedes total heart failure and death. The functioning of any system is dependent on the functioning of the larger systems of which it is a part, and also on its subsystems. On a broad level, the solar system is a subsystem of the larger system, the universe. The molecule is one of the smallest defined subsystems. On another level, the process of evolution is a system that operates slowly over long periods of time. There is sufficient knowledge about evolution to recognize the general patterns of its function, but there is much less knowledge about the larger systems of which evolution is a subsystem. We can look back and make postulations about the factors that influenced past evolutionary change, but our lack of knowledge about the larger systems reduces us to guessing about the future course of evolution.

From observing families I have attemped to define and conceptualize some of the larger and smaller family functioning patterns as they repeat and repeat, and as old patterns tone down and new ones become more prominent. The research started with schizophrenia in which one family member was in a state of total dysfunction and collapse, and the patterns so intense they could not be missed, but it required work with the entire range of human dysfunction to see the patterns in broader perspective. One of the most important aspects of family dysfunction is an equal degree of overfunction in another part of the family system. It is factual that dysfunctioning and overfunctioning exist together. On one level this is a smooth-working, flexible, reciprocating mechanism in which one member automatically overfunctions to compensate for the dysfunction of the other who is temporarily ill. Then there are the more chronic and fixed states of overfunctioning and dysfunction in which flexibility is lost. An example would be the dominating (overfunctioning) mother and passive father. The overfunctioning one routinely sees this as necessary to compensate for the poor functioning of the other. This might be valid in the case of temporary illness in one spouse, but in the chronic states there is evidence that the dysfunction appears later to compensate for overfunction in the other. However it develops, the overfunction–dysfunction is a reciprocating mechanism. In previous papers [12,13] I called this the overadequate-inadequate reciprocity. Symptoms develop when the dysfunction approaches nonfunctioning. Families often do not seek help until flexibility of the system is lost and the functioning of one member is severely impaired. When the mechanism advances beyond a certain point, anxiety drives the mechanism toward panic and rapid increase in both overfunction and dysfunction. The increased pressure can jam the circuits of the disabled one into paralyzed collapse. Even at this point, recovery can begin with the slightest decrease of the overfunctioning or a slight decrease in the dysfunction.

Some of the main functional patterns observed in families have been formulated into component concepts that comprise the family theory of emotional illness. It would be more accurate to say family dysfunction. The broad family patterns of emotional illness are also present in physical illness and social dysfunction such as irresponsible behavior and delinquency. The component concepts (subsystems) are among those I believe to be the most critical variables in human dysfunction. Symptoms in any part of the family are viewed as evidence of dysfunction, whether the symptoms be emotional, physical, conflictual, or social. There have been most promising results from the effort to view all emotional symptoms as evidence of family dysfunction rather than as intrapsychic phenomena.

The therapist also fits into this concept of the family as a system. This is a combination theoretical-therapeutic system in which theory determines therapy, and observations from therapy can in turn modify the theory. The original design, reported in another paper,[14] has been continued, although both the theory and therapy have been constantly modified. From the early days of the research there was increasing emotional detachment from the families. The more one observes families, the easier it is to detach from the narrow conceptual boundaries of individual theory; and the more one detaches from individual theory, the easier it is to see family patterns. The early family psychotherapy was predominantly observational, with questions to elicit more information about the observations. Over the years, research families have done better in family psychotherapy than those for whom the primary goal was therapy. This helped establish a kind of orientation which has made all families into research families. It has been my experience that the more a therapist learns about a family, the more the family learns about itself, and the more the family learns, the more the therapist learns, in a cycle which continues. In the observational process with early families, some were able to restore family functioning without much therapeutic intervention. The most successful families followed remarkably consistent courses in accomplishing this. Thereafter, it was possible to intervene and tell new families about successes and failures of former families and to save the new families endless hours and months of trial and error experimentation. In broad terms, the therapist became a kind of expert in understanding family systems and an engineer in helping the family restore itself to functioning equilibrium.

The overall goal was to help family members become system experts who could know the family system so well that the family could readjust itself without the help of an outside expert, if and when the family system was again stressed. It is optimum when the family system can begin a shift toward recovery with the important members of the family attending the hours. There were those in which the family became worse during the therapy, the helpless one becoming more helpless in response to the overfunctioning of the other. Some would struggle through this period and then move toward recovery; others would terminate. In these situations, it was found to be more profitable to work with one side of the reciprocity until the family was able to work together without increasing the bind. It is far easier for the overfunctioning one to tone down the overfunctioning than for the poorly functioning one to pull up. If the overfunctioning one is motivated, I see this one alone for a period of family psychotherapy in which the goal is to free the immobilized system and restore enough flexibility for the family to work together. From my orientation, a theoretical system that "thinks" in terms of family and works toward improving the family system *is* family psychotherapy.

With this theoretical-therapeutic system, there is always the initial problem of the therapist establishing the orientation of the system. Most families are referred with a diagnosis for the dysfunction. They think in terms of the medical model and expect that the therapist is going to change the diagnosed family member, or the parents may expect the therapist to show or tell them how to change the child without understanding and modifying their part in the family system. With many families, it is surprisingly easy for the therapist to establish this family orientation in which he stands alongside to help them understand and take steps to modify the system. To help establish this orientation, I avoid the diagnosis of any family member and other medical model concepts such as "sick" or "patient." I persistently oppose the tendency of the family to view me as a therapist. Instead, I work toward establishing myself as a consultant in family problems for the initial interviews, and as a supervisor of the family effort for the long-term process. When the therapist allows himself to become a healer or repairman, the family goes into dysfunction to wait for the therapist to accomplish his work.

From this discussion of the family as a system, I have avoided saying what kind of a system. The family *is* a number of different kinds of systems. It can accurately be designated a social system, a cultural system, a games system, a communication system, a biological system, or any of several other designations. For the purposes of this theoretical-therapeutic system, I think of the family as a combination of emotional and relationship systems. The term emotional refers to the force that motivates the system, and relationship to the ways it is expressed. Under relationship would be subsumed communication, interaction, and other relationship modalities.

There were some basic assumptions about man and the nature of emotional illness, partially formulated before the family research, that governed the theoretical thinking and the choice of the various theoretical concepts, including the notion of an emotional system. Man is viewed as an evolutionary assemblage of cells who has arrived at his present state from hundreds of millions of years of evolutionary adaptation and maladaptation, and who is evolving on to other changes. In this sense, man is related directly to all living matter. In choosing theoretical concepts, an attempt was made to keep them in harmony with man as a protoplasmic being. Man is different from other animals in the size of his brain and his ability to reason and think. With his intellectual ability he has devoted major effort to emphasizing his uniqueness and the differences that set him apart from other forms of life, and he has devoted comparatively little effort to understanding his relatedness to other forms of life. A basic premise is that what man thinks about himself, and what he says about himself, is different in many important ways from what he *is*. Emotional illness is seen as a disorder of man's emotional system, and man's emotional system is seen as basically related to man's protoplasmic being. I view emotional illness as a much deeper phenomenon than that conceptualized by current psychological theory. There are emotional mechanisms as automatic as a reflex and that occur as predictably as the force that causes the sunflower to keep its face toward the sun. I believe that the laws that govern man's emotional functioning are as orderly as those that govern other natural systems, and that the difficulty in understanding the system is governed more by man's reasoning that denies its existence than by the complexity of the system. In the literature there are discrepant views about the definition of and the relatedness between *emotion* and *feelings*. Operationally I regard an emotional system as something deep that is in contact with cellular and somatic processes, and a feeling system as a bridge that is in contact with parts of the emotional system on one side and with the intellectual system on the other. In clinical practice, I have made a clear distinction between feelings, which have to do with subjective awareness, and opinions, which have to do with logic and reasoning of the intellectual system. The degree to which people say, "I feel that . . ." when they mean, "I believe that . . ." is so commonplace that many use the two words synonymously. However valid the ideas behind the selection of these concepts, they did play a major part in the choice of concepts.

An attempt has been made to keep terminology as simple and descriptive as possible. Several factors have governed this. The effort to think of the family as a fluid, ever-changing, functional system was impaired by the use of the static, fixed concepts conveyed by much of conventional psychiatric terminology. Early in family research, the loose use of psychiatric terms, such as depressed, hysterical, and compulsive, interfered with accurate description and communication. An effort was made to prohibit the use of psychiatric jargon within the research staff and to use simple descriptive words. This was a worthwhile discipline. It is difficult to communicate with colleagues without using familiar terms. An effort was made to bridge this gap by the sparing use of familiar terms. In the early years I worked toward some kind of correlation of family concepts with psychoanalytic theory. In writing and professional communication, the use of certain familiar terms would evoke vigorous discussion about the proper definition and use of terms. When the discussions went beyond productive exchanges of views and into nonproductive cyclical debates that consumed both time and energy, I elected to describe the family phenomenon in terms that did not stir up debates, to advance the research as far as possible, and to leave integration of individual and family concepts for some future generation. Although there are inaccuracies in the use of the term family psychotherapy, I have retained it as the best working compromise between the theory and the practice, and for describing it to the professions to which it is related.

THE FAMILY THEORY

The central concept in this theory is the undifferentiated family ego mass. This is a conglomerate emotional oneness that exists in all levels of intensity—from the family in which it is most intense to the family in which it is almost imperceptible. The symbiotic relationship between a mother and child is an example of a fragment of one of the most intense versions. The father is equally involved with the mother and child, and other children are involved with varying lesser degrees of intensity. The basic notion to be conveyed at this moment is that of an emotional process that shifts about within the nuclear family (father, mother, and children) ego mass in definite patterns of emotional responsiveness. The degree to which any one family member may be involved depends on his basic level of involvement in the family ego mass. The number of family members involved depends on the intensity of the process and the functional state of individual relationships to the central mass at that moment. In periods of stress, the process can involve the entire nuclear family, a whole spectrum of more peripheral family members, and even nonrelatives and representatives of social agencies, clinics, schools, and courts. In periods of calm, the process can remain relatively contained within a small segment of the family, such as the symbiotic relationship in which the emotional process plays back and forth between mother and child with the father isolated from the intense twosome.

The term undifferentiated family ego mass has been more utilitarian than accurate. Precisely defined, the four words do not belong together, but this term has been the most effective of all in communicating the concept so that others might hear. Also, the four words, each conveying an essential part of the concept, have provided latitude in theoretical extension of the idea. Clinically, the best examples of the relationship system within the undifferentiated family ego mass are conveyed by the more intense versions of it, such as the symbiotic relationship or the *folie à deux* phenomenon. The emotional closeness can be so intense that family members know each other's feelings, thoughts, fantasies, and dreams. The relationships are cyclical. There is one phase of calm, comfortable closeness. This can shift to anxious, uncomfortable overcloseness with the incorporation of the self of one by the self of the other. Then there is the phase of distant hostile rejection in which the two can literally repel each other. In some families, the relationship can cycle through the phases at frequent intervals. In other families the cycle can stay relatively fixed for long periods, such as the angry rejection phase in which two people can repulse each other for years, or for life. In the rejection phase, each can *refuse* into a similar emotional involvement with another family member or with certain other people outside the family. Within the family emotional system, the emotional tensions shift about in an orderly series of emotional alliances and rejections. The basic building block of any emotional system is the triangle. In calm periods, two members of the triangle have a comfortable emotional alliance, and the third, in the unfavored outsider position, moves either toward winning the favor of one of the others or toward rejection, which may be planned as winning favor. In tension situations, the outsider is in the favored position and both of the emotionally overinvolved ones will predictably make efforts to involve the third in the conflict. When tension increases, it will involve increasing outside members, the emotional circuits running on a series of interlocking emotional triangles. In the least involved situations, the emotional process shifts about in a subtle process of emotional responsiveness, which might be compared to an emotional chain reaction. These mechanisms can be defined in the later stages of family psychotherapy in which it is possible to analyze the family emotional system. For instance, a smile in one family member might initiate an action response in another, and this initiate a reverie about a dream in another, which is followed by a change-the-subject joke in another.

There are three major theoretical concepts in the theory. The first has to do with the degree of differentiation of self in a person. The opposite of differentiation is the degree of undifferentiation or ego fusion. An attempt has been made to classify all levels of human functioning on a single continuum. At one end of the scale is the most intense version of the undifferentiated family ego mass in which undifferentiation and ego fusion dominate the field and there is little differentiation of self. The symbiotic relationship and the *folie à deux* phenomenon are examples of clinical states with intense ego fusion. At the other end of the scale the differentiation of self dominates the field and there is little overt evidence of ego fusion. People at this end of the scale represent the highest levels of human functioning. Another concept has to do with the relationship system *within* the nuclear family ego mass and the *outside* emotional forces from the extended family emotional system and from the emotional systems of work and social situations that influence the course of the process within the family ego mass. Important in this concept is the family projection process by which parental problems are transmitted to their children. The patterns of this process have been incorporated into a third concept which deals with the multigenerational interlocking of emotional fields and parental transmission of varying degrees of maturity or immaturity over multiple generations. For practical purposes, the term family ego mass refers to the nuclear family which includes the father, mother, and children of the present and future generations. The term extended family refers to the entire network of living relatives, though in the everyday clinical situation this usually refers to the three-generation system involving grandparents, parents, and children. The term emotional field refers to the emotional process in any area being considered at the moment.

The Differentiation of Self Scale is an attempt to conceptualize all human functioning on the same continuum. This theory does not have a concept of normal. It has been relatively easy to define "normal" measurements for all areas of man's physical functioning, but attempts to establish a "normal" for emotional functioning have been elusive. As a baseline for this theoretical system, a detailed profile of complete differentiation of self, which would be equivalent to complete emotional maturity, has been assigned a value of 100 on a scale from 0 to 100. The lowest level of no self, or the highest level of undifferentiation, is at the bottom of the scale. Some of the broad general characteristics of people at the various levels of the scale will be presented.

People in the lowest quarter of the scale (0 to 25) are those with the most intense degree of ego fusion and with little differentiation of self. They live in a feeling world, if they are not so miserable that they have lost the capacity to feel. They are dependent on the feelings of those about them. So much of life energy goes into maintaining the relationship system about them—into "loving," or "being loved," or reaction against the failure to get "love," or into getting more comfortable—that there is no life energy for anything else. They cannot differentiate between a feeling system and an intellectual system. Major life decisions are based on what feels right or simply on getting comfortable. They are incapable of using the differentiated *"I"* (I am—I believe—I will do—I will not do) in their relationships with others. Their use of "I" is confined to the narcissistic, "I want—I am hurt—I want my rights." They grew up as dependent appendages of their parental ego masses, and in their life course they attempt to find other dependent attachments from which they can borrow enough strength to function. Some are able to maintain a sufficient system of dependent attachments to function through life without symptoms. This is more possible for those in the upper part of this group. A no self who is sufficiently adept at pleasing his boss might be considered a better employee than if he had some self. This scale has nothing to do with diagnostic categories. All in the group have tenuous adjustments, they are easily stressed into emotional disequilibrium, and dysfunction can be long or permanent. The group includes those who manage marginal adjustments and those whose efforts failed. At the extreme lower end are those who cannot exist outside the protective walls of an institution. It includes the dead-enders of society, many of the lower socioeconomic group, and those from higher socioeconomic groups with intense ego fusions. I would see the hard core schizophrenic person at 10 or below on the scale, and his parents at no more than 20. In family psychotherapy, I have yet to see a person in this group attain a higher basic level of differentiation of self. Many attain reasonable alleviation of symptoms, but life energy goes into getting comfortable. If they can gain some symptom relief and a dependent attachment from which they can borrow strength, they are satisfied with the result.

People in the second quarter of the scale (25 to 50) are those with less intense ego fusions and with either a poorly defined self or a budding capacity to differentiate a self. This has to be in general terms because a person in the 30 range has many of the characteristics of lower scale people, and those between 40 and 50 have more characteristics of a higher scale. This scale provides an opportunity to describe feeling people. From 50 down it is increasingly a *feeling* world except for those at the extreme lower end who can be too miserable to feel. A typical *feeling* person is one who is responsive to emotional harmony or disharmony about him. Feelings can soar to heights with praise or approval or be dashed to nothingness by disapproval. So much life energy goes into "loving" and seeking "love" and approval that there is little energy left for self-determined, goal-directed activity. Important life decisions are based on what feels right. Success in business or professional pursuits is determined more by approval from superiors and from the relationship system than the inherent value of their work. People in this group do have some awareness of opinions and beliefs from the intellectual system but the budding self is usually so fused with feelings that it is expressed in dogmatic authoritativeness, in the compliance of a disciple, or in the opposition of a rebel. A conviction can be so fused with feeling that it becomes a "cause." In the lower part of this group are some fairly typical no selfs. They are transilient personalities who, lacking beliefs and convictions of their own, adapt quickly to the prevailing ideology. They usually go along with the system that best complements their emotional system. To avoid upsetting the emotional system, they use outside authority to support their position in life. They may use cultural values, religion, philosophy, the law, rule books, science, the physician, or other such sources. Instead of using the "I believe" of the more differentiated person, they may say, "Science has shown . . ." and it is possible to take science, or religion, or philosophy out of context and "prove" anything. It is misleading to correlate this scale with clinical categories, but people in the lower part of this segment of the scale, under stress, will develop transient psychotic episodes, delinquency problems, and other symptoms of that intensity. Those in the upper range of the scale will develop neurotic problems. The main difference between this segment and the lower quarter of the scale is that these people have some capacity for the differentiation of selfs. I have had a few families in the 25 to 30 range who have gone on to fairly high levels of differentiation. It is a situation of *possibility* but *low probability*. Most in this range will lose motivation when the emotional equilibrium is restored and symptoms disappear. The *probability* for differentiation is much higher in the 35 to 50 range.

People in the third quarter of the scale (50 to 75) are those with higher levels of differentiation and much lower degrees of ego fusions. Those in this group have fairly well-defined opinions and beliefs on most essential issues, but pressure for conformity is great and under sufficient stress they can compromise principle and make feeling decisions rather than risk the displeasure of others by standing on their convictions. They often remain silent and avoid stating opinions that might put them out of step with the crowd and disturb the emotional equilibrium. People in this group have more energy for goal-directed activity and less energy tied up in keeping the emotional system in equilibrium. Under sufficient stress they can develop fairly severe emotional or physical symptoms, but symptoms are more episodic and recovery is much faster.

People in the upper quarter of the scale (75 to 100) are those I have never seen in my clinical work and that I rarely meet in social and professional relationships. In considering the overall scale, it is essentially impossible for anyone to have *all* the characteristics I would assign to 100. In this group I shall consider those that fall in the 85 to 95 range which will include most of the characteristics of a differentiated person. These are principle-oriented, goal-directed people who have many of the qualities that have been called inner directed. They begin growing away from their parents in infancy. They are always sure of their beliefs and convictions but are never dogmatic or fixed in thinking. They can hear and evaluate the viewpoints of others and discard old beliefs in favor of new. They are sufficiently secure within themselves that functioning is not affected by either praise or criticism from others. They can respect the self and the identity of another without becoming critical or becoming emotionally involved in trying to modify the life course of another. They assume total responsibility for self and are sure of their responsibility for family and society. They are realistically aware of their dependence on their fellow man. With the ability to keep emotional functioning contained within the boundaries of self, they are free to move about in any relationship system and engage in a whole spectrum of intense relationships without a "need" for the other that can impair functioning. The "other" in such a relationship does not feel used. They marry spouses with equal levels of differentiation. With each a well-defined self, there are no questions or doubts about masculinity and femininity. Each can respect the self and identity of the other. They can maintain well-defined "self's" and engage in intense emotional relationships at the same time. They are free to relax ego boundaries for the pleasurable sharing of "selfs" in sexuality or other intense emotional experience without reservation and with the full assurance that either can disengage from this kind of emotional fusion and proceed on a self-directed course at will.

These brief characterizations of broad segments of the scale will convey an overall view of the theoretical system that conceives all human functioning on the same continuum. The scale has to do with *basic* levels of differentiation. Another important aspect has to do with *functional* levels of differentiation, which is so marked in the lower half of the scale that the concept of *basic* levels can be misleading. The more intense the degree of ego fusion, the more the borrowing and lending and giving and sharing of self within the family ego mass. The more the shifting of "strength" within the ego mass, the more likely the marked discrepancies in functional levels of self. The occasional brief shifts are striking. One of the best examples of this is that of the regressed schizophrenic person who pulls up to resourceful functioning when his parents are sick, only to fall back when they have recovered. Other shifts are so fixed that people wonder how one spouse so strong would marry another so weak. A striking example of this is the overadequate husband who might function well in his work at perhaps 55 on strength from a wife housebound with phobias, excessive drinking, or arthritis and a functioning level of 15. In this situation, the basic level would be about 35. Fluctuations in the upper half of the scale are present but less marked, and it is easier to estimate basic levels. People high on the scale have almost no functional shifts. Other characteristics apply to the entire scale. The lower the person on the scale, the more he holds onto religious dogma, cultural values, superstition, and outmoded beliefs, and the less able he is to discard the rigidly held ideas. The lower a person on the scale, the more he makes a federal case of rejection, lack of love, and injustice, and the more he demands recompense for his hurts. The lower he is on the scale, the more he holds the other responsible for his self and happiness. The lower he is on the scale, the more intense the ego fusions, and the more extreme the mechanisms such as emotional distance, isolation, conflict, violence, and physical illness to control the emotion of too much closeness. The more intense the ego fusions, the higher the incidence of being in touch with the intrapsychic of the other, and the greater the chance that he can intuitively know what the other thinks and feels. In general, the lower the person on the scale, the more the impairment in meaningful communication.

Relationship System in the Nuclear Family Ego Mass

An example of a marriage with spouses in the 30 to 35 range will convey an idea of several concepts in this theoretical system. As children, both spouses were dependently attached to parents. After adolescence, in an effort to function autonomously, they either denied the dependence while still living at home, or they used separation and physical distance to achieve autonomy. Both can function relatively well as long as they keep relationships distant or casual. Both are vulnerable to the closeness of an intense emotional relationship. Both long for closeness but both are allergic to it. The marriage for each duplicates essential characteristics of former ego masses. They fuse together into a new family ego mass with obliteration of ego boundaries and incorporation of the two pseudo self's into a common self. Each uses mechanisms, previously used in their families of origin, in dealing with the other. For instance, the one who ran away from his own family will tend to run away in the marriage. The most common mechanism is the use of sufficient emotional distance for each to function with a reasonable level of pseudo self. The future course of this new family ego mass will depend on a spectrum of mechanisms that operate *within* the family ego mass, and others that operate *outside* in their relationships within the extended family system.

Within the family ego mass, spouses use three major mechanisms to control the intensity of the ego fusion: (1) *Marital conflict,* in which each spouse fights for an equal share of the common self and neither gives in to the other. (2) *Dysfunction in one spouse.* A common pattern is a brief period of conflict followed by one spouse who reluctantly gives in to relieve the conflict. Both spouses usually see self as giving in, but there is one who does more of it. In another pattern, one spouse volunteers to be the no self in support of the other, on whom he (or she) becomes dependent. The spouse who loses self in this mechanism may come to function at such a low level that he (or she) becomes candidate for physical, emotional, or social illness. There are some marriages that continue for years with one functioning well and the other chronically ill. (3) *Transmission of the problem to one or more children.* This is one of the most common mechanisms for dealing with family ego mass problems. There are a few families in which ego mass problems are relatively contained within one of the three areas. There are a few with severe marital conflict but no impairment of either spouse and no transmission to the children. There are also a few with no marital conflict, no dysfunction in either spouse, and in which the entire weight of the marital problem goes into one child. There may be no significant symptoms until after adolescence, when the child collapses in psychotic dysfunction or other dysfunction of comparable degree. In most families, the problem between the spouses will be spread to all three areas. The few families in which the problem remains contained in one area are important theoretically. The fact that there are some families with intense marital conflict and no impairment of children is evidence that marital conflict does not, within itself, cause problems in children. The fact that serious impairment of children can develop in calm, harmonious marriages is further evidence that impairment of children can occur without conflict. The degree of the problem between the spouses can be assigned quantitative measures. The system operates as if there is a certain amount of immaturity to be absorbed by the system. Large quantities of this may be bound by serious dysfunction in one family member. One chronically ill parent can be a kind of protection against serious impairment of children. In the area of transmission to children, the family projection process focuses on certain children and leaves others relatively uninvolved. There are, of course, families in which the quantity of immaturity is so great that there is maximum marital conflict, severe dysfunction in one spouse, maximum involvement of children, conflict with families of origin, and still free-floating immaturity.

The mechanisms that operate *outside* the nuclear family ego mass are important in determining the course and intensity of the process *within* the nuclear family. When there is a significant degree of ego fusion, there is also a borrowing and sharing of ego strength between the nuclear family and the family of origin. In periods of stress the nuclear family can be stabilized by emotional contact with a family of origin, just as the nuclear family can also be disturbed by stress in the family of origin. In general, the intensity of the process in a nuclear family is attenuated by active contacts with the families of origin. There is one striking pattern illustrated by the following example: The father separated himself from his family when he left for college. There was no further contact except infrequent, brief visits and occasional letters and Christmas cards. He married a wife who maintained close contact with her family, including frequent exchanges of letters and gifts, regular family reunions, and visits with scattered members of the clan. Five out of six of the father's siblings followed the same pattern of separating from the family of origin. The mother was one of five siblings, all of whom married spouses who were brought into the emotional orbit of her family. This pattern is so common that I have called these *exploding* and *cohesive* families. The spouse who separates from his family of origin does not resolve the emotional attachment. The old relationship remains latent and can be revived with emotional contact. Through the active relationship with the cohesive family, the nuclear family system is responsive to emotional events within the cohesive extended family. There are other nuclear families in which both spouses detach themselves from families of origin. In these the spouses are usually much more dependent on each other, and the emotional process in the family tends to be more intense. The average family in which both spouses are emotionally separated from families of origin tends to become more invested in the emotional systems of work and social situations. An example is a family in which the principal outside emotional tie was the father's long-term emotional dependence on his boss at work. Within weeks after the sudden death of the father's boss, a teen-aged son was in serious dysfunction with a behavior problem. A brief period of "family" psychotherapy with the father alone restored the family emotional equilibrium sufficiently for the parents to work productively together toward resolution of the parental interdependence. Knowledge of the relationship patterns in the extended family system is important in understanding the overall problem and in devising a family psychotherapy program.

Multigenerational Transmission Process

One of the important concepts of this theoretical system is the pattern that emerges over the generations as parents transmit varying levels of their immaturity to their children. In most families the parents transmit part of their immaturity to one or more children. To illustrate this multigenerational pattern in its most graphic and extreme form, I shall start with parents with an average level of differentiation and assume that in each generation the parents project a major portion of their immaturity to only one child, thereby creating maximum impairment in one child in each generation. I shall also assume that in each generation one child grows up relatively outside the emotional demands and pressures of the family ego mass and attains the highest level of differentiation possible in that situation. It would be essentially impossible for this pattern to occur generation after generation, but it does illustrate the pattern. The example starts with parents at 50 on the scale. They have three children. The most involved child emerges at 35 on the scale, much lower than the basic level of the parents and a fairly maximum degree of impairment for one generation. Another child emerges with 50, the same basic level of the parents. A third grows up relatively outside the problems of the family ego mass and emerges with a level of 60, much higher than the parents. In considering the child at 35 who marries a spouse in the 35 range, the personality characteristics of this marriage would vary according to the way this family ego mass handles its problems. A maximum projection family would have a calm marriage and almost total preoccupation with the health, welfare, and achievement of the most involved child, who could emerge with a level as low as 20. They could have another who grew up outside the family ego mass with a level of 45, much higher than the parents. To have two children, one at 20 and another at 45, is hardly probable. The child at 20 is already in the danger zone and vulnerable to a whole spectrum of human problems. In his early years he might be an overachiever in school, and then in the postadolescent years go into an emotional collapse. With special help he might eventually finish school, spend a few aimless years, and then find a spouse whose "needs" for another are as great as his. At this level of ego fusion the problems are too great to be contained in one area. They will probably have a variety of marital, health, and social problems, and the problem will be too great for projection to only one child. They might have one child at 10, another at 15, and another who grows up outside the family mass to a level of 30, much above the basic level of the parents. The ones at 10 and 15 are good candidates for total functional collapse into states such as schizophrenia or criminal behavior. This illustrates former statements that it requires at least three generations for a person to acquire the level of no self for a later collapse into schizophrenia. In the average situation the immaturity would progress at a much slower rate. Also, in every generation there are children who progress up the scale, and in the average family the upward progression is much slower than illustrated in this example.

It is emphasized that the scale level figures used in the preceding examples are to illustrate the broad principles of the theoretical system. The shift in functional levels in the lower half of the scale is so responsive to such a variety of hour-to-hour and week-to-week shifts, through good years and bad, that approximate levels can be established only after having awareness of the particular variables most operative over a period of time for a given family. It is the general level and the pattern that are most important in the clinical situation. The levels in the multigenerational concept are strictly schematic and for illustrative purposes only. The postulations for this concept were derived from historical material covering three to four generations on approximately a hundred families, and ten or more generations on eight families.

There is one other theoretical concept that I have combined with my own work that is used with every family in psychotherapy. These are the personality profiles of the various sibling positions as presented by Toman in *Family Constellation*.[15] I consider his work one of the significant contributions to family knowledge in recent years. He presents the thesis that personality characteristics are determined by the sibling position and the family constellation in which one grows up. I have found his personality profiles to be remarkably accurate, especially for people in the midscale range of my Differentiation of Self Scale. Of course, he did his study on "normal" families and made no attempt to estimate other variables. He also did not consider the personality alterations of the child who was the object of the family projection process. An example of the shift is a family of two daughters. The older, the one most involved in the family emotional system, emerged with the profile of a younger "baby." The younger daughter, who was less involved in the emotional system with the parents, emerged with more of the characteristics of an older daughter. Most of his profiles contain a mixture of the adult and the infantile characteristics. The higher a person on the scale, the more the adult qualities predominate; the obverse is also true.

CLINICAL USE OF FAMILY PSYCHOTHERAPY

I hope that the theoretical concepts help the reader think more in terms of family systems rather than diagnostic categories and individual dynamics. Each point in the theory has application in clinical evaluation and in family psychotherapy. This section will be presented in three main parts: (1) survey of the family fields, (2) the process of differentiation of self in family psychotherapy, and (3) family psychotherapy principles and techniques.

Survey of the Family Fields

This is a term used to designate a family evaluation process used in the initial interview with every family I see. It is designed to get a volume of factual information in a brief time. The information is used with the family theory for a formulation about the overall patterns of functioning in the family ego mass for at least two generations. The formulation is used in planning the psychotherapy. Initially, it required a number of hours to get this information. With practice, and the careful structuring of the interview, and an average uncomplicated family, it is possible to do a survey adequately for planning the psychotherapy in one hour. This is different from the kind of evaluation in which the therapist may spend several hours with all family members together to observe the workings of the family relationship system. In the training of young therapists, considerable experience in observing multiple family members together is essential. It is not possible to *know* family without direct clinical observation, and it is not advisable to work with segments of families until one has a working knowledge of the whole. For the average family, the initial interview is with both parents, who can usually provide more information than one. In addition, it provides a working view of the marital relationship. If there is evidence that marital discord might interfere with the fact gathering, I often ask to see the one parent who has the most knowledge about the family. Some interesting developments come from this. Most families seek help when there is dysfunction in one or more of the three main stress areas of the nuclear family system: (1) marital conflict, (2) dysfunction in a spouse, or (3) dysfunction in a child. To illustrate this survey, I shall use a family referred for a behavior problem in a teen-aged child.

In surveying the family fields, I first want to know about the functioning in the nuclear family field and then how the functioning of the extended family field intergears with the nuclear field. A good starting point is a chronological review of the symptom development in the teen-aged child, with specific dates and circumstances at the time of each symptom eruption. Many symptomatic eruptions can be timed exactly with other events in the nuclear and extended family fields. The parents might report the child first played hooky from school "in the eighth grade," but it would convey much about the family system if one knew the day he played hooky was the day his maternal grandmother was hospitalized for tests for a feared cancer. Information about feeling and fantasy systems of other family members on that day would be helpful if it could be obtained.

The second area of investigation is the functioning of the parental ego mass since marriage. This emotional unit has its own system of internal dynamics that change as it moves through the years. The internal system also responds to the emotional fields of the extended families and to the reality stresses of life. The goal is to get a brief chronological view of the internal system as it has inter-responded with outside forces. This might be compared to two constantly changing magnetic fields that influence each other. The internal functioning is influenced by events such as closeness or distance and emotional contact with extended families, changes in residence, the purchase of a home, and occupational success or failure. Major events that influence both emotional fields are births within the central ego mass and serious illness or death in the extended family. Functioning within the ego mass can be estimated with a few questions about stress areas, which are marital conflict, illness or other dysfunction, and projection to a child. A change in stress symptoms might be related to internal dynamics or external events. The dates of changes are important. A change from a calm to a conflictual relationship might be explained by the wife as, "the time I began to stand up to him," when it would in fact be timed exactly with a disturbance in an extended family.

Important ego mass changes accompany the birth of children. The birth of the first child changes the family from a two-person to a three-person system. At an important event such as this, it is desirable to do a fix on the entire family system, including place, date, ages of each person in the household and the functioning of each, and a check on the realities in the extended families. It is desirable to get readings on the feeling-fantasy systems of various family members at stress points, if this is possible. A check on the family projection process is often easy by asking about the mother's fantasy system before and after the birth of the child. If it is a significant projection process, her worries and concerns have fixed on the child since the pregnancy, her relationship with this one has been "different," she has long worried about it, and she is eager to talk about it. An intense, long-term, projection process is evidence of a deeper and more serious problem in the child. A projection process that started later, perhaps following the death of an important family member, is much less serious and much easier handled in family psychotherapy. A projection process, usually between mother and child, *changes* the internal functioning of the family system. This much psychic energy from mother to child will change the psychic energy system in the family. It might serve to reduce marital conflict, but it might also disturb the husband to the point he would start spending longer hours at work, or he might begin drinking, or have an affair, or become emotionally closer to his parents. This survey is followed to the onset of symptoms in the child for which there are already nodal points that may be connected with dates and events in the parental relationship. The survey provides a picture of general functioning levels, responsiveness to stress, and evidence about the flexibility or rigidity of the entire system. It also provides a notion about the more adaptive spouse, who is usually the more passive. The adaptive one is much more than one who gives in on a controlled surface level. This involves the entire fantasy, feeling, and action system. A spouse who develops physical symptoms in response to an emotional field is in a cell-to-cell adaptiveness that is deep.

The next area of investigation is the two extended family fields in either order the therapist chooses. This is similar to the nuclear family survey except it focuses on overall patterns. Exact dates, ages, and places are very important. The occupation of the grandfather and a note about the marital relationship and the health of each grandparent provides key clues to that family ego mass. Information about each sibling includes birth order, exact dates of birth, occupation, place of residence, a few words about spouse and children, a note about overall life course, and frequency and nature of contact with other family members. From this brief information, which can be obtained in five or ten minutes, it is possible to assemble a fairly accurate working notion about the family ego mass, and how the nuclear parent functioned in the group. Siblings who do best are usually least involved in the family emotional system. Those who do poorly are usually most involved. Distance from other family members and quality of emotional contacts with family provides clues about the way the person handles all emotional relationships and whether this tends toward an exploding or cohesive family. A high incidence of physical illness often occurs in those with low levels of differentiation of self. The sibling position is one of the most important bits of information. This, plus the general level of family functioning, makes it possible to postulate a reasonably accurate personality profile to be checked later. In general, a life style developed in the family of origin will operate in the nuclear family and also in family psychotherapy.

Surveys of the family fields follow the same pattern for other problems, except for different emphases. Certain areas may require detailed exploration. It is always helpful to go back as many generations as possible. The overall goal is to follow the total family through time with a focus on related events in interlocking fields. The lower the general level of differentiation in a family, the greater the frequency and intensity of the related events. A secondary dividend of a family field survey is the family's beginning intellectual awareness of related events. The family emotional system operates always to obscure and misremember and to treat such events as coincidental. Family replies to an effort to get specific dates might go, "That was when he was about . . . 11 or 12 years old," and, "He must have been in the fifth grade," or, "It was about five or six years ago." It requires persistent questioning and mathematical computation to get specific information. The obscuring process is illustrated by a family in family psychotherapy. Ten days after the wife returned from her mother's funeral, her daughter developed nephritis. Some weeks later the wife was insisting that the daughter's illness preceded her mother's death. The husband's memory and my notes were accurate. In theoretical thinking, I have never been willing to postulate causality or go beyond noting that such events have a striking time sequence. I believe it may have to do with man's denial of dependence on his fellow man. I avoid glib dynamic speculations and record the family explanations as, "The family member *said*. . . ." I have never been able to use the related events early in psychotherapy. Early in family psychotherapy there was the temptation to show this to the family after the initial interview. Some families found reason to never return. My goal is to keep asking questions and let the calendar speak when others are able to hear.

The family field survey is primarily for the therapist in knowing the family and how it operates, and in planning the psychotherapy. If the symptoms develop slowly in the nuclear family, it is likely to be the product of a slow buildup in the nuclear family. If the symptoms develop more quickly, the situation deserves a thorough exploration for disturbance in the extended family. If it is a response to the extended family, it can be regarded as an acute situation and it is fairly easy to restore the family functioning. The following is an example of multiple acute problems following a disturbance in the extended family.

A 40-year-old woman was referred for a depression for which hospitalization had been suggested. Her husband belonged to a cohesive family of six siblings, all of whom lived within a few hundred miles of their parents. Two months before, his 65-year-old mother had a radical mastectomy of breast cancer. Two weeks after the operation, one of the husband's sisters had a serious automobile accident which required months of hospitalization. Six weeks after the operation, one of the husband's brothers had a son arrested for a series of delinquent acts, the first of which had occurred two weeks after the operation. After an initial interview with the depressed wife alone, the husband and wife were seen together. A few hours with the process focused on feelings about the mother brought rapid relief of the depression and set the stage for long-term family psychotherapy with both together.

The Process of Differentiation of Self

The basic effort of this therapeutic system is to help *individual* family members toward a higher level of differentiation of self. An emotional system operates with a delicately balanced equilibrium in which each devotes a certain amount of being and self to the welfare and well-being of the others. In a state of disequilibrium, the family system operates automatically to restore the former togetherness equilibrium, though this be at the expense of some. When an individual moves toward a higher level of differentiation of self, it disturbs the equilibrium and the togetherness forces oppose with vigor. In larger emotional systems, an individual may seek an ally or group to help oppose the forces of the system, only to find self in a new undifferentiated oneness with his allies (even a sect or minority group within the larger system) from which it is harder to differentiate than from the original oneness. Any successful effort toward differentiation is for the individual alone. Some of the forces that oppose the differentiation of self will be described later. When the individual can maintain his differentiation stand in spite of opposition, the family later applauds.

One of the important concepts in this theoretical system has to do with triangles. It was not included with the other concepts because it has more to do with therapy than the basic theory. The basic building block of any emotional system is the triangle. When emotional tension in a two-person system exceeds a certain level, it triangles a third person, permitting the tension to shift about within the triangle. Any two in the original triangle can add a new triangle. An emotional system is composed of a series of interlocking triangles. The emotional tension system can shift to any of the old preestablished circuits. It is a clinical fact that the original two-person tension system will resolve itself automatically when contained within a three-person system, one of whom remains emotionally detached. This will be discussed under "detriangling the triangle."

From experience with this therapeutic system, there are two main avenues toward a higher level of "differentiation of self." (1) The optimum is differentiation of a self *from* one's spouse, as a cooperative effort, in the presence of a potential triangle (therapist) who can remain emotionally detached. To me, this is the magic of family psychotherapy. They must be sufficiently involved with each other to stand the stress of differentiation and sufficiently uncomfortable to motivate the effort. One, and then the other, moves forward in small steps until motivation stops. (2) Start the differentiation alone, under the guidance of a supervisor, as a preliminary step to the main effort of differentiating a self *from* the important other person. This second avenue is a model for family psychotherapy with one family member. A third avenue is less effective: (3) the entire process under the guidance of a supervisor who coaches from the sidelines. Direct use of the triangle is lost, the process is generally slower, and the chances of an impasse are greater. As a general comment about differentiation, the highest level of differentiation that is possible for a family is the highest level that any family member can attain and maintain against the emotional opposition of the family unit in which he lives.

Family Psychotherapy Principles and Techniques

My optimum approach to any family problem, whether marital conflict, dysfunction in a spouse, or dysfunction in a child, is to start with husband and wife together and to continue with both for the entire period of family psychotherapy. In most families, this optimum course is not possible. Some 30 to 40 per cent of family hours are spent with one family member, mostly for situations in which one spouse is antagonistic or poorly motivated, or when progress with both is too slow. The method of helping one family member to differentiate a self will be discussed later. The method of working with the two parents evolved from several years of experience in which both parents and symptomatic child (usually postadolescent behavior and neurotic problems) attended all sessions together. An average course would continue a year or more. Family communication improved, symptoms disappeared, and the families would terminate, much pleased with the result. There was no basic change in the pattern of the parental relationship, postulated to be fundamental in the origin of the problem. On the premise that the entire family system would change if the parental relationship changed, I began asking such parents to leave the child at home and to focus on their own problems. These have been the most satisfying results in my experience. Many of the children who initiated the family effort were never seen, and others were seen only once. The parents who achieved the best results would continue about four years at once a week for a total of 175 to 200 hours with better results than could be achieved with any other psychotherapeutic method in my experience. The children were usually symptom free in a few weeks or months, and changes have gone far beyond the nuclear family into the extended family system. The time has been so consistently in the four-year range that I believe it might require this amount of time for significant differentiation of self. Some people can spend a lifetime without defining themselves on numerous life issues. I am now experimenting with less frequent appointments to reduce the total amount of time.

The basic process of working with husbands and wives together has remained very much the same over the years with some different emphases and modifications in theoretical concepts. In the past I stressed the communication of feelings and the analysis of the unconscious through dreams. More recently, it has been a process of watching the step-by-step process of externalizing and separating out their fantasy, feeling, thinking systems. It is a process of knowing one's own self, and also the self of the other. There have been comments such as, "I never knew you had such thoughts!" and the counterresponse, "I never dared tell anyone before, most especially *you*!"

The following is an example of two small differentiation steps with the emotional response of the other. One wife, after many hours of private thinking, announced, "I have decided to take all the thoughts, time, and energy that I have devoted to trying to make you happy and to put it into trying to make myself into a more responsible woman and mother. Nothing I tried really worked anyway. I have thought it out and I have a plan." The husband reacted with the usual emotional reaction to an "I" position by the other. He was angry and hurt. He ended with, "If I had realized it would come to this after fifteen years, I can tell you one thing, there never would have been a wedding!" Within a week he was happy with his "new" wife. Some weeks later, after much thinking by the husband, he announced, "I have been trying to think through my responsibilities to my family and to work. I have never been clear about this. If I worked overtime, I felt I was neglecting my family. If I spent extra time with the family, I would feel I was neglecting my work. Here is my plan." The wife reacted with emotion about his real selfish lack of concern finally showing its true color. Within a week that had subsided.

As spouses change in relation to each other, they disturb the emotional equilibrium in families of origin where there are the same emotional reactions and resolutions as between themselves. Most of these spouses have become the most responsible and respected in both extended family systems. The emotional opposition to change also occurs in social and work emotional systems. The main point to be communicated here is that a change in self disturbs the emotional equilibrium and evokes emotional opposing forces in all interlocking emotional systems. If two spouses can make the primary changes in relation to each other, it is relatively easy to deal with the other systems.

One of the most important processes in this method of psychotherapy is the therapist's continuing attention to defining his self to the families. This begins from the first contact which defines this theoretical and therapeutic system and its differences from others. It proceeds in almost every session around all kinds of life issues. Of importance are the action stands which have to do with "what I will do and will not do." I believe a therapist is in poor position to ask a family to do something he does not do. When the family goes slowly at defining self, I begin to wonder if there is some vague ambiguous area of importance about which I failed to define myself.

At this point, I shall describe *family* psychotherapy with one family member. The basic notion of this has to do with finding a way to start some change in the deadlocked family; with finding a way to get into contact with family resourcefulness and strength and to get out of contact with the sickness morass; and with getting some differentiation to rise out of the family quagmire. Actually, if it is possible to get some differentiation started in one family member, it can loosen up the entire family system. Communication of this idea has been difficult. To those who use a medical model and consider the therapeutic relationship the basic healing force in emotional illness, the idea is erroneous. I have used several different concepts in trying to write about the idea and a number of different angles in trying to teach it. There are those who heard it as "treating the healthiest family member instead of the patient, on the grounds that the healthiest is more capable of modifying behavior." This is an accurate description of the goal but it uses a "health" concept in the place of "sickness," which is still a medical model. A therapist who attempts to "treat" the healthiest with his medical orientation could either drive him away or make him into a "patient."

The conflictual marriage provides one of the best examples of working with one spouse. This is a clinical situation in which the emotional system is already fairly well locked in dysfunction before they seek help. A fair level of overt conflict is "normal," and it has to reach a relative state of dysfunction before they seek help. The marriage began with an almost idyllic model in which each devoted a high percentage of self to the happiness and well-being of the other. This I have called a fraudulent emotional contract in which it was realistically impossible for either to live up to the agreement. With this arrangement, the functioning of self *is* dependent on the other and, in that sense, any failure in happiness or functioning *is* the fault of the other. The emotional investment in each other continues; only it shifts into negative energy that accuses, indicts, and diagnoses. I believe the conflictual marriage is an enduring one because of the energy investment. The amount of *thinking* time that goes into the other is probably greater than calm marriages. With the intensity of emotional interdependence and the ability to utilize conflict, the conflictual spouses usually do not seek help until adaptive mechanisms are jammed. In a high percentage of conflictual marriages, I see one spouse alone for a few months to a year before calm working together is possible. Choice about the one to see first is easy when one is motivated and the other antagonistic. It is a little different when both are seen together and the repetitious accuse the other—excuse self continues in the interview. If they have any capacity to stop the cycle and look at the pattern, I continue with both together. If a vigorous effort to help them contain the cycle is not successful, I say that I consider this cyclical and nonproductive, that I am not willing to spend time this way, and that I want to see the healthiest, best-integrated one alone for a period of time to help this one gain some objectivity and emotional control. A request for the "healthiest" establishes a different orientation and changes their long-term diagnosing, "You are the sick one who needs a psychiatrist." I do not see spouses alternately. It invites triangling, neither really works at the problem, each expects the other to do it, and each tends to justify self to the therapist. My "I" stands, all based on experience, are in terms of what I will do and will not do, and are never in terms of what is best.

Since the process of working with one family member alone is similar in all situations, I shall describe the effort with the conflictual spouse in some detail. The early sessions go into a detailed communication of an orientation with the use of clinical examples and a blackboard for diagrams. In broad terms, the concept is one of withdrawing psychic energy from the other and investing it in the poorly defined ego boundaries. It involves the idea of getting off the back of the other by reducing the other-directed thinking, verbal, action energy which is designed to attack and change the other, and directing that energy to the changing of self. The changing of self involves finding a way to listen to the attacks of the other without responding, of finding a way to live with what is without trying to change it, of defining one's own beliefs and convictions without attacking those of the other, and in observing the part that self plays in the situation. Much time is devoted to establishing the therapist's self in relation to the one spouse. These ideas are passed along for their possible use in defining a self. They are told that others have found some of them helpful, that the effort will fail if they try them without incorporating them into self as their own beliefs, that they would be unrealistic to try something they could not really believe in, and it will be their responsibility to find other ideas and principles if these do not fit with their own selfs. They are assigned the task of becoming research observers and told that a major part of each hour will go into their report on their efforts to see self. I tell them about the predictable stages they can expect if their efforts are successful in defining self and containing the critical actions, words, and thoughts that have been trying to direct the life of their spouse. If they are successful at this, the first reaction will be a version of, "You are mean, selfish and vicious; you do not understand, you do not love, and you are trying to hurt the other." When they can listen to the expected attack without reacting, a milestone will have been passed. Then they can expect a withdrawal from the other which emphasizes, "To heck with you. I do not need you." This will be the most difficult stage. They might get depressed and confused and develop a whole spectrum of physical symptoms. This is the reaction of one's psyche and soma as it cries out for the old dependence and togetherness. If they can live with the symptoms without reacting, they can expect the other to make a new and different bid for affection on a higher level of maturity. It is usually not many days after that before the other spouse asks to take the therapy hour, and often not many hours before they can finally work together.

The life style of this low level of differentiation is the investment of psychic energy in the self of another. When this happens in the therapy, it is transference. A goal of this therapy is to help the other person make a research project out of life. It is important to keep self contained with the therapist as the other spouse. If the person understands the life-goal nature of the effort and that progress will slow down or stop with energy invested in the self of the therapist, he is in a better position to help keep the energy focused on the goal. If progress does stop, the family psychotherapy is shifted to a similar effort with the other spouse. It is not possible to use this differentiation of a self approach with two spouses. It results in intense triangling.

Work with one sick spouse depends on the problem and which one seeks help. If the well one seeks help, the sick one is near collapse. With these I work toward avoiding a relationship with the sick side of the family, and work toward relating to the well one about his problems with the sick one. Some of these families achieve remarkable symptom relief with a few appointments, but these people are not motivated for more than symptom relief. When the sick one seeks help, I maintain a detached, "Let's examine this and understand your part in the family problem." The cells of the sick spouse literally go into dysfunction in the presence of the other spouse, especially in those with severe introjective and somatic dysfunctions. If the other spouse is brought in too early, the therapy effort may terminate within a few hours. A goal is to propose family early and wait until the self of the sick one can operate in the presence of the other without going into dysfunction. There have been some excellent long-term results which include about six months with the sick one and some two years with both. Problems such as impotence and frigidity belong more in the area of relationship functioning. These can usually be converted to family within a few hours, and the response has been good. Impotence often disappears within a few weeks, and frigidity is rarely mentioned after a few months. Most of these go on with long-term family therapy for two years or more.

The problem of the triangled child presents one of the most difficult problems in family psychotherapy. From the initial family survey can come a fair estimate of the intensity of the process. If it is not too severe, the parents can focus on their own problems immediately, they almost forget about the child and, suddenly, he is symptom-free. Even with severe triangling, I do a trial run with both parents together to test the flexibility in the parental relationship. In the severe triangling or projection of the parental problem to the child, the parents are not able to leave the child out of their feelings, thoughts, and actions. There are the less severe versions in which parents try hard to work on their problem but the relationship between them is dull and lifeless. Life and self is invested in the child. The gut reaction, in which a parent's insides tie into knots in response to discomfort in the child, is common. After several years of symptom-relieving methods, including working with various combinations of family members, I began what I have called detriangling the triangle. This is too complex for brief discussion, but it involves helping one parent to establish an "I" position and to differentiate a self in the relationship *with the child*. If there is another magic in family psychotherapy, it is the family response when one parent can begin to differentiate a self from the amorphous we-ness of the intense undifferentiated family ego mass. One bit of clearly defined self in this sea of amorphousness can bring a period of amazing calm. The calm may quickly shift to other issues, but the family *is* different. The other parent and child fuse together into a more intense oneness that alternately attacks and pleads with the differentiating parent to rejoin the oneness. If the differentiating one can maintain a reasonable "I" for even a few days, there is an automatic decrease in the intensity of the attachment between the other two and a permanent decrease in the intensity of the triangle. The second step involves a similar effort by the other parent to differentiate a self. Now the parental relationship has come a little more to life. Then there is another cycle with each parent separately, and then still more life and zest between the parents. Differentiation proceeds slowly at this level of ego fusion, but there have been a few of these families that have gone on to reasonable levels of differentiation.

There are several other configurations of family psychotherapy with one family member, but this provides a brief description of the basic principles. It is used when the family system is so stalled that efforts to work with multiple family members increases the dysfunction, or when work with multiple members reaches a cyclical impasse. The effort is to help one family member to a higher level of functioning which, if possible, can restore function to the family system.

REFERENCES

1. Freud, S., "Analysis of a Phobia in a Five Year Old Boy," in *Collected Papers,* Vol. III, London, England, Hogarth Press, 1949, pp. 149-289.
2. Flugel, J. C., *The Psycho-Analytic Study of the Family,* London, England, Hogarth Press, 10th Impr., 1960.
3. Lidz, T., Cornelison, A., Fleck, S., and Terry, D., "The Intrafamilial Environment of the Schizophrenic Patient, II, Marital Schism and Marital Skew," *Amer. J. Psychiat.* 114:241-248, 1957.
4. Wynne, L., Rykoff, I., Day, J., and Hirsch, S., "Pseudo-mutuality in the Family Relations of Schizophrenics," *Psychiatry* 21:205-220, 1958.
5. Ackerman, N., "Interlocking Pathology in Family Relationships," in Rado, S., and Daniels, G. E. (Eds.), *Changing Concepts in Psychoanalytic Medicine,* New York, Grune & Stratton, 1956.
6. Bateson, G., Jackson, D., Haley, J., and Weakland, J., "Toward a Theory of Schizophrenia," *Behav. Sci.* 1:251-264, 1956.
7. Bell, J. E., *Family Group Therapy,* Public Health Monograph 64, 1961.
8. Dysinger, R., "The Action Dialogue in an Intense Relationship," paper read at Annual Meeting, American Psychiatric Association, Chicago, 1957.
9. Birdwhistell, R., *Introduction to Kinesics,* Louisville, Ky., University of Louisville Press, 1952.
10. Scheflen, A., "The Significance of Posture in Communication Systems," *Psychiatry* 26:316-331, 1964.
11. Bowen, M., "Family Psychotherapy with Schizophernia in the Hospital and in Private Practice," in Boszormenyi-Nagy, I., and Framo, J. L. (Eds.), *Intensive Family Therapy,* New York, Harper, 1965.

12. Bowen, M., "Family Relationships in Schizophrenia," in Auerback (Ed.), *Schizophrenia—An Integrated Approach,* New York, Ronald, 1959.
13. Bowen, M., "A Family Concept of Schizophrenia," in Jackson, D. (Ed.), *The Etiology of Schizophrenia,* New York, Basic Books, 1960.
14. Bowen, M., "Family Psychotherapy," *Amer. J. Orthopsychiat.* 30:40-60, 1961.
15. Toman, W., *Family Constellation,* New York, Springer, 1961.

14

Behavior Therapy in the Home: Amelioration of Problem Parent-Child Relations with the Parent in a Therapeutic Role

ROBERT P. HAWKINS
ROBERT F. PETERSON
EDDA SCHWEID
SIDNEY W. BIJOU

In recognition of the important part parents play in the behavioral (or personality) development of the child, various agencies dealing with child behavior problems have often utilized techniques whose goal is to modify parent-child relationships. For example, the parent of a child who exhibits deviant behavior may, himself, be given psychotherapy in order to change his behavior toward the child. Alternatively, the parent may merely be given advice as to how he should react differently toward the child, or both parent and child may be given psychotherapy and/or counseling. The technique employed is likely to depend on the type of therapist consulted and the therapist's theoretical orientation. A general discussion of therapeutic techniques with children has been presented by Bijou and Sloane (1966).

Traditional types of therapy have a number of deficiencies. First, the

Reprinted with permission of authors and publisher from *Journal of Experimental Child Psychology* 4(1):99-107, 1966.

This research was supported in part by a grant from the National Institute of Mental Health (MH-2232), U. S. Public Health Service.

child's behavior is seldom observed by the therapist, leaving definition of the problem and description of the child's behavior totally up to the parent. Second, the behavior of the parent toward the child is seldom observed. Thus considerable reliance is placed on the verbal report of the parent and child and on the imagination of the therapist. Third, when "practical suggestions" are made by the therapist, they may be so general or technical that it is difficult for the parent to translate them into specific behavior. Fourth, since no objective record is kept of behavior changes over short intervals, (e.g., minutes, hours, days) it is difficult to judge the effectiveness of the treatment.

Wahler et al. (1965) have developed a technique for effectively altering mother-child relationships in a laboratory setting, with objective records being kept of the behavior of both mother and child. The present study was an investigation of the feasibility of treatment in the natural setting where the child's behavior problem appeared—the home. As in the Wahler et al. studies, the mother served as the therapeutic agent. She received explicit instructions on when and how to interact with the child. The behaviors of both the mother and the child were directly observed and recorded.

METHOD

Subject

The child in this study was a 4-year-old boy, Peter S. He is the third of four children in a middle-class family. Peter had been brought to a university clinic because he was extremely difficult to manage and control. His mother stated she was helpless in dealing with his frequent tantrums and disobedience. Peter often kicked objects or people, removed or tore his clothing, called people rude names, annoyed his younger sister, made a variety of threats, hit himself, and became very angry at the slightest frustration. He demanded attention almost constantly, and seldom cooperated with Mrs. S. In addition, Peter was not toilet trained and did not always speak clearly. Neither of these latter problems was dealt with in the study.

Peter had been evaluated at a clinic for retarded children when he was 3 years old and again when he was 4½. His scores on the Stanford Binet, form L-M, were 72 and 80, respectively. He was described as having borderline intelligence, as being hyperactive, and possibly brain-damaged.

Procedure

The experimenters (Es), observing the mother and child in the home, noted that many of Peter's undesirable behaviors appeared to be maintained by attention from his mother. When Peter behaved objectionably, she would often try to explain why he should not act thus, or she would try to interest him in some new activity by offering toys or food. (This distraction method is often put forth by teachers as a preferred technique for dealing with undesirable behavior. Behavior theory suggests, however, that while distraction may be temporarily effective in dealing with such behaviors, repeated employment of such a procedure may increase the frequency of the unwanted set of responses.) Peter was occasionally punished by the withdrawal of a misused toy or other object, but he was often able to persuade his mother to return the item almost immediately. He was also punished by being placed on a high chair and forced to remain there for short periods. Considerable tantrum behavior usually followed such disciplinary measures and was quite effective in maintaining mother's attention, largely in the form of verbal persuasion or argument.

Prior to the study, the child's difficulties were discussed thoroughly with his mother. She was told that therapy might take several months, was of an experimental nature, and would require her participation. She readily agreed to cooperate.

Treatment consisted of two to three sessions per week, each approximately one hour in length. Peter's mother was instructed to go about her usual activities during these sessions. His younger sister was allowed to be present and to interact with him in her usual way. Peter was allowed to move freely through the main part of the house—the recreation room, laundry room, dinette, kitchen, and living room—because the wide openings between these areas made it possible to observe his activity with a minimum of movement on the Es' part. The Es never responded to Peter or his sister. When the children asked questions about them or spoke to them, they were told by the mother to "leave them alone; they are doing their work."

Initial observations showed that the following responses made up a large portion of Peter's repertory of undesirable behavior: (1) biting his shirt or arm, (2) sticking out his tongue, (3) kicking or hitting himself, others, or objects, (4) calling someone or something a derogatory name, (5) removing or threatening to remove his clothing, (6) saying "No!" loudly and vigorously, (7) threatening to damage objects or persons, (8) throwing objects, and (9) pushing his sister. These nine responses were collectively termed "Objectionable behavior" (O behavior), and their frequency of occurrence was measured by recording, for each successive ten-second interval, whether or not an O behavior occurred. This same method was used to obtain a record of the frequency of all verbalizations Peter directed to his mother and of the frequency of her verbalizations to him.

In order to assess interobserver reliability, two Es were employed as observers on eight occasions and three Es on one occasion. Since it was sometimes possible for an observer to detect when another observer had scored a response, the obtained reliability scores may be overestimated. For every session of observation each observer obtained total frequency scores for the O behaviors, the child's verbalizations, and the mother's verbalizations. When two observers were employed, proportion of agreement, in any one of these three classes of behavior, was calculated by dividing the smaller score by the larger. When three observers were employed, the three proportions for a class of behavior were averaged to obtain mean proportion of agreement. Agreement on O behaviors ranged from 0.70 to 1.00, with a mean of 0.88. Agreement on mother's verbalizations to Peter ranged from 0.82 to 0.98, with a mean of 0.94. Agreement on Peter's verbalizations to his mother ranged from 0.90 to 0.99, with a mean of 0.96.

Treatment was divided into five stages: the first baseline period, the first experimental period, the second baseline period, the second experimental period, and a follow-up period.

First Baseline Period. During this period Peter and his mother interacted in their usual way. Their behaviors were recorded by the *E*s, and after some 16 sessions, when an adequate estimate of the pretreatment rate of O behavior had been obtained, the next stage was begun.

First Experimental Period. Prior to the beginning of this period, the mother was informed of the nine objectionable behaviors which would be treated. She was shown three gestural signals which indicated how she was to behave toward Peter. Signal A meant she was to tell Peter to stop whatever O behavior he was emitting. Signal B indicated she was immediately to place Peter in his room and lock the door. When signal C was presented, she was to give him attention, praise, and affectionate physical contact. Thus, every time Peter emitted an O behavior, Mrs. S. was either signaled to tell him to stop or to put him in his room. On the first occurrence of a particular O behavior during the experimental session, Mrs. S. was merely signaled to tell Peter to stop, but if he repeated the same response at any subsequent time during that session, she was signaled to place him in his room. (This isolation period may be viewed as a period of time out from stimuli associated with positive reinforcement; see Ferster and Appel, 1961.) Occasionally, when *E* noticed that Peter was playing in a particularly desirable way, signal C was given and his mother responded to him with attention and approval. Mrs. S. was asked to restrict the application of these new behavioral contingencies to the experimental hour. She was told to behave in her usual way at all other times.

The period of Peter's isolation was not counted as part of the experimental hour, so each session consisted of one hour of observation in the main living area of the house. When placed in his room, Peter was required to remain there a minimum of five minutes. In addition, he had to be quiet for a short period before he was allowed to come out (a technique employed by Wolf et al. 1964). Since all objects likely to serve as playthings had been previously removed from the room, he had little opportunity to amuse himself. Neither Mrs. S. nor Peter's sister interacted with him during time out. On two occasions, however, it was necessary to deviate from this procedure. These deviations occurred when Peter broke windows in his room and called out that he had cut himself. The first time Mrs. S. entered his room, swept up the glass, reprimanded him for breaking the window, noted the (minor) nature of his injury and left. The second time she bandanged a small cut and left immediately. Peter broke a window on one other occasion but since no injury was apparent, the act was ignored.

Second Baseline Period. When, after six experimental sessions, the frequency of O behaviors appeared stable, contingencies were returned to those of the earlier baseline period. Mrs. S. was told to interact with Peter just as she had during previous (nonexperimental) observation sessions. This second baseline period consisted of fourteen sessions.

Second Experimental Period. After the second baseline period, the experimental procedure was reintroduced and continued for six sessions. Contingencies were identical to those of the first experimental period except that special attention for desirable play was excluded, save one accidental instance.

Follow-Up. For twenty-four days after the second experimental period there was no contact between the Es and the S. family. Mrs. S. was given complete freedom to use any techniques with Peter that she felt were warranted, including time out, but she was given no specific instructions. After this twenty-four-day interval (whose length was limited by the impending departure of one E) a three-session, posttreatment check was made to determine whether the improvements effected during treatment were still evident. These one-hour follow-up sessions were comparable to earlier baseline periods in that Mrs. S. was instructed to behave in her usual manner toward Peter.

RESULTS AND DISCUSSION

The frequency of Peter's O behaviors in each treatment condition is shown in Fig. 1. Asterisks mark sessions in which observer reliability was assessed. These nine reliability sessions are plotted in terms of the mean of the frequencies obtained by the different observers. During the first baseline period, the rate of O behavior varied between 18 and 113 per session. A sharp decrease occurred in the first experimental period; the rate ranged from one to eight per session. In the course of this period, Peter was isolated a total of four times, twice in session 17, once in session 18, and again in session 22. He received special

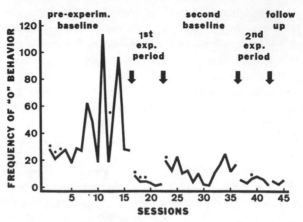

Fig. 1. *Number of 10-second intervals, per 1-hour session, in which O behavior occurred. Asterisks indicate sessions in which reliability was tested.*

attention twice in session 17, six times in session 18, and once each in sessions 20 and 21.

During the second baseline period, the rate of O behaviors varied between 2 and 24 per session. Although this was an increase over the previous experimental period, the frequency of response did not match that of the first baseline period. This failure to return to earlier levels may have occurred for several reasons. For example, midway through the second baseline, Mrs. S. reported considerable difficulty in responding to Peter as she had during the first baseline period. She stated she felt more "sure of herself" and could not remember how she had previously behaved toward her son. It was apparent that Mrs. S. now gave Peter firm commands when she wanted him to do something and did not give in after denying him a request. The *E*s also noted that Peter was receiving more affection from his mother. This increased affection, however, seemed to be due to a change in Peter's behavior rather than his mother's, since Peter had recently begun to approach her with affectionate overtures.

The rate of O behaviors in the second experimental period was comparable to that of the first experimental period, from two to eight per session. Special attention was (accidentally) given once in session 38.

Data obtained during the follow-up period show that Peter's O behaviors remained low in rate after the passage of a twenty-four-day interval. Mrs. S.

reported that Peter was well behaved and much less demanding than he had previously been. She stated that she had been using the time-out procedure approximately once a week. (It was the E's impression that not only the quantity but also the quality, i.e., topography, of O behaviors had changed. As early as the second baseline period it had been observed that O behaviors frequently lacked components which had been present earlier, such as facial expressions, voice qualities, and vigor of movement that typically constitute "angry" behavior.) Thus, it would appear that not only were the treatment effects maintained in the absence of the Es and the experimental procedures, but that they had generalized from the treatment hour to the remaining hours of the day. These developments were being maintained by the use of occasional isolation (contingent, of course, on the occurrence of an objectionable behavior) and other alterations in the mother's behavior.

Evidence that Mrs. S.'s behavior toward her child did change during the course of treatment is presented in Fig. 2, which shows the verbal interaction between Peter and his mother. It can be seen by comparing Figs. 1 and 2 that the frequency of O behavior and the frequency of the mother's verbalizations to Peter sometimes covaried. A positive correlation is particularly evident during the second baseline period, and a negative correlation during the follow-up. The correlation between O behavior and mother verbalization was determined for each of the five stages of the experiment. During the first and second

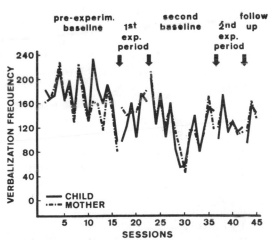

Fig. 2. Number of 10-second intervals, per 1-hour session, in which Peter spoke to his mother or the mother spoke to Peter.

baseline periods the correlations were 0.17 and 0.47, respectively, while for the experimental and follow-up periods they were −0.41, −0.20, and −0.71 in that order. None of these correlations differ significantly from zero. Combining these figures into nontreatment (baseline periods) and treatment (experimental and follow-up periods) yields correlations of 0.39 for the former and −0.41 for the latter. These coefficients were found to be significantly different from one another ($z = 2.48$, $p = 0.007$). This finding may indicate that Mrs. S., when left to her usual way of interbehaving with Peter, attended to (and thus maintained through social reinforcement) his undesirable behaviors while ignoring (extinguishing) desirable (non-O) responses. A number of studies (Allen et al., 1964; Harris et al., 1964; Hart et al., 1964; Wahler et al., 1965) have demonstrated that social reinforcement in the form of adult attention can influence the behavior of the young child. It is interesting to note that Mrs. S.'s proclivity to respond to Peter's O behaviors was reversed during the two experimental periods and thereafter.

Besides showing a relationship between the mother's verbalizations and Peter's O behaviors, a comparison of Figs. 1 and 2 also shows that the time-out procedure operated in a selective manner. Even though the isolation technique reduced the rate of undesirable responses, other classes of behavior such as verbalizations were not affected. This is evidenced by the fact that Peter's verbalization rate during the combined treatment periods did not differ significantly from his rate during nontreatment periods ($F = 2.24$; $df = 1$, 43; $0.25 > p > 0.10$).

The results of this study show that it is possible to treat behavioral problems in the home with the parent as a therapeutic agent. Home treatment may, in some cases, be more effective than treatment in the clinic, particularly when the undesirable responses have a low probability of occurrence in settings other than the home. Since it is widely held that many of a child's problems originate in the home environment, direct modification of this environment (including the behavior of other family members) may arrest the difficulty at its source. One limitation of this type of study, however, is the requirement of a cooperative parent. If this requirement can be met, the use of the parent as therapist can not only free the professional for other duties, but the parent, in learning to use techniques of behavioral control, may become generally more skillful in dealing with the responses of the developing child and more capable in handling any future difficulties that may occur.

REFERENCES

Allen, K. E., Hart, B. M., Buell, J. S., Harris, F. R., and Wolf, M. M., "Effects of Social Reinforcement on Isolate Behavior of a Nursery School Child," *Child Develp.* 35:511-518, 1964.

Bijou, S. W., and Sloane, N. H., "Therapeutic Techniques with Children," in Pennington, L. A., and Berg, I. A. (Eds.), *An Introduction to Clinical Psychology* (ed. 3), New York, Ronald, 1966.

Ferster, C. B., and Appel, J. B., "Punishment of S^Δ Responding in Matching to Sample by Time-Out from Positive Reinforcement," *J. Exp. Anal. Behav.* 4:45-56, 1961.

Harris, F. R., Johnston, M. K., Kelley, C. S., and Wolf, M. M., "Effects of Positive Social Reinforcement on Regressed Crawling of a Nursery School Child," *J. Educ. Psychol.* 55:35-41, 1964.

Hart, B. M., Allen, K. E., Buell, J. S., Harris, F. R., and Wolf, M. M., "Effects of Social Reinforcement on Operant Crying," *J. Exp. Child Psychol.* 1:145-153, 1964.

Wahler, R. G., Winkel, G. H., Peterson, R. F., and Morrison, D. C., "Mothers as Behavior Therapists for Their Own Children," *Behav. Res. Ther.* 3:113-124, 1965.

Wolf, M., Risley, T., and Mees, H., "Application of Operant Conditioning Procedures to the Behaviour Problems of an Autistic Child," *Behav. Res. Ther.* 1:305-312, 1964.

15

Techniques for Working with
Disorganized Low Socioeconomic Families

SALVADOR MINUCHIN
BRAULIO MONTALVO

Certain modifications in family therapy and in therapeutic style have shown themselves to be useful for dealing with disorganized families from the low socioeconomic population.[1] Elsewhere [2] we have described some of the modifications in therapeutic technique that we believe are warranted by obstacles to interpersonal problem solving such as the faulty mechanisms regulating communication and the undifferentiated cognitive style. This paper will focus on ways of using modifications in family structure to help family members increase their differentiation of affect and will touch on some difficulties inherent in working with this population.

Some of the structural features of these families must first be described. Disorganized families from the low socioeconomic population fluctuate between moments when members appear in relatively disconnected subsystems and other moments when these subsystems swiftly lose their boundaries and members mesh

Reprinted with permission of authors and publisher from *American Journal of Orthopsychiatry* 37:880-887, 1967.

intensely into an undifferentiated whole. Moreover, a marked discontinuity of behavior among individual family members is evoked by different subgroupings. In these families, personality features appear to be either more sharply inhibited or more sharply facilitated by such changes than is the case in more stable, differentiated families regardless of their socioeconomic position. This particular phenomenon evoked our interest in the therapeutic potential of intentional variations of subgroup composition.

Many workers in the field use and even vary subgroupings, but usually for the purpose of family diagnosis or as an incidental aspect of a therapy that centers largely on keeping the whole family together. Consistency in the composition of the family group is generally considered essential if family participants are to make explicit the hidden structural clashes that express family pathology. However, as an implied general model for working with families, we think these views may need modification in the light of our experience. For the families we have been describing, the therapist's accommodation to self-contained subsystems and the behavioral discontinuities they produce can enhance, rather than deter, the reintegration of family members into a more differentiated whole.

The active manipulation of family subgroups in their relation to the whole group seems to us an effective therapeutic strategy to sharpen affective experience. The traditional therapeutic emphasis is predicated on the reclaiming of "repressed" feelings, on the patient's own ability to define affect and to dislodge it from the totality of experience. This emphasis was developed for a patient population with a more differentiated psychological inner organization, but for the families discussed here, *therapy* must attempt to dislodge affect from amorphous experience and to modulate and expand the range of emotional events. Active alterations in the composition of groupings are such vivid and unescapable events that they facilitate sharper experiencing; the reorganization of contexts fosters the emergence and dislodgment of affect, as the examples below may show.

CHANGING GROUP COMPOSITION

The Parrington family is composed of the mother, her paramour, and eight children, the oldest 17. The children cluster into two age groupings: three adolescent girls from 13 to 17; five smaller children between 2 and 8 years old. Mrs. Parrington is a heavyset, bright Negro woman in her late thirties.

After several sessions with the total group, it became clear that two different dynamic centers prevailed in this family. One revolved around the three older daughters' need for autonomy, the other around nurturance and guidance needs. Mother was better able to deal with the younger group, by which her control was not challenged, than with the increasing need for autonomy and independence in her older daughters.

At first we divided the family along its own gross outlines, holding sessions alternately with the mother and the older girls and with the mother and the younger children, and later on, sessions with the whole family. Interspersed sessions of couple therapy were also included to begin assimilating the father of the youngest child, who was restricted by Mrs. Parrington to the role of peripheral male with only narrow parenting functions toward the rest of the children.

In working with the mother and adolescent daughters, the therapists found themselves in the midst of constant power interactions. The daughters would challenge their mother's authority and be repeatedly crushed under her capacity to outshout and intimidate them. For several sessions it was impossible to disentangle any thematic material beyond loud claims and counterclaims as to who was "right." Interactions among the siblings could never develop very far; the mother would instantly become embroiled with the daughters, automatically triggered into authoritarian behavior. The rigidity and pervasiveness of this operation robbed the co-therapists of freedom for therapeutic maneuvering. Therefore, it became imperative for the therapists to completely reorganize the situation, to stop this automatic triggering of impulsive reactions. So one therapist engaged the three daughters in sibling therapy, seeing them alone, while the mother joined the other therapist behind a one-way mirror for coobservational therapy.

During the first session with the three girls, the two oldest, Shirley and Maria, engaged in an argument as to who had started most of the beatings the week before. After a variety of escalating attacks and counterattacks consisting largely of assertions as to who was more stupid, Shirley said despairingly, "I wish you could learn to beat me back so I don't always wind up beating you so bad." The therapist seized this fleeting occurrence of a hazily expressed but different affect and made it a central issue. He froze the interaction by dramatically showing his surprise at Shirley's "protection" of her sister, and then led the girls to explore among themselves for other occasions in which "you show concern for your sister."

In this family, as in many others in this population, the language of aggression had covered the experience and the language of concern. The new issue fostered reorganization of several inner and outer events (memories and feelings about past incidents). The word concern framed different perceptions; the girls, and the mother behind the mirror, began to detect some positive affect in what had formerly seemed only familiar incidents of power interactions. This snatching and opening of a transitory affective nuance is crucial to the dislodging of affect in our families.

Though the incorporation of the word concern into the communication system was tenuous at the beginning, it established a frame of reference for later exploration of the confusions between tenderness and being a sucker which plagued the family. This active pursuit of strategic moments to introduce more subtle evaluative language is essential for any exploration of new affective dimensions.

The emergence among the siblings of the new affective cluster—concern—hinged on fundamental compositional moves. Had the mother been with the girls, the transaction between Shirley and Maria would have been short-circuited long before the appearance of this undelineated affect. The sister-to-sister sequence would have been quickly transformed into the usual transactions of control from mother to daughters.

The significance of compositional moves is also shown by the interaction between the mother and Maria about the girl's menstruation. Through a number of sessions the mother chastised and shamed Maria about her dirtiness and smelliness. Maria doesn't use sanitary napkins, but during her menstruations wears cotton and two or three pairs of underpants. The exploration of the why's and how's of this particular problem of Maria's continues to be submerged by her mother's attack upon her passive rebellion. The automatic mother-to-daughter conflict blocks any opportunity for examining Maria's own relationship to her menstruation. It may be that explorations leading to Maria's phobic fear of touching her genitals can be accomplished only in the compositional context of an individual interview and later in a sibling subgroup.

CO-OBSERVATION

Some general goals for the therapy of adults by the use of the one-way mirror warrant explication. This work entails the shifting of observational sets. The grown-ups in these families, especially the mothers, respond without "hesitation" and usually in a controlling fashion to their children; they overfocus on their children's negative behavior. When we put a mother behind the one-way mirror, we initially aim at reorienting her observations away from her offspring and toward the behavior of the therapist in the room with them. We consider this an essential intermediate experience, engineered to permit certain changes in affective thresholds—changes that seem necessary before a mother can concentrate either on learning to identify what behaviors in her children are blocked by her presence or on tackling the need to change her unrewarding patterns of relating to them. The therapist working with a mother in the observation room helps her focus initially on his cotherapist's operations with her children. She experiences a certain kinship between herself and the therapist with the children because he tends "to become like me."

A mother's sense of parity with the adult in the room with her children occurs almost inevitably because therapists as well as mothers fall prey to children's systems and to their capacity to organize adults into authoritarian or help-less positions. The experience of the mother behind the one-way mirror increases her self-esteem, after which sufficient relaxation and readiness usually develop that eventually her attention can focus on events among her children that express interactions other than anger, power, rebelliousness, and the like. She is moni-tored in this process by the co-therapist next to her, who by design treats her more as a peer or co-observer than as a patient. At first only an observer, she seems gradually to become capable of reflecting on and then analyzing the previously undiscriminated events in the other room.

At this point some tentative generalizations are in order concerning the advantages of a therapeutic model that centers on active use of compositional ploys, on dislodging affect, and on reliance upon observation more than introspection:

1. The therapy that uses varying subsystems seems to have qualities that correspond with these families' capacities for experience. Small subgroupings present interpersonal stimuli through a narrower interpersonal field, which is more manageable for our family members, who have limited capabilities in encompassing a field and in sustaining attention.

2. Smaller groups can buffer somewhat the impulsive nature of the responses of individuals in them, that is, the lack of hesitation and reflection that is usually elicited when they are impinged upon by multiple stimuli.

3. The group changes enhance the possibility that discrete rather than diffuse affects will be the prevailing experience. Changes in the composition of sub-groups are very noticeable interpersonal events (member inclusion or exclusion). They create more distinct affective reactions, improving possibilities for detecting the presence or absence of emotional response (as in the interchange of the Parrington sisters, when the absence of the mother made it possible for the girls to express a new affect which the therapist could snatch at and use). These group changes directly challenge the global and undifferentiated nature of the family's usual observations of self and others, providing grounds for training their undeveloped concepts of interpersonal causality.

4. The active manipulation of composition, the removal of the enactors of roles, exerts a direct pull on one of the most prominent mechanisms handicapping family members—externalization. Their tenacious reliance on the behavior of others as a projective target and as a means for organizing their own behavior is powerfully tested. Members cannot anchor their attention on the people whose roles and cues they usually rely on; they are compelled to consider alternative responses toward the others who are actually present.

The need for structuring stimuli in ways that will facilitate differentiated response runs through all the above considerations and facilitates work with families characterized by amorphous cognitive-affective systems. These considerations are also relevant for modifications of therapeutic styles.

THERAPEUTIC STYLES

The well-timed exaggeration or diminution of the therapist's own affective components is essential for promoting cognitive-affective reorganization and expansion, for dislodging affects, and for allowing the initial articulation of new interaffective patterns.

The Pedroso family presents an example of the latter. For this Puerto Rican family, composed of mother, father, and two sons, 13 and 10, we initiated therapy with the total group. During a session in the middle phase of therapy the younger child, Angel, teased the father about the way in which he combed his hair. The teasing insinuated that the father was homosexual. Soon the whole family, including the mother, was sharing in this teasing. The father was caught in the center of a family teasing alliance, but the teasing was presented as a joke, a mood that masked and curtailed in this system the actualization of other affects. The father felt confused and could only join in the joke, thus derogating himself.

At this point, the therapist could have intervened in different ways. He could have assumed an intrapsychic emphasis and dealt with the latent homosexuality of the father or with the unconscious homosexual tinge between father and son. He chose, however, to respond with intense and visible indignation. He got up from his chair and faced the father with raised arms, recruiting his attention, then turned to the mother and attacked her for joining with the children in this derogation of her husband, explaining that by doing so she was increasing the prevailing disrespect for both their executive positions as parents.

Two sessions later, the father joined the therapist, actually producing a response of indignation when a similar incident occurred. Following the father's indignant response, a frail complementary response of shame became available to the child. Shame as a new transactional product apparently emerged from circumstances in which the therapist's affective participation served as a model. A variety of sessions followed, each reinforcing the father's new stance. He increasingly defended his hitherto unclaimed rights as male and father of the family, thereby permitting moves to other organizational formats. Sessions between the father and sons with the mother behind the one-way mirror could have been employed later, with the father and sons addressing themselves even more specifically to their problems of learning respect for each other. The mother's task could have been focused on learning to detect those moments when her husband, as father, needed her help, checking her tendency to enter as the son's assistant in ridicule.

Since the presentation of this single incident does not do justice to the complexity of the therapeutic process, we will emphasize some of the areas of difficulties it illustrates that require special adaptation in therapeutic style. The Pedroso family incident exemplifies accommodation [3] in communication—a closing of the gap between the usual style of the therapist in cognition and communication and the style of the patient families in those same areas. The therapist might have said in words alone that he felt the father was derogating himself. He sensed, however, that if he used only verbal statements, his intervention would pass unnoticed by all but the most verbal members of the family. The language of movement was attended to by everyone.

Such operations are essential in the work with this population. Families that experience chronic frustration and impotence and fail to see how they can affect their own environment either remain immobile in situations in which directed differentiated movement is indicated or else respond by fast, random activity that serves only as a crude way of alleviating stress. They need from the therapist examples of well-timed responses that can use the same motoric modality in differentiated fashion in pursuit of a focus instead of in active but purposeless relatedness. In this incident, the therapist employed an almost physical territorial language, grounding his message in the more primitive cognitive and communicational systems through which our families communicate among themselves. His indignation was "enacted," [4] visible, difficult to ignore. It demanded little abstraction, inference, or introspection from the family, remaining close to the terms of the actual occurrence and aiming at facilitating the eventual retrieving of what had been vividly seen.

Generally, when we gear ourselves to the enactive modality in communicating with our families, avenues of direct communication that have previously been unavailable seem to become accessible. This is especially relevant in the initial periods of therapy for actualizing working grounds in which to intervene usefully. If instead of asking Mr. Pedroso, "Why does your son talk to you with disrespect?" the therapist challenges, "Can you help your child talk to you with respect?" the family appears far more capable of presenting and exploring interpersonal conflicts. Using this kind of stimulation toward the actual enactment of problems does not mean that therapists dismiss the task of assisting family members to avoid their tendency to constant action. It simply means that the participants are moved gradually, rather than abruptly, to more representational and symbolic levels.

Failure to employ such accommodations to the family's style of communication can lead to an unmanageable degree of suction. [6] The therapist may accept working in a field of noise. He may find himself having to talk across or around other people who are talking, thereby rewarding a basic feature in the family system—disordered communication—that accounts for much of its handicap in resolving interpersonal problems. In his frustrated attempts to communicate, he may also relate only with those members of the family who are likely to use his own logical language. The result is that the most disruptive children—the ones who cannot use verbal messages as a way of establishing their presence—disappear from the areas of interchange. They are left to establish their presence through further disruptive interaction.

To diminish the effects of suction and enhance the possibilities of accommodation, the training of therapists requires sensitizing them to these families' communicational styles and structural pull.

In the Pedroso family the therapist could have been recruited into the family's style of communication had he smiled at the moment when the family began ridiculing the father. He also could have been caught up in the family structure, protecting its current homeostasis, had he centered on the mother only instead of carefully spreading his response—first making Mr. Pedroso more central and insuring his attention and then confronting his wife. His spread attentuated the effects of his assuming the role of protector of the father, lessening the danger of reinforcing the man's weak position in the family.

To compensate for the effects of suction, we rely primarily on the therapist's experience in working with these families: he becomes alert to the manifold ways in which he may be pulled, and if his own anticipatory processes cannot rescue him from suction, he can rely on the co-therapist. Co-therapists can learn specific ways of buffering the effects of suction. Whenever one therapist is interacting directly with the family, the other can observe both the family and the co-therapist rather than the family alone, watching specifically for the way in which the family organizes his partner into behaving along lines that do not permit family change. When his turn to be active arrives, his partner can in turn engage himself in recovering distance and looking anew at the system.

Even when therapists are very skilled in these maneuvers, there are many instances of suction, but they can be used to the family's advantage. In some cases a supervisor systematically observers behind the one-way mirror and can enter the therapy room in order to disentangle the therapists from unwitting adaptations to negative family patterns. With some of the disorganized families this third therapist becomes an integral part of the therapeutic model. He enters free of the adjustments to prevailing group dynamics that are organizing the two therapists in the session, and he shares with the group his observations from behind the mirror. His particular advantage is that he is not involved in the thematic thread being pursued at the moment; his comments center of necessity on the overall structure and help free the therapists from entrapments in the family system. The surprise concomitant on his entrance and the "magic" and abrupt quality of his presence usually allow the family to fix and sustain special attention on his message. This enhances the likelihood that family members will remember the significance of the event as well as the implied interpersonal lesson he brings. For the therapists in the room, it involves not only a recovery of maneuverability but often the possibility of reorienting their task to direct immediate tensions toward family change. Because the third observer is not caught in the structure, he can often sense more clearly the necessary refashioning of the therapists' responses, and this may also yield therapeutic tension.

SUMMARY

Disorganized families from the low socioeconomic population require adaptations of traditional family therapy and therapeutic style that take into account their specific characteristics of communication, cognition, and ways of experiencing affect. Rather than treating the members of one family as a single unit, we have found it effective to treat various subgroupings by first working with the family's natural subgroupings, then changing the subgroupings as the situation may require and actively manipulating them in relation to the whole family group. Such an approach helps them experience their feelings more clearly.

Both changing the composition of the family subgroups and shifting observational sets help family members differentiate their global responses, fostering valuable transitions from observation to reflection which help them begin to see how they contribute to family disorganization and change their ways of behaving.

It is conceivable that similar adaptations may well apply to all disorganized families, not only to those of low socioeconomic position, and further study of that possibility seems warranted.

NOTES AND REFERENCES

1. The population we are considering is not homogeneous. For the present, our generalizations are made with the acknowledgment that they cannot possibly apply to all the people who fall into this socioeconomic group. Our attempt at preliminary classification is expanded in a book by the co-authors and others—*Families of the Slums: An Explanation of Their Structure and Treatment,* New York, Basic Books, 1967.
2. Minuchin, S., and Montalvo, B., "An Approach for Diagnosis of the Low Socioeconomic Family," *Psychiatric Research Report 20,* American Psychiatric Association, February, 1966.
3. Accommodation refers to those situations in which the therapist is generally in command of his moves, choosing roles and styles of communication congruent with those of the family to alter its homeostasis.

4. We have found Bruner's [5] early classification of three modes of coding and processing experience (enactive, iconic, and symbolic) very useful for the therapist in his attempts to couch his messages in ways that will be most accessible for family members.

5. Bruner, J. S., "The Course of Cognitive Growth," *Amer. Psychol.* 19:1-15, 1964.

6. Suction refers to those situations in which the therapist's choice of roles is restricted. He is compelled to behave in ways that he would not choose. This can occur when the therapist's behavior is being shaped by the family to protect its equilibrium. Suction is not necessarily countertransference. Different therapists come to behave in remarkably similar roles despite their different childhood histories and internal reactions.

16

Family Therapy

Family therapy studies of the past dozen years, as a recent review establishes,[1] have predominantly reflected the psychoanalytic viewpoint, even though striking departures from psychoanalytic theory and technique have been made by family therapists. For the most part, writers on technique [2-7] have essentially adhered to the view that to promote beneficial change in patients the therapist must formulate and communicate insights and work through unconscious resistances. Even such departures from psychoanalytic technique as those described by Satir [8] and Minuchin [9] recently seem to this writer fundamentally insight centered.

Among major contributors to family therapy theory and practice today, only Haley [10] has offered a clear alternative to the "insight-centered model," although he is joined to an extent by Jackson [11] and Brodey,[12] using somewhat different approaches. Haley maintains that the therapist secures beneficial change when he enforces a dominant *position* vis-à-vis patient, that is, to the extent that he

Reprinted with permission of author and publisher from *Archives of General Psychiatry* 16:71-79, 1967.

controls the relationship, decides what its goals shall be, and parries the patient's attempts to undermine his control. The therapist is skillful at setting up paradoxical situations in which the patient thinks he can "win" against the therapist, but loses. In the losing, the patient comes to accept the therapist's control and direction and changes accordingly.

As a result of experience in family therapy over the past five years, I am convinced that beneficial change, as Haley suggests, is a creative outcome of a struggle for control between the therapist and family members, but I believe that the skillful setting up of paradoxical situations is not sufficient as an explanation of change in family therapy, although it does provide a useful basis to consider what does bring about change. This paper will describe a technique which uses sources of therapeutic leverage believed unique to family therapy, although applications are possible in marital and, to a lesser extent, in group therapy. The technique arises specifically from the fact that family therapy is the transaction of a therapist with at least two or more persons who have had an extensive history of relating to one another.

Preliminary descriptions of technique and theoretical framework have been given elsewhere.[13, 14] A cornerstone of the technique is a definition of family therapy as follows: *it is the technique that explores and attempts to shift the balance of pathogenic relating among family members so that new forms of relating become possible.* This definition presumes Jackson's notion [15] that the family is a homeostatic system in which change in one part is likely to effect changes in other parts.

Another cornerstone of the technique that will be described in this paper is the fact that the expression of conflict in family therapy is like that in no other form of therapy, and that conflict generates the energy required to shift fixed patterns of relating among family members. The therapist must be an expert in searching out the main issues in the family, in keeping these issues in focus, and in exploring the sources and intensity of disagreement. Only in family therapy do patients come with an established history of conflict and with well-developed means for expressing or disguising it.

In the more comprehensive of the preliminary papers,[14] I described go-between process in family therapy in four variations rather commonly encountered. In two of the variations the initiative in conducting go-between process rests with the therapist. In the other two variations the initiative resides with the family members, that is, they conduct go-between process "against" the therapist as a means to forestall his attempts to control and direct the treatment. In this paper I hope to take up in much greater detail the steps in the go-between process and describe the theoretical structure in which the process is grounded.

GO-BETWEEN PROCESS:
ITS TERMS AND SOME DIMENSIONS

In the sections to follow terms and some dimensions of go-between process will be elaborated (1) from the point of view of the therapists vis-à-vis family, (2) in the context of the family's defensive tactics, and (3) in the context of phases of treatment, specifically onset and termination.

The Viewpoint of Therapist Vis-à-Vis Family

The therapist conducts go-between process when:

Term 1. (a) He probes issues in the family, establishes the existence of conflict by eliciting expressions of disagreement, and encourages the open expression of disagreement. (b) He exposes and otherwise resists the family's efforts to deny or disguise disagreement. (c) He encourages the expression of recent or current disagreement rather than rehashes of old. (d) He encourages expression of conflict between members who are *present* rather than absent from the treatment session.

Term 1 sets conditions for the therapist's encouragement of expression of conflict. Families differ greatly in the extent to which they will express it: some appear only too eager to do so; others are most reluctant. The therapist must be as wary of the first type of these families as the second, for the first type often generates a lot of superficial noisy disagreement and frequent deeper sources of disagreement are disguised. In these families members will engage in a great deal of mutual recrimination—bitterness, anger, and hostility are openly expressed. But the process might be labeled a pseudohostility. Wynne [16] has used this term and means by it a shared defense against recognizing feelings of tenderness, affection, or sexual attraction, but the writer uses it here to mean the expression of hostility which serves as a mask for a more pervasive, deeper-lying hostility. A pseudohostility may be directed by one family member against another toward whom the first does not really feel the greatest animosity, but whom he finds a convenient scapegoat.

A second and contrasting group of families will deny disagreements and even develop elaborate means for disguising them. Some of these families will appear genuinely puzzled when the therapist calls attention to sources of conflict. Family members appear confused, pained, even deeply hurt if the therapist persists in pointing out conflict. The members pride themselves on their rational approach to the solution of family problems, on their ability to find answers acceptable to all. Even from themselves they skillfully hide the fact that they simply have failed to deal with major problem areas—have swept them under the rug, as it were.

Because memory for detail is likely to be still fresh and emotions running high, the therapist conducting go-between process encourages families to talk about recent conflict as opposed to old. Sometimes therapists will encounter families whose members prefer to talk about their past problems, but this may be a skillful gambit to introduce doubt and uncertainty into the treatment situation—i.e., members have difficulty recalling precisely what was said, who was present, and so on. The therapist will have to judge how much of this recollection to allow, and in general will tend to discourage its expression.

Therapists will also encounter family members who prefer to talk about their conflict with a family member, relative, or friend who is not present in the treatment session. Since this process also tends to introduce doubt and uncertainty, the therapist conducting go-between process will in general tend to discourage its expression. Too much control is left in the hands of the member who presents his side of the disagreement. There will be times, to be sure, when the therapist will allow this expression, but only if he thinks it will open up sources of conflict between family members who are present.

The therapist conducts go-between process when:

Term 2. (a) He selects specific disagreements as especially worthy of discussion, rejects others as unworthy, and resists the family's expected efforts to establish its own rules of priority. (b) This selection is part of his move into the role of the go-between. He then seeks to establish his authority in the role and resists the family's expected efforts to displace him.

In a previous paper [14] on the topic it was stated that:

In family therapy the go-between may be very active, intrusive, and confronting or inactive and passive. He may move into the role of go-between by the device of attacking two parties he hopes to make into principals, or he may move into the role by calmly pointing out a difference between two parties. On the other hand, he may become a go-between by refusing to take sides in a dispute that has erupted, or he may become one by presenting a new point of view in a dispute [p. 165].

The point here is that in the role of go-between the therapist is constantly structuring, and directing, the treatment situation.

A case will be presented to illustrate the terms of go-between process, but term 2 in particular. A family was referred for therapy on the basis that a young daughter's poor school performance seemed to have origins in disturbed family living. The family was composed of the daughter, 9 years old, her brother, 13 years old, her 40-year-old mother, and 56-year old father. The family was of Catholic, Irish-German, and upper-lower religious, ethnic, and social status origins. The mother had completed high school, but the father only the fourth grade, and the difference in educational level was a serious source of conflict between them. The father was a steady jobholder who was married previously and had been involved in sexual misconduct with other women in his marriages. He considered his main problem to be his explosive temper and the fact that he could not get his children to be respectful to him. The mother began drinking heavily in her late teens, and referred to herself as an alcoholic up until five years ago, when she gave up drinking and joined Alcoholics Anonymous. There was also evidence of some sexual promiscuity on her part before her marriage to her husband fourteen years ago, but none since.

The mother reported that at times she believed she was losing her mind. She expressed bitterness toward her husband, who she said deserted her for another woman about the time she was pregnant with her now 13-year-old son. She believed the marriage started to deteriorate since that time. She expressed fear of her husband's quick temper, as did the children. Her son openly expressed bitter resentment of his father and hoped that his mother would separate.

A special source of resentment of the father was that his wife had taken their son into their bedroom, avowedly to attend to him more effectively during an illness, and had not moved him out in several months. She asked her husband to sleep in another room and he complied. Another source of the father's resentment was the chaotic condition of the home, although as it turned out he contributed to the chaos by bringing and storing in the house all sorts of odd, useless objects.

The therapist had little difficulty getting family members to verbalize conflict. (This was one of the noisy-type families referred to earlier, which seem only too eager to express their feelings.) But the conflict did not seem to go anywhere for the first few sessions: each member expressed opposition to another in such a way as to put the other in a bad light, and each seemed to know the means to put the other on the defensive. However, in the fourth session there was a break which the therapist was quick to take advantage of, and which will illustrate how the therapist conducting go-between process selects certain types of disagreements as especially worthy of discussion and rejects other types.

A week or so prior to the fourth session the father brought home a bicycle that was given to him by a friend. He told his daughter the bike was hers, that he had bought it from his friend for $10, and that he had had it repaired at an additional cost. His daughter accepted the bike and rode it, but it soon broke down. She took the bike for repair, but it broke down again, and again she returned the bike for repair, threatening the repairman that if he did not fix it properly this time or if he refused to fix it she would start screaming at the top of her voice right there in his shop. The man fixed the bike. But later it broke down again, and the girl decided to give it to her brother. Her brother repaired the bike and rode it for awhile before it again broke down and was put away in storage. In the meantime, the daughter got her mother to promise to buy her a new bike as a Christmas present.

As this incident was related mainly by the daughter to the therapist, it was apparent that it met the criteria of term 1 of go-between process in that disagreement was expressed about how the bike was purchased and who was to use it, all members involved were present and capable of telling their versions, and the incident had occurred recently and was still fresh in the memory. Because these criteria were met and because the incident seemed to epitomize so well the way conflict was handled (or rather mishandled) in the family, the therapist selected it for special attention. (A not insignificant factor influencing his decision was that the incident was one about which the father could talk with some show of control, that is, without such excitement or emotion that he would frighten other family members into quiet submission.)

The therapist specifically moved into the role of go-between by stating that he was puzzled by what actually happened in the bike incident and that in order to clear up the confusion he would ask each member to tell his version of the story. The therapist then acted to establish his *authority* as the go-between by indicating that he would not allow interference in the telling of stories. He was thus introducing an unusual structure for the family: they were not used to letting each talk without frequent interruption, for one thing, and without efforts at intimidation, for another.

First, the fuller details of the daughter's story were elicited. When she came to the point at which she threatened the bike repairman with screaming if he did not agree to fix the bike again, the therapist said he thought she was using a favorite tactic of intimidation of her father's. Then the son was directed to relate his story. (He countersuggested that his father should speak next, but this was disallowed since it was believed by the therapist that it would have helped to subtly undermine the type of procedure he had established.) The son voiced his resentment that the bike had not been given to him originally. He said he knew he would get it eventually because it was bound to break down; his sister would come to him to fix it, and then he would be able to claim at least part ownership. He complained that his father never gave him anything—giving the bike to his sister was just another example of the father's stinginess toward him.

In telling his story, the father stressed his good intentions and expressed resentment that they were doubted. He told how he had bargained skillfully with the original owner of the bike to get it for the lowest price, if possible for nothing. He told how he had taken the bike for renovation to a place he knew would do it for little money. He said he fully supported his daughter when she insisted the bike should be repaired properly by the repairman.

When it came the mother's turn to tell her story, she ruefully stated it was incidents such as this one that sometimes made her doubt her sanity. She said she actually felt relieved and reassured that the therapist had also expressed doubt and uncertainty about what really happened. In the following excerpt from the fourth session the mother relates how her husband and children frequently befuddle her:

THERAPIST: You've said that two or three times—that you were losing your sanity. What do you mean by that?

MOTHER: I told you when I first came here I had questions about my own sanity. When you live under these conditions and you hear it morning, noon, and night, after a while you do question your own sanity. Am I hearing this, or am I imagining it?

THERAPIST: What's the worst part of the whole thing? A lot is going on. A lot of it looks to be kind of harmless.

DAUGHTER (*referring to her brother*): He teases me—with the cat.

THERAPIST: Teasing is teasing. I'm asking your mother.

MOTHER: You mean about bickering back and forth?

THERAPIST: Whatever it is that drives you crazy.

MOTHER: Well, they'll tell me one thing and then there's a twist to the story. You saw it yourself. Each one told a slightly different version. After a while you just can't follow it. All these thoughts get in my head, and I think "Oh, my God, am I imagining this or is this so?" I find that the three of them—my husband, the children—are very much alike in this bit. Like even the interruptions! I don't think you could say I interrupted here today, but they do and it's constant. Nobody shows each other courtesy enough to hear each other out. . . . They all have to get heard, and they all consider their own feelings more important than anybody else's.

This excerpt and the description of the bike incident should show that the therapist as go-between provides the family with a new context in which to express and examine their conflicts. As go-between he acts as the broker in the context—for example, he insures that all parties understand his rules for examining the conflict, and he insures that all parties are fairly dealt with. He aims to fashion a context that is different from the established pathogenic patterns of relating among family members. Temporarily freed by the therapist's action from a vicious repetitive pattern, the family may experience the good feeling of more positive and productive relating and explore the possibility of new means to relate in the future.

In his excellent paper on marriage therapy, Haley [17] notes that the therapist is unavoidably a go-between or broker. He states that the mere presence of the therapist as a third party requires that the spouses deal differently with each other than they have in the past—particularly because the therapist is a third party who is a presumed expert in unraveling the meaning of human interaction. He points out that the marriage therapist may relabel or redefine the activities of the spouses with each other, and he may label the treatment situation as unique in other respects—e.g., as having rules which would not hold in ordinary situations.

The therapist conducts go-between process when:

Term 3. (a) He sides, either by implication or intentionally, with one family member against another in a particular disagreement. (*Siding is unavoidable,* for even if the therapist thinks he is maintaining a strictly neutral or objective position, the family still judges him to be partial. The problem of the therapist is to decide when and with whom to side *intentionally*—i.e., as a therapeutic tactic—and to decide with whom the family *believes* him to be siding.) (b) He may side with or against the entire family unit in a disagreement, as well as with or against single family members.

Haley, in his paper on marriage therapy,[17] notes that a therapist cannot make a neutral statement:

. . . his voice, his expression, the context, or the mere act of choosing a particular statement to inquire about introduces a directiveness into the situation [p. 25]. . . . When the therapist is being directive, coalition patterns are being defined and redefined, and a crucial aspect of this type of therapy is continually changing coalition patterns between therapist and each spouse.

This statement is equally true of family therapy: the therapist's most innocuous-sounding comment will be judged by family members as clear evidence that he favors the "position" of one member against another. Family members will *act* toward the therapist as if he were siding, and even *interpret* him as siding, however, he may choose to deny that such was his intention. (It is also true, to be sure, that therapists are rarely fully aware of all the ways in which they *actually may be siding* with one member against another, and may become defensive when this is *fairly* brought to their attention.)

In my opinion, not only is siding unavoidable in family therapy, it is a legitimate tactic of therapeutic value in shifting the balance of pathogenic relating among family members. *By judicious siding, the therapist can tip the balance in favor of more productive relating, or at least disrupt a chronic pattern of pathogenic relating.* By siding with one family member in a disagreement with another, the therapist throws weight to the position of the former. The effect of the therapist siding *against* all members often is for the members to minimize the extent of the disagreement, but it also moves them to examine more carefully the bases of the disagreement. The effect of the therapist siding *with* all members is often subtly disorganizing, for then they become confused as to what their own position should be vis-à-vis the therapist—in other words, it tends to undermine any stubborn shared family resistance to the therapist's interventions.

It is probably unwise for the therapist to give the message that he consistently sides with one member against others. It is advantageous for him to keep the family guessing as to *whether* he will engage in siding and *what* the tactics of his siding will be. The therapist must retain flexibility in the face of strenuous efforts by the family to get him to side predictably with one member or another, with the result that he becomes, in my opinion, a less effective therapeutic agent.

In the fourth treatment session with the family that has been described here, there were several instances of intentional siding by the therapist. For instance, he engaged in siding when enforcing his rule that family members could not interrupt each other in telling the story of the bike incident, for he did not enforce the rule *with equal vigor* for all members. For example, the therapist tended to halt the attempted interruptions of the father with considerably more vigor than such attempts of other family members, particularly when his attempts were directed against his son. In this the therapist showed an inclination to side against the father. One reason for this type of siding was that it seemed necessary to the therapist to guard against the danger that the father would undermine the therapist's rules of procedure by means of an outburst of temper. A correlated reason was to encourage other family members to speak their feelings more freely, especially the son, who was furious at his father for being continually browbeaten by him. In brief, the therapist was intentionally siding *against* the father and *with* other family members in enforcing his rules of procedure for the exposition of the bike incident.

In the fifth treatment session with the family, there was a good example of the therapist siding first with one member and then another in a disagreement as a therapeutic tactic to tip the balance of pathogenic relating. The father had accused his wife, in a typically inferential manner, of sexual misconduct with other men in the course of her work in Alcoholics Anonymous. The therapist encouraged the father to talk about his feelings of anger and jealousy which he, again characteristically, strenuously denied having. Turning then to the wife, the therapist asked her to respond to her husband's feelings of anger and jealousy based on his suspicions. In confirming the husband's *feelings,* despite his lack of confirmation of actual promiscuity by the wife, the therapist was implicitly siding with the husband against his wife. He was suggesting, in effect, that the husband's feelings were genuine and valid and that the wife was bound to consider and respond to them. The following excerpt from the fifth session is relevant to this point:

THERAPIST: The question is—your husband is showing jealousy.

MOTHER: Right. I've said this from the beginning.

THERAPIST: And you are responding in a funny kind of way. I don't know whether you're encouraging it or discouraging it.

MOTHER: You would have to understand AA. I don't know if you do. But each and every one of us helps each other out in maintaining sobriety.

FATHER: But a man don't help no woman, and the woman don't help no man! A man helps a man, and a woman helps a woman!

THERAPIST: Yes. Your husband is raising the question of men in particular, jealousy of the men. And you are not responding to that. You're putting it in terms of humanity. . . .

MOTHER: I've given in to every whim about jealousy. I've stopped kissing my kids and stopped hugging them.

THERAPIST: But you're still sleeping with your son.

MOTHER: He's in my bedroom, yes. . . .

THERAPIST: Maybe you've stopped kissing him, but you haven't stopped sleeping with him.

FATHER: Her son is not sleeping with her; he's sleeping in a twin bed.

THERAPIST: Are you defending her too now? (*Laughs*) Whose side are you on? I'm not implying anything. . . . This has been something that you brought up here today.

FATHER: That's right.

THERAPIST: You're angry about it.

FATHER: I'm not angry about it.

THERAPIST: You say you're not, and I say you are.

Shortly after this exchange, in which, by encouraging the husband to express his jealousy and by confronting the wife with her evasiveness, the therapist appears to side with the husband, the therapist then turns the tables; he now confronts the husband in such a way as to appear to side with the wife.

THERAPIST: . . . Is that what you're saying to him: "I need companionship? I need somebody?"

MOTHER: I certainly do need somebody. . . .

THERAPIST: "I need my son close to me because I get something from him that I don't get from somebody else." This I think is what your wife seems to say. She says, "I need something too. And whether you're jealous about it—well, that's just too bad. I need those things." That's what she's saying. . . .

FATHER: Well, I understand that, and I want to try my best to give her what she wants!

By siding alternately with the father and then the mother, the therapist believed he shook up their relationship and facilitated open expression of a bitter conflict between them that had been raging for some time but in a rather devious form. In the case of the father, the therapist insisted that he acknowledge his anger and jealousy in the presence of his family. In the case of the mother, the therapist insisted she express her yearning for warmth and emotional closeness. The therapist made it difficult for the parents to employ their usual techniques to avoid confronting each other with their actual feelings and attitudes. He promoted a more direct confrontation than was typical for them in their relationship, i.e., forced them to put aside the usual means both had developed to keep each other at a distance, and opened up the possibility of relating in a new way.

This discussion of siding and the illustrations given should make it quite evident how complex an issue it is in family therapy. Certainly related to it, for example, are the issues of transference and countertransference, although siding is not simply to be explained by either or both of these concepts because as conceived here, it means an *intentional* alignment of the therapist with the position of one family member against another for the purpose of tipping the balance of the relationship between them.

The Family's Defensive Tactics Vis-à-Vis Therapist

Families exhibit a marvelous array of tactics which serves to forestall the therapist in his conduct of go-between process. The therapist must be alert to these tactics and act to circumvent them. Three major defensive tactics may be listed. In the first, family members seek to lead the therapist astray by subtle denials or evasions of his allegations of conflict. For example, the therapist may call attention to an issue between two members on which there seems latent conflict. The members deny the allegation; they say they have never disagreed on the issue. (Technically, they may be telling the truth in the sense that they may never have actually *openly* disagreed on the issue.) The therapist is called on to either hit on some device to split the team, or give up the issue he introduced— an often not insignificant loss of face. As a face-saving device, I sometimes return to the issue introduced when it seems less anxiety provoking. This is a kind of therapeutic one-upmanship in that it defines the fact that the members have formed a coalition against the therapist, informs them of his awareness of the fact, and implies a sympathetic understanding of the needs that caused them to join forces against him.

A second defensive tactic of the family vis-à-vis therapist is encountered when a member assumes the role of spokesman and consistently comments on or explains the meaning of the family to the therapist. This role seems most often assumed in families by the mother, but sometimes it is assumed by the father, and infrequently by one of the children. In effect, the family spokesman is in the role of a go-between and as long as he occupies a go-between role the therapist's capacity to assume it is impaired. Sometimes the therapist will decide early in treatment to prohibit a member from taking the role of family spokesman; sometimes, however, he will temporize and permit the member to be the spokesman in the hope of learning more about the key dynamics of the family.

In either case, it is necessary for the therapist to identify the family spokesman early and restrain or check him at some time in the course of treatment.

A third defensive tactic is encountered when family members act toward the therapist as if he was a particular type of go-between, or when they act toward him as if he were consistently siding with a particular member against others. As an example of this type of tactic, the father in the family whose case has been presented would accuse his wife of some misconduct, then turn to the therapist and ask, "Am I right, or am I wrong?" He addressed the therapist as he might a judge who would decide a case, somewhat rigging his question to get the answer he wanted, which was to be in effect, "Yes, Mr. ——, you are perfectly right."

My practice, as therapist, is to respond to the father in one of three ways: (1) state that I was not a judge and that the purpose of family therapy was not to decide who in the family was right and who wrong; (2) ignore the father's question and change the subject; or (3) not answer the question directly, but turn to the wife and ask her to comment on the husband's accusation. By means of these responses the therapist takes steps to turn aside the father's attempt to cast the therapist in the role of the family judge, a particularly inflexible type of go-between in family therapy. In the third response, in which the therapist asked the wife to comment on her husband's accusation, there was an implicit message given to the effect: "There may be something to your husband's accusation and I would like you to defend yourself." The message could be interpreted as evidence that the therapist was mildly siding with the husband against the wife, but evidence not nearly so strong as that initially desired by the husband in his aim to cast the therapist as the family judge.

Change at Onset and Termination of Family Therapy

Go-between process constitutes, in the writer's opinion, an alternative to the psychoanalytical insight-centered model to explain the beneficial changes that may occur in family therapy. Onset and termination are key phases in relation to the issue of change. At onset, two points at issue between the family and therapist are the questions: "Is there something wrong with us?" and "If there is something wrong, how will you treat us as a family?" The family and therapist may be viewed as opponents on these questions. The therapist begins to conduct go-between process when he explores them with the family for areas of expected disagreement.

Some families, in their eagerness to convince the therapist at the onset that there is nothing wrong with them as units, will actually bring about some improvement. The change need not be perceived as the result of insight but as a function of the "bargaining" transaction between family and therapist on the question, "Is there something wrong with us? The family changes *in order to achieve a change* in the therapist's expected position. The change is calculated to be the least necessary to secure a change in the expected position of the therapist. By means of judicious siding, by taking the role of go-between, or by shifting between these two positions, the therapist hopes to control the bargaining transaction in accordance with his therapeutic goals.

By the tenth therapy session in the case of the family described in this paper, beneficial symptomatic changes had already begun to occur. In the tenth session the mother reported she had begun to clean up the mess in her house and had requested the cooperation of her husband and children in doing so. In this session also the mother reported that she had moved her son back into his own bedroom and that her husband was once again occupying the bed that adjoined hers. It also became evident that her husband had been less verbally abusive to her and her children during the preceding couple of weeks.

The writer suggests that these beneficial changes in the onset phase constituted moves to try to budge the therapist from a position the family members believed he was occupying. The writer believes the mother conceived of the therapy as a means to punish her husband for his misdeeds, and a means to persuade the therapist of the righteousness of her "cause" vis-à-vis her husband. When in the early sessions it became apparent that the therapist was not easily being sold on her viewpoint, she was compelled to introduce a more subtle means of persuasion. She would show the therapist that *she* could change but her husband could not, and thus the lack of a true foundation for the marriage would become even more apparent. It did not quite enter into her calculations that her husband *would* change in relation to (or as a result of) her own change and that his change would also be of a positive nature.

It has been my experience that sometimes dramatic improvement may follow upon *the therapist's notice of intention to terminate treatment because there has been no significant progress.* When the therapist puts the family on such notice he is using go-between process in the sense that he is siding against the family as a whole. He chooses to employ this powerful confrontation because he is convinced that only by means of it can he undercut a powerful family resistance to change.

I have had the privilege of seeing, both in cases of my own and of colleagues, dramatic improvement (even including the clearing up of bizarre symptoms in schizophrenics) following the therapist's notice of intention to terminate. It may be speculated here also that *what has produced the change is actually the family's strenuous effort to prevent change;* that is, a strenuous effort by the family to frustrate the therapist's avowed intention to withdraw from treatment. In confronting the family with his intention to terminate, the therapist conducts go-between process in accordance with term 3 stated in this paper, i.e., siding against the whole family as a means to shake up the system.

SUMMARY

Family therapy is defined in this paper as the treatment that examines and attempts to shift the balance of pathogenic relating among family members so that new forms of relating become possible. Go-between process is described as a technique that may be employed in family therapy to promote the shift of pathogenic relating. This process is grounded in the fact that the unique aspect of family therapy is that the so-called patients have had an extensive history of relating to one another.

The three terms of go-between process as conducted by the therapist are: (1) his definition of issues on which the family is in serious conflict and the expression of that conflict, (2) his taking the role of go-between or broker in conflicts, and (3) his siding with or against the family members in conflicts. As the therapist moves from one step to the next and back again, he exerts a critical leverage on the fixed patterns of relating among family members.

Families display a number of tactics which seem aimed at forestalling the therapist in his conduct of go-between process—in effect, they are a kind of counter go-between process conducted by the family. Three such tactics are: (1) the family denies or is evasive about the therapist's allegation of conflict; (2) with the complicity of other family members, one becomes the family spokesman and thus a kind of go-between who blocks the therapist's access to this critical role; and (3) the family attempts to trap the therapist into becoming an overrigid type of go-between, such as the family judge, or accuses him of siding unfairly with one family member against others.

It is a main hypothesis of this paper that families change in order to forestall the therapist's expected demands for much greater change, or in order to foil his other attempts to control the relationship. Illustrations of such change are given in which the *phase* of treatment seemed also a critical factor, that is, whether treatment was at the onset phase or termination. The notion of change entertained here is believed consonant with Haley's,[10, 17] which was designed to contrast with the insight-centered psychoanalytic model.

REFERENCES

1. Zuk, G. H., and Rubinstein, D.: "A Review of Concepts in the Study and Treatment of Families of Schizophrenics," in Boszormenyi-Nagy, I., and Framo, J. L. (Eds.), *Intensive Family Therapy,* New York, Harper, 1965, pp. 1-31.

2. Ackerman, J. W.: "Family-Focused Therapy of Schizophrenia," in Scher, S. C., and Davis, H. R. (Eds.), *Out-Patient Treatment of Schizophrenia*, New York, Grune & Stratton, 1960, pp. 156-173.
3. Bell, J. E., *Family Group Therapy*, Washington, D.C., Public Health Monograph 64, Department of Health, Education, and Welfare, 1961.
4. Bowen, M., "Family Psychotherapy," *Amer. J. Orthopsychiat.* 31:42-60, 1961.
5. Jackson, D. D., and Weakland, J. H., "Conjoint Family Therapy: Some Considerations on Theory, Technique and Results," *Psychiatry* 24:30-45, 1961.
6. Whitaker, C. A., Felder, R. E., and Warkentin, J., "Countertransference in the Family Treatment of Schizophrenia," in Boszormenyi-Nagy, I., and Framo, J. L. (Eds.), *Intensive Family Therapy*, New York, Harper, 1965, pp. 323-341.
7. Wynne, L. C., "Some Indications and Contraindications for Exploratory Family Therapy," in Boszormenyi-Nagy, I., and Framo, J. L. (Eds.), *Intensive Family Therapy*, New York, Harper, 1965, pp. 289-322.
8. Satir, V., *Conjoint Family Therapy*, Palo Alto, Calif., Science and Behavior Books, 1964.
9. Minuchin, S., "Conflict-Resolution Family Therapy," *Psychiatry* 28:278-286, 1965.
10. Haley, J., *Strategies of Psychotherapy*, New York, Grune & Stratton, 1963.
11. Jackson, D. D., "Aspects of Conjoint Family Therapy," in Zuk, G. H., and Boszormenyi-Nagy, I. (Eds.), *Family Therapy and Disturbed Families*, Palo Alto, Calif., Science and Behavior Books, 1969.
12. Brodey, W. M., "A Cybernetic Approach to Family Therapy," in Zuk, G. H., and Boszormenyi-Nagy, I. (Eds.), *Family Therapy and Disturbed Families*, Palo Alto, Calif., Science and Behavior Books, 1969.
13. Zuk, G. H.: "Preliminary Study of the Go-Between Process in Family Therapy," in *Proceedings of the 73rd Annual Convention of the American Psychological Association*, Washington, D.C., American Psychological Association, 1965, pp. 291-292.
14. Zuk, G. H., "The Go-Between Process in Family Therapy," *Family Process* 5:162-178, 1966.
15. Jackson, D. D., "The Question of Family Homeostasis, *Psychiat. Quart.*, Suppl. 34:79-90, 1957.
16. Wynne, L. C., "The Study of Intrafamilial Alignments and Splits in Exploratory Family Therapy," in Ackerman, N. W., Beatman, F., and Sherman, S. N. (Eds.), *Exploring the Base for Family Therapy*, New York, Family Service Association of America, 1961, pp. 95-115.
17. Haley, J., "Marriage Therapy," *Arch. Gen. Psychiat.* 8:213-234, 1963.

17

Approaches to Family Therapy

The clinicians who began to do family therapy in the early days were largely people who had been trained in the ideology and practice of individual therapy. Whatever their professions, their focus had been upon how to change a person. As they began to discover the new problem of how to change a family, each of them developed a unique approach. Often these therapists' approaches were different because they were innovating on their own and did not know that others were doing family therapy. As a result, a number of schools of family therapy have developed, each of which has its students and followers. New approaches continue to develop as more clinicians take up family therapy in different parts of the country and develop unique ways of working. Comparing different family therapists is difficult because they differ markedly in their techniques of intervening in families. However, as family therapists have gained experience they seem to have developed a shared body of premises about human

Presented at a divisional meeting of the American Psychiatric Association in New York, 1967. Reprinted with permission from *International Journal of Psychiatry* 9:233-242, 1970.

problems and the nature of change despite the fact that they work with families in quite different ways. Some family therapists, particularly those embedded in academic psychiatry or the tight professional organizations of a large city, do not seem to change their views with experience. However, most family therapists have gone through a similar transitional process and share a basic shift in ideas which comes from the experience of working with families. At least one can assume that the shift in ideas comes from exposure to families, since often family therapists shift to a common view even though they have not been exposed to the work of other family therapists. At about the time a family therapist passes his two hundredth family, he usually changes his perspective markedly and finds himself in a different conceptual world from the one in which he was trained. One way to describe this shift in thinking about therapy is to describe where a family therapist begins and where he often ends. Contrasting the premises of a beginning family therapist with those of a therapist who has had many years of family experience can help clarify what is new in the family therapy field.

Method versus Orientation

The beginning family therapist tends to see family therapy as a method of treatment—one more procedure in a therapist's armentarium. As he gains experience, the therapist begins to view family therapy not as a method but as a new orientation to the arena of human problems. This conceptual difference has practical results. For example, when asked "What are the indications and contraindications for family therapy?" the beginning family therapist will attempt to answer the question. The more experienced family therapist will appear puzzled since he finds himself defining any kind of therapy as a way of intervening in a family. Having shifted his unit of diagnosis and treatment from the single person to the processes between people, he defines psychopathology as a relationship problem. He cannot say that this person should receive individual therapy and that person family therapy because he views individual therapy as one way of intervening in a family. The therapist who treats a wife may be dealing with the woman's fantasies, fears, hopes, and so on, but by seeing the wife and not seeing the husband the therapist is intervening in a marriage in a particular way. The family therapist might also interview only the wife, but it would be with the assumption that her problem involves the context in which she lives and that the treatment must change that context. Even if drugs are given only to one person, the family therapist does not see it as drug therapy in the usual sense; it is the introduction of a drug into a family system with consequent concern about who is being labeled as the patient or labeled as the one who is at fault as a result of this act.

The contrast between family therapy seen as an orientation and family therapy seen as method is similar to the contrasting approaches in psychiatry forty years ago when psychodynamic theory developed. It was not a question of deciding whether the neurological method of treatment or the psychodynamic method of treatment was indicated; the issue was the difference in conceptual framework between the two approaches because each represented a different way of thinking about the psychiatric problem. Similarly, one cannot contrast individual and family therapy as two different methods; they are not comparable at that level.

Color the Patient Dark

The beginning family therapist tends to emphasize the individual patient as the focus of treatment and the remainder of the family as a stress factor. He may even have a style of family treatment which is called interviewing the patient in the presence of his family. The more experienced family therapist gives family members more equal weight and struggles to find a better term than patient for the family member who is chosen to be *it*. The terms used are the identified patient, or the supposed patient, or the person in pain, or the person expressing the symptom, and so on. While the beginner tends to see a particular individual as a container of psychopathology or a person with a low stress threshold, the more experienced therapist sees the family system as needing some individual to express the psychopathology of the system. For example, if a child becomes agitated and is quieted, the mother will become agitated, and if mother and child are quieted, then the father or a sibling will become agitated because the system is of such a nature that this is necessary. In a similar way, the beginner tends to see the family as a collection of persons who are describable with the past language about individuals. He sees relationships as a product, a projection, of intrapsychic life. For example, he will emphasize why a wife is being mistreated by a sadistic husband: the husband is expressing this aggression, and the wife is satisfying her masochistic needs. The more experienced family therapist sees intrapsychic process as a product of the relationship situation. He will describe such a couple as involved in a game in which they must both contribute behavior which keeps the distressing sequence going. In a similar manner, the beginner often sees the child as a victim of the parent's strife or as a scapegoat, while the more experienced will view the child as a contributor and an essential part of a continuing sequence of events among all the people involved. As a result of this difference, the beginning therapist tends to intervene to get a person to shift his ideas or behavior while the more experienced therapist intervenes to change a sequence of behavior involving several people. For example, in an interview the father will be interrogating the child and the child will weakly protest. At a certain point the mother will come to the support of the child and attack the father. The father will back down and apologize. After a while, the sequence will begin again and repeat itself. When the more experienced family therapist has seen the sequence occur, he will intervene at a certain point to change it when it starts again. He might intervene while the father is interrogating the child, just before the mother comes in to attack the father, or just before the father backs down when the mother attacks. His goal is to give the sequence a different outcome, and he may or may not point out to the family the nature of the sequence. The beginning family therapist will tend to see the behavior in smaller units, and he will usually intervene to indicate to the father that he should not behave as he is doing, or to help him understand why. He will be thinking about the father's motivations and possibly his history with his own father rather than about the current sequence that is happening in the family.

Where Is History?

When we watch the beginner at work, he seems much more interested in history than the experienced family therapist. He tends to see the family as a collection of individuals who have introjected their pasts, and the therapeutic problem as lifting the weight of this programming out of their inner space. The more experienced family therapist learns to see the present situation as the major causal factor and the process which must be changed. He inquires about the past only when he cannot understand the present and thinks the family can discuss the present more easily if it is framed as something from the past. Assuming that what is happening now has been happening for a long time, the therapeutic problem is what is happening now. At times a therapist may emphasize the past when he is trying to define a time when the family members were enjoying each other more; this is a way of labeling the current problem as a temporary upset as well as clarifying a goal of the therapy. In general, the more experienced the family therapist, the more he assumes that a current problem must be currently reinforced if it is continuing to exist.

What Is Diagnosis?

The beginner tends to put more emphasis upon diagnosing and evaluating the family problem and prefers to gather information before intervening. He tends to use diagnostic ideas in an individual language, and he prefers to try to define in as much detail as possible the family dynamics. The more experienced family therapists tend to find themselves always working with minimal information. Since they view the opening session as important to the ultimate therapeutic outcome, particularly when it is a time of family crisis, they wish to intervene as rapidly as possible to take advantage of this opportunity to bring about change. Therefore they intervene as soon as they have some grasp of what is going on; they do not like to delay therapy for diagnosis and evaluation. Many of them think careful diagnosis is more to allay the anxiety of the therapist than to benefit the family. In their discussion, such therapists spend less time talking about differences in family dynamics and more time talking about ways they have intervened to bring about changes. Generally they like to end the first therapy session with some therapeutic aim accomplished so that the family has gained something from the immediate encounter and knows what the therapeutic experience will be like. This action-oriented point of view does not mean that family therapy is always brief therapy. Often it is long term, but it is brief when it can be. Whether treatment is short or long term, most experienced therapists share an awareness of how much can be accomplished with active intervention at a time when a family is in crisis and unstable. Some experienced family therapists say that, if adolescent schizophrenia is not resolved with family treatment, the case has been mishandled. However, they are referring to family treatment at the time of acute onset of the family crisis and not after the adolescent has been hospitalized and the family has stabilized. When hospitalization is involved, family treatment can become interminable because each improvement leads to renewed hospitalization.

The more experienced therapist looks upon long-term therapy as necessary to accomplish particular ends rather than meritorious in itself. If the job can be done quickly, it is done that way. It is also typical of more experienced therapists to see change as occurring in discontinous steps, and they peg a change when they achieve one so that the family continues on to the next stage of development and does not slip back. Instead of the desultory movement one sees in the beginner's family treatment, the more experienced therapist tends toward a developmental improvement in the family.

Is the Therapist Part of the Diagnosis?

A major difference between the beginner and the more advanced family therapist is the way the beginner tends to leave himself out of the diagnosis. He describes the family as a set of problems independent of him, much as the individual therapist used to describe the patient's productions in therapy as if they were independent of the therapist. The more experienced therapist includes himself in the description of a family. For example, the beginner will say that the family members are hostile to each other; the more experienced therapist will say the family members *are showing me* how hostile they are to each other. This is not a minor distinction. As a consequence, the more experienced person does not think of the family as separate from the context of treatment; he includes himself in that context. He will consider, for example, whether the particular difficulty he sees between a husband and wife is created by the way he is dealing with the couple. A vignette can illustrate this. An experienced therapist was supervising a beginner by listening to a tape recording, and after hearing five minutes of a first session with a family the supervisor said that several minutes had passed and the therapist had not yet made a therapeutic intervention. The beginner replied that it was an evaluation interview and that he had been gathering information about the family problem. The experienced supervisor replied, "Evaluation of a family is how the family responds to your therapeutic interventions." This example illustrates how much more rapidly the experienced person prefers to work, and how he sees the family problem in terms of how the family responds to *him*. From this viewpoint, there are not different diagnostic categories of families, but rather there are different families in different treatment contexts. An important aspect of this contextual view is the realization by experienced therapists that they must take not only the family into account, including the extended kin who always influence a family, but also other helping professionals who may be involved. In some cases a family has been divided up with each fragmented part being treated by some professional, often without the professionals' knowledge of each other. A classic instance, which may be a record, is a family in California which had fourteen professional helpers involved. To deal with the family unit, the experienced therapist finds he must also deal with the wider treatment morass or the total ecological system. The beginner tends to see the other helpers as irrelevant until he gains experience.

In relation to diagnosis, a sharp difference between the beginner and the experienced therapist is the concern with using a diagnosis which defines a solvable problem. Unless the diagnosis indicates a program for bringing about change, it is considered irrelevant by the more experienced therapist. The usual psychiatric categories are rarely used not only because they apply only to individuals but also because they have nothing to do with therapy. The beginner tends to think of diagnosis as something that he has not created but which exists independent of him and with which he must live. For example, a family therapist who was a beginner and worked in the conservative network of a large city posed a question to a more experienced family therapist from the provinces. She said that she was working with a family, and that after three diagnostic sessions she and the family had decided that the problem was a symbiotic tie between a mother and her daughter which was unresolvable. She asked, "What would you do with this problem?" The experienced therapist replied that he would never let that be the problem, and she did not understand what he meant. She saw the problem not as one which she defined but as one which was independent of her with which she must struggle even though she defined it as unsolvable. Given the same family, the experienced therapist might have concluded with the family that, when the daughter began to move toward independence, the mother became upset and there was open conflict between mother and father. This diagnosis indicates ways of bringing about change, and by the third session an experienced therapist would already have begun a change rather than dwell on diagnosis.

The Positive View

The beginning family therapist tends to feel that it is helpful to the family to bring out their underlying feelings and attitudes no matter how destructive these might be. He interprets to family members how they are responding to each other and expressing their hostility through body movement, and so on. Often he feels this is a way of giving meaning to the family members. The more experienced family therapist has less enthusiasm for the idea that interpreting feelings and attitudes brings about change. In particular, he does not feel it is helpful to confront family members with how much they hate one another. Instead, he tends to interpret destructive behavior in some positive way, for example as a protective act. His premise is that the problem is not to make explicit underlying hostility but to resolve the difficulties in the relationships which are causing the hostility. Therefore the more experienced therapist is sparser with interpretations except when using them tactically to persuade family members to behave differently. At times the beginner may seem to be torturing a family by forcing them to concede their unsavory feelings about each other. The more experienced therapist feels that this is a waste of time and not therapeutic. For example, a beginning family therapist working with the family of a schizophrenic observed the mother pat her son on the behind. He could not overlook this opportunity to help her by interpreting this behavior as the product of an incestuous desire, with the result that mother and son avoided each other even more than previously. A more experienced family therapist would probably have congratulated the mother on being able to show some affection toward her son. Although more experienced family therapists do not emphasize negative aspects of family living, they are quite willing to bring out conflicts if doing so is necessary to break up a particular pattern.

The Problem Is the Method

The beginning family therapist, like the beginner in any field, would like to have a method which fits everyone who comes in the door. Being uncertain, he would like to have a set of procedures to follow each time. The more experienced family therapist tends to feel that any set procedure is a handicap;

each family is a special problem which might require any one of several different approaches. Instead of fitting the family to a method, he tries to devise a way of working which varies with the particular family before him. In contrast, the beginning family therapist tends to set rules which include seeing the whole family for a set length of time at set regular intervals. Most family therapists began to work with families by always seeing the whole family group, but as they gained experience they found this too restricting. With experience, they shifted to seeing the whole group sometimes to get a total portrait of the situation, but then they might interview a single person, or a marital pair, or the siblings, or any combination that seemed appropriate for the problem involved. They might also see a family regularly or quite irregularly, and they might have a session of several hours at certain points to save months of more regularly spaced sessions. There is also a willingness to experiment when a particular approach is not working. As a result, some family therapists are now trying out multiple family therapy and network therapy where not only the family but friends and neighbors are brought into treatment sessions.

Equal Participation

When the experienced family therapist interviews the whole family group together, he puts special emphasis upon getting all the members to participate. If a family member is not speaking, the therapist becomes uncomfortable and tries to involve him. Often the experienced family therapist will turn the family upon each other so they talk together rather than to him, and when he does this he wants them all to talk. The beginner often focuses upon one person at a time and tends to have the family members talk largely to him rather than to each other.

The Factional Struggles

When a therapist intervenes in a family, whether he interviews one person or the whole family group, he is caught up in the struggle of family factions with each other. The beginner tends to side with some part of the family. Often he sides with the child patient against the victimizing parents, or if he is older he may side with the parents against the child. In marital struggles the beginner is likely to find himself joining one spouse against another. The more experienced family therapist appears to assume quite flatly that if the therapist sides with one part of a family against another there will be a poor therapeutic outcome. This is particularly true if he joins one faction while denying that he is doing so, which often happens if the therapist still responds to one person as the patient but is trying not to. When experienced therapists take sides, they state this explicitly and announce that they are doing so, usually defining it as temporary.

Live Supervision

Since the vital part of bringing about change is the way the therapist behaves in a session, the experienced person wants to know what is happening when he is supervising a trainee. The beginer tends to think in terms of traditional supervision, where he makes notes about what happened and carries them to his supervisor for discussion. This kind of delayed, content-oriented conversation arouses little enthusiasm in the experienced family therapist. He prefers to watch the trainee in a session through a one-way mirror or on videotape so he can give instructions in the technique of interviewing, which is the essence of therapy. More commonly, the experienced family therapist supervises live by watching a session and calling in on the phone to suggest changes, calling the trainee out to discuss what is happening, or entering himself to guide the session. In this way a trainee learns to do what should be done at the moment something happens, not later, when the opportunity to change his form of intervention has long passed.

Emphasis upon Outcome

The beginning family therapist tends to emphasize what is going on in the family; the more experienced therapist emphasizes what therapeutic results are happening in terms of quite specific goals. Some beginners become so fascinated with family history, family dynamics, and the complex interchanges in the family that they lose sight of the goals of treatment. Often the beginner will seem to define the goal as proper behavior by the family—if the family members are expressing their feelings, revealing their attitudes, and the therapist is making sound interpretations, then therapy is successful. The more experienced family therapist emphasizes whether the family is changing, and he shifts his approach if it is not. This does not mean that family therapists scientifically evaluate the outcome of their therapy, but it does mean that outcome is a constant focus as well as a subject of conversation among experienced family therapists. They talk about family dynamics largely in relation to family change. The willingness of therapists to shift their approach if it is not working is one of the factors that makes family therapy difficult to describe as a method. Not only will a particular therapist's approach vary from family to family, but his way of working evolves innovations from year to year as he attempts to produce better results.

What family therapists have most in common they share with a number of behavioral scientists in the world today. There is an increasing awareness that psychiatric problems are social problems which involve the total ecological system. There is a concern with, and an attempt to change, what happens with the family and also the interlocking systems of the family and the social institutions in which the family is embedded. The fragmentation of the individual into parts or the family into parts is being abandoned, and there is a growing consensus that a new ecological framework defines problems in new ways and calls for new ways in therapy.

18

Enduring Effects of Videotape Playback Experience on Family and Marital Relationships

IAN ALGER

PETER HOGAN

Videotape equipment has opened exciting new possibilities in therapy, teaching, and research. The importance of the immediate playback and its effect in therapy have been described by several workers including Moore,[7] Cornelison,[4] Kagan,[6] and the present authors.[1, 5] The fact that so much objective data on the tapes themselves is available for review again and again has application not in the therapy itself but also in the area of research.

Assessing change in behavior has always been most difficult, but the comparison of television recordings of couples and families over a period of time provides a new dimension in measurement. No one can be present in a situation and perceive, much less remember, all the complexities of behavior. Comparison of therapists' dictated notes on a session to the television recording of the same session reveals the limits and personal bias in one person's observation and recall. Patients, too, are unaware of much of the interaction in a session, and also of

Reprinted with permission of authors and publisher from *American Journal of Ortho-psychiatry* 39:86-94, 1969.

much of the change which may be occurring over a period of time. Comparison by them of serial video recordings provides convincing evidence that change has occurred.

In this paper, the authors will describe some of the clinical effects of the use of videotape playback in family and marital therapy, focusing particularly on the long-term or enduring influence of the experience. In terms of research these observations are presented as clinical material only, but the way has been opened for a thorough research project into the measurement through videorecordings of change in behavior. In many centers such work is now in progress.

In addition to facilitating a measurement of behavioral change, videorecording also contributes to an understanding of the nature of human behavior. Therapy with natural groups, such as families and couples, is evidence of growing acceptance of the concept that no individual can be understood in isolation. The videorecording is a superb technique for capturing the context of a situation as well as the multiplicity of cueing and other communicational behavior. Insight therapy traditionally was considered to a large degree a verbal therapy; the idea of acting out was discouraged. But the consideration of behavior in terms of an interpersonal field led to a broadened understanding, and developments in communication theory such as the double bind [2] concept also increased the basis of our understanding. Kinesics,[3] a study of communication through body movement and gesture, adds further richness to our understanding. The videorecording makes it possible for those involved in a situation to suddenly stand back and observe themselves in the midst of an interactional situation. No longer will a particular experience occur only once; now it can be repeated as often as desired, and over any period of time. One of our patients aptly described the method as a "time mirror."

There is a marked difference between viewing one's behavior on videotape and viewing it in an actual mirror. First, with videotape there is a virtual image and not a mirror image. But perhaps of greater importance is the possibility of more completely separating the observing self from the participating self. In mirror observation, you still have immediate control over the movement of your body in the mirror image, but with videorecording the observing person can only observe and cannot any longer influence the behavior he is watching himself perform. It is essentially because of this phenomenon that a patient is able to become an equal partner with the therapist in the observing and research function of therapy. The effect of this is the development in the patients of a greater sense of personal involvement. When a person observes something for himself rather than having it "pointed out" to him, he more readily integrates his new awareness without the feeling of being directed to do so by someone else.

EQUIPMENT

The actual equipment used will be described briefly. Since less expensive equipment became available in 1965, there has been a continuing development in the field. Refinements and innovations appear with increased frequency. Therefore, anyone wishing to purchase or lease equipment should have a survey made of his particular requirements so that the best current videorecording equipment suited to his specific needs can be obtained.

The essential elements are a videorecorder, a camera, suitable lenses, and proper lighting and seating arrangements. All the equipment can be concealed behind a one-way mirror, or the camera alone can be concealed behind a heavy-mesh cloth so that focal point is behind the cloth. In our method, most of the equipment and the camera are not concealed by deliberate design. It is felt that the procedure is not distracting, and the openness supports one of our therapeutic goals in attempting to integrate therapy with the rest of a person's life.

The camera and recorder can be operated by remote controls if desired. The therapist can do this himself, or an operator at another location can monitor the action and control the cameras. In our work, we either have the camera in fixed focus for a married couple or have a camera operator present. At times, members of the family have been asked to operate the camera. This has often produced a dual result. First, the family member may reveal a great deal about his own feelings in the way he chooses his scenes. Second, he tends to develop a different perspective on the total situation when he is in place behind the camera. Several patients have commented that they realized after the experience of operating the camera they had found a new perspective in the way they were looking at any situation in which they were later involved.

When a wide-angled lens is used, one can observe the interrelatedness of each participant's behavior. This is especially valuable in determining family interaction and in highlighting established family patterns and covert agreements. A zoom lens is valuable for focusing on a person's facial expression, and such a picture often has great impact. Special effects can be obtained through the use of generators, allowing the use of split-screen images. In this way, two people confronting each other can be placed side by side on the viewing screen. In more elaborate installations, several cameras can be used to good advantage to obtain shots from different angles. In such a situation, an operator is usually placed in a position at a monitor console to choose the shots to be recorded.

METHOD OF USE

So much for discussion of the actual equipment. The method of use can be varied. In one of our usual sessions, a videorecording is made of the first ten or fifteen minutes of a regular session. The recording is then played back to all participants, with the instruction that anyone can ask that the tape be stopped at any point in the replay. Therapists as well as patients may stop the tape to comment on anyone's behavior or on their own reactions, either as they appear on the recording or as they remember feeling them at the time of the actual session. Patients may be likely to pick up discrepancies between their observed behavior and their remembered feelings. The therapist may more likely be able to comment on complex patterns of interaction and the cueing and following behavior.

A second way to use the recording is to have the camera operating throughout a regular session with the understanding that at any point anyone may ask that the recording be stopped and the particular section just recorded be played back. This allows an immediate and ready way to check an observation or to review an action that one person observed but another family member missed.

A third method is to record a session entirely, or in large part, and then replay it in its entirety with no stops in order to allow the impact of the complete unfolding of the interaction.

All these methods can be used in an immediate session, or the videorecordings of one session can be played back at a later session. For example, some of the clinical excerpts used in this paper came from a session in which a married couple viewed the recording of their initial joint therapy session which had occurred over a year earlier.

It is clear that the videorecording is actually a technique, or tool, which has impact in its own right but which lends itself as an adjunct to many styles of therapy. The way in which this technique is used, therefore, will vary greatly with each therapist's style and conceptualization and practice of psychotherapy.

LONG-RANGE EFFECTS

In other papers,[1, 5] the authors have discussed some of the immediate or short-range effects of the videotape playback experience. One such effect is "image impact," which has been used by us to describe a person's reaction to the initial viewing of his own image. Another short-range effect is the "second-chance phenomenon." When, on playback, a person becomes aware of a feeling he was experiencing during the original episode, he then has a second chance to communicate this feeling to the others present in a more direct way. The *après vu* phenomenon has a similar basis. On replay, one may become aware of behavior in another person which was not seen earlier. He then has a new opportunity with this afterview to react to that person in light of the new awareness.

The long-range, or enduring, effects of the playback experience have two aspects. The first concerns the effectiveness of playback with repeated use over a period of time. The second has to do with the residual effects of a single or closely connected series of exposures after a longer interval.

The first aspect involves adaptation to confrontation. It is common experience that when playback is used to help someone learn new maneuvers in sports, for example, there is a gradual lessening of the effect after two to three weeks of daily exposure. In other words, the viewer tends to become used to his image in that situation, and so the freshness of the observer role is diminished. One, in a sense, becomes functionally blind to one's own image. Undoubtedly, there is some of this pattern when the playback is used in a therapy situation. Certainly observation reveals that one becomes less sensitive to one's actual physical appearance. However, even after many months of use patients still find new impact on viewing themselves. One explanation of this may be that the behavior is constantly changing (in a way that is different than when a person is continually practicing a special figure in ice skating); that is, the behavior is changing in reference to the current set and context, and to the altering ways that other people in the situation are behaving. Thus, although a pattern in one individual may be repetitive in one sense, it also is related to different cues at different times, and the total experience continues to have a freshness which counters mechanical adaptation in the personal response. The further implication of this is that a person viewing himself on different days in different contexts will see that his behavior can be extremely varied. Not only do family members become aware of this wide range of possible behavior, but therapists too may be startled (and possibly encouraged) to realize that they behave in very different ways at different times and with different patients. An awareness is developed that we are not just static personalities that can be labeled but rather very responsive and adaptive human beings with a wide repertoire of responses and reactions.

One couple we treated viewed their original session about a year and a half later. Many of their comments about the original session were the same as they had been at the time of the immediate playback during the original session, but there was now even greater emotional reaction to some of the original behavior they felt they no longer exhibited to the same degree. The discrepancy between the inner feelings and the behavior which apparently belied the presence of those feelings seemed even more apparent on the new viewing. In this session, the recognition of covert anger was especially emphasized by both husband and wife, and they both commented on the marked change which had occurred during the interim in their capacity to be more in touch with their angry feelings and to express the anger more directly. This same reviewing experience confirmed a finding of Nielsen.[8] He found that reconfrontation induced in the couple many of the feelings from the original episode, and that with the new viewing these feelings were now seen in wider perspective and with more acceptance. It has not been our experience that the counterevaluation described by Nielsen is frequently found. He stated that on review several months after an original filming a person would have a different evaluative reaction than he originally had. We found, in our examples, that the initial reaction was more strongly affirmed on the new viewing.

Repetitive use of the playback method has the effect of increasing sensitivity to a family communication pattern. In one family, for example, the husband began to relate his feeling of frustration when he tried to discipline his son. Almost before he was started, his wife interrupted and began to elaborate and modify the description. As this happened, the husband shifted position several times, turned his head away from his wife, and stared up towards the ceiling. When this pattern was noted on the replay, he became aware of angry feelings and, at the same time, thought that he should listen to his wife. In turn, the wife reported that she felt anxious when he began to talk about difficulties with their son and wanted to make sure that the son's side was fairly presented. As soon as the husband turned away, she realized, she had more anxiety and consequently tried to reduce this by talking more, which only caused further withdrawal on his part. Once this pattern was identified several times, the cycle became interrupted as soon as one partner mentioned the anxiety cycle. Eventually, the husband became very alert to his shift of position and would immediately identify the now familiar communication pattern. Both were then able to communicate more directly about their anxieties, and clarification resulted. Thus, repeated viewing of playback permits sensitization to a communication pattern, and eventually all that is needed is a slight cue to make one of the family members open up the communication by saying something like, "Here we are at the same old game again!"

CASE EXAMPLES

The residual effects from playback can be very profound, even from a single experience. Image impact often has not only an immediate marked effect but a sustained effect. After a single viewing, one married woman kept referring to her "chicken-pox voice" and to "that frozen puss!" Up to six months later, she would frequently make appropriate references to these qualities, and use them in a metaphorical way to describe a pattern of relating to which she was now quite sensitively aware. The "chicken-pox voice" referred to a tone of arrogant belligerence she had detected when she once asked the therapist what chicken pox looked like.

One patient continues to refer to an image of himself from a videotape playback session approximately six months earlier. During the actual therapy session, the wife referred to the husband's detachment, his emotional lack of connection, and his unwillingness to struggle with these factors in his relationship with her. This husband accepted, as he usually did, his wife's definition of his behavior—until he watched the playback segment. At that point he realized that while he was somewhat detached he was struggling to make contact, and could respect himself for it. During the playback his wife was also able to see this effort. He has since frequently recalled that image of himself as he saw it on the TV screen to help sustain his self-esteem, and to confirm his genuine effort in responding to his wife.

Another example which was quite dramatic continues to figure in the ongoing relationship of another husband and wife. The husband saw himself for the first time as cringing and servile before his wife, although he had been told about this behavior many times in individual therapy sessions. As he watched the screen, his reaction was so intense that sweat stood out on his forehead. He said that he couldn't stand to watch it again. He did, however, watch several more times, and then determined to stand up to his wife regardless of the consequences. Since then he has been able to persist in this determination, with the result that a more respectful relationship between them continues to develop.

Therapists also can experience a lasting effect from a vivid realization of their own behavior during videotape playback. Dr. Hogan recalls, and still associates frequently, to the image of himself having an angry exchange with a patient. Following the actual session, he recapitulated in a two-hour period most of the work he had done in his personal analysis concerning his anxiety about uncontrolled anger. More important, while he had become fairly comfortable with his own expression of anger, he realized through seeing this image how people could experience him in a more menacing and threatening way than he himself had been aware of. In another videotape session, Dr. Alger on replay saw himself frozen and paralyzed during the interview, even though at the time he had subjectively experienced himself as listening in an interested way. Since that realization, whenever he finds himself frozen in the position of an "interested" listener, he is reminded of that video image and actively moves to alter the situation.

A startling series of moves in one videotaped segment of a joint marital therapy session had profound and lasting effect on the relationship. The husband had begun to discuss his feelings about a situation in the home when the wife interjected by asking if she could question something. The husband suddenly looked dazed as the wife continued her interruption. As if in a trance, the husband began to follow every physical move the wife made as she moved forward in her chair, then back, then slightly forward and back again. As this sequence was played and replayed on the videotape, the husband became more and more aware of how much he let himself be taken over by his wife's directions, so that he was following her in almost automated puppet style. The shocking image of himself rocking back and forth in resonance with her cues stayed with him, and from that time on he was increasingly able to protect himself from this kind of dependent resignation. After a full year the impact of that scene is still powerful, and is still being used by him.

A husband and wife who had been seen separately and in joint session were seen as a family with their two sons. On replay, it became immediately evident that the father and the two sons were in almost constant rapport. Their physical movements coincided and posturing was imitated among the three of them, while the mother appeared to be very isolated in the family group. On viewing this videotape playback, the father became more aware than ever before of his wife's exclusion and he felt sympathy for her loneliness. After several weeks, the recollection of that scene remained with him, and he has used it frequently to reorient himself in the family situation in an attempt to reach out to his wife and to counter the isolating structure that had developed.

Another family session involved a mother and father and their twin daughters who were then 16 years old. In the session, it was clear that there was a coalition of the father and the two daughters against the mother. On playback, one daughter recognized her mother's isolated position and felt very empathetic towards her mother. Following this, she was able to make a new kind of personal connection with her mother, and over eighteen months later this new quality of relationship still persists.

During a family session with a mother and father and their 5-year-old son, the son kept trying to gain his father's attention while the mother was talking. The father continually avoided his son's attempts, and tried to act as if he was unaware of the son's presence. On playback, the father recognized immediately how he was avoiding his son but said that at the original time he was completely unaware that this was going on. The recognition gained during playback has remained, and the father now is much more receptive to his son and is more sensitive when he begins to disconnect and withdraw.

A final example of lasting impact will be given, although it does not really fit into the patterns described already. This example cannot be adequately explained, only reported. One married couple had a young son, age 6, who, over a period of several years had a severe problem with chronic constipation. Many medical approaches had been suggested by pediatricians, and still the problem persisted. The mother and father participated in one videotaped session, which had great impact for them. Among other things, they became aware of the degree of distance between them and of the great difficulty each had in expressing feeling, particularly anger, in an open and direct way to one another. The couple worked by themselves for awhile and later reported that the impact from seeing their impasse on videotape had been lasting, and that from that time on they had been able to work more effectively in establishing open communication with one another. What was especially startling was that from the day following that session until the present time, nearly two years later, the son has had no further problem with constipation. One can only speculate that the alteration in the parents' communication, and their renewed efforts at working towards greater understanding in their marriage, resulted in an alteration in the family constellation which reflected itself even in the son's physiology!

CONCLUSION

Since 1965 the authors have used the videotape playback technique with over seventy-five families and marital couples in their private practices. On the basis of this experience, it is felt that the addition of this tool for providing immediate self-confrontation has made a significant contribution to therapy. Not only does it make immediately available more objective data concerning the therapeutic process, but it also encourages a more intensive emotional involvement in the process of therapy itself. In addition, the nature of the therapeutic endeavor is felt as a more equal and cooperative activity, since both patients and therapists have equal access to the objective record of what transpired. This aspect of the involvement and the cooperative feeling is described by the wife of one couple as follows:

That first videotape session was the first time in therapy that I didn't feel on trial. You know when you first catch yourself out at something, I mean that the first time you have to realize that yes this is something negative about you, about one's self, this is a very painful impact. The painful impact of this realization that— Oh! Christ! I am like that. I do do that. I am radiating anger or hostility or I am covering up or something like that—this painful piece of knowledge about yourself that makes you feel so bad. You know, when we were looking back I would see it for myself and the first overwhelming baffled feeling, that sort of all-down-the-drain-punch-in-the-eyes came to me by looking at it. And then when somebody stopped it and said it, the way you said it was so much milder than the way I was already saying it to myself that I hardly felt—I didn't feel at all that you were attacking me, which is the way I felt before. Because you usually were saying it in such a milder way and such a nicer way than I had just been saying it to myself that I was sort of relieved. I didn't feel like you came down on me with boots, but that you were pointing something out very gently. I had already sort of come down on myself with boots. You know, when I saw myself do it, I would say Oh, God!

Because of this, when one of you pointed out something to me, it came to me as a sort of helpfulness as a gentle calling to my attention this or that or the other that I felt that I could listen to and felt that I could take it and I felt like I could go on and explore it further and deeper.

The use of the playback also serves to clarify complex behavior patterns and sequences in the actual context of their occurrence, and is especially useful in relating verbal and nonverbal levels and channels of communication within these contexts.

The final point, and the central one as far as this paper is concerned, is that the impact from the playback experience can be both effective on repeated trials over a period of time, and also that the residual effect can be clinically quite significant and lasting and can have a major influence on a person's adaptation over a period of months and even years. In brief, the experience of videotape confrontation can help produce insight of a meaningful and lasting nature. It can also be helpful to a person in contacting and taking responsibility for his own feelings and behavior, in expressing those feelings more directly when desired, and in maintaining his own direction in life.

REFERENCES

1. Alger, I., and Hogan, P., "The Use of Videotape Recordings in Conjoint Marital Therapy," *Amer. J. Psychiat.* 123(11):1425-1430, 1967.
2. Bateson, G., et al., "A Note on the Double-Bind," *Family Process* 2:154-162, 1963.
3. Birdwhistell, R., "Contribution of Linguistic-Kinesic Studies to the Understanding of Schizophrenia," in *Schizophrenia,* New York, Ronald Press, 1959.
4. Cornelison, F., and Tausig, T., "A Study of Self-Image Experience Using Videotapes at Delaware State Hospital, *Delaware Med. J.* 36:229-231, 1964.
5. Hogan, P., and Alger, I., "Use of Videotape Recording in Family Therapy," presented at Annual Meeting of American Orthopsychiatric Association, 1966.
6. Kagan, N., et al., "Stimulated Recall in Therapy Using Videotape—A Case Study, *J. Counseling Psychol.* 10:237-243, 1963.
7. Moore, F., et al., "Television as a Therapeutic Tool, *Arch. Gen. Psychiat.* 12:217-220, 1965.
8. Nielsen, G., *Studies in Self-Confrontation,* Copenhagen, Munskgaard, 1964.

19

A Reevaluation of "Psychiatric Help When Divorce Impends

CARL A. WHITAKER

MILTON H. MILLER

It was Hippocrates who said, "Physician, at least do no harm!" In attempting to provide aid to those couples who are experiencing marital discord, the members of the family, the would-be friend, and the psychiatric clinician alike may well take heed. Marriage is a complex matter and divorce no less so. Each marital unit represents a system all its own—no two are alike. When trouble occurs, no simple formula gained from past success will necessarily apply.

Before consulting a psychiatrist, most couples in difficulty have struggled together for long periods and have talked individually with their friends, possibly with their minister, occasionally with the lawyer. Then, one or both turn for assistance to the psychiatrist. We suggest that in a circumstance where divorce impends the ordinary and customary styles of reacting to an appeal for help characteristic of general psychiatric practice may be inappropriate, ineffectual, or, at worst, substantially detrimental.

Reprinted with permission of authors and publisher from *American Journal of Psychiatry* 126:57-64, 1969.

Although the courts have held that "a high degree of intelligence is not essential to understand the nature of the marriage contract," the significance of that contract and the factors that go into its maintenance or its dissolution are by no means well understood. Many "well-adjusted marriages" dissolve, whereas other marriages, characterized by storm, travail, highs and lows, episodic fisticuffs, jealousy, recrimination, and occasional trips to the lawyer appear to sustain and satisfy.

Key words in understanding a marriage appear to be "engagement," "involvement," "locked in together." It is ordinarily a lessening of "engagement" in a marriage that leads to a provocative act by one partner or the other. Thus, in a cool marriage with a marital temperature dropping slowly toward the freezing level, there may occur an incident that on the one hand seems to provoke divorce but that may, conversely, represent an impetus for "reengagement," "reinvolvement," "getting locked in together." The provocation for divorce may constitute simultaneously a possibility for a heightening of engagement in a marriage that had grown stagnant. Clearly a turning point. Enter the psychiatrist.

PROVOCATION LEADING TO ENGAGEMENT NOT WITH THE MATE BUT THE THERAPIST

Case 1. Mrs. B., desperately agitated, thinking of suicide, tearful, was referred to a psychiatrist by her girl friend. Mrs. B had been separated from her husband for three weeks as a result of his great anger when she confessed an act of infidelity one week before. Her husband of seven years—rather critical and cold, a frequently unfaithful man—was powerfully hurt by what his wife told him and after a week of passionate rejection and reconciliation, he struck her and she left.

She was in great turmoil, as was her husband, who was quite certain that she had left him to return to her lover. Her lover was, however, in Mrs. B's eyes, something of "an innocent bystander." During the first few interviews with the therapist she was terribly depressed and anxious, alternately defensive, ashamed, and filled with proclamations of love for her husband, followed by statements of indignation at his treatment of her and determined announcements of her intention to seek redress.

Mrs. B. was a sensible, proud woman, 30 years old, the product of a somewhat distant home with considerably older parents. In her marriage she and her husband appeared to take turns in periods of anger, hurt, and withdrawal. They had difficulty coming together in a loving way. They alternated in turning down the heat on their marriage burner. She was more outwardly loving, though masochistic; he was more domineering, perhaps less secure. Together they developed something of an indifferent marriage. Indeed, they were unaware of how involved they could be with each other until the interval after Mrs. B.'s infidelity.

Because of the level of the patient's despair, the therapist saw her two or three times each week in a supportive manner during a period of four or five weeks after she first consulted him. He attempted to play a non-decision-making role, reflected her feelings, expressed confidence in her ability to make an ultimately sound decision, questioned her about the coldness in the marital relationship, but at the same time reassured his patient that the problem in the marriage was not hers alone.

Four weeks after Mrs. B. was first seen, there was a joint interview with the husband. However, the husband was greatly threatened by what he experienced as a coalition against him. He responded with a belligerent assault on his wife, calling her "a cold whore" and warning the therapist not to be deceived by the wife as he had been, etc. The husband was incapacitated when he faced his wife's newest allegiance and he put on a very bad performance. He felt outnumbered, outgunned, in danger of assault or humiliation.

The impact of this interview was perhaps decisive in leading to the divorce that followed. The therapist concluded privately, "He's worse than she told me." In the succeeding weeks both the husband and wife were involved in casual sexual contacts outside the marriage. Approximately three months after the initial separation, both the husband and wife had discovered that there was little steam left within the marriage. The glue had dried with the partners separate. The engagement, weakened before, had become a disengagement.

For Mrs. B., however, her hours with the therapist assumed the central position in her life. She was grateful to her therapist for his support to her during the most trying period in her life. Her husband, from whom she became divorced three months later, continued to resent the therapist very much and referred to him as "her $30 lover." She appreciated the fact that her doctor had not tried to influence her decision. From our vantage point, he was more influential than she knew.

THE IMPACT OF A DIAGNOSIS—A SICK MATE OR A MARITAL PROBLEM

Case 2. Professor R., a 36-year-old language instructor, called to request an appointment with a psychotherapist. When questioned over the telephone, he explained that he was very concerned about his inability to consummate his marriage of three and one-half months. When he was asked to come with his new wife for the first appointment, he protested that the problem was strictly his, that he had had psychotherapy off and on for a number of years, and that there were matters he did not want to discuss in the presence of his bride. The therapist was insistent, however, and after some protest the two appeared together for the first appointment.

The husband proved to be a most eccentric man. He was deeply entangled with his widowed mother, a woman given to spiritualism and a belief in the living occult and who, over the years, had demonstrated a determination to protect her son against sinfulness. The mother had opposed the marriage. She appeared to take poorly to strangers.

The husband had experienced transient homosexual contacts throughout most of his life but he had never experienced sexual intercourse. Although he had informed his wife about past periods of homosexuality, she had not been discouraged about marrying him. She had been a graduate student in her husband's department and had "loved him from afar" for many years. She was, however, very upset about his inability to consummate the marriage. She proclaimed her love for her husband, as he did for her. She was alternately self-castigating and very angry with him. She was 33 years old, had never been married, but had had a few prior sexual experiences.

Psychiatric examination revealed a very eccentric and narcissistic man, creative but extremely conflicted in the sexual area. He carried to that first interview a Rorschach protocol, one product of a psychiatric examination he had undergone a few years earlier. The protocol hinted broadly, and perhaps not incorrectly, at a psychotic diagnosis. His manifest problems were considerable; the latent problems overwhelming.

The patient's wife appeared to be a much more stable person. She was very attractive, shy, extremely proper, and very female. It is easy to become overidentified with the sexually deprived mate in a psychotherapeutic circumstance and she was that kind of person. Despite the obvious problems of the husband and the apparent stability of the wife, this couple was viewed as sharing in a 50-50 way a need for help to resolve the heterosexual difficulties of the marriage. Despite efforts, first by one, then by the other, to gain an individual appointment, they were always seen together.

After a period of approximately six weeks of reassurance, support, and relatively gentle interpretation, the husband and wife together had successfully consummated their union. They were lovingly proud of having worked through a very difficult problem together, an achievement undiluted by major involvement of a third person. The couple was seen at intervals over the next six months, always together. They were first seen some seven years ago and since that time Christmas cards with the growing family pictured and an occasional letter from both speak of the successful union.

The therapist saw himself as a catalyst to the love and desire for success that was present in this union. Had one person been labeled in the marriage as "the sick one" (albeit with some basis), a less desirable outcome might well have resulted. And importantly, there was time later to go toward a more elaborate therapeutic endeavor if necessary. The demonstration of psychopathology, the search for a basis for the husband's anxiety, analysis of his homosexual conflicts, or the explication of the wife's reason for picking a sexually reticent mate were not precluded later if this simple, more direct intervention in the marriage was not successful.

In this instance the husband was not without reason for seeking psychotherapy. He qualified by most standards as warranting psychiatric therapy.

The therapist's choice, however, was to take no step to take the action out from the marriage and to take as few steps as possible that put him, the therapist, into the marriage. The therapist viewed his task as one of getting the mother-in-law out of the bedroom, replacing a former student with a wife, assuring the husband that it was okay to enter the bedroom, and keeping himself, the therapist, out of that bedroom. Perhaps most important, the therapist elected to assign heavy weight to the fact of the marriage, recognizing its fragility but affording it particular reverence nonetheless.

RETURNING THE UNWANTED MATE TO A PARENT OR A PSYCHIATRIST

It is always good to know that one's mate of twenty-five years will not be badly hurt by being divorced and/or that one could divorce one's mate and at the same time, in absentia, take care of her (or him). One way is to provide a rich divorce settlement. Another is to find a lover for the abandoned mate. A third system is to return the mate to his or her parents; a fourth is to find a psychiatrist who will take over.

Case 3. Mr. D., a 44-year-old lawyer, confronted his wife with the news that although he loved her he loved his partner's wife even more, and he wanted a divorce. Their marriage of twenty-two years had been quite civilized and in some ways rather productive and fruitful.

He had become a very successful man in his profession. Apparently he had been somewhat threatened by the departure of the older of their two girls for college and on that occasion, two years earlier, he had his first extramarital encounter. Puzzlingly, this first affair, although supposedly unknown to the wife, seemed to warm up the marriage slightly and moved it from its rather habitual and civilized form into a period of brief excitement. This did not last too long, however.

Mrs. D., a socially active club woman, was devoted to her family but somewhat on the distant side. She was extremely upset following her husband's announcement, and her husband immediately referred her to a psychiatrist in order to help her through the difficult period. The psychiatrist saw Mrs. D. several times, then insisted that the husband should come for an appointment. At that time, Mr. D. explained his deep affection for his wife and his expectation that they would always be, in one way or another, friends, voiced great concern about her suicidal threat, and with great feeling repeated his hope that the doctor would take good care of this woman. That evening, as if to underscore her husband's words, Mrs. D. made a suicidal attempt, ingesting ten sleeping capsules.

The psychiatrist found himself catapulted into caring for this woman in the hospital and, despite his ambivalence, accepted her as a psychotherapy outpatient. He worked with Mrs. D. through the enormous ordeal of her impending divorce, saw her through the anger, despair, animosity, and humiliation of the divorce itself, and worked with her for another year afterwards. The loss of her husband was, she felt, endurable only because of the assistance that he had provided.

Two years later the husband, who had ultimately failed in his attempt to marry his partner's wife because of the latter's reconciliation with her husband, committed suicide.

USE OF THE TELEPHONE DURING ENFORCED SEPARATION

Case 4. Mr. R., a handsome, likeable, 28-year-old married, unemployed, thrice hospitalized only son in a prominent Milwaukee family, returned to his parent's home unexpectedly in the middle of the night from the Texas university community in which he and his wife had been living. His wife remained in Texas. He seemed mildly dazed, had been drinking heavily, and spoke in vague terms about his inability to find meaning, etc. Diagnostically, he seemed to be on a seriously troubled continuum with severe character problems and poor controls, strong sexual conflict, alcoholism, and, more ominously, a strong paranoid predilection. Attempts to arrange therapy at the time of earlier hospitalization had, as with so many of this man's plans, washed away.

He had been married for three years to a college classmate. His wife was teaching in a Texas high school. He had drifted out of college five years earlier, and his work record in the succeeding years had been very spotty. He was somewhat vague about the status of the marriage but had been living with his wife prior to coming to his parents' home. He had left the evening before without much discussion with her.

In considering this young man's situation, the psychiatrist felt that one of his solid therapeutic assets, and he had few, was a three-year-old marriage to an apparently more stable and loyal wife. The therapist asked the patient to be in touch with the wife the first day by telephone. The second day, therapist, patient, and wife, by three-way phone, held a ten-minute discussion of treatment plans, reviewed the possibility of continuing therapy "there or here," reviewed the wife's ideas as to reasons for current trouble and her explanation as to why previous recommendations for therapy had been overlooked, etc.

Mr. R. had a long history of ineffectual moves in the face of stress. Drifting from the marriage toward his home appeared to be the newest in that series. He needed help. It developed that there were psychiatrists in Texas as well as Wisconsin.

DISCUSSION

The psychiatrist confronts a number of complex professional questions when he is called upon for assistance by a person who is one of a marital pair. He walks a fine line between wishing not to intrude into the intimacy of a marriage and, at the same time, honoring his own credo, which holds that any person who needs professional help should find an answer to his appeal. As a result of these often conflicting pressures clinicians have explored various therapeutic deployments and assignments to make it possible to work with a married person without disturbing the marital relationship. A number of patterns have been tried, but as yet no predictably satisfactory system of intervention has been developed.

Intervening therapeutically on one side or another in a marriage remains a risky business. A number of unsatisfactory results develop. It may be well to list a few examples of what we mean. There are a great many instances of prolonged individual therapy for one or both mates followed by divorce; therapists have worked in prolonged psychotherapy with one partner who does very well in psychotherapy, matures, and grows, while the mate is unable to keep pace; there are those particularly uncomfortable occasions in which a patient sustains a dreadfully barren marriage by embarking on a prolonged "therapeutic marriage" with a doctor that becomes intractable because the termination of therapy threatens the termination of "both marriages."

Of course, the technique of deployment of one or more therapists is perhaps less important than the attitudes of the therapist, his sense of his own therapeutic role, and his unconscious fantasies about the patient (or patients) and the possibility of the patient's divorce. When the therapist is asked to mediate in an impending divorce situation and he agrees to work with one or both of the pair, his own feelings about himself, his own marriage, and his patient's marriage will inevitably play an important role in determining what happens next. The most natural course is to go where his own life is going, i.e., if he himself has never been divorced, he can watch the marital pair progress toward divorce or reunion and extrapolate from his observations answers to questions of what could happen in his own marriage.

The third option, perhaps the ordinary stance, is for the therapist to move toward a state of apparent neutrality, asserting, "I am neutral. I will not take sides. The matter of a divorce is for them to decide. I want for them what they want." The patient or patients, however, particularly in the kind of stressful situation represented by marital discord, may utilize the therapist's "neutrality" to project onto him a sense of support for their private decision making, thereby moving on toward their own fantasied objective.

The patient or the couple may pick a side for the therapist, put him on that side, and act as if he said "okay" even though he does not know what side they have put him on. They may make it clear to each other that the therapist wants them to get divorced and thinks that they should become divorced because he frowns at the end of the second hour, or they may decide that the therapist obviously wishes them to stay together since he smiled when they talked about the good old days.

The stance of neutrality is comfortable for the therapist. In theory, when he assumes no responsibility, he may be in a position of such strategic weakness as to contribute negatively to the outcome of the therapy. That weakness may be understood in this way: The gradual, manageable psychotherapeutic transference that often occurs in one-to-one relationships is not easily available in therapy with a couple. The couple are ordinarily substantially "transferred" to each other. Unless the therapist moves in such a way as to displace the mate, he becomes a kind of bystander and he is either a catalyst in their relationship or he is nothing. When the therapist elects to talk seriously with the couple about their impending decisions, which after all may be the result of ten or twenty years of struggle and ambivalence, he faces an almost insurmountable problem. He ordinarily lacks the power needed to move such an entrenched team.

Even when the marital tie is a very powerful one and where divorce is not an imminent question, treating a married person and hoping that the result will generalize into the marriage usually does not work. Where the marital tie is weak and divorce threatens, intervention with one of the pair seems routinely to be disruptive. We are impressed that moving unilaterally into a marriage relationship, taking one of the two as the patient and referring or ignoring the mate, is very often a tactical blunder.

What is the alternative? A psychiatrist ordinarily moves toward a person who calls for help and offers to listen to him and to see him again. What should he do when there is a marriage in question? The therapist ordinarily feels that in almost any situation something useful can come from honest and open discussion. What should he do if one member of a marital pair wishes to talk unbeknown to the mate? What should the therapist do when there is a suggestion that one member of a marital pair is emotionally disturbed and needs some kind of assistance?

CONCLUSIONS

We believe that psychiatric intervention when divorce impends cannot be regarded as a routine matter. The therapist should view his entrance into the situation as calling for his broadest perspective. He must see what is going on between him and his patient, already a difficult task. Even more than that, he must see what is implied by the fact that he and his patient are sitting down together without the mate. Any move by the therapist that discounts the significance of the marriage may be unexpectedly influential. Thus, the ordinary medical system of replying affirmatively to a request for help by one person in a marriage, excluding the other, may in effect be an intervention favoring divorce.

In working with a married individual, or with a couple who contemplate divorce, the therapist confronts a system under stress. He would do well, ordinarily, to respect the marriage as a continuing fact until the legal divorce is complete. No matter what the degree of complexity, no matter how seemingly collapsed the patient's marriage is, the therapist should not presume to discount its ongoing power, its possibility of resurrection, its beating heart. If there is to be a death certificate, the trial judge of a divorce court of record is the one to sign the document.

Accepting in therapy one member of a troubled couple should be viewed by the therapist as very possibly a step toward preventing a reconciliation. For many couples on the verge of divorce, the therapist becomes an alternate mate no matter how scrupulous his efforts to avoid it. In the history of many, many ongoing marriages, one finds episodes of apparent cruelty, of separation periods, of affairs, of litigation, along with an episodic move toward divorce followed by reconciliation. Therefore, the therapist should be aware that he may be intervening and changing a process that, when nature takes its course, will heal. In a general way, we feel that the burden of proof is on the therapist who elects to work with a couple in such a way as to take the action out of a marriage, either in the first or during subsequent interviews.

Divorce inevitably has many ramifications for children and families of origin. These others, significant others, should be considered for inclusion in the psychotherapy. Our own experience suggests that involving the children and parents of a couple in the midst of marital discord is often a powerfully helpful device. The majority of our patients who were asked to bring family members in for interviews have agreed and in no case did we regret their presence. That the technique is often a useful one we feel quite sure. We are less certain why. Whether the inclusion of other family members offers an opportunity for correcting basic discord or whether its usefulness rests upon a symbolic proof of the seriousness with which the therapist views the possibility of dissolution of the marriage, we are unable to decide. Bringing the other family members in, however, coincides with our general philosophy that it may be better to err on the side of too much respect for the fact of the marriage, particularly in the early interviews.

We often find it necessary to remind ourselves that as therapists we are in no position to offer a real substitute relationship for the mate who will be disappearing, not at the time, not in one month, six months, nor in a year, and certainly not four years hence. This may be especially relevant if the therapist himself is comfortably married and enjoys a marriage where there is parity, affection, and reliability. A comfortably married person is rarely able to anticipate or appreciate the loneliness, despair, and tedium in the life of a divorced person. Even statistical studies that appear to demonstrate rather conclusively that divorce is hardly a road to happiness [1] tend to be forgotten when one is working with an aggrieved, or apparently aggrieved, member of a marital pair.

An observation passed down through the generations advises that almost any couple during a lifetime of marriage could find ample opportunity to break up, depending upon who is around when divorce impends. We hope that it will not be one of us.

REFERENCE

1. Srole, L., Langner, T. S., Michael, S. T., Opler, M. K., and Rennie, T. A. C., *Mental Health in the Metropolis: The Midtown Manhattan Study,* New York, McGraw-Hill, 1962.

DISCUSSION

WILLIAM C. NORMAND, M.D. (New York, N. Y.): Drs. Whitaker and Miller deserve thanks for bringing to our attention some important ethical and scientific issues that thoughtful psychotherapists frequently must face. The main point— that in a marital crisis the usual ways of reacting to an appeal for help may be harmful—is a valuable one, with which I agree. I would propose, however, that this issue presents a special aspect of the general question of how we carry out an initial interview and arrive at a treatment plan, whatever the precipitating circumstances.

In other words, it is the question of whether to treat and, if so, whom should we treat and how. To focus on the marital crisis issue, all couples in trouble are unique, as the authors note, and decisions about treatment should be based on an initial appraisal that carefully evaluates ego strengths and weaknesses, environmental opportunities and limitations, and the nature of the interactions among the significant people involved.

Evaluations of people in marital crises suggest that at least four possible categories may be used to describe their situation:

1. Husband and wife are substantially normal people in an adequate environment. Treatment should be joint and limited to helping them resolve the crisis and preserve the marriage.

2. Both parties are significantly sick, but their psychopathology is complementary and the chance for substantial improvement with intensive treatment is small. Joint, limited treatment, as above, would seem indicated to preserve what they have, which, though unsatisfactory, is better than nothing.

3. Both husband and wife are sick and both are motivated for therapy; the

circumstances suggest a good chance for improvement of one or both. Here treatment, I believe, should be intensive and either joint or individual, with the same or different therapists depending on the appraisal and the circumstances. Intensive therapy does disrupt the status quo, and the outcome in some cases may thus be divorce.

4. Both are sick but one significantly less so than the other. Here the issue is more complex and difficult. Treatment of the healthier member alone, or of both when the sicker of the two cannot respond very well to therapy, may indeed lead to divorce. Should we deny a person, for this reason, the richer life possible as a result of intensive therapy? My personal opinion is that we should be as careful as possible in our appraisal and then recommend treatment for everybody concerned as needed, preferably individual, and let the chips fall where they may.

The authors emphasize the moral issue—a psychiatrist should not contribute to a divorce which might be detrimental to the interests of the patient and his spouse. I agree, where it concerns the first two above-mentioned categories. With regard to the latter two, however, and especially the fourth, there is a significant possibility that the rift may widen and finally lead to a divorce. I would therefore like to emphasize the other side of the moral coin (with the ever-present caution that the matter is complex and does not present a simple either/or).

I believe that we as physicians should be careful lest we contribute to the maintenance of a marriage that is pathological for one or both parties and that might dissolve unless we intervene to save it. Here I may be diverging from Drs. Whitaker and Miller. In the case of the professor who had been unable to consummate his marriage, they state: "Perhaps most important, the therapist elected to assign heavy weight to the fact of the marriage, recognizing its fragility but affording it particular reverence nonetheless." I submit that a psychiatrist's attitude toward marriage should be one of informed concern, by an expert, for the individuals who are involved. I believe that our job as professionals is to see as clearly as possible the conscious and unconscious forces involved in our patients and their families and in ourselves, and to foresee as clearly as possible the effects of our interventions. The harmful effects of countertransference, discussed by the authors, are less likely to occur when therapists have been adequately analyzed.

Another general issue on which I would like to comment has to do with engagement in therapy of individuals with character disorders. They frequently marry people who also have character disorders, whose psychopathology fits, so that a way of life, an equilibrium state, develops between them. This state may be undesirable from many viewpoints, but it serves the psychic purpose of decreasing anxiety or, in more severe cases, of preserving the intactness of the ego. Like all neurotic functioning, however, it does so at a cost in spontaneity, productivity, and pleasure.

In such cases, the individuals tend not to seek help while the relationship "works." However, such equilibrium states are notoriously unstable and involve the sort of periodic outbursts described by Drs. Whitaker and Miller: "storm, travail, highs and lows, episodic fisticuffs, jealousy, recrimination, and occasional trips to the lawyer." The authors persuasively argue that at these times of crisis the therapists should try to preserve the marriage and carry out more intensive therapy later, if indicated.

Again I concur with regard to many cases, but not all. One should consider the danger of missing an opportunity to engage one or two sick people in intensive therapy. Once the storm is over, the reestablishment of the pathological equilibrium state may make treatment difficult or impossible. In the case of the professor whose marriage was preserved by brief, supportive therapy, there apparently was no further treatment. This may have been the best treatment possible in the circumstances. However, one might wonder about this outcome in the light of the rather severe psychopathology of the professor and the probability of emotional disorder in the wife.

Marriages that involve complementary psychopathology may generate an emotional atmosphere destructive in subtle ways both for the adults concerned and for their children, who may suffer from this home environment and in turn develop psychiatric disorders.

In conclusion, let me again thank Drs. Whitaker and Miller for a stimulating and thought-provoking presentation.

20

Therapy Techniques of the Family Treatment Unit

FRANK S. PITTMAN, III
DONALD G. LANGSLEY
KALMAN FLOMENHAFT
CAROL D. DEYOUNG
PAVEL MACHOTKA
DAVID M. KAPLAN

The Family Treatment Unit at Colorado Psychiatric Hospital, between 1964 and 1969, was largely concerned with studying some of the relationships between acutely psychotic patients, their families, and psychiatric hospitals. One part of the unit's overall activity was the effort to keep patients out of the psychiatric hospital while providing crisis therapy for the entire family, with the expectation that chronicity and subsequent hospitalization rates would be reduced.

Despite the well-known disadvantages of psychiatric hospitalization,[12] the effort to keep people out of such institutions can be overvalued. Psychiatric hospitals are places, not treatment, and keeping someone out does not guarantee he will be treated any more than putting him in would provide such a guarantee. The Family Treatment Unit's patients were chosen randomly from those about to be admitted to Colorado Psychiatric Hospital, after psychiatric evaluation had determined that they were too sick to be treated more conservatively. The

The Family Treatment Unit was partially supported by a grant from the National Institute of Mental Health (MH-1577), U. S. Public Health Service.

259

only selection criteria, beside immediate need for hospitalization, were that the patient live with some relative over 16 years old, that his home lie within an hour's drive of the hospital, and that no court order require his hospitalization. Most patients were adolescents or young to middle-aged adults, working or lower middle class, and diagnosed as schizophrenic or depressed.

The treatment approaches are related to certain theoretical assumptions.[5, 8] The request for psychiatric hospitalization can be seen as part of the process of crisis and resolution. Crisis, the state of things at a time of impending change, is characterized by disruption of usual roles and rules, increased tension, suspension of long-term goals, and revival of past conflicts. The crisis state is resolved by making indicated changes to incorporate or remove the stresses which have precipitated it.

Stresses, i.e., forces tending to distort, come in all shapes and sizes. There are bolts from the blue, such as an accidental death or the house burning down. There are developmental stresses, as adolescence, retirement, or the arrival of children. There are predictable recurrent stresses, such as seasonal unemployment, summer vacation from school, the mother-in-law's annual visit, and broken washing machines. There are extrafamilial stresses, such as a relative's will, a therapist's vacation, or a friend's divorce. There are retroactive stresses, as the revelation of an old secret or a new insight into a past event. Whatever the stress, it requires some change in the family. The crisis can be resolved, and in most families usually is, by taking some action to remove or incorporate the stress, perhaps by a change in role assignments, a change in rules, a change in goals, or even a change in the way in which the family views its past. The degree of crisis seems less related to the severity of the stress or the amount of change required than to the family's ability or willingness to recognize the need for change and make changes which consider both the current realities and the adaptive capacities of the individual family members.

Certain families do not resolve crises easily. At times of crisis, they may avoid necessary change, scapegoat individuals inside or outside the family, threaten dissolution, ignore current reality while battling over past issues, or simply fail to define the situation. If the resolution to a crisis is faulty, tension rises and unbearable pressure may be placed on one member of the family to make an impossible change, to ignore his perceptions of the need for change, or to escape. A susceptible family member at this point may become symptomatic, may behave in a manner unacceptable to the family, or may seek escape through suicide, psychosis, and/or psychiatric hospitalization.

Treatment, therefore, is basically an effort to clarify this crisis process to the family and to establish in the family an atmosphere in which the patient can recompensate, the immediate crisis can be resolved, and the family can become better prepared to handle or even avoid future crises. The process of such treatment, requiring an average of five office visits and one home visit over a three-week period, may be considered to consist of seven steps,[7] which may be simultaneous rather than consecutive.

1. Immediate aid: The family is seen at once by a psychiatrist, a social worker, a nurse, or all three. This may occur at any hour of the day or night, and the promise is made of immediate availability around the clock from that moment on.

2. The problem is defined as a family crisis: Absent members of the household are called in and significant extended family is included. The history of events leading up to the crisis is obtained, and the interactional aspects of the crisis are stressed. Any attempts to avoid defining the family crisis by considering the problem to be craziness within one member, and arrive at a faulty resolution, such as hospitalization of that member, are blocked. Likewise, there is a blockage of efforts to escape the family crisis by running into the hospital.

3. Focus on the current crisis: The current crisis is defined. The past is used to throw light on the present and past strengths are stressed, but the distinction is made between the present unbearable crisis state and the bearable problems for which psychiatric hospitalization was not requested.

4. General prescription: Excessive regression is blocked. Reassurance and support are given. Drugs are used freely for tension and symptom relief for any member of the family.

5. Specific prescription: Tasks are assigned for resumption of functioning and for resolution of the crisis state. As the crisis process is defined, specific resolutions are recommended.

6. Negotiation of role conflicts: The conflicts in role assignment and performance, in overt and covert family rules, in goals and in history, which have almost invariably preceded the crisis and prevented proper crisis resolution, are negotiated with the family members. A long-term referral may be made for continuation of this.

7. Management of future crises: The availability of the treatment team for subsequent crises is stressed. If referral is made, this availability is stressed with the referral source.

Of the 186 hospitalizable patients who underwent this treatment process with their families, 87.5 percent remained completely out of a psychiatric hospital for at least six months and most of these returned rapidly to their usual level of functioning. Followup and comparison with a hospitalized control group revealed that this approach was in some ways superior and in all respects at least as effective as the usual inpatient treatment in achieving the goals of recompensation, return to functioning, avoidance of chronicity, maintenance of family stability, and reduction of subsequent hospitalization.[9]

This form of treatment bears little resemblance to more analytic therapies, in which the goals are ambitious and change and improvement are expected to follow insight into the historical roots of the conflicts and symptoms. Likewise, there are important differences from the usual family therapy in which the goals may involve the same sort of insight and maturation for each family member or the achievement of some ideal of family health. Not only are the goals different, but also the problems being dealt with are different from the neurotic and interactional conflicts usually considered appropriate for family therapy, the roots of which lie in child guidance and marriage counseling.

The Family Therapy Unit's techniques were developed gradually, empirically, and often painfully, within the framework of the presenting challenge.[1, 13, 16] Any preconceived concept of a single proper structure for an interview was the first thing that had to be discarded. Useful meetings varied in length from a few seconds to four nearly nonstop hours. The number of therapists in the room ranged from none to four or five at one time, but was usually one or two. The number of family members seen together went as high as nine, and the group included people of all ages and of such obscure biological relationships as the identified patient's stepfather's first wife's second cousin. The importance of extended family is undeniable.[2] In addition to actual relatives, sessions included pets, boarders, friends, lovers, homosexual partners, ex-wives, landladies, employers, probation officers, ministers, divorce lawyers, and anyone else who might be involved in the current crisis. Ordinarily the first interview included only the members of the household and extended family who were intimately involved. Initially, any member of the household was included unless there was some good reason to exclude him. This applied to small children also, since much understanding of how the family operates can be obtained from seeing the whole group together. Occasionally a peripheral member was disruptive or inhibiting and was excluded for that reason in further contacts. At other times, there was someone whose connection with the family was ending, for instance, the wife's ex-lover, and involving him might have provided him with a reentry into the situation. In general, anyone involved was seen, or at least interviewed by phone, and then negotiations continued with whatever combination of people might most naturally negotiate the conflictual issues. Ordinarily, therapy narrowed down to the two or three people most directly involved in the crisis and included the decision-making hierarchy of the family. Even the identified patient might be excluded early in treatment. Family therapy might involve, all along, only one family member, perhaps not the identified patient.

The setting for therapy sessions was somewhat less diverse, though therapy was conducted wherever the therapists and patients happened to be. The therapist's office gives him an advantage by defining his role and that of the patients who have come to his office in a certain way. Likewise the patient's home gives the patient an increased opportunity to reveal his health, to retain his dignity, and to maintain freedom of movement when anxious. While the therapist's office or the patient's home has some advantages for privacy, comfort, and convenience, informal, even accidental, meeting places structure the relationship in a way which could have advantages too.

The telephone was used freely. There are advantages to seeing people face to face, but such encounters are far from necessary. Once a relationship is established, there is little that can be done in the office that can't be done by telephone, except perhaps evaluating a new symptom, conducting negotiations with a large group, or giving an injection.

The ideal physical arrangement would not be constant, but it might begin with an initial interview of about an hour and a half with two therapists and the identified patient, his spouse or parents, and whoever else accompanied him to the psychiatric emergency room. This would be followed within twenty-four hours by a home visit, at which time small children and any other members of the household could be seen interacting as part of the family. By this point, it should be clear who else needs to be seen or included, as the mother-in-law or divorce lawyer, and who should be excluded as peripheral or a "flame fanner." (A flame fanner is someone whose role in the family has become important as a reaction to the crisis, for instance, the relative who moves in to "help" the sick patient by usurping his role or the role of the therapist and keeping the crisis going to retain this role.) At times outside relatives or friends would be turned temporarily into useful extensions of the therapists, for instance, by providing a temporary home for an angry adolescent who refuses to live with her parents until some conflicts are settled.

After the immediate crisis situation is understood, and the team has seen whoever wants to be seen and whoever needs to be seen, a few more interviews, preferably in the therapist's office, can be held at intervals of several days to a week to negotiate issues between two or three family members, usually the identified patient and the one or two family members whose role in the family is to pass on the appropriateness of behavior, family rules, and role functioning.

If someone does not want to be involved, he can be first invited, then firmly persuaded to come in. If this fails, he might be met at his work or at home. This rarely fails, but the team might have to settle for telephone contacts with him. Only once did someone hang up the telephone on the unit team. Once it is clear what each family member needs to do, subsequent contacts can be completely by telephone, except for those members who need the reinforced support offered by face to face contacts, often for fifteen minutes or less.

In this process most of the techniques involve direct and straightforward communication, instructions, or advice. There are some techniques, however, which are more manipulative or subtle. In the first of the seven steps, the provision of immediate aid, the therapists offer availability and a high degree of support, reassurance, and sometimes even a promise of results in exchange for cooperation. There is some seduction in this, with the therapist subtly conveying great confidence in his ability to handle the immediate situation if his directives are followed. (Fortunately the therapists' experiences gave them this confidence, so it rarely needed to be reinforced specifically, as it was at times in the early history of the Family Therapy Unit.) In times of crisis, this air of assurance is usually what the family wants. The family which is frightened at the prospect of taking the patient home can be greatly reassured by knowing that the therapist will be at their home later that afternoon or the next morning and will be beside his telephone meanwhile. They can also be reassured by the therapist's feeling that there is "nothing" he can't handle.

In the vital second step, defining the crisis as a family problem, can come the most delicate manipulations the therapist performs. Fortunately, in most "nonschizophrenic" families, the family already sees the problem as a family problem. Opening complaints have included, "He's been wild and irrational since his parents visited," "I've felt no point in living since my wife left me," "She resents us so that we can't control her," or even "He tries to kill himself everytime his father gets drunk, but I'm afraid it would wreck the only social life in the marriage for his father to quit drinking." When the patient is schizophrenic, has been seen by other psychiatrists, or has been psychiatrically hospitalized before, the situation may be quite different.[10] The opening complaint may be "She's just gone crazy and has to be in the hospital again," "Dr. Blank says I should have never married a schizophrenic woman," "Dr. Blank says it'll take years in the hospital, maybe forever," "I'm just run-down," "He's so disturbed, he's even blaming me," "If you think I'm to blame, just tell me and I'll leave him forever," or "I know you'll blame my parents, but it's just me—I've never been any good—they'll tell you that." To attack such a definition head on may lead only to an overt power struggle.

It may be helpful to focus immediately on the least involved member present, the one with least to gain by accepting such a definition, and teasing out his doubts about this way of seeing it. The patient may be ignored while the individual problems of other family members are explored for the group. If no one in the group is willing to dispel this scapegoating definition, the history of the events leading to the symptoms is undertaken. If this fails, a discussion of family crises in the past year is undertaken and the therapist may comment that it is easy to see what the patient is reacting to (even if the therapist is somewhat unclear). Any clues which arise from the interaction in the session are focused on gently and supportively.

A maneuver which is interesting and, in small doses, useful is for the therapist to calmly refuse to acknowledge the patient's pathology. This is a schizophrenogenic move that may precipitate decompensation of the family, and therefore is best followed by an explanation of how disruptive it must be to the patient to have his perceptions ignored in this manner.

If all else fails, the patient may be seen individually and it can then be reported truthfully to the family that the patient's craziness is reserved for them and diminished when away from them, and therefore must be a way of telling them something about the relationships.

Despite the many manipulations that may go into this process of defining the crisis as a family problem, it is best for the family to arrive at this definition themselves. Blaming of the family must be avoided, and support for them must be steady. Likewise, the patient must not be overprotected, for fear of supporting the symptoms. The ideal attitude to the patient is one of intolerance of the symptoms with maintenance of sympathetic respect for the message underneath.

This leads to an important maneuver, perhaps the most important maneuver of all. The patient's symptom is translated to the family as a comment on the problems in the current situation upon which more direct communication was ignored or seemed impossible. Symptoms as weapons are identified when applicable. In all cases, symptoms must be made coherent to the family. In other words, symptoms are seen as arising from the crisis within the family, not as arising from incomprehensible conflicts within the patient. It may be necessary to admit the craziness of a patient's behavior, in order to be appropriately sympathetic with the family's efforts to control or tolerate it, but this can coexist with acknowledgement of the significance of the (perhaps symbolic) content of the behavior. This may require communicating with each family member on a somewhat different level, with symbolic conversation with the schizophrenic patient in his own chosen language, interspersed with concrete translations for the other family members. In practice this has been likened to the theater of the absurd.[4]

An example of this was the case of a house painter who became a contractor in an effort to please his wife. He soon began talking about the meaning of red paint spots on one ladder and green paint spots on another ladder. He stayed home from work to explore these meanings. As his ideas became wilder and more incoherent and as his income dropped, his wife became frightened and brought him to be hospitalized. In discussing the difference between painting and contracting, he commented that he was not a smart man and that contracting required him to think about too many things, such as when to "start" and when to "stop" and what colors to use. This symbolism was translated to the wife, and she was able to assure him that her love was not dependent on the prestige of his job, as he had feared. He was encouraged to return to painting (with the green ladder). Meanwhile, though his symptoms continued for a few days, his wife was comfortable with him at home because his previous craziness now made sense to her and she could give him the reassurances he was requesting so obliquely, often in the symbolic language he was using.

The third step, focusing on the current crisis, requires the therapist to realize that there has been a time, usually quite recently, when all members of the family functioned satisfactorily, or at least well enough for no one to request psychiatric hospitalization. Some families may need to be reminded of this from time to time, but the therapist, trained to view current problems as evidences of childhood conflicts, may have to constantly fight his training to maintain his perspective. On a home visit, the physical evidence of past functioning can be seen and discussed, usually for the therapist's benefit, but sometimes for that of the family. When this perspective is difficult for the family, past successes can be discussed. With marital partners, there may be discussion of how they were initially attracted to one another, a maneuver which may stop a battle that has gotten out of hand.

Step four, the general prescription for relief of tension, involves many things, among them the therapists's availability and confidence, the efforts to make the patient's behavior understandable to the family, reminders of the fact that all this chaos is temporary, the rapid pace of the therapy, the atmosphere in which responsibility is carefully divorced from blame, and a family-therapist relationship that is warm. It helps for therapists and family to like one another and enjoy one another.

A good temporary reliever of tension is medication, and this is used freely, often massively, for the patient and sometimes for other members of the family. It often helps to give everyone a good night's sleep before proceeding further. A particularly agitated patient may require medication by injection. Then the whole family is instructed to go home or back to work. There is rarely any objection to returning home, though occasionally a temporary alternative for someone may have to be found, such as a relative's or friend's house, a boardinghouse, or, in one case of a woman who refused to be under the same roof with her husband, the trailer behind the family home. In the rare situation in which the family refuses to take responsibility for the patient, it may be necessary to insist, from "We think this way is best for such and such reasons" to "This is the way we operate and this is the way it will be." Avoiding psychiatric hospitalization, particularly for the first time, is worthwhile but not vital. If both the patient and the family are insistent and will not attempt alternatives, overnight hospitalization is useful and allows for rest and the effect of drugs before proceeding anew.[6]

Usually during this first interview the situation is clarified for the therapists, even if not for the family. The person who *must* understand what is going on is the therapist—the family can catch up later. At this point comes the fifth step, specific prescription, or the assignment of specific tasks. This may not be necessary and it may not be very obvious, but usually one or more or all members of the family are given some direct advice or a piece of homework to do, something which involves returning to functioning, making a commitment to solving the crisis, or even making the specific changes required by the stress which produced the crisis. Tasks could include the performance of some fearful but necessary act, such as making a telephone call to an employer or a lawyer, the call being made from the Family Therapy Unit offices with the team's support. More complex examples could involve the taking, by force if necessary, of a school-phobic child or work-phobic man to school or work.[15] The task could be in the nature of a truce. In one family, reported in detail elsewhere,[3] the mother had quit cooking or cleaning the house in anger at her son's refusal to fix the washing machine. Without solving the basic battle of whose move was next, two tasks were given to be done simultaneously: the mother was told to clean the kitchen, and the son was told to call the washer repairman. In another case, a couple was told to write a letter together, rather than continue the battle over whose responsibility it was to write it. A couple may be advised to go out together, to discuss the budget, or just to quit talking about something. If the tasks are not performed, the focus of treatment from that point on becomes the obstructionism. If the tasks are performed, the situation is improved. In either case, each family member has something tangible to concern himself with, which makes continued blaming of the patient unlikely.

The sixth step in the treatment process may be the most time consuming, but it seemed the easiest and the least distinctive aspect of the Family Therapy Unit's operations. The involved family members are seen together to negotiate the conflictual areas. There is an effort to preserve the integrity of the family's uniqueness and to keep the focus on those issues that led to the crisis. For example, a family may be of the *Doll's House* type,[14] a relationship in which one spouse, usually the wife, is kept dependent and secluded while the husband protects her from adult responsibility and freedom. A crisis may occur when some outside friend or relative or agency encourages her rebellion. Her abortive attempt at emancipation, which fails because she prefers her doll's house, leads to guilt with anxiety, depression, or even overt psychosis. Despite all the pathology, the couple may like it this way and the appropriate therapeutic effort may be to return the wife to her doll's house without guilt, without the need to rebel, but perhaps with the freedom to request a few adult comforts from her husband.

There is a danger of working for more change than anyone really wants. It may also be that one member, perhaps the identified patient, is less interested in change than in a professional confirmation of his perceptions of how mistreated he is. It should also be remembered that a slight change in a familiar situation may seem like a profound one to the family.

A return to the status quo with only a few changes may be a possibility in many families, but developmental stresses require a different solution. When an adolescent inevitably matures sexually and her parents would prefer that she remain a child, the status quo cannot be recovered and new rules and role expectations must be carefully negotiated.[7]

During these negotiations, one family member may feel the need to deny his involvement, since any admission would necessitate rather profound changes in the way he must operate in the family. When it is clear that changes will have to be made, it must be realized that in most families there is one family member, who is probably not the patient, who has the power to facilitate or prevent any change. This person must be an ally of the therapists. He may need support and reassurance about his past performance, a careful avoidance of blaming, and a clear endorsement of his good intentions. This can all be combined with an unmistakable statement of his role in the crisis and his need to change. If these things are combined, they are more likely to be accepted. For instance, "I can imagine how painful it must be for you to realize after all these years that your wife's problems could have been avoided if you'd just refrained from all those affairs—which you obviously would have done if you'd known how she felt about them. How do you feel about her not telling you until now?"

The incestuous family [11] presents a striking example of denial of responsibility. In father-daughter incest, the mother denies it is going on because if she did not, she would have to resume her discarded role of wife and mother. This can be handled by focusing on the consequences of the denial itself, more subtly than this, but with this message: "It must be hard; if you believe the incest story, you say you can't live with the guilt and you'd have to act, by becoming a wife and mother again—if you don't believe it, they may continue having sex and resenting you behind your back, in your own bed. Have you considered just begging the issue and moving back to your husband's bedroom?" A message of support and challenge may be included, i.e., "If they'd only told you before how they felt about your resignation as a woman, you would have returned home and prevented this, wouldn't you?" Once the good intentions have been established, the question of why they couldn't tell her can be approached.

The point of these machinations is to support each family member's good intentions, however invisible in his actions, and place him in a situation in which his good intentions can be proved by change in his behavior. Any fears of change can be explored directly. The point has been made that therapy is basically a series of binds from which the patient can escape only by giving up his symptom—it becomes more painful and embarrassing to retain it than to give it up. Of course, the therapist tries to avoid forcing anyone into a role which is realistically beyond his intellectual, physical, or emotional potential.

There are people with so little pride that they cannot be shamed or maneuvered into change. Perhaps they can be rewarded by other family members, or even threatened. Usually the family knows of some method which could work. In particularly impossible situations, it may be best to recommend changes, not try to seek agreement to them, then terminate, and let the family members approach them in their own good time.

There are situations in which negotiations are nearly impossible. If one member is alcoholic, he may agree to anything and run from everything he has agreed to. The only thing possible here may be to avoid the trap of trying to stop the alcoholic from drinking and turning therapy into just another game for him and his family to play while the immediate issues get lost. Negotiations may also be difficult when there is a threat of imminent family disruption. Rather than try to hold the constantly battling couple together, it may be best to support separation—knowing this may drive them together in alliance against the therapists.

Since this entire series of approaches was developed for crises, they are most applicable to acute situations, recent onset of dysfunctioning, and new symptoms. Acute schizophrenia, depressions (neurotic or psychotic), and adolescent problems may occur in crises and may be relieved in crisis therapy. When chronic problems remain, referral is made for the family or a new contract made for long term therapy. One member may be so limited in his adaptability that he cannot readily adjust to a new situation, and individual referral may be indicated. Often the loss of a therapist is the precipitating stress, and finding a new therapist is the key to resolving the crisis.

When termination is made, the team assures the family of "continuing availability for future crises." Termination becomes a problem when the short-term nature of the treatment has not been conveyed clearly in the beginning.

Brief therapies, using this and other models, rely heavily on nonspecific factors, including drugs, the confidence of the therapists, and availability. Nonetheless, it would seem to those involved in the Family Therapy Unit experience that several of the techniques are of major importance. These are the focus on the crisis, the orientation toward rapid return to function, and the respect for the family's uniqueness.

It must be kept in mind in the discussion of manipulative maneuvers that most families can be treated quite well with a totally straightforward approach.

The maneuvers are reserved for the situations in which the straightforward approaches fail, and they are often explained afterwards in order to keep the relationship honest. Respect, on both sides of the therapy relationship, is too valuable to risk losing.

In summary, the Family Therapy Unit has developed a series of techniques, some of which are reported here, which spring from a nontraditional view of the nature of mental illness and the purpose of therapy. The techniques have proved workable, which may lend some support to the value of looking at crises and therapy in this way.

REFERENCES

1. Flomenhaft, K., Kaplan, D. M., and Langsley, D. G., "Avoiding Psychiatric Hospitalization," *Soc. Work,* October, 1969, pp. 38-45.
2. Flomenhaft, K., and Kaplan, D. M., "Clinical Significance of Current Kinship Relationships," *Soc. Work* 13:68-75, 1968.
3. Haley, J., and Hoffman, L., "Cleaning House: An Interview with Frank Pittman, III, Kalman Flomenhaft, and Carol DeYoung" in *Techniques of Family Therapy,* New York, Basic Books, 1967, pp. 361-471.
4. Kanton, R. E., and Hoffman, L., "Brechtian Theater as a Model for Conjoint Family Therapy," *Family Process* 5(2):218-229, 1966.
5. Kaplan, D. M., "A Concept of Acute Situational Disorders," *Soc. Work,* Vol. 7, No. 2, 1962.
6. Kritzer, H., and Pittman, F. S., III, "Overnight Psychiatric Care in a General Hospital Emergency Room," *Hosp. Community Psychiat.* 19(10):21-24, 1968.
7. Langsley, D. G., Fairbairn, R. H., and DeYoung, C. D., "Adolescence and Family Crises," *Canad. Psychiat. Ass. J.* 13:125-133, 1968.
8. Langsley, D. G., Kaplan, D. M., Pittman, F. S., III, Machotka, P., Flomenhaft, K., DeYoung, C. D., *The Treatment of Families in Crisis,* New York, Grune & Stratton, 1968.
9. Langsley, D. G., Pittman, F. S., Machotka, P., and Flomenhaft, K., "Family Crisis Therapy—Results and Implication," *Family Process* 7:145-158, 1968.
10. Langsley, D. G., Pittman, F. S., and Swank, G. E., "Family Crises in Schizophrenics and Other Mental Patients," *J. Nerv. Ment. Dis.* 149:270-276, 1969.
11. Machotka, P., Pittman, F. S., III, and Flomenhaft, K., "Incest as a Family Affair," *Family Process* 6:98-116, 1967.
12. Pittman, F. S., III, "A Comprehensive Emergency Service as an Alternative to Hospitalization," in McGee, R. K. (Ed.), *Planning Emergency Treatment Services for Comprehensive Community Mental Health Centers, Conference Proceedings,* Gainesville, Fla., University of Florida, 1967, pp. 33-42.
13. Pittman, F. S., III, DeYoung, C. D., Flomenhaft, K., Kaplan, D., and Langsley, D. G., "Crisis Family Therapy," in Masserman, J. H., *Current Psychiatric Therapies,* Vol. 6, New York, Grune & Stratton, 1966, pp. 187-196.
14. Pittman, F. S., III, and Flomenhaft, K., "Treating the Doll's House Family," *Family Process* 9(2):143-155, 1970.

15. Pittman, F. S., III, Langsley, D. G., and DeYoung, C. D., "Work and School Phobias: A Family Approach to Treatment," *Amer. J. Psychiat.* 124(11):93-99, 1968.
16. Pittman, F. S., III, Langsley, D. G., Kaplan, D. M., Flomenhaft, K., and DeYoung, C. D., "Family Therapy as an Alternative to Psychiatric Hospitalization," in *Psychiatric Research Report 20*, Washington, D.C., American Psychiatric Association, 1966.

21

Family Therapy: A Radical Change

JAY HALEY

There have been two major developments in the field of therapy in the last twenty years. One approach has its origin in learning theory and is represented by the variety of therapies which come under the heading of conditioning. The other approach developed out of systems theory, perhaps, and is expressed in the variety of different family therapies now being practiced. Of the two, family therapy is the greatest departure from past ideas. The conditioning therapies offer a new emphasis upon changing behavior, they offer a systematic set of operations for bringing about change, and they have placed a new emphasis upon evaluating the outcome of therapy. However, in the conditioning approaches the unit with the problem and the focus of treatment continues to be the individual. A therapist with a psychodynamic background might disagree with the conditioning therapists, but he can easily understand them. In contrast, family therapy requires new ways of thinking about human dilemmas and what to do about them.

This paper was presented at *El Primer Congreso Argentino de Psicopatologia Del Grupo Familiar,* Buenos Aires, 1970.

A field of knowledge usually develops by students' learning from their teachers and building upon the ideas that have gone before. The field changes as ideas are discarded and added, but the process is incremental because the basic framework remains the same. Occasionally, however, there is a discontinuous change in a field of endeavor. When this happens, the ideas of the past are not building blocks but become stumbling blocks in grasping a new way of thinking. Many of the innovators of family therapy argue that their approach represents a discontinuous break with past ideas. It is based upon a new set of premises and is not merely a new method of treatment. From the family view, what was once considered individual therapy is seen as *one* way of intervening into a family or other natural group.

The family view and the traditional way of thinking about therapy can be contrasted to clarify this change. Traditionally the unit of diagnosis and treatment was a person. Diagnosis was a classification of a person into a type, and therapy was an attempt to change him. What motivated a person to do what he did was assumed to be an idea, emotion, or force within him, and his interpersonal situation was secondary. What was important was the ways a person perceived his situation, what expectations he had, and how he responded to the interiorized images carried over from the past. Psychodynamic therapy was based upon a theory of repression and largely centered upon making a person consciously aware of his motivations and his inner dynamics. Conditioning therapy sought to change the learned perceptions and responsive behavior which had been programmed in the individual by his past experience. Group therapy with artificial groups of strangers brought together was based upon an idea of changing each individual unit in the group.

Most clinicians throughout the first half of this century were trained in this framework of individual theory and shared the basic premise that a person was the problem and the focus of therapy. At midcentury, a change came about. The unit of diagnosis and treatment changed from one person to a dyad, at least, of two people. This might seem a minor shift, but carried to its logical conclusion it requires a revolutionary revision of clinical views.

Just why a change came about in the 1950's is not clear. It would be too simple an explanation to say that in the field of psychiatry the cause was dissatisfaction with the individual unit, even if that were so. By the 1950's many people felt that the psychiatric diagnostic system was inadequate. It was necessary for school textbooks and for medical records, but the diagnostic categories could not deal with the complexities of individual variation or the changing behavior of people who just would not stay in the categories. Moreover, it was a system of classification which was irrelevant to therapy. At that time there was also dissatisfaction with the outcome of individual treatment. Evaluation of therapy outcome was just beginning, but it was becoming obvious that individual therapy was just not curing sufficient people to be worth the time and expense. Therapists began to experiment with new innovations as they faced an increasing population of therapeutic failures. A few people were also beginning to notice that if a patient did change in individual therapy there were consequences among other people in his family.

It seems more likely that the shift from the individual unit in psychiatry was part of a more general change to an emphasis upon social units. In the 1950's, a variety of different fields became more socially oriented. The field of ethology developed when investigators of animal behavior gave up looking at the individual animal in the zoo or the laboratory and began to examine them in their natural environments. In psychological experiments, the relationship between subject and experimenter was studied in the experimenter bias investigations. Hospitals began to be looked at as total institutions. In business and other organizations there was more of an emphasis upon a system and less upon the individual and his character. The cybernetic ideas of systems penetrated a variety of fields in the social sciences, bringing increasing concern with the context of a person and his relationships with others.

THE DYAD

In psychiatry, the shift took place in a number of areas. A first step was a change in the explanation of schizophrenia. Of all individuals, the schizophrenic had been thought to be an isolated unit—he was withdrawn from reality into a fantasy world and therefore his interpersonal situation was not relevant. Yet it was in schizophrenia that a major shift occurred when it was discovered that schizophrenics had mothers. In 1948 the term schizophrenogenic mother was coined by Frieda Fromm-Reichmann, and in 1951 John Rosen had a chapter in *Direct Analysis* called "The Perverse Mother." The importance of this idea was not that mothers were falling from grace, but rather that the unit with the problem was shifting from a person to a dyad.

When it was first suggested that psychosis was a product of a mother-child relationship, the theory was only etiological. The mother had done something in infancy which scarred the child and affected his later development. Yet rather quickly it began to be argued that psychotic behavior was the response of the child—who might be 40 years old—to what his mother was doing with him at that moment. Once the hypothesis was posed that schizophrenia was a product of a certain kind of relationship, a problem became apparent. There were no languages for describing relationships, no theoretical models, and no means of testing the relationship between two people. Previous research had tested a person. Yet if one wanted to investigate whether a mother and schizophrenic child were relating to each other differently from a mother and normal child, it was necessary to make measurements of their behavior with each other. With less severe pathologies, the same shift in unit took place. Symptoms of a person began to be described as responsive behavior to another person. A "problem" of a person began to be defined as a type of communication with someone else.

In the 1950's two major changes took place in the field of psychotherapy: individual therapy became defined as an interchange between two people, and therapists began to try to change a relationship rather than an individual. Prior to 1950 one could read descriptions of therapy and rarely learn what a therapist said or did. The patient's thoughts, dreams, feelings, fantasies, or fears were described, but the therapist was left out except as a projection of the patient. When audiotape recordings and film were brought into the field of therapy, it became obvious that the therapist was acting as well as the patient. The patient responded to his inner ideas, but he also responded to the interest, disinterest, words, movements, and silences of the therapist. Even the dreams of patients were observed to conform in content with the ideological biases of the therapist. Many therapists became uncomfortable when they were described as part of the interchange with a patient and preferred to emphasize how the patient misperceived them because of transference distortions.

With the idea of a dyad as a unit, therapists began to bring two persons into treatment sessions. Mothers and children were seen together, and husbands and wives were treated together in the same room. With this change, the goal of therapy shifted from trying to change a person to trying to change sequences of behavior between intimates. Therapists sought to influence a mother and child, or a husband and wife, to deal with each other differently. There was no precedent for this kind of therapy. At first clinicians carried over the ideas developed in individual therapy by treating a husband and wife together but thinking of them as individuals and trying to give each one insight into unconscious processes. Later there was a shift to helping each spouse become aware of what he was doing to the other. In time, clinicians began to think of the unit as a dyad and not two individuals. They also increasingly doubted whether insight and awareness were causal to change in the patterns of a dyad.

As an illustration, it was noted that a husband and wife follow rules in their behavior with each other and that these rules can require a limited range of behavior. For example, a couple might follow the rule that the wife criticizes the husband and he defends himself. If one ignored the content of what they said and observed this pattern, the rule was evident whether they were talking about sex, his work, the involvement of in-laws, or other kinds of issues. It was possible to test this rule by pointing it out to the couple. One could say, for example, "I notice that you criticize your husband and he defends himself." The wife would reply, "Well, that's necessary because he never quite does what he should." The husband would add, "Well, I try." Making people aware of the rule often seemed only to increase the behavior and in fact to provide new support for it. The therapist could go further and ask for a change with a directive. He could say to the husband, "Now, I want you to make a criticism of your wife." The husband would struggle to think of one, and then he might say "Well, my wife talks a good deal." The wife would respond, "That wasn't a very good criticism," and the husband would say, "It is the best one I would think of." The pattern had easily reestablished itself. How to change that pattern became a new focus for therapy.

THE TRIAD

As many clinicians began to grasp the idea of a dyad, and as social scientists focused upon a relationship between two people, the unit began to shift to a larger one. More and more one heard references to a triangular unit, a triad, rather than a dyad. This shift coincided with the discovery that schizophrenics had fathers. When an attempt was made to explain why a mother and child behaved as they did, the description seemed incomplete if the father was not included. When a mother behaved helplessly with her child, it was noted that her helpless behavior had a function in relation to her husband. For example, if she handled the child well, the husband disengaged himself but if she dealt with the child inadequately the husband became more involved with the family. In other units besides families the descriptions emphasized a unit of three as an explanation of behavior. Stanton and Schwartz in their book on the mental hospital in 1953 pointed out that a patient had a psychotic episode when there was a covert disagreement between his therapist and ward administrator. This observation was made quite independent of family therapy observations in families of schizophrenics, where it was reported that a child behaved in a psychotic way when there was a covert conflict between his parents.

With this shift to a unit of three, it became clear that a child could be responding not only to his mother or to his father but to the relationship between his parents even if he was not present at the moment. A child could fail when he left home to go to college, and that failure could be at least partially accounted for by the disruption at home when he left.

A language adequate for individuals or for dyads proved inadequate for talking about three people. For example, one could divide dyadic relationships into two kinds: *symmetrical,* where the pair exchange the same sort of behavior, and *complementary,* where they exchange different behavior. Yet how could this language be used when the unit to be described was three people? New models became necessary and available with this new unit. With a triad one could talk about coalitions of two against one, which was not possible with an individual or dyadic description. Ideas from games theory began to enter the field along with concepts from role theory, information theory, and communications theory.

The range of possible therapeutic innovations opened up along with the range of possible theoretical approaches. In the 1950's a number of therapists began to bring whole families into treatment sessions with a goal of changing the relationships among the family members. Often a therapist began to do this without knowing that others were doing it too. Within a few years, about ten or twelve distinct schools of family therapy had developed and different approaches continue to appear today. These different family therapists do not necessarily share a common method, but they share the idea that the unit with the problem is more than one person and many of them have shifted to a unit of a triad or larger.

The conditioning therapists have begun to enlarge their unit and carry out family treatment. Previously a conditioning therapist would reinforce a child for correct behavior. Now conditioning therapists are training a mother or a father to condition the child. Instead of thinking of a person being reinforced, they are thinking of reciprocal reinforcement; the response of one person is the stimulus to another which provokes a response. However, conditioners have not shifted to a unit of three, perhaps because learning theory has no triadic unit. A conditioner does not describe the way a child is used as a communication vehicle between his parents; he can only describe how mother deals with child and how father deals with child. His family descriptions consist of a set of dyads, and so his approach differs from family therapists who have moved to larger units.

Example from Different Points of View

To communicate how diagnosis changes if one thinks in different units, an example can be offered. Let us say that an adolescent commits some delinquent act, such as stealing a car. He is a boy from a proper middle-class family and not a gang delinquent. When we try to explain his motive for the act, our explanation will differ with our unit of observation.

If our unit is the boy, we must explain that he stole the car because of something about him and his nature. We might say that he is immoral, that he has a weak conscience, that he is expressing feelings of adolescent rebellion against the establishment, or that he lacks impulse control. We could also explain it in terms of his needs or thoughtlessness, or we could consider what a car might mean to him symbolically. The variety of causal possibilities would necessarily involve only him since he is defined as the one with the problem.

If we think in terms of a dyad, we would include at least two people in our description. We might say that the act was done in relationship to a peer, or we could say that his mother or his father was not firm enough in giving him proper discipline. His mother had been too permissive with him, or his father encouraged this kind of behavior because he got vicarious satisfaction out of the boy's misbehavior. Our explanation could vary, but the problem would be the boy and one other person.

Should the investigator make his description in terms of three people, he would describe the act as part of a triangular interchange. For example, many family therapists say that when a marital couple is about to break up and seek a divorce, their child will get in difficulty in some way. The parents pull back together to deal with the problem child, and the marriage stabilizes. From this view, the child is helping to hold a family together by his delinquent act. This is only one of many possible triangular explanations of behavior, but it illustrates the way many family therapists see the function of a child problem in a marital relationship. They see the child as a communication vehicle between the parents. As another example, his mother and father might be in conflict over the father's masculinity but they cannot deal with this directly with each other. Therefore they disagree over whether or not the son is too effeminate, with the mother saying he is and father saying he is not. The child must behave just effeminate enough to provide mother a position, and just masculine enough to support father's view. When the parents deal with this conflict directly with each other, the child is free to be different.

It would seem evident that each of these explanations of a problem is "true" depending upon which unit of observation is being considered. However, the choice of therapeutic intervention will be determined by the explanation.

From these different vantage points, the same therapeutic encounter appears quite different. For example, a therapist can be treating a wife for "anxiety spells." If he thinks in terms of an individual unit, he sees her problem as an expression of her inner nature. She has fears within her related to her past. An observer who thinks in dyads would include two people in the description of the woman. He might say, for example, that the anxiety has a function in the woman's relationship with her husband. Or he might argue that the woman is continuing to have anxiety because she must have a problem to continue to associate with the therapist. The assumption would be that the "anxiety spells" were a way for two people to communicate with each other.

If the observer thinks in units of three, he would have as his unit the therapist and the woman and her husband. He would say that, by seeing the woman alone in therapy, the therapist was intervening into her marriage in a particular way. He might suggest that the husband was paying the therapist to see his wife so she would not ask too much of him. Or he might describe the consequences for the husband when his wife is going to another man to talk about him. His emphasis could be on the effect on the loyalty in marriage when a therapist sees only one of the spouses. For example, he would be concerned with the effect on a marriage when the wife tells experiences to her therapist that she does not tell her husband. "Anxiety" might even be described as the wife's response to being in a triangle with husband and therapist, whatever the reason for the "anxiety" that originally brought her into therapy.

All of these observers will be talking about the same case. Their ideas about what is wrong and what needs to be changed will vary because of the descriptive unit they choose to examine. Each will feel that anyone who focuses on the other unit is being superficial and overlooking the important factors in the case. Whether agreement can occur depends to some extent on how discontinuous the change is from thinking in a unit of one to thinking in a unit of two to thinking in units of three or more.

THE LARGER UNIT

In recent years the unit has shifted to yet a larger one. By the end of the 1950's, family therapists were talking about the importance of the extended kin, and through the 1960's the emphasis has been upon the ecological setting of the family. Some family therapists are uncomfortable with the word family because they are thinking of any natural group—a group with a past and future together. With this shift has come the treatment of several generations and also interviews with the family plus the significant other people involved with it, including other professional helpers. As the unit has grown larger, sociological theories have entered the field. Durkheim proposed in the last century that every group needs a deviant member. The function of the deviant is to behave improperly so that the others in the group can know the proper rules of behavior. He argued that, if a group did not have a deviant member, it would produce one in order to function. If this is so, then every natural group, whether family or other, will always need a deviant member. Therapists who change that member will be forcing the group to produce another deviant member. This idea has implications for therapy which perhaps had best not be considered.

The 1960's have been a time of considering the social context of the family, much as the 1950's considered the family context of the individual. There has been an increasing awareness that the family is but one of multiple social groups which must be taken into account in therapy. For example, in the case of a child with school phobia, the problem might reside in the family or in the school or at the interface of family and school. A delinquent's behavior might involve his family or a peer group or the conflict between them. The development of community mental health centers and a new concern with families in poverty has made it necessary to consider larger social contexts than the family. The intervention of the government in a family with a welfare program, the deprivation in a neighborhood, or the cultural rules followed by a family become part of the portrait of a psychiatric problem. A symptom might involve not only two or three people; it might be a product of an overcrowded housing condition which affects all the people involved in an adverse way. In this period therapists are learning to think of community influence and also gaining experience in working at the interface of conflicting groups. The street, the job, or the home might be the setting in which a therapist works, and therapists dealing with mobile young people with drug problems will even do therapy in the park where networks of young people gather. Therapists are moving out of their offices into the community with consequences to their practices and to their theoretical framework.

DIFFERENT PREMISES

The clinician who shifts from thinking about a person as a problem to thinking of a dyad, a triad, or a larger unit as the problem is shifting to a new set of premises about human dilemmas and their solutions. Some of his premises must shift to the opposite of those in which he was trained. The premises of family therapists can be summarized, keeping in mind the fact that family therapists are a heterogeneous group, differing in their concepts as well as their ways of working with families. In the field today there are also beginning family therapists with an individual ideology who might disagree with therapists who have many years of experience in dealing with families. Granting the different views, most family therapists tend toward a common view as they gain experience, partly because the logic of the change in unit leads them toward common premises. Some of the views held in common can be described as they appear in the ways a family therapist gathers information, makes a diagnosis, and intervenes to bring about change.

Gathering Information

When a family therapist interviews, he wishes to find out what is happening in people's lives right now. Since he assumes that psychopathology is a response to a current situation, he does little review of history or examination of the past. When gathering information, he wants to observe the family members dealing with one another. Even if he does not regularly treat the family together as a group, he prefers at least one session so he can observe their interaction. Because of his interest in sequences and patterns of behavior in the family, he would rather observe than listen to a person's report about his family. What someone says might or might not be related to what is actually happening and often provides little information relevant for designing a therapeutic intervention.

When family members talk, the family therapist listens to them in a special way. He does not take what they say as merely a report about their inner states or their perception but is concerned with the function of the statement in the situation. For example, if a woman says, "I am unhappy," it is not received as merely a statement about her feelings but as a message to other people. It might be a request that another person do something about her being unhappy, or it could be a bid for a coalition with a therapist against other family members, and so on. The third ear of the family therapist is listening to the effect of a person's statements on other people.

It is structural information which most concerns a family therapist. He wants to know if there is a breeching of generation lines, such as one parent siding with a child against the other or a husband siding with his mother against his wife. He wants to know how the child is used as a vehicle of communication between the parents. He is concerned with the coalition of the child within his sibling structure as well as with the involvement of extended kin financially and otherwise. When dealing with families with multiple problems, he wants to know how many other professionals are involved with the family in what ways.

Perhaps the most important information for the family therapist is the ways the family responds to his interventions. How the family uses him in their struggle with one another and whether or not they do as he asks is of crucial importance. For example, if the father says he has difficulty talking with his adolescent son, the family therapist wants observable information about that difficulty. He will ask father and son to talk together right then in the session so that he can learn how they deal with one another and how much the mother intrudes upon them. Only by action under observation can a therapist gain this information. Ideally, the gathering of information and the intervention to produce a change occur simultaneously in the therapy session.

Family Diagnosis

Most family therapists have become reluctant to think of an individual as normal, neurotic, or psychotic and with that change they abandon most individual diagnosis. It is assumed that a person who is called neurotic is behaving in a way different from the person defined as normal because he is responding to a different situation. When a situation is seen as psychotic, rather than a person, the inevitable question raised is whether or not a normal person placed in a psychotic situation would be diagnosed as psychotic. The fact that psychotics appear to behave in such extreme ways becomes explainable when the extreme situation in which they live is examined.

When one accepts the idea that a problem involves more than one person and is a response to a current situation, it necessarily follows that symptomatic behavior is appropriate behavior. The symptom has an adaptive function in the person's intimate relationships and is not irrational or maladaptive. The diagnostic question is what sort of situation is provoking this kind of adaptation. For example, if a person is depressed, the question for the family therapist is not what type of person is this or what past experiences have led to this behavior. It is what function does the depression have in the current situation and how is it appropriate to what is happening.

From the family view, if symptoms persist the social situation requiring them is perduring. It is also assumed that "spontaneous" change in symptoms can occur because family life changes over time. Not only do families have structures which differ from one another, but each family must go through stages which have different characteristics. For example, a young man might show various problems, including psychotic behavior, when living in a particular social situation with his parents. When he marries he can change, if that marriage helps him disengage from his parents in a successful way by creating a new social structure which includes a normal base outside the family.

The logic of the family view leads to a reversal of traditional thinking about the cause of behavior. Rather than assume that a person has a predisposition to collapse into abnormality under stress, it is assumed that each person's stressful situation is different. Similarly, rather than assume that a person seeks out certain kinds of relationships because of his inner dynamics, it is assumed that his dynamics are a result of the relationships in which he lives. What was considered primary and secondary gain is reversed.

The diagnostic unit for the family therapist is no longer the individual, but it is also not the family. Such a therapist assumes that the way the family is behaving is influenced by the ways he deals with them and therefore he includes himself in the diagnostic unit. Just as he has the premise that the family or the hospital milieu influences psychotic behavior, he assumes that the therapeutic context helps determine what is said and done. He is examining not merely how the family members respond to each other but how they respond in his presence. The formulation of a family "problem" is inevitably a joint venture between therapist and family from this point of view.

Perhaps the most important premise about diagnosis for the family therapist is his concern with how changeable a family is. He is interested in diagnosing how the family responds to his therapeutic interventions; therefore, diagnosis can only occur as a result of therapeutic action.

How to Change

When the unit with the problem is defined as two or more people, inevitably therapy has as its goal a change in the ways people deal with one another. The communicative sequence between intimates is the focus of change. With this focus, ideas about lifting repression, expressing emotion when alone with a therapist, or becoming aware of how one deals with other people are peripheral matters. The cause of change centers in the way the therapist intervenes in the family and requires a different sequence of behavior among the members. The family therapist might interview one person or the whole family, but he is actively requiring different behavior.

There have been few explanations of why people change in therapy proposed in the brief history of this art. Originally the idea was that insight into unconscious processes within a transference framework caused change. Next, there was the notion that helping a person become aware of how he dealt with other people caused him to change because of the assumption that he could consciously control his behavior. When the unit is more than one person, the cause of change must include more than one person. Typically the family therapist talks to family members about understanding each other because they expect this, but he does not necessarily assume that this will cause them to change. He tends to see the change occur because of the ways he has introduced himself into a person's intimate network. How he sides with different family members, how he encourages or requires them to deal differently with each other, and how he shifts the responsibility for change back upon the family is considered central to change. Essentially the family therapist is introducing complexity into a narrow and rigid system.

The family approach is a radical departure from many previous premises about therapeutic technique. For example, most family therapists assume that bringing out hostility or exploring unsavory behavior in the family can prevent, rather than encourage, change. There is an emphasis upon creating a positive framework within which family members can be motivated to deal with each other differently. There is also an emphasis upon outcome more than upon the process of therapy. If change is not happening, the therapy is not going well no matter how well the family talks about their problem or expresses their emotions. As part of this emphasis upon outcome, most experienced family therapists have a problem rather than a method approach. What they do with a family will vary with the family. They might interview a husband and wife for one type of problem, the nuclear family for another, or the whole family including extended kin and significant other people for yet another. Therefore family therapy is not as easily described as psychoanalysis or behavior therapy, where there is a set method to follow whatever the problem.

Because the family therapist sees abnormal behavior as adaptive to an abnormal situation, he assumes the person cannot change unless his situation changes. He also assumes that the abnormal behavior might reappear again if a situation requires it. He has given up the illusion that therapy will "clear" a neurosis or a psychosis from inside a person and that he will never be abnormal again. When people are seen as responding to social situations and being driven by the responses of other people, the question of free will arises in a new form. Therapists, as well as patients, are seen as responding to their situation. For example, a therapist might have the illusion that he can change his therapeutic theory and practice if he chooses. Yet clearly his interpersonal context largely determines his ideas as well as what kinds of therapy he will do.

THE EFFECT ON THE PROFESSIONS

As part of the shift in premises about the nature of a problem and what to do about it, the helping professions must change. Traditionally a psychiatric problem was thought of as medical. Therefore it was correct that a medically trained psychiatrist be the primary authority and have the greatest status and salary. Social workers and psychologists were thought of as auxiliary personnel. When the unit shifts from one person to two or more, the medical framework must be abandoned. Psychiatric problems become defined as social dilemmas. If the unit is a husband and wife, a mother and child, or a whole family, it is not appropriate to think of a disease model, or an illness model, or to think of sickness and health.

As the unit of treatment changes and the problem is redefined, inevitably the professions must change. As an example, in a child psychiatric facility when the unit with the problem was the child, the treatment was in a medical framework and all the professionals had a function that was related to their training. Typically, the child psychiatrist treated the child, who was the sick unit, the social worker saw the parents, and the psychologist tested the child. If the child was put in custody, a psychiatric nurse took care of him under medical supervision. In a child treatment facility today, and more commonly in adult clinics, the psychiatrist can treat the whole family, the social worker can treat the whole family, and the psychologist can treat the whole family. There are also several major programs training nurses in family therapy. What has traditional training in a profession to do with this new type of therapy? Since no particular profession has shown superior skill or better training in family treatment, why should one of them have more status or salary than another? A therapist is now often judged on his merit—the success of his therapy—not upon his professional background. Perhaps that is the most radical change introduced into the field by family therapy.

22

Deviation-Amplifying Processes in Natural Groups

LYNN HOFFMAN

One of the most interesting concepts contributed by general systems theory to the study of human behavior is what Magoroh Maruyama calls deviation-amplifying mutual causal processes. In describing them, he says,

Such systems are ubiquitous: accumulation of capital in industry, evolution of living organisms, the rise of cultures of various types, interpersonal processes which produce mental illness, international conflicts, and the processes which are loosely termed as "vicious circles" and "compound interests"; in short, all processes of mutual causal relationships that amplify an insignificant or accidental kick, build up deviation, and diverge from the initial condition.[1]

Pointing out that most systems thinkers have focused on what he calls the first cybernetics—deviation-*counteracting* processes or negative feedback—Maruyama suggests that more attention be given this second cybernetics, which he sees as an essential agency for change in living forms.

The phenomenon of positive feedback has usually been looked at from the point of view of its destructive effects on a given system.* Norbert Wiener discusses it in terms of mechanisms like control feedback elements in guns, observing that if the feedback element is pushed beyond some optimum point, it will begin to overcorrect, making wider and wider arcs until the oscillation causes the machinery to break down.[2] Garrett Hardin, a biologist, analyzes this same process as it applies to social systems.[3] Describing a number of homeostatic models, both man-made and natural, he doubts that a true homeostatic system can ever exist unregulated in human affairs, owing to the tendency for vested interests to build up. Social power, he observes, is inherently a process of positive feedback. But herein lies danger. All systems, according to Hardin, possess a homeostatic plateau (limits within which the system is self-correcting), but "beyond the homeostatic plateau, at either extreme, lies positive feedback and destruction." [4]

Both Hardin and Wiener betray the bias of many thinkers who are grounded in communications theory in that they equate any movement toward randomness or chaos with something undesirable. Maruyama, on the contrary, finds this a value. Along with some examples of destructive positive feedback cycles, he cites others which increase the survival potential of a given system. Thus he gives a cybernetic framing to a Darwin-like theory of deviation that embraces change of any sort.

Although insights like these have been applied to fields such as economics or international relations, surprisingly little use of them has been made by sociologists or psychologists. An exception can be made of two groups. Writers identified with the sociology of deviance, e.g., Erving Goffman, Howard Becker, and Kai T. Erikson, have long been familiar with the deviation-amplifying process leading to the creation of a deviant. The other group is represented by researchers in family communication: Gregory Bateson, Jay Haley, Don Jackson, and a growing number of therapists-turned-researchers who are working with whole families. Some of the clinically oriented members of this group are still trying to interpret family theory in terms of various modifications of Freudian psychodynamics. Others, such as the writers mentioned above, have focused on investigating the properties of the family as a "system" and the role of symptomatic behavior in maintaining the equilibrium of that system. Bateson, in fact, in a book published in 1936 called *Naven,* had already begun to interest himself in the problem of how self-corrective and deviation-amplifying processes jointly interact in social systems. This was long before anybody ever thought of observing these processes directly in families.[5]

* The question of what is a system is a vexing one. The most common definition seems to be: any entity the parts of which covary interdependently with one another, and which maintains equilibrium in an error-activated way.

In general, one can say that the writers on the sociology of deviance have tended to be more interested in factors that promote differentiation and the family theorists in forces that maintain the *status quo,* but the work of both groups seems to converge usefully toward some central point. This paper will attempt to explore where that point might be. I will begin by describing briefly the research that has been done in family theory and the sociology of deviance and then see how it can be fitted in with the ideas of the "systems" theorists. My purpose is to bring together the thinking of these scholars and practitioners as it illustrates the function of deviants in families and other natural groups, with some implications for therapy as well.

FAMILY THEORY

This line of research is one of the few which has taken an explicitly cybernetic view of social relationships. It has been closely connected with the family therapy movement because this different way of treating emotional illness was logically suggested by family theory and in part grew out of it. However, family theory is more than an adjunct of therapy. It is a different way of looking at behavior which could be described as a kind of communications research focusing on the ongoing relationships of people in intimate groups.

In the early 1950's, a number of psychotherapists working with schizophrenics made the independent observation that, if the patient got better, someone else in the family would break out with a problem. It was almost as if the family required the presence of a person with a symptom. At the same time, the researchers mentioned above (members of a communications research project led by Gregory Bateson in Palo Alto, California) had started observing families with schizophrenic members directly. They did this initially in an effort to see whether the schizophrenic member might have learned how to communicate in a bizarre fashion by growing up in a bizarre home. Not only did the group find evidence for this assumption, but it was impressed by the extent to which the family encouraged, even demanded, the patient's bizarre behavior. Efforts of a therapist to make him better were often frustrated by the family. Noting the obstinacy with which change was resisted, even when it meant the improvement of a loved one, Jackson coined the term family homeostasis, and described family interaction as "a closed information system in which variations in output or behavior are fed back in order to correct the system's response." [6] Haley elaborated on this, comparing the family to a servomechanism with a governor:

Granting that people in ongoing relationships function as "governors" in relation to one another, and granting that it is the function of a governor to diminish change, then the first law of human relationships is as follows: *When one person indicates a change in relation to another, the other will act upon the first so as to diminish and modify that change.*[7]

Although the emphasis of the group was mainly on deviation-counteracting processes, the work of Maruyama was well known to its members. The idea of deviation amplification seemed to fit what Jackson observed while working with families in therapy and often referred to as a runaway. This would be any positive feedback process which escalated rapidly, leading to a breakdown, a blowup, or some such violent result. Jackson often stated that he preferred to work with a family where this kind of movement was taking place. With a very immovable family, especially one with a chronic schizophrenic, he would sometimes try to start a runaway as a therapeutic gambit.[8] This could be done by "prescribing the symptom," that is, by increasing the angle of deviance of the patient from the rest of the family. Alternatively, the therapist could reinforce any family member's behavior, pushing it to continue in the same direction in a kind of *reductio ad absurdum*. Such interventions would presumably threaten the "homeostasis" of the family so that family members would grasp more readily at the therapist's suggestions in reestablishing a balance.

To some extent, the Bateson group became identified with an idea of the family as an equilibrium-maintaining entity. This was partly because of the popularity of Jackson's phrase family homeostasis, and partly because so much of the group's research was done with families which had an extremely restricted range of behavior. Experiments devised by Haley showed a greater rigidity of communication patterns (e.g., order of speaking) in families where somebody had a symptom than in families where nobody did, or at least where none had been identified.[9] Also, one of the group's first questions was whether a family could be said to behave as a "system" at all, that is, whether all families had a greater patterning in their communications than one would expect if these communications were ruled by chance. This question was answered in the affirmative by Haley in the research cited above.

The sociology of deviance writers, whom I shall take up next, also recognizes the homeostatic function of deviant behavior for a group, but this has been a theoretical assumption more or less taken for granted. Actual research has focused on how a deviant gets that way, that is, on the deviation-amplifying aspect of the process. Both aspects are, as I shall show in more detail later, facets of the same whole.

THE SOCIOLOGY OF DEVIANCE

This school's most obvious ancestor is Durkheim, who contended that many categories of behavior we think of as dysfunctional, such as crime, perform a socially useful role in accentuating common norms and heightening group cohesion.[10] However, Durkheim did not go so far as to call such behaviors part of the normal division of labor, as recent sociologists have done. For him, it was a pathological manifestation arising from a condition of "anomie." According to Durkheim, this condition arises when the division of labor—developed to an extreme in complex, modern societies—is not working well, so that an appropriate meshing of skills to opportunities does not take place.

A more recent group of social theorists, represented by Robert Merton and Albert Cohen, have revived Durkheim's concept of "anomie" as a way of explaining deviant behavior, in particular deviant subcultures such as gangs.[11] According to this view, deviance is a response to the mismatch between goals legitimized by the society and the individual's real chances for achieving them. It is this disjunction between goals and means that forces people to go outside the norms to find satisfaction.

Sociologists like Goffman and Becker, themselves deviants from the mainstream of American sociology as typified by the heavily normative approach of Parsons, do not accept this view because it ties deviance too closely to an idea of dysfunction. They pick out a particular strand in Durkheim's thinking and push it further: the idea that the presence of deviants may be essential to the stability and survival of social groups. One can note here that a systems framework for studying social groups is being introduced. Kai T. Erikson, the most systems oriented of the writers on deviance, describes this shift explicitly, and at the same time offers a good definition of what a social system is:

In recent years, sociological theory has become more and more concerned with the concept "social system"—an organization of society's component parts into a form which sustains internal equilibrium, resists change, and is boundary-maintaining.[12]

He goes on to consider the role of deviant behavior in such systems, saying,

Perhaps some communities can retain a sense of their own territorial identity only when they keep up an ongoing dialogue with deviants who mark and publicize the outer limits of space; perhaps some families can remain intact only if one of their members becomes a visible deviant to serve as a focus for the rest.[13]

Erikson criticizes the "anomie" position that assumes that deviance is a sign of disorder, saying that the deviant is "a relevant figure in the community's overall division of labor." [14] Here he echoes Goffman who, in pioneering studies of deviance like *Asylums,* speaks of the "career" of being a mental patient or a prison inmate.[15] According to this view, the town "needs" its drunkard just as the village does its idiot, and if the place falls vacant, somebody else may be appointed to fill it.

Thus it comes about that deviance is no longer seen as an attribute of the individual but as a property of the group. Durkheim first dramatized this thought when he called attention to the remarkably consistent rates of suicide characteristic of different nations.[16] More recent writers like Eliot Freidson have extended the idea by wondering whether agencies that deal with deviance may not, over time, develop their own stable rates or "quotas." [17] From arguments like these, it follows that it is meaningless to look for the causes of deviance in individual motivations, circumstances, or life histories except as these factors feed into a larger circular process which is the transaction between the social group and the deviant-elect. Out of this conviction have come a large number of studies of deviant careers covering a variety of lawbreakers, misfits and fringe people; Howard Becker's *Outsiders* is perhaps the best-known example.[18] Most of these studies rest on the assumption that deviance is what has been so labeled and go on to analyze the process of labeling in minute detail.

But before going on to survey this literature, perhaps we should see what writers with a general systems orientation have to say about the forces that promote differentness and those that promote sameness in living systems in general, not just human society. From these writings, we may be able to extract some useful generalizations that can be applied to the deviation-amplifying processes that go on between the individual and his group.

POSITIVE AND NEGATIVE FEEDBACK LOOPS

Maruyama points out that the survival of any living system (here defined as any self-maintaining entity, from closely bounded units like the cell to loosely bounded units like the family) depends on two important processes.* One is morphostasis, which means that the system must maintain constancy in the face of environmental vagaries. It does this through the error-activating process known as negative feedback; the simple house thermostat is usually given as an example. The other process is morphogenesis, which means that at times a system must change its basic structure. This process involves positive feedback loops and is deviation amplifying, as in the case of a successful mutation which allows a species to adapt to changed environmental conditions.[19]

Another way to look at these two processes is in terms of what Walter Buckley, following W. Ross Ashby, calls variety and constraint. Constraint is synonymous with pattern, structure, regularity. It goes away from a random state, toward what communications theorists call negentropy. No living system could survive without pattern or structure. On the other hand, too much structure, too

* For an imaginative analysis of the prototypical "living system," see Miller.[20]

much negentropy, will kill it. This is why there must always be, as Buckley explains it,

. . . some source or mechanism for *variety*, to act as a potential pool of adaptive variability to meet the problem of mapping new or more detailed variety and constraints in a changeable environment.[21]

As described so far, the two types of feedback—that which produces and that which inhibits deviance—would seem to have simply divided functions. Negative feedback is conservative and promotes the *status quo*; positive is radical and promotes change. But this is far from the whole story. Buckley, in talking about the "vicious circle or spiral or escalation," says that "it is not at all certain whether the resultant will maintain, change or destroy the given system or its particular structures."[22] One can think of examples: the growth of monopolies might lead to such total inequity that social revolution would result, *or* it could inspire a movement toward antitrust legislation. The death of a religious or political heretic might reinforce the system he repudiated, *or* his martyrdom might lead to a revision of the entire order.

Maruyama paints an even more complicated picture. He points out that it is possible to have both positive and negative mutual-causal loops counterbalancing one another in any given situation (by loop he means a series of mutually caused events in which the influence of any element comes back to itself through other elements). As an example, he offers a vector diagram showing forces and counterforces impinging on the growth of a city. Factors such as number of people, migration level, modernization, sanitation facilities, amount of garbage per area, bacteria per area, and number of diseases are shown to form a number of interrelated positive and negative loops increasing or decreasing the population. If the number of inverse mutual causal influences in a feedback loop is even, the influences will cancel each other out and the effect will be deviation amplifying; if it is odd, the result will be the opposite. But this will still not indicate the overall outcome, because whether the system as a whole will respond in a deviation amplifying or counteracting way depends on the strength of the loops. Maruyama does not, unfortunately, have any idea as to how such a product might be measured, leaving us merely with the statement that "an understanding of a society or an organism cannot be attained without studying both types of loops and the relationships between them."[23]

TIMING AND STAGES

But there is another way to look at feedback loops. What is important is not only the relative strength of these loops and the way they are combined but *timing*. Bateson, in *Naven,* develops a model for social systems that takes this factor into account. When he first wrote the book, he was struggling with a "dynamic equilibrium" model involving two types of process. One was any movement leading to differentiation, which he called schismogenesis; the other included movements which operated to counteract such schisms. In an epilogue added in 1958, Bateson recast these concepts in the light of information theory and came up with a formulation close to that of Maruyama. "Schismogenesis" now resembles the "progressive exponential change" of positive feedback, and the corresponding corrective tendencies have become negative feedback processes leading to the maintenance of a steady state.[24]

Bateson goes on to observe that, in assessing a self-correcting system, a particularly important factor is the state of the system itself in regard to its own homeostasis. Using the analogy of a steam engine with a governor, he states that, in response to an event or message, one of two pathways may be taken. The system may either seek a steady state or go in the direction of a runaway. But which outcome will prevail depends on timing, on whether the event hits the system at a moment of stability or at a time when it is extremely precarious.[25] Hardin says the same thing when he states that "An act which is harmless when the system is well within its homeostatic boundaries may be quite destructive when the system is already stressed near one of its limits." [26] This is, of course, what Jackson and other family therapists realized when they tried unsuccessfully to introduce changes into families which were not in crisis and why at times they would deliberately try to make the family "system" exceed its limits.

Another aspect of feedback processes which is related to timing is that they often occur in alternations or stages. Bateson calls attention to inverse progressive changes, as when an increase in mutual hostility between a couple reaches some built-in limit and shift toward mutual affection takes place.[27] Such an oscillation usually implies an overall stability.

A different case is one described by Maruyama where a deviation-amplifying process can, over a period of time, change into a deviation-counteracting one. In other words, there can be a drift toward increasing differentiation which at some point loses its somewhat adventitious nature and stabilizes. Maruyama cites as examples the principle of diminishing returns, or a culture which develops through a series of favorable mutual causal events but finally stops expanding and produces mechanisms to preserve the *status quo.*[28]

One might add that the process can go the other way, as when a stable system moves into a period of disequilibrium. Deviation-amplifying chains characteristic of this sequence seem to divide along Maruyama's and Hardin's different ideas about the nature of positive feedback. There is the gradual process by which a variation takes hold, and there is the runaway that develops when a system's error-activating mechanisms break down. The two types of positive feedback may *not* be related—for instance, a drift toward deviation may occur all by itself and not in connection with any systemic form—but they may also be stages of a larger process. An example is the behavior of animal populations like the lemmings which live in an environment where there is an unlimited food supply and few competing species to act as a check to increase. These populations will periodically start to overexpand, in the manner of the first type of positive feedback. Then they will suddenly adopt a self-destructing behavior, like the march of the lemmings to the sea, as if a limit in the plateau regulating numbers of animals has been reached and a runaway (literally) is triggered off which does away with the excess.

But here a difficult question presents itself. Can this sequence really be said to go in the direction of a deviation-amplifying result? From the point of view of the lemming population as a whole, if not from that of the subgroup that gets destroyed, the entire series of events has operated to reinstate the *status quo*. At this point it becomes obvious that to clear up the confusion one must bring in a concept of levels.

LEVELS

So far, we have been looking at the effect of feedback loops on one particular system. What is all too seldom realized is that feedback in living systems must always be viewed in terms of *several levels of system at once*. The fact that there is a hierarchy of living systems is not a new discovery, although it is not always related to cybernetic theory. Herbert Simon has offered the thought that the complexity of natural phenomena could be better understood if it were realized that one is always dealing with "layers" or "nests of Chinese blocks," in sequences of increasing inclusion, such as individual, primary groups, organizations, social systems, or, in biology, gene, cell, organ, organism. Any activity taking place in one of these layers will obviously be operating simultaneously in at least one other.[29]

Bateson, who is always aware of levels, makes a similar point when he notes that the study of interaction always involves at least two pieces of information: "a statement about participating entities and a statement about that larger entity which is brought into being by the fact of interaction." [30] He then adds that an important source of destructive interaction can be a discrepancy between the goals of two systems on different levels:

For example, a self-maximizing tendency may lead to the destruction of some larger system which was instrumental and necessary to the existence of the self. In special cases, the self-destruction of the smaller entity is instrumental to the survival of the larger system.[31]

The struggle of social theorists to discriminate between an open aim and an unacknowledged consequence in human events, embodied in pairs of terms like conscious/unconscious, overt/covert, or manifest/latent, may in many instances have to do with this same fact that any action taking place in a social field will touch at least two contiguous systems. Merton comes close to suggesting this in an essay on manifest and latent function. Listing Durkheim as one of many thinkers who have, without realizing it, used a concept of latent function, he observes that

Emile Durkheim's similar analysis of the social functions of punishment is also focused on its latent functions (consequence for the community) rather than confined to manifest functions (consequence for the criminal).[32]

Examples of behavior affecting more than one system at a time are cited continuously by family researchers; in fact, it was the surmise that the individual sufferer from mental illness could not be understood *without* looking at the consequences of his illness for the family group that started family therapy on its way. Following this line of thought, Haley observed the double consequence of symptoms of all kinds: the effect on the individual, which was to make him less responsible and more helpless, and the effect on his family relationships, which was to give him a lever for enormous control.[33] The Bateson group used the word overt, as opposed to covert, to distinguish between the openly acknowledged purpose and the unadmitted result.

Holding fast to this concept of levels, it now becomes clear that any feedback loop may have deviation-amplifying *and* counteracting effects at the same time, depending on which system one is looking at. Tragic drama is suggestive in regard to this point. What the Greeks called hubris, inadequately translated as overweening pride and somehow linked to the tragic hero's downfall, closely resembles our old friend the positive feedback chain of social power. Once set in motion, this chain is deviation *amplifying* from the point of view of the hero, whose deviance in relation to his group is increased to the point that he is eventually cast out, brought low, or otherwise destroyed. It is deviation *counteracting* from the point of view of his society, in that out of the ashes of the hero's downfall supposedly rises a new social peace. An alternative explanation might be that the society uses the aftermath of the debacle to recalibrate the setting for its own equilibrium. Thus a tragedy may essentially describe a morphogenetic change (change *in* the homeostatic setting) rather than a morphostatic change (change *governed by* the homeostatic setting). However one defines what is going on, it is clear that, without some such multilevel view, one will not begin to understand it.

In the next section, I will put away this oppressively complex apparatus I have conjured up and narrow down to the exchanges between two especially interesting systems: the individual and his group. In particular, I will consider the literature on social typecasting.

THE TYPECASTING OF DEVIANTS

Most of the studies in this area read like contributions to the sociology of occupations, except that the term occupation is extended to cover delinquency, mental illness, and the like. However, a respectable few are concerned with the circular causal processes that increase the difference between a person and his group so that he is perceived unfavorably. A classic example is Merton's treatment of racial stereotyping, "The Self-Fulfilling Prophecy." [34] For a number of more recent studies in the same vein, the reader is referred to the anthology by Rubington and Weinberg, *Deviance/The Interactionist Perspective*.[35] Two representative essays from this volume can be cited here: Edwin T. Lemert's "Paranoia and the Dynamics of Exclusion," which notes the way the paranoic's expectations of hostility from the people around him promote the very reaction he fears; and Frank Tannenbaum's "The Dramatization of Evil," which traces the mutually escalating animosity between an adolescent and his community until he is finally labeled a delinquent.

Although these writers, like many in this field, note the presence of a vicious cycle, they do not tend to think in cybernetic terms. An exception is Leslie T. Wilkins' "A Behavioral Theory of Drug Taking." [36] Wilkins explicitly applies Maruyama's mutual causal concepts to the typecasting process. He explains how an addict "outlaw group" is created through the mutually reinforcing effect of social definition on self-image, and how the further step of placing addicts together in rehabilitation or detention centers amplifies their difference from the community (and likeness to each other) even more. Using this framework, Wilkins makes an intelligent criticism of systems of control which are directed toward the individual deviant rather than the process which creates him.

Using the concept of scapegoating rather than typecasting, family theorists have also developed a literature on a deviant: the symptomatic member of a family. The best example of such a study is perhaps Vogel and Bell's "The Emotionally Disturbed Child as a Family Scapegoat." [37] * According to these

---

* Although family therapists in the East have tended to use the term "scapegoating" for the process that creates a deviant in a family, other writers about deviance have not used it much. This brings up an interesting problem. It is easily noticed that scapegoating is a mutual causal process, despite the implication that the scapegoat is the victim and everyone else is taking advantage of him. Nevertheless, the word is weighted in favor of the underdog and is hard to use objectively. Perhaps this is why more rigorous researchers are not partial to it.

authors, such children are invariably involved in the tensions between their parents. The parents, by projecting their conflicts on the child, maintain a reasonably harmonious relationship, although the cost to the child's development may be great. A major contribution of the article is the description of the way the child is selected and then inducted into his role. Some chance characteristic of the child—it need not even be an obnoxious trait so long as it differentiates him—will be singled out and then developed, increasing the contrast between himself and everybody else in the family. The authors do not see this as a mutual causal process in Maruyama's sense, but it answers the description very well.

In looking over the literature on typecasting and scapegoating, one finds two emphases. The first is on behavior as it functions on different levels of systems. Researchers studying the family as a system and most of the contributors to the sociology of deviance write from this standpoint. The other emphasis is based on traditional, individual-oriented ideas and gravitates to concepts like projections, expectations, or roles. Into this category falls much clinical writing on behavior like delinquency or mental illness, especially when the writer is a psychiatrist or social worker with psychodynamic training.

From the point of view of this paper, the individual-oriented approach badly misrepresents the subject. For instance, to speak of the role of the scapegoat is to act as though this were a *persona* with fixed characteristics rather than an aspect of a process. Scapegoating, if one thinks about it, is a term which applies to one stage only of a shifting scenario: the stage where the person is cast out of the village.* The deviant can begin like a hero and go out like a villain, or vice versa. There is a positive-negative continuum on which he can be rated depending on which stage of the deviation process we are looking at, which sequence the process follows, and the degree to which the social system is, as Hardin says, "stressed."

At the same time, the character of the deviant may vary in another direction, depending on the way his particular group does its typecasting. Which symptoms crop up in members of a group is itself a kind of typecasting. Thus the deviant may appear in many guises: the mascot, the clown, the sad sack, the erratic genius, the black sheep, the wise guy, the saint, the idiot, the fool, the impostor, the malingerer, the boaster, the villain, and so forth. Literature and folklore abound with such figures.

It will thus make a difference in any study of deviance whether one chooses

* Webster's defines scapegoating as: "in ancient Hebrew ritual, a goat, turned loose in the desert, upon which the sins of the people had been symbolically transferred, hence, one who bears the blame for others." (*Webster's New School and Office Dictionary*, New York, Crest Giant, 1966.)

to depict one's subject in cross section, by phase or type, or to trace it in terms of a longitudinally viewed, shifting career. One of the problems with early family research was the attempt to see a typology of families according to symptom: the "schizophrenic" family, the "delinquent" family. More recently, it has been realized that what is needed are longitudinal studies that will show the varying nature of the family deviant over time, or the use made of different family members in changing succession, as need arises and persons offer themselves.

The second emphasis mentioned above, the systems emphasis, is congruent with this picture of deviance as an ever-shifting process. Unfortunately, if one looks in the literature that takes this point of view for a consistent idea about the meaning of deviant behavior for either the individual or the group, one does not find it. A loose collection of ideas will accordingly be set down in the next section, in an attempt to find some points of agreement.

VIEWS ON THE MEANING OF DEVIANCE
FOR SOCIAL SYSTEMS

First, there is the cohesion view. Most writers on the sociology of deviance agree with Durkheim that the main function of the deviant for the group is to promote solidarity and highlight rules and norms. A good summary of this position can be found in Dentler and Erickson's "The Functions of Deviance in Groups." [38] Arlene Daniels, in an essay on scapegoating in a sensitivity training group, makes the further point that this morale-building function seems to come to the fore in groups where anxiety and hostility are encouraged.[39]

Second, there is the view that emphasizes the danger to the group. This idea is played down by many of the writers on deviance in their efforts to show that deviance is adaptive rather than dysfunctional, but a few recognize it. Daniels, in the article cited above, remarks that the process of scapegoating may only serve to keep a precarious system from collapse, and points out other risks. Another factor not always noticed is that scapegoating can interfere with a group's ability to deal with reality. Family therapists often comment on the curious way in which the people in a family with a deviant member will feel that there is nothing wrong with them in contrast to the one who is "sick" or "bad." This is not surprising if it is remembered that one is dealing with a positive feedback chain, which does not report errors but goes on convincing the system of the rightness of its ways. A system in the grip of unabated, positive feedback is in danger of failing to be cognizant of reality factors, pursuing a delusive course, and eventually paying the price. Euripides may have been talking about this when he said, "Those whom the gods wish to destroy they first make mad." *

Third is a view which emphasizes the *mediating* function a deviant may have in situations where people are in conflict. Researchers first studying or working with families of schizophrenics were amazed by the way the patient's symptoms would flare up when attention was focused on some crucial disagreement, particularly one between the parents. Jackson felt that this type of activity served a diversionary purpose and termed it a "rescue operation." [40] The family therapy literature, as typified by the Vogel and Bell article mentioned above,[37] almost uniformly emphasizes the way in which the parents of an emotionally disturbed child, who are often in serious, if unadmited, conflict, can unite around their common concern for him. Thus the hostility between them is submerged and a surface harmony prevails.

Observations like this led to the belief that, whatever else "schizophrenia" might be, it was always associated with a split in the family. Haley speculates on schizophrenia as a conflict of groups in his essay, "Toward a Theory of Pathological Systems," and suggests that schizophrenia is a name for behavior that results from mediating in many family triangles.[44] In families where profound differences exist between the parents, which often means between whole kin groups, a need for family unity will reward ambiguous communication which keeps the peace. Certain persons will be singled out to handle this task. Such persons will not make sense to outsiders, and may even be thought mentally ill, but within the family context this ability not to make sense is encouraged, because it helps the family to stay together.

---

* It is possible to think of deviation-amplifying mutual causal processes as the very stuff of which delusions are made. It is not coincidence that the classic study by Charles Mackay, *Extraordinary Popular Delusions and the Madness of Crowds,* contains many examples of deviation-amplifying processes: two stock market bubbles, the boom in tulip bulbs in seventeenth century Holland, witch-hunting, and so forth.[41] One can see a delusion as the outcome of a process which, being self-validating and unable to report errors, promotes its own truth. However, this "truth" is only valid from the point of view of an individual unit involved in it. If it could be seen in the context of the next system up, it would be contradicted or revised. Here, although the subject cannot very well be explored in a footnote, one begins to get another way to look at Bateson's concept of the double bind. [42] This he described as a message which seemed to contradict itself but which could be unraveled if one saw that each conflicting meaning referred to a different level of logical type. Jackson, looking at the same thing from the point of view of a relationship, identified it as a vicious cycle in which each person perceives the other as the binder.[43] My point is that the confusion of levels Bateson was talking about can be seen as a confusion about what is taking place on *levels of actual systems,* not just on levels of classification. This latter emphasis has led some of the followers of Bateson to analyze human interaction as if it could all be reduced to an exercise in logic. The direction picked up by Jackson, one Bateson was also in agreement with, seems to me to be a more fruitful one.

A few—not many—sociologists writing on deviance have also observed that the presence of a deviant may be vital to the management of conflict. An example is another study by Daniels, "The Social Function of the Career Fool," describing a young man who was the misfit and clown of a group of recruits undergoing training for the Air Force.[45] This person was invaluable as a butt for hostilities and a source of comic relief, as well as a living comment against everything the military stood for. In this way he mediated between the anxieties of the men and the demands of an inflexible social situation. Daniels makes the generalization that

One can expect the formation of stabilized deviant roles as the precipitates of social interaction in which clashing interests may themselves be stabilized through the persons who play out the deviant roles.[46]

In summarizing these views, one can say that all of them make a connection between the presence of a deviant and the survival of the group. But there is another connection, one which was brought out in the last two paragraphs, between the type of process that splits a group in two and that which casts up a deviant. It is this lead that I shall follow in the next section. To do so, I will go back to *Naven* and look more closely at Bateson's concept of schismogenesis. It is possible that this concept will begin to show us how deviation-amplifying processes may, in the context of a larger circuit, act upon each other in mutually self-regulating ways.

SCHISMOGENESIS

It was in trying to puzzle out the meaning of an obscure ceremony called naven in a New Guinea tribe he was studying that Bateson first began to elaborate on this idea. His original definition of schismogenesis was "a process of differentiation in the norms of individual behavior resulting from cumulatve interaction between individuals." [47] This was before Bateson had rethought this concept in the light of cybernetic theory, but the examples he came up with were all of deviation-amplifying processes: the mutual-causal processes at work in family relationships, mental illness, culture contacts, international rivalries, the rise of political leaders, and so forth. In applying this category of schismogenesis to interpersonal relationships, Bateson went on to distinguish between two types. One he called symmetrical, meaning the competitive rivalry that sometimes threatens to split a group down the middle. The other was complementary, meaning the progressive differentiation that takes place between two unequal parties, one of whom is dependent on the other.

The way Bateson applied these ideas to the naven ceremony was this. He noticed that this ritual took place whenever kin groups in this very competitive, headhunting society approached an imbalance in relative standing. This could occur when a clan gained a new member through marriage or birth. Or it could be when a child achieved an important first; his first fish spearing or canoe building, especially his first homicide. The ritual of naven which then ensued consisted of the child's uncles on his mother's side dressing up like filthy hags, clowning outrageously, and offering themselves as "wives" to the child. A characteristic accompanying gesture would be to rub the cleft of the buttocks down the child's leg. In addition, the father's female relatives would dress up like men, and there would be an exchange of gifts and food between the two sides of the child's family.

In his first attempt to understand the naven, Bateson saw it as a kind of societal glue, acting to strengthen the weak affinal ties to the child's maternal relatives in this strongly patrilineal group. Decades later, in the epilogue added to the 1958 edition, he began to refine his thinking about schismogenesis and to apply cybernetic principles to this idea. Looking back, he picked out the emphasis on complementary relationships in the naven. The ritual seemed to include not only travesties on the parent-child roles, which were complementary by nature, but on the male-female roles, which were also highly differentiated in a complementary direction. This contrasted with the intensely symmetrical competitiveness of the men in the different clans and moieties. Going back to his distinction between the two types of schismogenesis, Bateson wondered whether there might not be a reciprocal action between complementary and symmetrical forms in this society, so that each corrected the excesses of the other:

With self-corrective circuits as a conceptual model, it was now natural to ask whether there might exist, in this culture, functional connections such that controlling factors would be brought into play by increased schismogenic tension. . . . The answer was immediately evident. The *naven* ceremonial, which is an exaggerated caricature of a complementary sexual behavior between *wau* [uncle] and *laua* [nephew] is in fact set off by overweening symmetrical behavior. When *laua* boasts in the presence of *wau*, the latter has recourse to naven behavior.[48] *

Bateson found that the process went the other way too, so that extremes of complementary behavior were controlled by extremes of symmetrical behavior.

* Hardin describes similar social rituals directed against one person achieving too much power, like the statement of the early bishops who had to say "Nolo episcopari" ("I don't want to be a bishop") as part of their oath of investiture, or the threat of an "ostracism" (a vote to send a man into exile) which members of the Athenian Assembly knew could be brought against any one of them.[49]

What Bateson is saying, however, is not just that there are opposing tendencies in the society that counteract one another, but that one type of splitting process can be used to counteract another. This is an unusual thought. Yet as Bateson elaborates on it, it begins to make sense. The reader is particularly referred to the section on schismogenesis in *Naven* which illustrates various ways in which a threatened split in relationships can be relieved by splitting of another type or along another line of strain.[50]

We are now beginning to get at a possible way to describe the interplay between deviation-amplying and counteracting processes in natural groups in which deviants play a crucial part. Of all such groups, the family is the most important to study because it may be the prototype for every other ongoing group. And so I will take a look at the family, using some of the ideas already discussed. In particular, I shall focus on the peculiar phenomenon of what I shall call irresistible runs.

IRRESISTIBLE RUNS

In talking about homeostatic mechanisms, writers like Hardin assume that, if a homeostatic plateau is exceeded, a disastrous deviation-amplifying process will set in which will destroy the system. Yet in families that come into therapy (the only kind family researchers have been able to study closely—a weakness in the field) one finds constant small runs—positive feedback chains which look as if they might turn into runaways but never do. These runs can be escalating arguments such as Jackson noted in his work with what he called (following Bateson) symmetrical couples.[51] Or they can take place in a marriage where husband and wife have defined their roles in a complementary manner, with one seemingly the "strong" one and the other "weak." Such a pair, as Jackson says, "can be viewed as a mutual causative system, whose complementary communication reinforces the nature of the interaction."[52] Or one can have similar spirals of hostility between parent and child, as in the interchange William Taylor cites as an example of recurrent states in families in a recent article on family interaction.[53] These runs are almost irresistible, as anyone who has ever been caught in one or watched one knows, and they repeat and repeat like a broken record, never reaching any conclusion.

What are these forms, and why do they occur? A guess will be hazarded that they are a response to a system that is constantly threatening to exceed its homeostatic plateau. Why else would one have so many positive feedback chains that abort? It is even possible that the many redundancies of communication noted by researchers in families with disturbed members, particularly the disturbed child-parents triangle, are all feedback chains of this type.*

This explanation implies that there *is* something in family systems resembling a homeostatic plateau. Although no family researcher has, to my knowledge, used the idea of such a plateau in interpreting family behavior, Bales has used it in speaking of small group behavior.[54] Noting that it does not seem true that a successful meeting will have fewer negative than positive reactions by group members, Bales remarks that there seems to be a kind of optimum balance on which this success depends. Let there be a departure to one side or the other and trouble will arise. Bales finds this most true when there is an excessive rate of disagreement: "Apparently, when ill feeling rises above some critical point, a 'chain reaction' or 'vicious circle' tends to set in. Logic and the practical demands of the task cease to be governing factors." [56] In fact, says Bales, groups when they reach this point can hardly accomplish anything at all.

In the same way, there seems to be a certain range within which family functioning is maintained. In families where a member is deemed to be "abnormal," this range may be an extremely narrow one.† Let us set up an example which might make this metaphor more real. Assuming, along with therapists like Virginia Satir, that the relationship between the parents is one of the key variables governing pathology in the family, the setting for closeness and distance between the parents would be very important.[57] Suppose a husband is always exceeding the setting for distance from his wife because of a prior setting for closeness with one of his parents. One might then expect to find in the family a recurrent mutual causal sequence of some sort. This sequence might take the form of the bickering noted by Jackson, where each spouse, feeling the "victim" of the other, provokes the very hostilities that justify his own. Or it may take the form of an increasing withdrawal, where distant behavior provokes even more distant behavior in reciprocal fashion. Before such a run can become a runaway, a child or other family member will often move in to block the escalation—the rescue operation noted by Jackson—and divert the hostilities and concern of the parents to himself. Thus he substitutes a safe deviation-amplifying process for one that threatens the family at its base.

One can think of another sequence: if two parents who engage in a withdrawal contest go too long without contact, a child and one parent may get into a run of mutual causal hostilities which is blocked when the other parent moves

* Haley's findings of an extraordinary rigidity in the order of speaking in this triangle have been confirmed by a similar study done recently by Waxler and Mishler.[55]

† Dr. Richard Fisch, of the Mental Research Institute in Palo Alto, California, has used the term "the ten foot pole" to describe the narrow range of closeness and distance that seemed to limit the relationships of some of the married pairs that came to him for therapy.

in to defend the child. This sequence then serves to reestablish a connection between the parents, albeit an unfriendly one. One can imagine runs countering runs in this way in a kind of periodic seesaw, and observation of families confirms that at times this is exactly what happens.

Of interest here is Bateson's idea that it is possible for one schismatic process to ward off another. As an example, he mentions a marriage where the roles are extremely complementary, being based on assertion/submission. He suggests that, should the schismogenetic strain from this pattern grow too intense, the development of a symptom in one of the spouses will provide a new complementarity with less divisive implications. Another example is where two warring factions in a group get together against an outside third party. Here the line of schism is shifted to a spot less threatening to the unity of the group, though, as Bateson points out, this second schismogenesis may be even more difficult to control than the first.[58] Bateson does not cover the instance of scapegoating, but one can see that this form entails the use of an *inside* third party, and that it has to involve a complementary relationship. The deviant in a family (or group) is usually a person of weak standing. Often he is a child. By being placed on the edge of the group, he becomes even less powerful—at least in the obvious sense. The advantage to the family of locating the schismatic process on this line rather than on the line between the parents is obvious.*

"PATHOLOGICAL" BALANCE

The question can still be asked: what keeps patterns like these so firmly installed? Why do they not break down? Perhaps the answer can be found in our concept of levels: the imbalance in the nuclear family is serving to correct an imbalance in the larger kin system, and is embedded not only in the equilibrium-maintaining mechanisms of that system but in many of its subordinate parts. These may be other nuclear families, dyads within families, single persons, or organs within those persons. Just as one cannot tamper with any one element in what the biologists call an ecosystem without taking account of its effect on the whole, so one cannot change much in a family or a member of a family

* Taylor says that another reason for the popularity of this device—which he calls the single deviant arrangement—can be traced to an increase in "emotional income" gained by every person in the group at the expense of the deviant. What he does not say is that, comfortable as this arrangement may be for the other family members, it is bound to produce strains in their relationships with other systems outside. Perhaps this is lucky, otherwise there would be no reason for groups to behave any other way. The thought does come to mind that one reason why families with a solidly entrenched deviant so often shun contact with the outside world is that more contact would reveal that their increased "emotional income" is a matter of inflation, not real gain.[59]

without affecting a larger field. This includes other social systems impinging on the family as well. Although one cannot say that such a "field" has a homeostasis as Jackson thought the family had a homeostasis, the combined effect of many systems leaning on or pulling against one another may add up to the kind of stability for which the ecosystem is such a good analogy.

To make this idea a bit more concrete, let us look at the interplay of feedback influences, both deviation amplifying and counteracting, in the hypothetical case of a child whose deviant behavior serves to heal a parental split. First of all, the same process which amplifies the deviance of the child is deviation counteracting in regard to the marital dyad. Moving to yet another level of system, one could say that the very consequence of having a "sick" member may be deviation amplifying for the nuclear family if it interferes with important family functions. For instance, the family line may die out with that generation if the sick member is an only child who becomes unable to have a family of his own. But if one shifts to the next level, the extended kin group, a deviation-counteracting effect may reappear. The inability of the parents to form a strong tie may be due to the fact that one or both of them are still being used to mediate relationships in their own families of origin. If so, they are performing a homeostatic function for the larger group. Given this prior arrangement, it is possible that all the others have to follow. Whatever the case, it is clear that any intervention that tries to reverse the deviation-amplifying sequences in this set without figuring out how to deal with the deviation-counteracting sequences will fare badly.

To sum up, one could say that a family which is off balance in regard to its own system, because it is helping to maintain the balance of larger ones, will be perpetually exposed to the destructive effects of positive feedback chains. In an effort to compensate, some of these will be used to counter others. Any form which serves to prevent a split in the family, like the child whose behavior serves as a diversion, can be thought of as a naven for a badly balanced system. Alternative navens, following Bateson's argument, might be for one of the spouses to develop a symptom and heal the split by becoming more dependent on his partner, or for the family to achieve a united front by scapegoating some outsider. Some families use an uneasy mix of all three strategies, or yet others.

A word should be put in here to the effect that *all* families become periodically unbalanced; they have to, as the power relationships between the generations shift over time. And all families experience the stresses that produce vicious cycles in interpersonal relationships. What is different in families that seem to have members in the deepest trouble is the way these cycles continually repeat, without ever forcing the family to change in a morphogenetic direction, because a form like the child deviant, or a symptomatic member, is there to prevent such a change.

There is one final question to ask: if family pathology can be so stable, what is it that finally causes it—as sometimes happens—to break down?

WHEN THE NAVEN FAILS

The reason that this happens has never satisfactorily been answered. Haley takes the view that there are really two parts to achieving true mental patient-hood: a long period of training in the right family setting, learning to mediate in many triangles, *and* the proper accreditation by an authorized psychiatric source.[60] The two types of deviation-amplifying process alluded to before come to mind: a condition of deviance gradually arrived at, followed by some crisis that ushers in a runaway. Of course, what constitutes a crisis to a family can only be answered in the specific instance. But one can surmise that any sudden shift in the arrangement of homeostatic checks and balances in the kinship group and its subsystems will cause an upset that the family may be unable to handle. A very obvious threat of this sort would be the departure of a key person who is helping to stabilize the family. Children who are being used in this way often erupt with disturbances when they come to the age when they would normally leave home, and the next system up—the community—is often brought in to restore equilibrium.

Is this a well-deserved end, then, to the pathological balance? Not always. The officials to whom society gives the power to act in these situations often authorize the family to go on using the person who is the key to their naven as before. But there is a difference. Previously, as the distance between the parents would periodically widen, using our hypothetical example, the child would produce the behavior that caused it to close up again. But—important point—he was not yet your true scapegoat; he was not hated, feared, extruded. It is society that comes in and turns the fault that intermittently opens up between the family and the child into a permanent chasm. The scapegoating process—redefined here as a way of relocating the split in the family—is only made easier by hospitalization or institutionalization. The family is free to continue with it without having to deal with inconvenient protests.

Thus does society move in to take a deviation-amplifying role, replacing the family's comparatively benign naven ceremonies with its own degredation ceremonies, as Goffman calls them. The person so honored is now stigmatized and placed outside the pale. However, what promotes deviance on the level of one system, can inhibit it on another. Society is the beneficiary of the deviation-*counteracting* effect produced by a deviant on his group, which is to reaffirm its solidarity, its belief in itself, and in the righteousness of its ways.

But herein lie the very seeds of its destruction (back to a deviation-*amplifying* aspect again!), not in terms of the present structure of the group but of its future ability to adapt and change. One could say that every single-deviant arrangement is one coffin nail more for the group. Over the long range, the process has implications for the eventual destruction of the group due to loss of flexibility and risk of error. It is at this point that the vista offered by the biologists becomes a comforting one, with their talk of variety pools and the role of deviance in forcing new solutions. To quote another systems thinker, Roget Nett:

Since the creative strength of a society must be sought in the capacity of individuals to evaluate, extend, correct, and ultimately to alter existing definitions and understandings (a process which is, in effect, deviation), the problem of ordering a society becomes one of utilizing the vital element—deviation—in social-organizational context.[61]

A DEVIATION-AMPLIFYING MUTUAL
CAUSAL THERAPY

The above remarks are all very well in the abstract, but can they be applied to the arrangements that exist for controlling deviant persons? Is there really a way to "utilize the vital element—deviation—in social-organizational context?" Some of the new approaches to therapy, at least, are beginning to come up with an answer. These approaches do not treat deviance as though it were a disorder inside the individual but deal directly with the interpersonal processes that produce it. Family therapy was, of course, the pioneering invention. The network therapy of Ross Speck and the ecosystems view of E. H. Auerswald are logical extensions of this method. The multiple family therapy of Peter Laqueur, the brief crisis work with families of Donald Langsley and David Kaplan's group in Denver, and Murray Bowen's work with triangles in kinship systems are still other variations.

With these developments, the task of the therapist is being redefined. Haley has observed that therapy was traditionally based on a notion implying that the patient is like a machine that has broken down, and that the therapeutic task is to put him back together. However, if one thinks in terms of systems and their tendency to rigidify rather than undergo change, one takes an opposite view. The problem then is that the patient is caught in an increasingly inflexible set of patterns, and the task is to loosen them up. Therapy may require the introduction of complexity rather than the restoration of order.*

A good example of this different approach to therapy is Salvador Minuchin's

* Personal communication.

technique for inducing crisis in families with the aim of changing the structure of the system. Minuchin and Barcai, in their article "Therapeutically Induced Family Crisis," differentiate between emergency activity and crisis activity, much as Maruyama distinguishes between morphostatic and morphogenetic change.[62] In the family they describe, the repeated and possibly fatal hospitalization of a child for diabetic acidosis was seen by family members as an emergency to be handled by getting her to the hospital. There was no perception of crisis, which might have pushed the family to make changes in family patterns which were triggering the attacks. Because of this, Minuchin and his co-workers set out to upset the equilibrium of the family. This equilibrium seemed to depend on using the attacks of acidosis to counteract the strains engendered by a years-long circular feedback process between the husband's dependency and the wife's control. By blocking some of the lesser strategies used to deflect these strains, the therapy team engineered a series of crises which had the virtue of uncovering the parents' difficult relationship and forcing them to invent new techniques to deal with it. The patient's attacks, although intensifying at first, dropped sharply after a few weeks. As one might predict, this movement corresponded to an increase in the problems experienced by everybody else. But the change that had been achieved in a short time, using small, planned changes in apparently peripheral areas of family interaction, seemed to confirm the rationale of the therapy, which was directed toward working with mutual causal processes throughout.

I have picked out Minuchin's article here because it gives an extraordinarily clear view of how the concepts we have been considering on an intellectual level can be applied to an actual instance of family distress. It is probable that all therapists work instinctively with mutual causal processes, even though they do not formulate the matter in this way. But to identify and then work purposely with something resembling a natural law of human behavior is a step in a remarkable direction. The thought arises that it may be possible to harness the forces of deviation and put them to domestic use much as the forces of electricity were harnessed and put to use. The family therapist Carl Whitaker once said, "The family is a matter of life and death voltages." He might also have observed that these same voltages can be used to light a home.

SUMMARY

This paper has investigated the ideas of general systems writers who are concerned with deviation-amplifying processes (positive feedback) and has related them to the work of researchers studying deviant behavior in families and other natural groups. A look at the way systems writers treat deviation-amplifying processes gives us two main perspectives. Some see positive feedback as the destructive activity that takes over when a system's error-activating mechanisms break down. Others maintain that this process is as vital as negative feedback, as it enables living systems to adapt to changing environments through random deviation selectively amplified by natural events.

These writers agree that there are many positive and negative feedback chains operating in any situation and that the results are not easy to predict. A runaway in a social system may force it to recalibrate, or it may produce a deviant who will lock the *status quo* back into place. In part, the homeostatic status of the system will determine the outcome. There are also different stages or types of mutual causal processes. There is the drift that may go toward or away from random, and then there is more systemic activity such as is evidenced by a runaway. Finally, there is the problem of levels. The same feedback process may have a deviation-amplifying effect on a system on one level and the opposite effect on a system the next level up. Thus it is difficult to decipher the cybernetic processes at work in a given field at the same time.

Family researchers and writers on social deviance have also been interested in these processes, but have not always seen the matter in cybernetic terms. The family theorists have focused on the equilibrium-maintaining effect on the family system of the process that produces a symptomatic member. The sociologists have been more concerned with the induction process that leads to a deviant career. Each group is looking at the same thing but from the point of view of different systems. Thus, one sees the deviation-*counteracting* effect, and the other the deviation-*amplifying* one. Both schools agree that the presence of a deviant seems to promote group cohesion and is most in evidence when the group is beset with inner strains.

In families, symptom behavior is similarly seen to mediate conflict between the parents or between two sides of the family. Applying a cybernetic framework to studies of family interaction suggests the further idea that the many redundancies noted in communication in "abnormal" families can be described as positive feedback chains set off by the continual threat of a split that might destroy the group. In particular, the idea that such a split may be offset by other, less costly schismatic forms serves to explain how a "pathological" family equilibrium is maintained.

Finally, it is suggested that most of the control systems set up by our society to handle deviance simply reinforce the mutual-causal processes that feed into it. This can also be dangerous for the society, as too much scapegoating makes its institutions more rigid, hence more fragile. A welcome sign is the emergence of philosophies and methods of therapy which see the patient as the key to the pathological balance of a set of ongoing relationships. The task then becomes one of recalibrating these relationships, usually in a freer and less restricted direction, rather than attempting to rehabilitate or control the person who is sustaining them.

REFERENCES

1. Maruyama, M., "The Second Cybernetics: Deviation-Amplifying Mutual Causal Processes," in Buckley, W. (Ed.), *Modern Systems Research for the Behavioral Scientist*, Chicago, Aldine, 1968, pp. 304-313.
2. Wiener, N., *The Human Use of Human Beings*, New York, Anchor, 1954, p. 25.
3. Hardin, G., "The Cybernetics of Competition: A Biologist's View of Society," in Shepard, P., and McKinley, D. (Eds.), *The Subversive Science: Essays Toward an Ecology of Man*, Boston, Houghton Mifflin, 1969, pp. 275-295.
4. *Ibid.*, pp. 286-287.
5. Bateson, G., *Naven*, London, England, Cambridge University Press, 1936.
6. Jackson, D. D., "The Question of Family Homeostasis," *Psychiat. Quart. Suppl.* 31:79-90, 1957.
7. Haley, J., *Strategies of Psychotherapy*, New York, Grune & Stratton, 1963, p. 189.
8. Haley, J., and Hoffman, L., *Techniques of Family Therapy*, New York, Basic Books, 1968, p. 227.
9. Haley, J., "Research on Family Patterns: An Instrument Measurement," *Family Process* 3:41-65, 1964.
10. Durkheim, E., *The Division of Labor in Society*, G. Simpson (Tr.), New York, Free Press, 1960.
11. Cohen, A. K., *Deviance and Control*, Englewood Cliffs, N.J., Prentice-Hall, 1966, Chapter 7.
12. Erikson, K. T., "Notes on the Sociology of Deviance," in Becker, H. (Ed.), *The Other Side*, New York, Free Press, 1964, p. 12.
13. *Ibid.*, p. 19.
14. Erikson, K. T., *The Wayward Puritans*, New York, Wiley, 1966, p. 19.
15. Goffman, E., *Asylums*, New York, Anchor, 1961, pp. 127-168.
16. Durkheim, E., *Suicide*, New York, Free Press, 1951.
17. Freidson, E., "Disability as Social Deviance," in Rubington, E., and Weinberg, M. S. (Eds.), *Deviance/The Interactionist Perspective*, New York, Macmillan, 1968, p. 119.
18. Becker, H., *Outsiders: Studies in the Sociology of Deviance*, New York, Free Press, 1963.
19. Maruyama, *op. cit.*, p. 304.
20. Miller, J., "Living Systems: Structure and Process," *Behav. Sci.* 10:337-379, 1965.
21. Buckley, W., "Society as a Complex Adaptive System," in Buckley, W. (Ed.), *Modern Systems Research for the Behavioral Scientist*, Chicago, Aldine, 1968, p. 491.
22. *Ibid.*, p. 500.
23. Maruyama, *op. cit.*, p. 312.

24. Bateson, G., *Naven* (rev. ed.), Stanford, Calif., Stanford University Press, 1965.
25. *Ibid.,* pp. 288-289.
26. Hardin, *op. cit.,* p. 287.
27. Bateson, *Naven* (rev. ed.), p. 197.
28. Maruyama, *op. cit.,* p. 312.
29. Simon, H., "Comments on the Theory of Organization," *Amer. Polit. Sci. Rev.* 46:1130-39, 1952.
30. Ruesch, J., and Bateson, G., *Communication: The Social Matrix of Society,* New York, Norton, 1951, p. 287.
31. *Ibid.,* p. 289.
32. Merton, R. K., *On Theoretical Sociology,* New York, Free Press, 1967, p. 115.
33. Haley, *Strategies of Psychotherapy,* Chapter 1.
34. Merton, R. K., *Social Theory and Social Structure,* New York, Free Press, 1968, pp. 475-490.
35. Rubington, E., and Weinberg, M. S., *Deviance/The Interactionist Perspective,* London, England, Macmillan, 1968.
36. Wilkins, L. T., "A Behavioral Theory of Drug Taking," in Buckley, W. (Ed.), *Modern Systems Research for the Behavioral Scientist,* Chicago, Aldine, 1968, pp. 421-427.
37. Vogel, E. F., and Bell, N. W., "The Emotionally Disturbed Child as the Family Scapegoat," in Bell, N. W., and Vogel, E. F. (Eds.), *The Family,* New York, Free Press, 1960, pp. 382-397.
38. Dentler, R. A., and Erikson, K. T., "The Functions of Deviance in Groups," *Soc. Probl.* 7:98-107, 1959.
39. Daniels, A. K., "Interaction Through Social Typing: The Development of the Scapegoat in Sensitivity Training Sessions," in Shibutani, T. (Ed.), *Festschrift in Honor of Herbert Blumer,* 1969.
40. Haley and Hoffman, *op. cit.,* p. 205.
41. Mackay, C., *Extraordinary Popular Delusions and the Madness of Crowds,* New York, Noonday, 1962.
42. Bateson, G., Jackson, D. D., Haley, J., and Weakland, J. H., "Toward a Theory of Schizophrenia," *Behav. Sci.* 1:251-264, 1956.
43. Jackson, D. D., and Weakland, J. H., "Conjoint Family Therapy: Some Considerations on Theory, Technique and Results," in Jackson, D. D. (Ed.), *Therapy, Communication and Change,* Palo Alto, Calif., Science and Behavior Books, 1968, p. 270.
44. Haley, J., "Toward a Theory of Pathological Systems," in Zuk, H., and Boszormenyi-Nagy, I. (Eds.), *Family Therapy and Disturbed Families,* Palo Alto, Calif., Science and Behavior Books, 1969, pp. 11-27.
45. Daniels, A. K., "The Social Function of the Career Fool," *Psychiatry* 27:219-229, 1964.
46. *Ibid.,* p. 229.
47. Bateson, *Naven* (rev. ed.), p. 175.
48. *Ibid.,* p. 289.
49. Hardin, *op. cit.,* pp. 288-289.
50. Bateson, *Naven* (rev. ed.), pp. 187-197.
51. Lederer, W. J., and Jackson, D. D., *The Mirages of Marriage,* New York, Norton, 1968, pp. 161-173.

52. Jackson, D. D., "The Role of the Individual," address to Conference on Mental Health and the Idea of Mankind, Annual Meeting, Council for the Study of Mankind, Chicago, Ill., 1964.

53. Taylor, W., "Research on Family Interaction, I, A Methodological Note," *Family Process* 9:221-232, 1970.

54. Bales, R. F., "In Conference," in Amitai, E. (Ed.), *Readings on Modern Organizations,* Englewood Cliffs, N.J., Prentice-Hall, 1969, pp. 147-154.

55. Waxler, N. E., and Mishler, E. G., "Sequential Patterning in Family Interaction," *Family Process* 9:211-220, 1970.

56. Bales, *op. cit.,* p. 150.

57. Satir, V., *Conjoint Family Therapy,* Palo Alto, Calif., Science and Behavior Books, 1964, Chapter 1.

58. Bateson, *Naven* (rev. ed.), p. 269.

59. Taylor, *op. cit.,* pp. 226-227.

60. Haley, J., "The Art of Being Schizophrenic," *Voices* 1:133-147, 1965.

61. Nett, R., "Conformity-Deviation and the Social Control Concept," in Buckley, W. (Ed.), *Modern Systems Research for the Behavioral Scientists,* New York, Aldine, 1968, pp. 409-414.

62. Minuchin, S., and Barcai, A., "Therapeutically Induced Family Crisis," in Masserman, J. H. (Ed.), *Science and Psychoanalysis,* New York, Grune & Stratton, 1969, pp. 199-205.

23

Social Network Intervention

ROSS V. SPECK

CAROLYN L. ATTNEAVE

In social network intervention we assemble together all members of the kinship system, all friends and neighbors of the family, and, in fact, everyone who is of significance to the nuclear family that offers the presenting problem. In our experience, the typical middle-class urban family has the potential to assemble about forty persons for network meetings. These meetings are held in the home. Gathering the network group together in one place at one time provides great therapeutic potential. The assembly of the tribe in a crisis situation probably originated with prehistoric man. Tribal meetings for healing purposes are well known in many widely varying cultures. Social network intervention organizes this group force in a systematic way.

THE INTERVENTION TEAM

When a social network is assembled, they meet with a team of network intervenors. It is doubtful if this type of therapy should routinely be undertaken

312

by one person working entirely alone. The first strategy, then, is the selection of a team. Preferably the team should be made up of two or three people who know one another well enough to have considerable trust in one another and who are familiar with each other's styles of relating and of general behavior. Division of roles and skills is important, but not a prerequisite. A particularly happy combination occurs when one of the team is skilled in large group situations, easily able to command the flow of attention and energy of a network, and knows when and how to turn it loose on itself.

The role of the leader is somewhat like that of a good discussion leader or a good theatrical director (particularly if he or she knows the Stanislavsky techniques). A sense of timing, empathy with emotional highpoints, a sense of group moods and undercurrents, and some charismatic presence are all part of the equipment that is desirable. Along with the ability to dominate, the leader must have the confidence that comes with considerable experience in handling situations and knowing human beings under stress. Equally important is his ability to efface himself, to delegate and diffuse responsibility, emphatically and pointedly, rather than to collect it for himself. This last characteristic is essential and often overlooked. One neophyte team commented that in their networks they did all the talking. By comparison, networks organized by experienced teams deceptively appear to run themselves. In fact, in several instances the team has been known to leave at about 11 o'clock, only to be told the next day, "We didn't even notice you'd gone until after 12:00—and we kept right on talking until about 1:30."

The other team members should also have some of the leader's characteristics, but may contribute special skills. If the network includes several generations, it is often helpful to have one youth and one grandparent type on the team so that mingling between team and network and participation by many of the network will be facilitated. Also, suppression of manic, overanxious, or inopportune comments is easier if the network member concerned is matched in style and status by a team member. Team members who blend easily with the total network can effectively help focus the smaller groups into which the network divides, such as committees, buzz sessions, or free-floating conversations.

It should be pointed out that if the team has three or more members, one member will often be selected as a scapegoat and be telephoned or vilified whenever the network or any part of it is angry at the leader or frustrated by its own impotence. The scapegoat role may as well be anticipated, even though one cannot always predict before the first meeting whom the network will choose for this sacrificial position.

An important skill that should be represented in the team is familiarity with nonverbal encounter techniques and their impact on groups and individuals. Emphasis on the scientific, cybernated aspect of the world has caused the importance of feelings and emotions to be overlooked to such an extent that most rituals are omitted or even ridiculed while the youth of the land cry out for meaning and for some way of learning how to "feel." Not only are the nonverbal reactions of the group extremely sensitive cues and clues for the intervention team, but when the team plays upon them to build a nonverbal network experience a ritual takes place. The tension released by jumping, shouting, or screaming, the calming effect of group swaying, the solidarity that comes from huddling and handclasping, all of these knot the network together in a way that merely meeting and talking cannot do. One often notes that, if a pattern of nonverbal openers has been utilized in the first meeting, the network members feel uneasy if it is omitted at the next meeting. That newcomers or latecomers are most easily melded into a social setting via informal nonverbal ritual is almost self-evident if one observes the number of rituals that form part of common courtesy, such as offering chairs, moving over, touching, exchanging meaningful looks, etc.

The experienced intervention team scattered in the crowd can respond to the leader's directions spontaneously and dramatically, catalyzing contagion and drawing everyone into participation. If a dignified "doctor" is willing to take off shoes and sit on the floor, or look at the ceiling and let out a rebel yell or war whoop, or close his eyes and sway while the whole group is looking, then it becomes safe for the housewives and husbands, the kids and the parents, the relatives and the neighbors to do so, too.

Also, quick verbal and nonverbal exchanges of information are easier for a team that is used to working together. The leader may need to have a piece of information, understand a relationship, see a development of insight or resistance in some subsection of the network. When space and organization permit, small conferences make information flow easy and help the leader utilize the team to verify impressions, check strategy, switch roles, or just let off steam. However, when conditions are too crowded or the session activities do not permit *sub voce* team conferences, postural and body communications are important and the ability to break in or to toss the ball quickly and deftly about the team becomes more important. Network sessions last three or four hours, and leadership is strenuous. For the team to keep optimally fresh, some spelling off, as well as change of pace, is desirable.

The teamwork exhibited by the professional intervenors is sometimes fundamental as a model for the network. The effect of the teamwork model is most quickly seen in the network's activists, but the more passive members also learn that it is safe to fumble, to stick one's neck out, and to trust one another.

In one first network session involving a teen-age drug user and his friends and family, the network youth group was most reluctant to discuss openly their use of and experience with various drugs, as well as their ideas about drug use, until the matched youth team member spoke up frankly about his own curiosity and experience. While challenging this peer, the network youth found that the network's older generation was both interested in and attentive to their views. Once stereotyped defenses were down, the older members of the network were amazed to find themselves feeling defensive about diet pills and tranquilizers. Discussion was facilitated when the older team member insisted that discussion was relevant and necessary. The leader then capitalized on the commonality demonstrated, instead of the confusion in role reversals, and shifted the pressure away from stereotypes about drug addictions and onto the more pertinent relationships involved. Team member support allowed the leader to capitalize on the mirror-imaging between the generations—a task which otherwise would have been much more difficult.

Goals of the Intervention Team

Naturally the personality, physique, and aura of each individual denote some of the limits of his or her role on the team. The common goal of the team is something else, and whatever the ingredients, the team must be committed to it, regardless of the division of labor.

The goals of all network intervention are to stimulate, to reflect, and to focus the potential within the network to solve one another's problems. By strengthening bonds, loosening binds, opening new channels, facilitating new perceptions, activating latent strengths, and helping to damp out, ventilate, or excise pathology the social network is enabled to become the life-sustaining community within the social matrix of each individual. This does not happen if the intervenors act like therapists toward patients, since implicit in the therapeutic contract is delegation to the therapist of responsibility for healing, even though eventually most therapies provide a terminal phase where responsibility for self is returned to the patient or family.

However, the intervention team must be on guard at every turn to deflect therapist attempts and keep the responsibility within the network itself. This means being able to live with one's own curiosity when the network activists gain enough confidence to take over. It means real, not pseudo, confidence in network members, who know the problems, the landmarks and terrain of the distressed person's life space. They must be free to do the thinking and acting that will evolve more practical and efficient solutions than the professional could. It means the willingness of team members to be available to consult without being drawn in, and it means considerable clinical experience and intuition to be able to make quick and decisive judgments. Above all, it implies a shared working philosophy of faith in human beings and satisfaction in seeing them rise to occasions rather than a faith in a professional mystique and a need to be central and depended upon.

If this goal and faith is part of the fiber of the team, it is communicated to the network in a positive and safe manner. Even suicidal and homicidal gestures can usually be controlled and handled by the network. The professional judgment that quickly evaluates both the gesture and the network strengths is important. It takes a good deal of acumen to know when it is safe to say "Leave him out in the rain—when he gets wet he will come in, and he ought to find you drinking coffee in the kitchen, not hanging out the window whining."

We have found that in every network there are members whom we call activists. These network activists perceive the need for someone to take over temporarily, and they require support from the team when filling the breech. It takes guts on the part of a network committee of activists to sit with parents around the clock while they let their boy learn what it is like to earn his own living. It takes compassion to invite a defensive embattled couple to dinner, a card party, or a style show and make them comfortable amongst guests and strangers. It takes reserves of patience to find job after job for an inept and unwilling depressed person, and to help him succeed almost in spite of himself so that he finds out that he can "be somebody." Moreover, it takes considerable courage for most professionals to turn these responsibilities over to someone else who has nothing but his or her humanity, concern, and horse sense to guide him through the traps professionals know so well.

The experienced team has often observed that, if they wanted to, they could shift any network over to individual and family therapy and be busy for the rest of their professional careers. For it is not just the index patient's distress that is dealt with, but that of many other families and individuals in the network. As they bring their distress to the surface, the network deals with it. The network team working through the activists enables the network to begin the important human task of solving one another's problems. The ambivalence of one set of parents is resolved when they find someone dealing with parallel problems down the block. One man's need for manual labor is matched by someone else's inside track to a hideaway that is available. This is the way that society has always functioned best—whether in extended families, small communities, clans, communes, or fraternal organizations. It is this potential within any group of forty or more people related by common concern for one another that can be unchained by the network effect. *There is no other single goal—not cure, not treatment, but enabling people to cope and to share their strengths in coping and also in reaping enjoyments and pleasures that restore their potentials and set them up to handle the inevitable next crisis of living.*

When these goals are clear, the skills needed by the team are relatively simple to define. The ability to relate to people, to sense group and subgroup moods and strengths, and to facilitate, focus, and reflect back confidence. The particular disciplines and techniques are raw materials, not prerequisites. The intervention team will blend them with experience and use any and all when appropriate.

Sequences and Patterns

With experience, too, comes the sense of an order to the events that transpire, and a pattern falls into shape. This makes it easier to work with the numbers of people involved and their subgroupings. It makes sense of the highs and lows, the ploys and counterploys, and the permutations behind the seemingly infinite changes each network rings on the organizational possibilities of human social relationships.

Not all these paterns have been identified and explored yet. It is part of the fascination of network study and intervention that there are unmapped vistas and old mountains to be climbed before new ones are glimpsed. The sequences and patterning sketched here may after some years seem like the early maps of the new world that showed California as an island and connected the Great Lakes to the western seas. Had the earlier explorers waited for the surveyors, and later perhaps the aerial photographers, before opening trade routes and establishing outposts, the wilderness would remain and the cities of Europe and the coastal plain of the United States would be even more crowded and explosive than they are now.

The assembly or prenetwork phase has already been well described. The opening session is usually considered one of a series, although on two occasions a single network meeting has been held and subsequent follow up indicated that the network effect had productive effects persisting for well over a year. Theoretically the one session intervention might be the ideal, but it is doubtful that it will be very often approximated when a network has to be assembled and created around the distress of an individual and his family. The experience of many religious groups who rely on the network effect of a conversion experience, as in revival meetings, suggests that even though this is a potent force it has to be renewed periodically or the group falls back into fragmentation. Other groups provide for renewal at a lesser peak through family reunions, seasonal festivals, life cycle celebrations of birth and marriage, and passage from one stage of the life cycle to the next, including death. Network intervenors need to be cognizant of this and, if possible, direct the energy of the network toward some such self-recharging cycle of its own, within whatever context seems appropriate to the group.

The principal reasons for continuing meetings beyond the tossing of the first rock into the pool are the need for practice, learning and development of insight, since one trial learning is usually not very permanent or predictable. The reinforcement that comes with shared coping experiences tends to make the network a stabilized social unit that can continue to function without professional coaching. A series of six meetings seems to be satisfying to all concerned, and practical, although sometimes three or four are adequate. The first session is usually one that ends on a high pitch of excitement and discovery of one another within the group. The reality of the fact that the professionals are not going to take over at some point or another is not always clear to the network at this time, and in fact the illusion of professional protection and sanction may be very important at this point to free the members of the network to explore one another more spontaneously. Hope and communication are both characteristic of this phase.

The strategy for the first session is plotted by the team on the basis of acquaintance with the problem gathered in the prenetwork discussions with the family about its distress. The leader will count on quick feedback from team members of subgroupings and moods as the network gathers. Individual team members arriving early and watching the host family and others can quickly sort out the alignments and the feelings as well as the relationships from the kinesics, the voices, and the clusterings.

New team members often ask "What do I do?" The answer is simple: Set the example of friendly interest, open communication, and unobtrusive returns of the ball whenever anyone moves to put the professional in charge. If asked, identify yourself by name and, if pressed, by occupation or professional role. If not asked, let people assume you are another member of the network, because for the next few weeks that is what you will become. Use whatever social skills seem appropriate, establishing human contact with as many people as possible, but also do a lot of listening and observing. Locate the refreshments, the bathrooms, the cloakrooms, the kitchen, the back door, the fans, the extra chairs, the ashtrays, the telephone and its extensions. Help move furniture if necessary. Get to know the people and the environment thoroughly as quickly as possible. If there are pets, identify them and their names and dispositions. Likewise, the children. Above all, don't get caught with the team standing grouped together staring at the people like zoological specimens. Never seem to be talking at length about any interest that cannot be shared with part of the network. It is not only rude; it is also destructive of morale.

Be prepared for many anxieties and much fear at the first session. Very few people will have any idea why they are there, and there will be many who are apprehensive about the distress of the family who invited them, about the risks they may be taking themselves, and about much that they have read and heard and misinterpreted about the whole profession of psychotherapy. In fact, those who have had experience with such marathons as group or individual therapy may be even more wary than the completely naive. This anxiety has its function, since, as the session relieves it, the relaxation and confidence is a potent reinforcement for continuing with the network intervention model. However, the clinical skill and ability to relieve false fears and to focus feelings realistically can be important at this stage.

Once the group has gathered, the leader takes charge. He needs to introduce himself with an outline of the problem and the network intervention methodology. This is a brief sales pitch and, like many similar openings, has impact beyond the cognitive level. Information may not be retained so much as a sense of purpose and direction.

Almost immediately after this introduction the leader introduces encounter-sensitivity techniques. This rapidly inducts the network into what we have called a group high where enthusiasm, activism, and polarization can break down ordinary social barriers and defenses which isolate each network member prior to the assembly. A fight for control is often noted here as the distressed person, his family, or a network member attempts to not participate. The team scattered through the group stimulates, initiates, and infectiously pulls the fringers into the group. During this prelude the leader often establishes control not merely of the network but, through it, of the dissidents and distressed persons in a highly significant fashion. These nonverbal periods need not be long: three, five, or ten minutes at most. But they do seem to be the first big breakthrough that begins the realignment of network bonds and binds.

These nonverbal rituals should end with the group feeling solidified, in contact with one another, and quiet. At this point, the leader quickly forms a structure for dialogue and discussion.

In conducting a new session, the leader's sense of timing is crucial, including his ability to shift the tempo and adapt the rate of change, introduce themes, and provide the staccato and legato marks that build to crescendos of maximum impact.

In introducing dialogue, the leader shifts the members' positions to form an appropriate grouping. The physical arrangements depend on the setting, which are usually the living room and dining room of homes. Frequently, people are seated on the floor as well as chairs, sofas, and stairways. One format that is adaptable to many such settings is the use of concentric circles.

An inner circle of six to ten people is rapidly designated and asked to sit on the floor in the center. These are the more outgoing, often younger members whose talk will stir up ripples and begin to polarize the group. Sometimes an outer group is designated because the older, less immediately involved group have naturally seated themselves on the comfortable peripheral furniture. At times there is a middle group interposed by the apparent vagaries of seating and furniture arrangement. This middle group may serve as a buffer or mediator between the inner and outer groups, which will soon be polarized by the task assignments of the conductor.

The leader not only selects the most communicative group first, but also arranges to polarize issues by dividing along generational lines, or in some other way dramatizing the tensions and differences that exist. He sets a topic for discussion and controls the outside group to prevent interruptions. This keeps the discussion focused, with everyone promised, and later given, their turn for similarly interruption-free expression.

Often a fairly neutral, but subtly loaded question is good for a kick off, like "What do you think of John?" or "How many of you have used drugs?" or "What do you think the basic problem in this family is?" No one is allowed to escape from commentary, but no one is embarrassed. Skill at giving the sanction for open expression is of paramount importance, and both leader and team need to be alert to protect individuals even while encouraging openness.

The purpose of the multiple circles is to produce more intense interaction in smaller subgroups of six to ten persons. The forty-plus group of the assembled network is too large a group for free group discussion. Also, the advantage of multiple polarization (within each subgroup) allows the development and synthesis of various dialectics. It is important to elicit competitive polarities with diverse opinions and resolve some of these. The wide range of topics discussed helps the network begin to select and focus on the major issues to be dealt with in order to resolve the predicament in a nuclear family. Each subgroup is given its turn to interact, with the other subgroups instructed to not interrupt and to listen. Later each will have a chance to criticize what has been said by the other subgroups. An empty chair in the inner circle is an excellent device to use when there is pressure to be heard by peripheral members. If the group is large and active, two empty seats may be placed in the inner circle. Anyone not in the focal group may take the empty chair to signal a desire to speak. Having spoken, he is then obliged to return to the outer group and give way to someone else. Other devices of this nature are within the repertoire of every group leader or skilled teacher who uses discussion techniques. The important thing is to get the group talking to one another rather than holding a socractic dialogue with the professionals or rehashing old arguments among themselves.

As the discussion gets several ideas going and some confrontations emerge, the focal group is shifted off the center stage and another group is brought forward before premature resolutions are frozen into the system. At first it appears that very little is being settled. This phase is a kind of brainstorming. The leader and team are setting the ground rules for widespread participation and much airing of opinions, suggestions, ideas. The objective is to get out in the open misinformation that the group can correct, as well as information that the group can validate.

An important rule is no polite secrets. Indeed, the professional network intervenor not only does not promise confidentiality but establishes the precedent that there will be none. The team helps see to it that this is carried out. At first, the reverse of the usual professional ethics seems to shock everyone. Soon the network members demonstrate their relief at being able to speak openly about things they have already observed but could not deal with. "We knew you and John disagreed, but you would never let us help you understand before. . . ." "I was embarrassed after that night you drank too much at my house because you never gave me a chance to say I felt the same way. . . ." "I was angry because you didn't let me know about Aunt Minnie's funeral for three months, so I didn't think you cared. . . ."

It is quite usual for people to think that their secret fears, foibles, and worries are hidden when they are patently obvious. It is also true that often people only know half-truths about one another, when the whole picture makes far better sense. But most heartening of all is not only the way people can take it when truths and secrets are shared, but also how within a social network the resources for supportive acceptance appear, along with a common sense, hardheaded approach to the things that need to be changed.

The sequence of polarizing, shifting, and refocusing, with everybody listening is timed to end again with a restatement of a specific problem. At the end of the session, buzz groups or a free-floating refreshment and visiting period is in order. Before breaking up, the leader designates the next time to meet and sets the assignment of a specific, task-oriented topic with this in mind. This is usually enough to get everyone talking, and as soon as that is assured the team exits with minimal attention to goodbyes, beyond the bare amenities, until the next meeting.

INITIATING THE NETWORK PROCESS

Consider a case in its initial phases, where decisions as to the strategy to be employed have not yet been made. A nuclear family consisting of a mother and father in their late 40's, a 25-year-old daughter, and an 18-year-old son (Jim) came to the clinic for help following Jim's acute psychotic episode, during which he thought his mind was being tape recorded and his thoughts played over the local radio stations. He also thought that the telephone system in the house was monitored by outside wires and enlisted the aid of his parents in tracing the wiring throughout the house in a frantic effort to cut off this source of outside interference. It was fascinating to learn that the sister worked at a local radio station taping spot announcements and advertisements, and that she resisted the initial efforts to involve her in any family conferences.

At the first session with the whole family, an attempt was made by the intervention team to find out just what kind of help the family was looking for. Among the possibilities were hospitalization for the son, psychotherapy for the whole family conjointly, and the assembly of their loosely knit social network with an attempt at network intervention by our team. A potential goal in the minds of the team was the mobilization of a peer-supporting network that might enable Jim to move out of the house and find employment and social relationships more appropriate for his age and status. The family was opposed to hospitalization, and at first resisted family therapy by using the sister's work as an excuse for all being unable to attend. They were intrigued by, but even more frightened of, the thought of network intervention, insisting that it would be impossible to assemble the forty persons which we gave as a minimum number necessary. Jim began to assert himself at this point and expressed reluctance to include his friends and peers in the same network as his parents' peers and kin.

What we are trying to communicate by this anecdote is that the resistance to any form of therapy or intervention rests on the lack of familiarity with it. People are unable to conceptualize the processes and change modalities about to be unleashed. Human beings universally resist change, and those in distress are usually most defensive in the face of a choice about whether to introduce a new element or not. If they have never heard of network intervention, the vast majority of people will want to proceed cautiously.

In fact, both the intervenors and the nuclear patient nexus prefer as simple an intervention as feasible. However, where the simple measures such as counseling, individual psychotherapy, group therapy, and family therapy have also been rejected, and where they seem inadequate to solve the family's predicaments, the potential network intervenor has to expand his own horizons and begin formulating strategies around a new theoretical base. This is essential to get himself into a network set. Once he is able to do this, it is not extraordinarily difficult to guide the family into thinking about themselves and their problems in network terms. We believe that this line of thinking does not involve any unusual problem, but we underline the seemingly obvious fact that, *unless one thinks in a new frame of reference,* the likelihood of the intervenor's being overwhelmed by the difficulties he perceives often prevents him from doing the obvious.

To round off the illustration, the family in question, even before actually completing their own network assembly, discussed the idea with many others. A new family called the clinic and startled the intake worker by saying, "We have a son with a problem just like Jim's, and the Jenkinses have told us about how you assemble networks to help solve it. Do you think you could do one for us?"

The Assembly Process: Advantages of Rapid Assembly

Once again it might be well to examine the predicament, the distress, and the forces suggesting the appropriateness of network intervention. In this case a 42-year-old mother had four children under school age. The oldest, a girl, was not presented as having any problems. The next, a 3-year-old boy, was dramatically frightening everyone, mother, siblings, baby-sitters, neighbors, and kin by grabbing knives and threatening to kill them. He appeared to be trying to avenge his father's murder, which all the children and the mother had witnessed. The killing was the aftermath of a neighborhood quarrel, when an older son of a neighbor, under the influence of drugs, invaded their home and stabbed the father in the presence of his family, who were watching a TV program.

The third sibling was severely damaged from birth defects affecting his central nervous system and was quite hyperactive. The last sibling, born after the father's death, was mongoloid and was in need of corrective plastic surgery.

Although the mother was not overtly depressed, she was drained of energy from coping with the four small children. She had moved from her previous home because of the overwhelming associations of loss and terror. She had lost contact with many of her old friends and had no extended kin since she had grown up in foster homes. However, there were some foster sisters as potential network participants.

The usual rationale for intervention in a case of this sort involves the treatment of the mourning and loss problems of mother and child(ren) and the search for social agencies to relieve the mother of some of the more pressing and energy-draining responsibilities in caring for defective children. One might suggest relieving the mother of her burdens by simply assuming them or handing them on to other professionals, if one were to follow the sick-and-needy-person model. However, a rapid assembly of interested and able friends, neighbors, relatives, and, if indicated, agency personnel, the foster families of the past, and perhaps the church-related persons of the present could provide a large enough group to stimulate considerable change. Presented with the predicaments and given the responsibility to jointly participate in their solution, both mother and network members, under the stimulus of the network effect, may generate some innovative and creative solutions, support the control needed for the abreacting boy, help the mother not only mourn but find and form new nexus and clustering relationships. All this could be accomplished in a much more efficient and self-perpetuating fashion than the conventional assumption of professional responsibility and patient dependence.

Slower Assembly: Advantages and Disadvantages

Most reports of the assembly and creation of networks for therapeutic intervention deal with cases in crisis where there is virtually no option but rapid decisive action. We recently had experience with the assembly and creation of a loosely knit social network around a nuclear family with a son who had had an acute psychotic episode and was on the verge of hospitalization because of delusional ideas, erratic behavior, and family turmoil. Unique features in the network preassembly phase included reluctance of the family to do anything about their predicament but call and talk to the social worker for hours. They refused to relinquish control over their own situation; yet they kept asking for help. After accepting (hesitantly) the idea of network assembly, they reasserted this control by disregarding the instructions merely to call and invite all the people that they and their son knew for a meeting at a given time and place. Instead they made a series of visits. They spent a couple of hours with each of about ten such friends, telling them about the network idea and discussing their own problems. Only after several weeks of this did they get into gear and begin phoning and settling specifics of time and place.

This slow-paced use of five or six weeks to mobilize the network is unique in our experience in the assembly and creation of networks and raises the following hypothetical formulations and theoretical questions:

1. Slow assembly, controlled by the rate of dissemination of information which feels most comfortable to the nuclear nexus, sets the network-effect phenomenon into operation before the large assembly. Much of the network interventive action has already occurred before the larger meeting. Assembly in this case could confirm and validate actions and perceptions already shared, and could focus energy displaced by the directions already set in motion. The first actual meeting of the network might somewhat resemble a second- or third-stage meeting of a more rapidly assembled network.

2. Some danger of stasis might occur because the family has already selected its own system out of the available social matrix. In our experience the rapid assembly and creation of the network in a chaotic crisis situation seems to have the advantage of multiple foci which could be relatively easily rocked or shaken loose by various strategies in order to introduce new structures and form new vincula. The rapid assembly of social networks, within ten days or two weeks of our being consulted about a crisis situation, makes up the largest number of our interventions. It is our clinical impression that more significant changes in occupation, in role performance, and in network relationships (vincula) occurred when crisis situations forced the rapid assembly of the network. However, we have not yet seen enough slow assembly cases to be sure of these speculations.

3. One related type of impasse is the polarization which may result if the nuclear nexus controls the slower process of assembly. If there is sufficient binding, knotting, and stacking of vincula, the assembly presents the intervenors with a dialectic so energized that the task of disalignment and realignment is staggering. One wonders what elements of good fortune would have to be added to technique to

implode the plexus and produce the network effect. The potential violence unleashed if the implosion is successful may spill over to involve police action or other disagreeable effects.

This risk is particularly probable if the polarization occurs around two or more clusters within the network. The intervenors are then set up for a large-scale reenactment of the classical situation where a well-meaning mediator attempts to reconcile a battling couple and gets clobbered by each of them.

4. On the positive side, however, the slow assembly process, if contact is maintained with the distressed nexus, allows the intervenors access to more information than is usually available when rapid assembly is utilized. In one particular case, the son with the schizophrenic label revealed that he and his friends had been using a variety of drugs, including marijuana, hashish, barbiturates, amphetamines, and possibly mescaline and LSD. Because of the experience of one of the authors with similar cases on the psychedelic drug scene, he had a strong clinical hunch that the psychotic process would not be as ingrained as in cases where drugs were used in the absence of peer relationships, or in cases where drug use had not been part of the clinical picture.

When the intervention team has advance information, it is possible to set goals for the network assembly that involve other less loaded areas of concern, which may enable the polarized factions the find common elements around which to reform. These might include appropriate employment for the son, who had graduated from high school six months before and was not yet motivated either for work or further education, and possibly moving the youth out of his home into a semistructured or somewhat loosely peer-supervised living arrangement—a pad in the center of the city, for instance.

At this point in time, there is simply not enough experience to provide the criteria for selecting appropriate cases for slow assembly versus rapid assembly of the network. Nor is there evidence to decisively rule either process in or out as a method of choice.

INVOCATION OF PREEXISTING NETWORKS

The invocation and utilization of a preexisting group which possesses the membership variety characteristic of a social network is not as common as creating a new social network via the assembly method. It seems applicable where minority group members depend upon tribal-style assemblies, or where the nuclear nexus in distress centers much of its life around some organization such as a church or temple, a cousin's club, a block organization, or the like. If this group provides the heterogeneity of most rapidly assembled networks, much the same processes can occur. If, however, it has factions, some of the dangers of the slow assembly process, such as selectivity of polarized clusters and stasis, may apply. In any case, such as group can add impetus to the network effect if it can be properly amalgamated in the network and involved in the task of solving the predicament of the distressed nexus.

Technical differences often center on how to arrange to invoke the network. It is usually not enough for the intervenors and the nuclear family or distressed individual to agree on the network idea. Preferably, one or more members of the intervention team should already be known, by reputation if not personally, to a plexus or authority figure in the group around which the network can be invoked. If it is a rather formal group, at some point the priest, medicine man, club president, or other role-assigned figure will have to be consulted. Usually a clustering person who has vincula with the authorized role representative can effect the team's introduction to the power structure.

Once introduced, the intervention team should demonstrate that they have no desire to take over the group or to reform it, as well as show mild positive empathy for its avowed goals and activities. If the team conveys the idea that the nexus in distress is somehow caught in a bind which prevents full utilization of the supports offered by the group, some expression of need for revitalizing the whole group is called forth from its leaders. From this point on the intervenors are on familiar ground, using their discretion in communicating confidence in the network effect's multiple impact without promising miracles.

Some differences in intervention technique will probably be required because some of the rituals familiar to the group have potential affect-laden charges that can be utilized in place of innovative nonverbal techniques to loosen binds, form bonds, and to stimulate growth of new vincula. Nonuse of a ritual response when it is expected is also effective in developing new perceptions and awareness.

Peer Networks: Special Cases

Peer networks are powerful social agencies in contemporary culture. They seem to be age-graded stratification phenomena with varying limits; probably a maximum span of about fifteen years is typical for older people and a narrower span for youth.

One needs first of all to recognize that peer networks exist and are as potent a force as the multigenerational networks if they can be properly invoked to assemble. They have varying degrees of tightness from a loose network to highly structured groups. When the generally loose-knit associations are assembled, the process is much like that of the creation of a network for a family, but the actual creation of a network of peers from scratch has not seemed feasible. Rather it seems more effective to take advantage of natural groupings, which abound.

Two natural sources of peer networks are adolescents' and work associations. An example of a hippie peer social network and its interventions was seen in the course of a long-term observation in a pad. A group of college students who had formerly been part of a fraternity formed the plexus of the network. A formal fraternity group had been broken up because of the group use of drugs, and this nucleus rented a large old Victorian home and set up a commune living arrangement. Although several members dropped out of college, most of them eventually graduated.

The intervenor gained access to the peer group through the development of a therapeutic relationship with one of its members when he panicked after prolonged use of LSD and other psychedelic drugs plus amphetamines. When he described his living arrangements, he was asked if we could meet with all the persons who customarily assembled in his pad, and the result was our seeing from six to twenty of his peers on typical weekly visits.

Over the course of a year we got acquainted with about a hundred youths at this pad, many of whom comprised peripheral members of the peer system of the original nexus. Some of these peripheral members were connecting links with drug-dealing networks. Others were pad crashers who were freaked out or were runaways looking for a place to hide. At different times the peer network provided for one or more young persons in acute "schizophrenic crisis," who were allowed the isolation and security they needed, a chance to talk about their panic, and generally secure subcultural approval for the "trip" they were on in their personal distress. Network intervention in this instance was a matter of operating largely as part of a validating cluster with those involved at any particular time, and of utilizing the natural setting as innovatively as the youth who had adopted the life style in the first place.

By contrast, interventions with work associates as a peer network seem stiff and formal. On one occasion, the authors, together with Mrs. Jean Barr, were invited by a professional group of about 150 persons to do a network intervention on the vincula and structure of their organization. This group seemed to have a number of problems, among them an affective tone of depression ascribed to uncertainties about the usefulness of the organization. There was also an unperceived exclusion of new members and a general fearfulness about the general political climate expressed in much small talk about the manipulations of city and county governments and the availability of funds.

The disruption of the usual seating structure, business agenda, and task orientation of the group's annual meeting loosened the habitual bonds rather quickly. Some nonverbal group process techniques furthered the evocation of more fundamental relationships stripped of formal role restrictions. Freely formed subgroups were used, who were then directed to develop a polarized dialogue, and the heightening and relaxing of tensions to prevent clear-cut crystallization was carried out by the team during the course of a whole day, during which not more than ten people dropped out or were replaced by latecomers. The network session itself ended on a good high note, and the intervenors left the group with a feeling that the goals of involving the newer and younger members and revitalizing the relationships at many levels had been well initiated.

As in the case of invoking existing networks, the invocation of professional associations, unions, service clubs, and other formal peer group networks needs to be done at the invitation of someone in executive authority. Interestingly enough, the organization itself, as well as an individual or plexus within the peer group, may be the social unit in distress and may request help with its own predicaments. An outside intervention team is probably best utilized for this type of "therapeutic" activity, since any member of the group who could set off the network effect would probably be quickly organized into the hierarchy of the group structure or ejected by counterpressures from the threatened establishment in its resistance to change.

THE NETWORK EFFECT

Early in our experiences with various kinds of networks, we became aware of a phenomenon that seems appropriately called the network effect. Originally it was noted that a new process had been set in motion which had little to do with the intentions of the network intervenor. It was a bonus that in some ways made network therapy seem more fun and more interesting, but it seemed tangential to the goal-directed tasks of therapy. Later reflection and discussion have raised some theoretical questions which strongly suggest that perhaps this network effect accounts for much of the impact of the various types of network intervention, and that it is an essential characteristic of social behavior in a basic and fundamental way.

The network effect eludes description because it is largely nonverbal and unconscious. It might be more easily recognized removed from the therapeutic setting and examined in social settings, where it occurs spontaneously. For instance, in Preservation Hall in New Orleans, old black men from the early Dixieland era improvise jazz nightly. The audience of habituées and tourists begins the evening relatively unrelated to one another, at separate tables, and in couples or small groups. Under the mystical, religious, tribal, hypnotic, musical spell they become closely knitted together. They sit tightly pressed. The small group boundaries dissolve. They clap, sway, beat out rhythms, and move their bodies in a united complex response. The group mood is a euphoric high, and the conventional binds dissolve. New relationships melt away the conventional barriers of status, generation, territory, and sex. Young white women, lower-class black men, older spinsters, and hippie youths recognize a mutuality and express it in gesture, contact, and verbal expression. This lasts until the musicians give out and the people leaving form some new bonds. They leave in groups they might not have ever contemplated before they came. For those brief hours they have become involved with one another and with humanity in general in new ways, with new feelings, new relationships, new bonds. However briefly, they have been a part of a social network and they have felt its effect.

Other examples are rampant in the contemporary and historical scene. Religious revival meetings, tribal healing ceremonies, and alumni association "big game" celebrations are time-tested institutionalized examples of this process at work. Newer phenomena such as the Woodstock festival, peace marches, civil rights activities, and revolutionary militant group meetings are contemporary examples. Although neither might like to admit it, some hope of expressing this process unites the Lions Club in its group-singing climax to its regular meeting and the Beatles with their tribal photos as a trademark on their record albums. The network effect is a turn-on phenomenon of group interaction. Once people have made this initial change, they can never step into the same river of human relationships again.

Sometimes they do try, and indulge in all the defensive countermaneuvers used to repress or neutralize any other strong affective experience. This produces its own resonance and can produce counterwaves of new network effects if many people are involved. Utilizing and harnessing the network effect and steering it as it begins to carom about a group is one of the essential strategies of network intervention technique. The evocation of the effect is probably one of the strategies common to the variety of interventions involving networks, and the different foci used may help evolve a typology or classification that will make discussions more meaningful.

Perhaps a metaphor will help at this point: If the water in a deep pool represents the binding and bonding between people, the widening ripples following the fall of a large rock into the pool are the visible network effects changing the apparently smooth surface and stirring the whole mass into new relationships. Counterripples collide as the waves reach boundaries or are drawn into eddies that preexisted, setting up apparently never-ending patterns. More complex patterns can be quickly achieved by skipping small rocks off the water surface, by sending a boat across, or by opening a new channel. But unless something persistently stimulates the water, either by changing the flow or organizing new splashes, the pattern eventually subsides again, leaving the surface calm but the original relationships realigned.

In our clinical experience we have discovered the equivalent of all these phenomena and are considering the varying desirability of permanent and transient changes that can be effected. For instance, in the case of one young schizophrenic girl who was symbiotically bound to her mother, activation of several network members broke through the usually reticent relationships enough for them to find her an apartment, physically move her into it, and support her through the initial phases of disorientation as the symbiotic bonds gave way to more personal ego boundaries. The ripple effects were observed as the ringleader of this network group, who had been unemployed for several months, spending his time writing poetry, began to look for a job. In a matter of weeks the associated efforts had transformed him from a sloppy-looking, bitter, depressed, and angry young man into a clean-cut business executive type with medium long hair (no value judgment intended.) Another member who had participated in breaking the index girl's symbiotic binds temporarily separated from her husband, saying that she had finally found the strength to stand up to him and renegotiate the relationship. The example could be spun out to illustrate the reactions that affected employment, marital, personal, and interactional patterns in the lives of at least a dozen members of the social network over the next six or eight weeks.

It would seem that the network effect begins once members realize that they are now part of a special human cluster. Therapeutic intervention labels this as a network and works within the newly formed associative groupings— tightening vincula, stimulating nexi, and coalescing clusters. The use of this vocabulary illustrates that the professional is not immune to the strong drive observed in most groups to try to develop rules that regularize and give the new associative bonds some permanence in the network-effect experience.

While these definitions will prove of some use later in this discussion, at present the phenomena can be described as first an experience of a new feeling of freedom. There are fewer rules, at least fewer formalized rules, in the new context. The network intervenors try to keep this openness, this sense of new options, alive so that the network members learn for themselves how to be innovative and creative. Learning is rapid as they discard regulations which do not work or which are limiting and begin to cherish a certain looseness of regulations which potentiates freedom. This sense of freedom, validated through shared intimate experience, is a high, a euphoric experience which energizes the group with confidence so that they can begin to tackle their everyday problems. Their success is partially due to the fact that their problems have been redefined by the new group culture, which strips off old labels, collapses old roles, and punctures old bags that are difficult to get out of. This last allusion is particularly apt, since the contemporary rediscovery and reapplication of this network effect in a therapeutic context belongs as much to the hippies and young radicals of today as to the professionals. A never-ending parade of examples of reinvented social values and cultural forms, as well as new realities, confronts anyone who looks for it in the contemporary scene.

When we began to conceptualize in this way we began to get rid of the "sick" model for many patients, and this felt good. We also began to get rid of the "healer" model for the therapist, and this left us uneasy—particularly in figuring out how to collect fees for an as yet undefined service, to a new population, in intuitively defined ways. Tradition tells society what is acceptable to the majority of the group by defining what is sick. When called upon, therapists take the sick person and tell him he must become like the majority, for which the system will reward him. What hasn't always been realized in using this model is that this system needs a certain number of persons to scapegoat—to define as sick—in order to define itself. Thus if one person gets over his needs for being scapegoated he has to be replaced by someone else. An alternative left for a patient is to find that being sick is more fun and to remain chronically ill. In either case, therapists are apt to find themselves in the middle of a cybernated pegboard game in which, if you press down one peg, sometimes two or three more pop up. Most of the time, only one pops up—but only occasionally and apparently by chance do no pop-ups occur.

The network effect can scramble the cybernated pegboard, open new feedback connections, make everybody both an experimenter and a validater of new options. Suddenly the only acceptable and needed epithets are WOW! FANTASTIC! RIGHT ON! and *no one is sick.*

IN CONCLUSION: SOME THOUGHTS ABOUT HUMAN SOCIAL SYSTEMS

In our world today, some workers in the social sciences have to become organized in their thinking about behavior and the modification of behavior in large human groups. In the McLuhan world of instant tribalization, each of us is influenced by mass behaviors—from protests to festivals. We are involved positively or negatively in the characteristics of what Abbey Hoffman has called the Woodstock nation or what Roszak has called the counterculture. This has some implications of a polarization of mankind into youth and adults which may be due to a fragmentation of social networks which in the past held generations together with a sense of unity in time and space.

Youths fear the destructive potentials of the cybernated technocratic world, which they feel have led to the imminent destruction of both man and nature. Adults, on the other hand, feel that we have an affluent and manageable system which can be exploited further to bring health, happiness, and security to the "motivated." Like it or not, this is the predicament facing mankind today. Therapists need to be willing to begin to experiment and study these human group phenomena at levels which have during the past couple of centuries been thought of as political. Unless we do this, it is questionable how relevant therapy, or indeed the social sciences in general, is going to be. The culture is changing so rapidly that the old methods of intervention with individuals, families, and groups are not meeting the requirements of the situation.

Rapid social change creates identity confusion in both the adult generation and in youth. Prescribed models for behavior no longer function effectively, and results of actions cannot be anticipated with confidence. This is readily seen in the way youth have established radical changes in dress codes and opened up to public view many relationships that were cloaked in Victorian mystery. They have also shaken up the adults as they have demonstrated their social and political skills in large assemblies, and as they have openly challenged many institutions disliked by the over-thirty generation who felt change could only occur slowly. Granting that there are many variables contributing to effectiveness, and that youth are not always successful in avoiding violence or achieving change, there is still ample evidence that they have established some new forms and uses of social relationships.

Such social mutations create new tensions and precipitate distress which should not be interpreted as a new guise for old pathologies. Clinically, adolescents seen today are not the same as the youth of the past two or three generations. They appear depressed and hopeless, but they admit it rather than blame themselves. They see the world situation as hopeless, and they are hungry —but for dialogue, not therapy. They are suffering from real distress of the soul, and so are their parents, teachers, and peers. Intuitively they sense something more than they can express about this change.

If the psychotherapist is to maintain relationships with human beings in this predicament, if he is to be of any value in relieving distress, he has to innovate.

It seems to us that social network intervention has much promise as a constructive innovation. It provides a chance for the healing of torn bonds and the gentle freeing of binds. Network intervention may be able to evoke the potential capacity of. people to creatively and cooperatively solve their own problems as an antidote to the aura of depersonalized loneliness characteristic of postindustrial society.

Bibliography of Family Therapy

This is a reasonably complete list of articles and books on family therapy. Excluded are papers on family diagnosis, dynamics or research.

Ackerman, N. W., *Treating the Troubled Family,* New York, Basic Books, 1966.

Ackerman, N. W., "Family Psychotherapy—Theory and Practice," *Amer. J. Psychother.* 20:405-414, 1966.

Ackerman, N., Beatman, F., and Sherman, S. (Eds.), *Exploring the Base for Family Therapy,* New York, Family Service Association, 1961.

Ackerman, N. W., Lieb, J., and Pearce, J. K. (Eds.), *Family Therapy in Transition,* New York, Little, Brown, 1970.

Alexander, I. G., "Family Therapy," *Marriage and Family Living* 25:146-154, 1963.

Alger, I., and Hogan, P., "The Use of Videotape Recordings in Conjoint Marital Therapy," *Amer. J. Psychiat.* 123:1425-1430, 1967.

Alger, I., and Hogan, P., "Enduring Effects of Videotape Playback Experience on Family and Marital Relationships," *Amer. J. Orthopsychiat.* 39:86-96, 1969.

Anderson, D., "Nursing Therapy with Families," *Perspect. Psychiat. Care* 1:21-27, 1969.

Appel, E., Goodwin, H. M., Wood, H. P., and Askren, E. L., "Training in Psychotherapy: The Use of Marriage Counseling in a Univeristy Teaching Clinic," *Amer. J. Psychiat.* 117:709-711, 1961.

Arlen, M. S., "Conjoint Therapy and the Corrective Emotional Experience," *Family Process* 5:91-104, 1966.

Arnold, A., "The Implications of Two-Person and Three-Person Relationships for Family Psychotherapy," *J. Health Hum. Behav.* 3:94-97, 1962.

Attneave, C. L., "Therapy in Tribal Settings and Urban Network Intervention," *Family Process* 8:192-210, 1969.

Auerswald, E. H., "Interdisciplinary vs. Ecological Approach," *Family Process* 7:202-215, 1968.

Augenbraun, B., Reid, H. L., and Friedman, D. S., "Brief Intervention as a Preventive Force in Disorders of Early Childhood," *Amer. J. Orthopsychiat.* 37:697-702, 1967.

Bannister, K., and Pincus, L., *Shared Phantasy in Marital Problems: Therapy in a Four Person Relationship,* London, England, Tavistock Institute of Human Relations, 1965.

Barcai, A., "An Adventure in Multiple Family Therapy," *Family Process* 6:185-192, 1967.

Bardill, D., "Family Therapy in an Army Mental Hygiene Clinic," *Soc. Casework* 44:452-457, 1963.

Basamania, B. W., "The Emotional Life of the Family: Inferences for Social Casework," *Amer. J. Orthopsychiat.* 31:74-86, 1961.

Beatman, F., "The Training and Preparation of Workers for Family-Group Treatment," *Soc. Casework* 45:202-208, 1964.

Beatman, F., Sherman, S., and Leader, A., "Current Issues in Family Treatment," *Soc. Casework* 47:75-81, 1966.

Beecher, W., and Beecher, M., "Re-Structuring Mistaken Family Relationships," *J. Individ. Psychol.* 13:176-181, 1957.

Beels, C. C., and Ferber, A., "Family Therapy: A View," *Family Process* 8:28-332, 1969.

Behrens, M., and Ackerman, N., "The Home Visit as an Aid in Family Diagnosis and Therapy," *Soc. Casework* 37:11-19, 1956.

Bell, J. E., *Family Group Therapy,* Public Health Monograph 64, U.S. Department of Health, Education, and Welfare, 1961.

Bell, J. E., "A Theoretical Position for Family Group Therapy," *Family Process* 2:1-14, 1963.

Bell, J. E., "Contrasting Approaches in Marital Counseling," *Family Process* 6:16-26, 1967.

Belmont, L. P., and Jasnow, A., "The Utilization of Cotherapists and of Group Therapy Techniques in a Family Oriented Approach to a Disturbed Child," *Int. J. Group Psychother.* 11:319-328, 1961.

Berman, G., "Communication of Affect in Family Therapy," *Arch. Gen. Psychiat.* 17:154-158, 1967.

Berman, K., "Multiple Family Therapy," *Ment. Hyg.* 50:367-370, 1966.

Blinder, M. G., Colman, A. D., Curry, A. E., and Kessler, D. R., MCFT: Simultaneous Treatment of Several Families," *Amer. J. Psychother.* 19:559-569, 1965.

Bodin, A., "Conjoint Family Therapy," in Vinacke, W. (Ed.), *Readings in General Psychology,* New York, American Book, 1968, pp. 213-219.

Bodin, A., "Family Therapy Training Literature: A Brief Guide," *Family Process* 8:272-279, 1969.

Bodin, A., "Videotape Applications to Training Family Therapists," *J. Nerv. Ment. Dis.* 148:251-262, 1969.

Boszormenyi-Nagy, I., "The Concept of Schizophrenia from the Perspective of Family Treatment," *Family Process* 1:103-113, 1962.

Boszormenyi-Nagy, I., "The Concept of Change in Conjoint Family Therapy," in Friedman, A. S., et al., *Psychotherapy for the Whole Family,* New York, Springer, 1965.

Boszormenyi-Nagy, I., "Intensive Family Therapy as Process," in Boszormenyi-Nagy, I., and Framo, J. L. (Eds.), *Intensive Family Therapy*, New York, Harper, 1965.

Boszormenyi-Nagy, I., "From Family Therapy to a Psychology of Relationships: Fictions of the Individual and Fiction of the Family," *Compr. Psychiat.* 7:408-423, 1966.

Boszormenyi-Nagy, I., and Framo, J., "Family Concept of Hospital Treatment of Schizophrenia," in Masserman, J. H. (Ed.), *Current Psychiatric Therapy*, Vol. 2, 1962, pp. 159-165.

Boszormenyi-Nagy, I., and Framo, J. L. (Eds.), *Intensive Family Therapy: Theoretical and Practical Aspects*, New York, Harper, Row, 1965.

Boverman, M., and Adams, J. R., "Collaboration of Psychiatrist and Clergyman: A Case Report," *Family Process* 3:251-272, 1964.

Bowen, M., "Family Psychotherapy," *Amer. J. Orthopsychiat.* 31:40-60, 1961.

Bowen, M., "Family Psychotherapy with Schizophrenia in the Hospital and in Private Practice," in Boszormenyi-Nagy, I., and Framo, J. L. (Eds.), *Intensive Family Therapy*, New York, Harper, 1965.

Bowen, M., "The Use of Family Theory in Clinical Practice," *Compr. Psychiat.* 7:345-374, 1966.

Brodey, W. M., "The Family as the Unit of Study and Treatment: Image, Object and Narcissistic Relationships," *Amer. J. Orthopsychiat.* 31:69-73, 1961.

Brodey, W. M., "On Family Therapy: A Poem," *Family Process* 2:280-287, 1963.

Brodey, W. M., and Hayden, M., "Intrateam Reactions: Their Relation to the Conflicts of the Family in Treatment," *Amer. J. Orthopsychiat.* 27:340-355, 1957.

Brody, E. H., and Spark, G., "Institutionalization of the Aged: A Family Crisis," *Family Process* 5:76-90, 1966.

Brody, S., "Simultaneous Psychotherapy of Married Couples," in Masserman, J. H. (Ed.), *Current Psychiatric Therapies*, Vol. 1, 1961, pp. 139-144.

Bulbulyan, A., "Psychiatric Nurse as Family Therapist," *Perspect. Psychiat. Care* 7:56-68, 1969.

Burks, H., and Serrano, A., "The Use of Family Therapy and Brief Hospitalization," *Dis. Nerv. System* 26:804-806, 1965.

Carek, D. J., and Watson, A. S., "Treatment of a Family Involved in Fratricide," *Arch. Gen. Psychiat.* 11:533-543, 1964.

Carroll, E. J., "Treatment of the Family as a Unit," *Penn. Med. J.* 63:56-62, 1960.

Carroll, E. J., "Family Therapy—Some Observations and Comparisons," *Family Process* 3:170-185, 1964.

Carroll, E. J., Cambor, C. G., Leopold, J. V., Miller, M. D., and Reis, W. J., "Psychotherapy of Marital Couples," *Family Process* 2:25-33, 1963.

Chandler, E., Holden, H., and Robinson, H., "Treatment of a Psychotic Family in a Family Psychiatry Setting," *Psychother. Psychosom.* 16:333-347, 1968.

Charny, I. W., "Family Interviews in Redefining a 'Sick' Child's Role in the Family Problem," *Psychol. Rep.* 10:577-578, 1962.

Charny, I. W., "Integrated Individual and Family Psychotherapy," *Family Process* 5:179-198, 1966.

Charny, I. W., "Marital Love and Hate," *Family Process* 8:1-24, 1969.

Clower, C. G., and Brody, L., "Conjoint Family Therapy in Outpatient Practice," *Amer. J. Psychother.* 18:670-677, 1964.

Cohen, I. M., "Family Structure, Dynamics and Therapy," in Cohen, I. M. (Ed.), *Psychiatric Research Report 20,* Washington, D.C., American Psychiatric Association, 1966.

Cooper, S., "New Trends in Work with Parents: Progress or Change," *Soc. Casework* 42:342-347, 1961.

Coughlin, F., and Wimberger, H. C., "Group Family Therapy," *Family Process* 7:37-50, 1968.

Coyle, G. L., "Concepts Relevant to Helping the Family as a Group," *Soc. Casework* 43:347-354, 1962.

Curry, A. E., "Therapeutic Management of Multiple Family Groups," *Int. J. Group Psychother.* 15:90-96, 1965.

Curry, A. E., "Toward the Phenomenological Study of the Family," *Exist. Psychiat.* 6:35-44, 1967.

Cutter, A. V., and Hallowitz, D., "Diagnosis and Treatment of the Family Unit with Respect to the Character-Disordered Youngster," *J. Amer. Acad. Child Psychiat.* 1:605-618, 1962.

Cutter, A. V., and Hallowitz, D., "Different Approaches to Treatment of the Child and the Parents," *Amer. J. Orthopsychiat.* 32:152-158, 1962.

Davies, Q., Ellenson, G., and Young, R., "Therapy with a Group of Families in a Psychiatric Day Center," *Amer J. Orthopsychiat.* 36:134-147, 1966.

Dicks, H. V., *Marital Tensions: Clinical Studies Toward a Psychological Theory of Interaction,* New York, Basic Books, 1967.

Duhrssen, A., "Präventive Massnahmen in der Familie," *Psychother Psychosom.* 16:319-322, 1960.

Dwyer, J. H., Menk, M. C., and C. V. Houten, "The Case Worker's Role in Family Therapy," *Family Process* 4:21-31, 1965.

Eist H. I., and A. U. Mandel, "Family Treatment of Ongoing Incest Behavior," *Family Process* 7:216-232, 1968.

Elkin, M., "Short-Term Counseling in a Conciliation Court," *Soc. Casework* 43:184-190, 1962.

Erickson, M. H., "The Identification of a Secure Reality," *Family Process* 1:294-303, 1962.

Feldman, M. J., "Privacy and Conjoint Family Therapy," *Family Process* 6:1-9, 1967.

Ferber, A., and Mendelsohn, M., "Training for Family Therapy," *Family Process* 8:24-32, 1968.

Fisch, R., "Home Visits in a Private Psychiatric Practice," *Family Process* 2:114-126, 1964.

Fisher, S., and Mendell, D., "The Spread of Psychotherapeutic Effects from the Patient to his Family Group," *Psychiatry* 21:133-140, 1958.

Fitzgerald, R. V., "Conjoint Marital Psychotherapy: An Outcome and Follow-Up Study," *Family Process* 8:261-271, 1969.

Fleck, S., "Psychotherapy of Families of Hospitalized Patients," in Masserman, J. H. (Ed.), *Current Psychiatric Therapies,* Vol. 3, New York, Grune & Stratton, 1963.

Forrest, T., "Treatment of the Father in Family Therapy," *Family Process* 8:106-118, 1969.

Fox, R. E., "The Effect of Psychotherapy on the Spouse," *Family Process* 7:7-16, 1967.

Framo, J., "My Families, My Family," *Voices* 4:18-27, 1968.

Framo, J. L., "The Theory of the Technique of Family Treatment of Schizophrenia," *Family Process* 1:119-131, 1962.

Framo, J. L., "Rational and Techniques of Intensive Family Therapy," in Boszormenyi-Nagy, I., and Framo, J. L. (Eds.), *Intensive Family Therapy*, New York, Harper, 1965.

Freeman, V. J., "Differentiation of 'Unity' Family Therapy Approaches Prominent in the United States," *Int. J. Soc. Psychiat.*, Special Ed. 2:35-46, 1964.

Freeman, V. S., Klein, A. F., Riehman, L. M., Lukoff, I. F., and Heiseg, V. E., "Family Group Counseling as Differentiated from Other Family Therapies," *Int. J. Group Psychother.* 13:167-175, 1963.

Friedman, A. S., "Family Therapy as Conducted in the Home," *Family Process* 1:132-140, 1962.

Friedman, A. S., "The Incomplete Family in Family Therapy," *Family Process* 2:288-301, 1963.

Friedman, A. S., Boszormenyi-Nagy, I., Jungreis, J. E., Lincoln, G., Mitchell, H., Sonne, J., Speck, R., and Spivack, G., *Psychotherapy for the Whole Family*, New York, Springer, 1965.

Fry, W. F., "The Marital Context of an Anxiety Syndrome," *Family Process* 1:245-252, 1962.

Gehrke, S., and Kirschenbaum, M., "Survival Patterns in Family Conjoint Therapy," *Family Process* 6:67-80, 1967.

Gehrke, S., and Moxom, J., "Diagnostic Classifications and Treatment Techniques in Marriage Counseling," *Family Process* 1:253-264, 1962.

Geist, J., and Gerber, N. M., "Joint Interviewing: A Treatment Technique with Marital Partners," *Soc. Casework* 41:76-83, 1960.

Glick, I. D., and Haley, J., *Family Therapy and Research: An Annotated Bibliography of Articles and Books Published 1950-1970*, New York, Grune & Stratton, 1971.

Glower, C. G., and Brody, L., "Conjoint Family Therapy in Outpatient Practice," *Amer. J. Psychother.* 13:670-677, 1964.

Goodwin, H., and Mudd, E., "Indications for Marriage Counseling: Methods and Goals," *Compr. Psychiatry* 7:450-461, 1966.

Goolishian H. A., "A Brief Psychotherapy Program for Disturbed Adolescents," *Amer. J. Orthopsychiat.* 32:142-148, 1962.

Goolishian, H. A., McDonald, E. G., MacGregor, R., Ritchie, A. M., Serrano, A. C., and Schuster, F. P., *Multiple Impact Therapy with Families*, New York, McGraw-Hill, 1961.

Gralnick, A., "The Family in Psychotherapy," in Masserman, J. H. (Ed.), *Individual and Family Dynamics*, New York, Grune & Stratton, 1969.

Gralnick, A., "Family Psychotherapy: General and Specific Considerations," *Amer. J. Orthopsychiat.* 32:515-526, 1962.

Gralnick, A., "Conjoint Family Therapy: Its Role in Rehabilitation of the Inpatient and Family," *J. Nerv. Ment. Dis.* 136:500-506, 1963.

Green, R., "Collaborative and Conjoint Therapy Combined," *Family Process* 3:80-98, 1964.

Greenberg, I. M., Glick, I. D., Match, S., and Riback, S. S., "Family Therapy: Indications and Rationale," *Arch. Gen. Psychiat.* 10:7-25, 1964.

Greene, B., "Management of Marital Problems," *Dis. Nerv. Syst.* 27:204-209, 1966.

Grosser, G. S., and Paul, N. L., "Ethical Issues in Family Group Therapy," *Amer. J. Orthopsychiat.* 34:875-884, 1964.

Grotjahn, M., "Analytic Family Therapy; A Survey of Trends in Research and Literature," in Masserman, J. H. (Ed.), *Individual and Family Dynamics*, New York, Grune & Stratton, 1959.

Grotjahn, M., *Psychoanalysis and the Family Neurosis*, New York, Norton, 1960.

Grotjahn, M., "Clinical Illustrations from Psychoanalytic Family Therapy," in Green, B. (Ed.), *The Psychotherapies of Marital Disharmony*, New York, Free Press, 1965.

Grotjahn, M., "Indications for Psychoanalytic Family Therapy," in Rosenbaum, S., and Alger, I. (Eds.), *The Marriage Relationship, Psychoanalytic Perspectives*, New York, Basic Books, 1968.

Grotjahn, M., and Treusch, J. V., "Psychiatric Family Consultations, The Practical Approach in Family Practice for the Personal Physician," *Ann. Intern. Med.* 66: 295-300, 1967.

Guerney, B., and Guerney, L. F., "Choices in Initiating Family Therapy," *Psychotherapy* 1:119-123, 1964.

Gullerud, E. N., and Harlan, V. L., "Four-Way Joint Interviewing in Marital Counseling," *Soc. Casework* 43:532-537, 1962.

Hahn, I., "Family Therapy: A Child-Centered Approach to Disturbed Parent-Child Relationships," *Penn. Psychiat. Quart.* 4:58-62, 1964.

Haley, J., "Whither Family Therapy?" *Family Process* 1:69-100, 1962.

Haley, J., "Marriage Therapy," *Arch. Gen. Psychiat.* 8:213-234, 1963.

Haley, J., *Strategies of Psychotherapy*, New York, Grune & Stratton, 1963.

Haley, J., "Approaches to Family Therapy," *Int. J. Psychiat.* 9:233-242, 1970.

Haley, J. (Ed.), *Changing Families: A Family Therapy Reader*, New York, Grune & Stratton, 1971.

Haley, J., and Hoffman, L., *Techniques of Family Therapy*, New York, Basic Books, 1967.

Hallowitz, D., "Family Unit Treatment of Character-Disordered Youngsters," *Social Work Practice*, New York, Columbia University Press, 1963, pp. 84-101.

Hallowitz, D., Clement, R. G., and Cutter, A. V., "The Treatment Process with Both Parents Together," *Amer. J. Orthopsychiat.* 27:587-601, 1957.

Hallowitz, D., and Cutter, A. V., "The Family Unit Approach in Therapy: Uses, Process and Dynamics, *Casework Papers*, New York, Family Service Association, 1961.

Handel, G., *The Psychosocial Interior of the Family*, Chicago, Aldine, 1967.

Handlon, J. H., and Parloff, M. B., "The Treatment of Patient and Family as a Group: Is It Group Psychotherapy?" *Int. J. Group Psychother.* 12:132-141, 1962.

Hansen, C., "An Extended Home Visit with Conjoint Family Therapy," *Family Process* 7:67-87, 1967.

Harms, E., "A Socio-Genetic Concept of Family Therapy," *Acta Psychother.* 12:53-60, 1964.

Hawkins, R. P., Peterson, R. F., Schweid, E., and Bijou, S. W., "Behavior Therapy in the Home: Amelioration of Problem Parent-Child Relations with the Parent in a Therapeutic Role," *J. Exp. Child Psychol.* 4:99-107, 1966.

Hoffman, L., and Kantor, R. E., "Brechtian Theater as a Model for Conjoint Family Therapy," *Family Process* 5:218-229, 1966.

Jackson, D. D., and Bodin, A., "Paradoxical Communication and the Marital Paradox," in Rosenbaum, S., and Alger, I. (Eds.), *The Marriage Relationship, Psychoanalytic Perspectives*, New York, Basic Books, 1968.

Jackson, D. D., and Satir, V., "A Review of Psychiatric Developments in Family Diagnosis and Family Therapy," in Ackerman, N. W., Beatman, F. L., and Sherman, S. N. (Eds.), *Exploring the Base for Family Therapy*, New York, Family Service Association, 1961.

Jackson, D. D., and Weakland, J. H., "Schizophrenic Symptoms and Family Interaction," *Arch. Gen. Psychiat.* 1:618-621, 1959.

Jackson, D. D., and Weakland, J. H., "Conjoint Family Therapy: Some Considerations on Theory, Technique and Results," *Psychiatry* 24:30-45, 1961.

Jackson, D. D., and Yalom, I., "Family Interaction, Family Homeostasis, and Some Implications for Conjoint Family Psychotherapy," in Masserman, J. H. (Ed.), *Individual and Family Dynamics*, New York, Grune & Stratton, 1959.

Jolesch, M., "Casework Treatment of Young Married Couples," *Soc. Casework* 43: 245-251, 1962.

Jones, W., "The Villain and the Victim: Group Therapy for Married Couples," *Amer. J. Psychiat.* 124:351-354, 1967.

Kaffman, M., "Short Term Family Therapy," *Family Process* 2:216-234, 1963.

Kaffman, M., "Family Diagnosis and Therapy in Child Emotional Pathology," *Family Process* 4:241-258, 1965.

Kardener, S., "The Family: Structure, Pattern, and Therapy," *Ment. Hyg.* 52:524-531, 1968.

Kaylina, E., "Psychoanalytic Psychotherapy with a Couple Considered as Brief Therapy," *Acta Psiquiat. Psicol. Amer. Alt.* 14:311-316, 1968.

Kempler, W., "Experiential Family Therapy," *Int. J. Group Psychother.* 15:57-71, 1965.

Kempler, W., "Experiential Psychotherapy with Families," *Family Process* 7:88-99, 1967.

Kimbro, E., Taschman, H., Wylie, H., and MacLennan, B., "Multiple Family Group Approach to Some Problems of Adolescence," *Int. J. Group Psychother.* 17: 18-24, 1967.

King, C., "Family Therapy with the Deprived Family," *Soc. Casework* 48:203-208, 1967.

Klapman, H., and Rice, D., "An Experience with Combined Milieu and Family Group Therapy," *Int. J. Group Psychother.* 15:198-206, 1965.

Knoblochova, J., and Knobloch, F., "Family Psychotherapy," in *Aspects of Family Mental Health in Europe*, Public Health Paper 28, World Health Organization, 1965.

Kohl, R. N., "Pathologic Reactions of Marital Partners to Improvement of Patients," *Amer. J. Psychiat.* 118:1036-1041, 1962.

Kwiatkowska, H., "Family Art Therapy," *Family Process* 6:37-55, 1967.

Laing, R. D., and Esterson, A., *Sanity, Madness and the Family*. London, England, Tavistock, 1964.

Landes, J., and Winter, W., "A New Strategy for Treating Disintegrating Families," *Family Process* 5:1-20, 1966.

Langsley, D., and Kaplan, D., *The Treatment of Families in Crisis*, New York, Grune & Stratton, 1968.

Langsley, D. G., Pittman, F. S., Machotka, P., and Flomenhaft, K., "Family Crisis Therapy—Results and Implications," *Family Process* 7:125-158, 1968.

Laqueur, H. P., and LaBurt, H. A., "Family Organization on a Modern State Hospital Ward," *Ment. Hyg.* 48:544-551, 1964.

Laqueur, H. P., LaBurt, H. A., and Morong, E., "Multiple Family Therapy," in Masserman, J. H. (Ed.), *Current Psychiatric Therapies, Vol. 4*, New York, Grune & Stratton, 1964, pp. 150-154.

Laqueur, H. P., LaBurt, H. A., and Morong, E., "Multiple Family Therapy: Further Developments," *Int. J. Soc. Psychiat.*, Special Ed. 2:70-80, 1964.

Laqueur, H. P., Wells, C., and Agresti, M., "Multiple-Family Therapy in a State Hospital," *Hosp. Community Psychiat.* 20:13-20, 1969.

Laskin, E., "Breaking Down the Walls," *Family Process* 7:118-125, 1968.

Lefer, J., "Counter-Resistance in Family Therapy," *J. Hillside Hosp.* 15:205-210, 1966.

Lehrman, N. S., "The Joint Interview: An Aid to Psychotherapy and Family Stability," *Amer. J. Psychother* 17:83-94, 1963.

Leichter, E., and Shulman, G., "The Family Interview as an Integrative Device in Group Therapy with Families," *Int. J. Group Psychother.* 13:335-345, 1963.

Leveton, A., "Family Therapy as the Treatment of Choice," *Med. Bull. U.S. Army Europe* 21:76-79, 1964.

Lidz, T., *The Family and Human Adaptation*, New York, International Universities Press, 1963.

Lidz, T., Fleck, S., and Cornelison, A., *Schizophrenia and the Family*, New York, International Universities Press, 1965.

Lieberman, L. P., "Joint Interview Technique—An Experiment in Group Psychotherapy," *Brit. J. Med. Psychol.* 30:202-207, 1957.

Lindberg, D. R., and Wosmek, A. W., "The Use of Family Sessions in Foster Home Care," *Soc. Casework* 44:137-141, 1963.

MacGregor, R., "Multiple Impact Psychotherapy with Families," *Family Process* 1:15-29, 1962.

Mackie, R., "Family Problems in Medical and Nursing Famililes," *Brit. J. Med. Psychol.* 40:333-340, 1967.

Markowitz, I., "Family Therapy in a Child Guidance Clinic," *Psychiat. Quart.* 40:308-319, 1966.

Markowitz, I., Taylor, G., and Bokert, E., "Dream Discussion as a Means of Reopening Blocked Familial Communication," *Psychother. Psychosom.* 16:348-356, 1968.

Martin F., and Knight, J., "Joint Interviews as Part of Intake Procedure in a Child Psychiatric Clinic," *J. Child Psychol. Psychiat.* 3:17-26, 1962.

Marx, A., and Ludwig, A., "Resurrection of the Family of the Chronic Schizophrenic," *Amer. J. Psychother.* 23:37-52, 1969.

Mendell, D., and Fischer, S., "A Multi-Generation Approach to the Treatment of Psychopathology," *J. Nerv. Ment. Dis.* 126:523-529, 1958.

Mereness, D., "Family Therapy: An Evolving Role," *Perspect. Psychiat. Care* 6:256-259, 1968.

Messer, A., "Family Treatment of a School Phobic Child," *Arch. Gen. Psychiat.* 11:548-553, 1964.

Midelfort, C. F., *The Family in Psychotherapy*, New York, McGraw-Hill, 1957.

Midelfort, C. F., "Use of Members of the Family in Treatment of Schizophrenia," *Family Process* 1:114-118, 1962.

Miller, D., and Westman, J. C., "Family Teamwork and Psychotherapy," *Family Process* 5:49-59, 1966.

Minuchin, S., "Family Structure, Family Language, and the Puzzled Therapist," *Amer. J. Orthopsychiat.* 34:347-348, 1964.

Minuchin, S., "Conflict Resolution Family Therapy," *Psychiatry* 28:278-286, 1965.

Minuchin, S., Auerswald, E., King, C., and Rabinowitz, C., "The Study and Treatment of Families that Produce Multiple Acting-Out Boys," *Amer. J. Orthopsychiat.* 34:125-134, 1964.

Minuchin, S., and Montalvo, B., "Techniques for Working with Disorganized Low Socioeconomic Families," *Amer. J. Orthopsychiat.* 37:880-887, 1967.

Minuchin, S., Montalvo, B., Guerney, B., Rosman, L., and Shumer, F., *Families of the Slums,* New York, Basic Books, 1967.

Mitchell, C., "The Use of Family Sessions in the Diagnosis and Treatment of Disturbances in Children," *Soc. Casework* 41:283-290, 1960.

Mitchell, C., "A Casework Approach to Disturbed Families," in Ackerman, N. W., Beatman, F. L., and Sherman, S. N. (Ed.), *Exploring the Base for Family Therapy,* New York, Family Service Association, 1961.

Miyoshi, N., and Liebmna, R., "Training Psychiatric Residents in Family Therapy," *Family Process* 8:97-105, 1968.

Morrison, G., and Collier, J., "Family Treatment Approaches to Suicidal Children and Adolescents," *J. Amer. Acad. Child Psychiat.* 8:140-154, 1969.

Mosher, L. R., "Schizophrenogenic Communication and Family Therapy," *Family Process* 8:43-63, 1969.

Mudd, E. H., *The Practice of Marriage Counseling,* New York, Association Press, 1951.

Nakhla, F., Folkart, L., and J. Webster, "Treatment of Families as In-Patients," *Family Process* 8:79-96, 1968.

Osberg, J. W., "Initial Impressions of the Use of Short-Term Family Group Conferences," *Family Process* 1:236-244, 1962.

Ostby, C. H., "Conjoint Group Therapy with Prisoners and Their Families," *Family Process* 7:184-201, 1968.

Parloff, M. B., "The Family in Psychotherapy," *Arch. Gen. Psychiat.* 4:445-451, 1961.

Pattison, E. M., "Treatment of Alcoholic Families with Nurse Home Visits," *Family Process* 4:75-94, 1965.

Patton, J. D., Bradley, J. D., and Hornowski, M. J., "Collaborative Treatment of Marital Partners," *North Carolina Med. J.* 19:523-528, 1958.

Paul, N. L., "Effects of Playback on Family Members of Their Own Previously Recorded Conjoint Therapy Material," in Cohen, I. M. (Ed.), *Psychiatric Research Report 20,* Washington, D.C., American Psychiatric Association, 1966.

Paul, N. L., "The Use of Empathy in the Resolution of Grief," *Perspect. Bio. Med.* 11:153-169, 1967.

Paul, N. L., and Grosser, G. H., "Family Resistance to Change in Schizophrenic Patients," *Family Process* 3:337-401, 1964.

Paul, N. L., and Grosser, G. H., "Operational Mourning and Its Role in Conjoint Family Therapy," *Comm. Ment. Health J.* 1:339-345, 1965.

Perlmutter, M., Loeb, D., Gumpert, G., O'Hara, F., and Higbie, I., "Family

Diagnosis and Therapy Using Videotape Playback," *Amer. I. Orthopsychiat.* 37:900-905, 1967.

Pittman, F., DeYoung, C., Flomenhaft, K., Kaplan, D., and Langsley, D., "Crisis Family Therapy," in Masserman, J. H. (Ed.), *Current Psychiatric Therapies,* Vol. 6, New York, Grune & Stratton, 1966, pp. 187-196.

Pittman, F., DeYoung, C., Flomenhaft, K., Kaplan, D., and Langsley, D., "Therapy Techniques of the Family Treatment Unit," in Haley J. (Ed.), *Changing Families; A Family Therapy Reader,* Grune & Stratton, 1971.

Pollack, O., and Brieland, D., "The Midwest Seminar on Family Diagnosis and Treatment," *Soc. Casework* 42:319-324, 1961.

Rabiner, E. L., Molinski, H., and Gralnick, A., "Conjoint Therapy in the Inpatient Setting," *Amer. J. Psychother,* 16:618-631, 1962.

Rakoff, V., Sigal, J., and Epstein, N., "Working-Through in Conjoint Family Therapy, *Amer. J. Psychother.* 21:782-790, 1967.

Rashkis, H., "Depression as a Manifestation of the Family as an Open System," *Arch. Gen. Psychiat.* 19:57-63, 1968.

Ravich, R. A., "Short-Term Intensive Treatment of Marital Discord," *Voices* 2:42-48, 1966.

Reding, G. R., and Ennis, B., "Treatment of the Couple by a Couple," *Brit. J. Med. Psychol.* 37:325-330, 1964.

Reding, G. R., Charles, L. A., and Hoffman, M. B., "Treatment of the Couple by a Couple, II, Conceptual Framework, Case Presentation, and Follow-Up Study," *Brit. J. Med. Psychol.* 40:243-252, 1967.

Reidy, J. J., "An Approach to Family-Centered Treatment in a State Institution," *Amer. J. Orthopsychiat.* 32:133-141, 1962.

Richter, H., "Familientherapie," *Psychother. Psychosom.* 16:303-318, 1968.

Ritchie, A., "Multiple Impact Therapy, an Experiment," *Soc. Work* 5:16-21, 1960.

Rubinstein, D., "Family Therapy," in Spiegel, E. A. (Ed.), *Progress in Neurology and Psychiatry,* Vol. 18, New York, Grune & Stratton, 1963.

Rubinstein, D., "Family Therapy," in Spiegel, E. A. (Ed.), *Progress in Neurology and Psychiatry,* Vol. 20, New York, Grune & Stratton, 1965.

Rubinstein, D., and Weiner, O. R., "Co-Therapy Teamwork Relationships in Family Therapy," in Zuk, G. H., and Boszormenyi-Nagy, I. (Eds.), *Family Therapy and Disturbed Families,* Palo Alto, Calif., Science and Behavior Books, 1967.

Sager, C., "The Development of Marriage Therapy: An Historical Review," *Amer. J. Orthopsychiat.* 36:450-468, 1968.

Sager, C., "Transference in Conjoint Treatment of Married Couples," *Arch. Gen. Psychiat.* 16:185-193, 1967.

Sager, C., "An Overview of Family Therapy," *Int. J. Group Psychother.* 18:302-312, 1968.

Satir, V., "The Question for Survival: A Training Program for Family Diagnosis and Treatment," *Acta Psychother. Psychosom.* 11:33-38, 1963.

Satir, V., *Conjoint Family Therapy,* Palo Alto, Calif., Science and Behavior Books, 1964.

Satir, V., "The Family as a Treatment Unit," *Confin. Psychiat.* 8:37-42, 1965.

Schaffer, L., Wynne, L. C., Day, J., Ryckoff, I. M., and Halperin, A., "On the Nature and Sources of the Psychiatrist's Experience with the Family of the Schizophrenic," *Psychiatry* 25:32-45, 1962.

Scheflen, A. E., *Stream and Structure of Communicational Behavior,* Philadelphia,

Eastern Pennsylvania Psychiatric Institute. Behavioral Studies Monograph 1, 1965.

Scherz, F. H., "Multiple-Client Interviewing: Treatment Implications," *Soc. Casework* 43:120-125, 1962.

Schuster, F. P., "Summary Description of Multiple Impact Psychotherapy," *Texas Rep. Bio. Med.* 17:426-430, 1959.

Searles, H. F., "Family Treatment and Individual Therapy," in Boszormenyi-Nagy, I., and Framo, J. L. (Eds.), *Intensive Family Therapy*, New York, Harper, 1965.

Serrano, A. C., and Wilson, N. S., "Family Therapy in the Treatment of the Brain Damaged Child," *Dis. Nerv. Sys.* 24:732-735, 1963.

Shellow, R. S., Brown, B. S., and Osberg, J. W., "Family Group Therapy in Retrospect: Four Years and Sixty Families," *Family Process* 2:52-67, 1963.

Shereshefsky, P. M., "Family Unit Treatment in Child Guidance," *Soc. Casework* 8:63-70, 1963.

Sherman, M. H., Ackerman, N. W., Sherman, S. N., and Mitchell, C., "Non-Verbal Cues and Re-enactment of Conflict in Family Therapy," *Family Process* 4:133-162, 1964.

Sherman, S. N., "The Sociopsychological Character of Family-Group Treatment," *Soc. Casework* 45:195-201, 1964.

Siporin, M., "Family-Centered Casework in a Psychiatric Setting," *Soc. Casework* 37:167-174, 1956.

Sluzki, C., and Bleichmar, J., "The International Approach to Marital Therapy," *Acta Psiquiat. Psicol. Amer. Alt.* 14:325-328, 1968.

Smith, V. G., and Hepworth, D. H., "Marriage Counseling with One Marital Partner; Rationale and Clinical Implications," *Soc. Casework* 48:352-359, 1967.

Sonne, J. C., and Lincoln, G., "Heterosexual Co-Therapy Team Experience During Family Therapy," *Family Process* 4:177-197, 1965.

Sonne, J. C., Speck, R. V., and Jungreis, J. E., "The Absent-Member Maneuver as a Resistance in Family Therapy of Schizophrenia," *Family Process* 1:44-62, 1962.

Speck, R. V., "Family Therapy in the Home," *J. Marriage Family* 26:72-76, 1964.

Speck, R. V., "The Home Setting for Family Treatment, *Int. J. Soc. Psychiat.*, Special Ed. 2:47-53, 1963.

Speck, R. V., "Psychotherapy of the Social Network of a Schizophrenic Family," *Family Process* 6:208-214, 1967.

Speck, R. V., and Rueveni, U., "Network Therapy—A Developing Concept," *Family Process* 8:182-191, 1969.

Stachowiak, J., "Decision-Making and Conflict Resolution in the Family Group," in Larson, C., and Dance, F. (Eds.), *Perspectives on Communication*, Milwaukee, Speech Communication Center, University of Wisconsin, 1968, pp. 113-124.

Stachowiak, J., "Psychological Disturbances in Children as Related to Disturbances in Family Interaction," *J. Marriage Family* 30:123-127, 1968.

Strean, H. S., "A Family Therapist Looks at Little Hans," *Family Process* 6:227-234, 1967.

Tharp, R., "Marriage Roles, Child Development and Family Treatment," *Amer. J. Orthopsychiat.* 35:531-538, 1965.

Tharp, R., and Otis, G., "Toward a Therapy for Therapeutic Intervention in Families," *J. Consult. Psychol.* 30:426-434, 1966.

Thormen, G., *Family Therapy—Help for Troubled Families*, New York, Public Affairs Pamphlet 356, February, 1964.

Treusch, J. V., and Grotjahn, M., "Psychiatric Family Consultations," *Ann. Intern. Med.* 66:295-300, 1967.

Vikersund, G., "Family Treatment in Psychiatric Hospitals," *Psychother. Psychosom.* 16:333-338, 1968.

Wahler, R. G., Winkel, G. H., Peterson, R. F., and Morrison, D. C., "Mothers as Behavior Therapists for Their Own Children," *Behav. Res. Ther.* 3:113-124, 1965.

Warkentin, J., "Psychotherapy with Couples and Families," *J. Med. Ass. Georgia* 49:569-570, 1960.

Warkentin, J., and Whitaker, C., "Serial Impasses in Marriage," in Cohen, I. M. (Ed.), *Psychiatric Research Report 20,* Washington, D.C., American Psychiatric Association, 1966.

Warkentin, J., and Whitaker, C. A., "The Secret Agenda of the Therapist Doing Couples Therapy," in Zuk, G. H., and Boszormenyi-Nagy, I. (Eds.), *Family Therapy and Disturbed Families,* Palo Alto, Calif., Science and Behavior Books, 1967.

Watson, A. S., "The Conjoint Psychotherapy of Marriage Partners," *Amer. J. Orthopsychiat.* 33:912-923, 1963.

Weakland, J., "Family Therapy as a Research Arena," *Family Process* 1:63-68, 1962.

Whitaker, C. A., "Psychotherapy with Couples," *Amer. J. Psychother* 12, 18-23, 1958.

Whitaker, C. A., Felder, R. E., and Warkentin, J., "Counter-Transference in the Family Treatment of Schizophrenia," in Boszormenyi-Nagy, I., and Framo, J. L. (Eds.), *Intensive Family Therapy,* New York, Harper, 1965.

Whitaker, C. A., and Miller, M. H., "A Re-Evaluation of 'Psychiatric Help' When Divorce Impends," *Amer. J. Psychiat.* 126:57-64, 1969.

Wilkinson, C., and Reed, C., "An Approach to the Family Therapy Process," *Dis. Nerv. Sys.* 26:705-714, 1965.

Williams, F., "Family Therapy: A Critical Assessment," *Amer. J. Orthopsychiat.* 37:912-919, 1967.

Wyatt, G. L., and Herzan, H. M., "Therapy with Stuttering Children and Their Mothers," *Amer. J. Orthopsychiat.* 32:645-659, 1962.

Wynne, L. C., "The Study of Intrafamilial Alignments and Splits in Exploratory Family Therapy," in Ackerman, N. W., Beatman, F. L., and Sherman, S. N. (Eds.), *Exploring the Base for Family Therapy,* New York, Family Service Association, 1961.

Wynne, L. C., "Some Indications and Contraindications for Exploratory Family Therapy," in Boszormenyi-Nagy, I., and Framo, J. L. (Eds.), *Intensive Family Therapy,* New York, Harper, 1965.

Zierer, E., Sternberg, D., Finn, R., and Farmer, N., "Family Creative Analysis: Its Role in Treatment," *Bull. Art. Ther.* 5:87-104, 1966.

Zuk, G. H., "Preliminary Study of the Go-Between Process in Family Therapy," in *Proceedings of the 73rd Annual Convention of the American Psychological Association,* Chicago, 1965.

Zuk, G., "The Go-Between Process in Family Therapy," *Family Process* 5:162-178, 1966.

Zuk, G. H., *Family Therapy and Disturbed Families,* Palo Alto, Calif., Science and Behavior Books, 1966.

Zuk, G., "Family Therapy," *Arch. Gen. Psychiat.* 16:71-79, 1967.

Zuk, G., "Family Therapy: Formulation of a Technique and Its Theory, *Int. J. Group Psychother.* 18:42-57, 1968.

Zuk, G., "Prompting Change in Family Therapy, *Arch. Gen. Psychiat.* 19:727-736, 1968.

Zuk, G., "The Side-Taking Functioning in Family Therapy," *Amer. J. Orthopsychiat.* 38:553-559, 1968.

Zuk, G. H., and Rubinstein, D., "A Review of Concepts in the Study and Treatment of Families of Schizophrenics," in Boszormenyi-Nagy, I., and Framo, J. L. (Eds.), *Intensive Family Therapy,* New York, Harper, 1965.

Index

Cohesion of group and deviance, 297-299, 308
Collective cognitive chaos, 104
Communication
  accommodation to family style of, 208-209
  analysis of processes in, 129-130
  denial of meaning and relation, 60-62
  and differences of opinion, 38
  double bind concept in, 16, 28-29
  expression of negative feelings, 120-121
  facilitation of, 163
  incongruent messages in, 29, 30, 129
  interpretation of messages in, 26-27, 38, 75, 76
  in low socioeconomic families, 204-205
  maternal verbalizations affecting child, 199-200
  modalities of, 165
  in multiple family therapy, 89
  multiplicity of messages in, 29
  need for improvement in, 84-85
  nonverbal reactions in groups, 313-314, 319
  patterns within families, 23, 288
  rational specific statements with overall disorder, 50-51, 104
  terminology of, 5
  with therapist by individual family members, 22, 23, 138
  videorecordings of patterns in, 237-246
Complementary and symmetrical behavior patterns, 299-301
Conditioning. See Behavior therapy
Confidentiality as ethical issue, 118, 123
Conflict
  as expressed in family therapy, 213, 214
  and go-between role of therapist, 215-218
  mediation of, and symptom behavior, 298 308
  and schizophrenia, 298
Conflict-resolution therapy, 146-157
Conflicts of interest between patient and family, 123-125
Constraints and variety, 290-291
Co-therapists, family members as, 73
Counterresistance, varieties of, 56, 63
Countertransference, 70, 125, 126

and interaction in families, 32-33
management of, 80
in multiple family therapy, 92
Crisis
  changes in, 292, 307
  and multiple impact therapy, 36-44
  and therapeutic results, 8, 292
Crisis therapy, 259-270, 306
Culture of family affecting therapist, 45-63
Cybernetic view of social relationships, 5, 274, 287-288, 30

Defensive tactics of family, 222-223
Definition of family, changes in, 6
Delinquency, dynamics in, 295
Denial
  in multiple family therapy, 91
  role of, 50-55, 58-59, 61, 214, 268
Dependency and hospitalization, 10-11
Determinism, psychic, 57-58, 61
Deviance
  function of, 2-3, 279, 297-299, 308
  sociology of, 288-290
  typecasting of, 295-297
  utilization of, 306-307
Deviation-amplifying processes, 285-309
Deviation-counteracting processes, 292, 294, 301, 304, 305, 308
Diagnosis
  emphasis on, 230-231
  impact of, in marital problems, 249-251
  mechanisms in, 281-282
  orientation affecting, 273, 277-279
Differentiation of self, 86, 172-176
  and relationship with child, 190-191
  as therapeutic goal, 184-185
  time required for, 186
Disagreement, expression of, 214
Disorganized families. See Low socioeconomic families
Displacement in multiple family therapy, 91
Dissociations
  patterns in families, 49
  trading of, 102-104
Distancing, devices for, 22, 104-105
Distraction affecting behavior, 195
Divorce, ethical issues in, 247-258
Dormant problems, emergence of, 124-125

Double bind concept, 16-18, 28-29, 162, 165, 238, 298
Dreams in multiple family therapy, 90
Drug taking, dynamics in, 295
Drug therapy, use of, 266
Dyad as treatment unit, 273, 274-276
Dysfunction
  in children, 177, 190-191
  in one spouse, 177, 188-190
  and overfunction mechanisms, 167-169

Ecosystems, 4, 6, 303, 304, 306
Ego mass, undifferentiated, 171-176
Emotional equilibrium. *See* Homeostasis
Emotional illness, concepts of, 169-170
Enuresis in marital couple, 65-68
Equilibrium in families. *See* Homeostasis
Ethical issues in therapy, 116-126
  and confidentiality, 118, 123
  and conflicts of interest, 123-125
  and countertransference, 125, 126
  and goals of therapy, 119-120
  and impending divorce, 247-258
  and social values, 117-118
Evaluation of family, 181-184
Experiential family therapy, 133-145
  conflict-resolution in, 146-157
  indications for, 134
  resistance in, 137, 140
Exploratory family therapy, 96-114
  contraindications, 107, 111
  indications for, 100
  individual therapy with, 110
  selection of participants, 106-108
  therapists available for, 111-114
Extended family, 4, 6, 172, 183
  in crisis therapy, 262
  and imbalance in nuclear family, 303-304
  importance of, 279-280
  in network therapy, 312-332
Externalization, problems of, 103

Familiarity, effects of, 147-148
Family theory, 15-18, 127-131, 171-180, 287-288
  in clinical practice, 159-191
Fathers. *See* Parents
Feedback mechanisms, 285-291, 308

Feelings, perception of, 170, 174
Films of family behavior, 5, 152, 240-242
Folie à deux phenomenon, 49, 171, 172
Follow-up studies. *See* Results of therapy
Fragmentation in families, 56, 58, 61, 62
  institutionalization of, 104
Frigidity, therapy of, 190
Functioning patterns in families, 167-170

Generalization process, 148
Goals of therapy, 10, 19, 47, 72, 79, 84-85, 119-120, 168, 184-185, 189, 235, 283
  changes in, 275-276
  and communication, 130
  in crisis therapy, 260-261
  in experiential therapy, 136
  in exploratory therapy, 100
  in network therapy, 315-317
  in traditional psychiatry, 10
Go-between process, 214-225
  changes resulting from, 223-225
  defensive tactics in, 222-223
Group therapy, 5, 47-48, 82-83, 273
  compared to family therapy, 106-107

Historical aspects of family therapy, 1-12, 14-15, 118-119, 160-162, 273-276
History taking, 181-184, 280-281
  and current family problem, 230
  See also Interviews
Home visits
  in behavior therapy, 193-200
  in crisis therapy, 263, 266
  in network therapy, 318-321
Homeostasis in families, 16-18, 28-29, 49, 114, 287-288
  and breakdown of stable pathology, 124, 305-306
  and emotional equilibrium, 171-172, 187
  limit in plateaus of, 293, 301
  between nuclear family and extended kin, 303-304
  and pathological balance, 28-30, 303-305, 308
  timing related to, 292
Hospitalization
  avoidance of, with crisis therapy, 259-270
  conjoint therapy in inpatient setting, 46, 69-81

School phobias, 4, 267, 279
Selection of cases for family therapy, 77-78, 87-88, 106-108
Self-differentiation. *See* Differentiation of self
Self-esteem of parents as ethical issue, 121
Separation problems in adolescence, 101-102
Siblings of patients, role of, 18-19, 180
Siding of therapists with family members, 219-222, 234
Skew families, 29
Social context of family, 279-280
Social network intervention, 312-332
 See also Network therapy
Social reinforcement, effects of, 200
Social typecasting of deviants, 295-297
Social values as ethical issues, 117-118
Socioeconomic groups, low. *See* Low socio-economic families
Sociology of deviance, 2-3, 279, 288-290, 297-299, 308
Solidarity of family as ethical issue, 121
Spokesman, identification of, 222-223
Spontaneity in experiential therapy, 135
Stability of family pathology. *See* Homeostasis
Stabilization of group and function of deviance, 297-299, 308
Stereotyping, racial, 295
Stresses in families, types of, 260
Subsystems in families, 166, 167
 variations in, 202-207
Supervision of trainees, 235
Symbiotic attachments, pathological, 75, 86, 89, 171, 172
Symmetrical and complementary behavior, 299-301
Symptom formation
 chronological review of, 181
 and interactional process, 127-131
 and mediation of conflict, 298, 308
 prescription of, 288
 as result of crisis, 265
Systems theory, 166-170, 272, 274
 and cybernetics, 5, 274, 287-288, 308
 and management of deviance, 285-309

Tape recordings of sessions, 152

Task assignments, value of, 149-150, 267
Teaching of family therapy, 6-7
Teams of therapists, 36-44, 312-321
Techniques of therapy, 18-28, 185-191
 in behavior therapy in home, 194-197
 in conflict-resolution therapy, 149-150
 in crisis therapy, 261-270
 in experiential therapy, 138-140
 and framing of therapy, 22-26
 in individual therapy, 30-32
 in initial discussions, 18-22
 with low socioeconomic groups, 202-210
 in multiple family therapy, 89-90
 in multiple impact therapy, 38-43
 and mutual causal processes, 306-307
 theoretical principles in, 28-30
Telephone discussions, use of, 252, 263
Termination of therapy, 224
Theory of family systems, 15-18, 127-131, 171-180, 287-288
 in clinical practice, 159-191
Therapists
 accommodations to family style of communication, 208-209
 advice to family members, 27, 47
 authority of, 91, 215, 217
 as catalyst when divorce impends, 247-258
 in conflict-resolution therapy, 155
 as decoder of communication, 26-27, 38, 75, 76
 defensive tactics against, 222-223
 defining of self to families, 187, 189
 ethical problems of, 116-126, 247-258
 for exploratory therapy, 111-114
 and family systems, 168
 in go-between process, 214-225
 goals of. *See* Goals of therapy
 interchange with patients, 275
 interpretations by. *See* Interpretations
 interventions by. *See* Interventions by therapist
 parents as, 193-200
 as part of diagnosis, 231-233, 282
 private communication with, by family members, 22, 23, 138
 professional background of, 284
 reactions to family culture, 45-63

as scapegoats, 313
shifts in approaches to therapy, 227-236
siding with family members, 219-222, 234
supervision of, 235
teams for multiple impact therapy, 36-44
traditional views of, 2-4, 8-12, 15, 193-194
viewpoint vis-à-vis family, 214-222
Thought disorders, transactional, 104
Timing
 and feedback processes, 291-293
 for introduction of therapy, 122
Traditional therapy. *See* Individual therapy
Training in family therapy, 6-7, 235
Transactional thought disorders, 104
Transference
 avoidance of, 164
 in experiential therapy, 136
 and interaction in families, 32-33, 49, 78, 189
 in multiple family therapy, 91

and role of interpretations, 7, 9
Transmission of problems to children, 177, 179-180, 190
Triad as treatment unit, 276-279
Triangles in kinship system, 172, 185, 190-191, 296, 302, 306
Typecasting of deviants, 295-297
Types of families, studies of, 7-8

Undifferentiated family ego mass, 171-176
Units of treatment, broadening of, 4, 6

Variety and constraints, 290-291
Verbalizations. *See* Communication
Videotape playback
 case examples of, 242-245
 long-range effects of, 240-242
 method of use, 239-240

Work associates as peer network, 327-328
Work phobias, 267